NOT NECESSARILY THE NEW AGE

NOT NECESSARILY THE NEW AGE

Critical Essays

Edited by Robert Basil

PROMETHEUS BOOKS
Buffalo, New York

91 90 89 88   4 3 2 1

Library of Congress Cataloging-in Publication Data

Not necessarily the New Age: critical essays.

    1. New Age movement—United States. I. Basil,
Robert, 1959–
BP605.N48N68   1988   133   88-12635
ISBN 0-87975-490-7

For Miles,
in awe
of the real

TABLE OF CONTENTS

THE POLITICS

A MEMOIR

THINKING OUR WAY THROUGH

INTRODUCTION
Robert Basil

My reason for putting this collection of essays together was exceedingly practical: I wanted to read a balanced and multifaceted examination of the religious phenomenon known as the New Age movement. I worked for a magazine that critically examined religion and religious institutions, and there was no book that offered an intelligent tour of the movement. Professionally, I found that to be an annoyance. My editor suggested that if I wanted such a tour, I would have to give it myself, or give it with the help of others who felt the need for a book like this one. You are holding the result of the latter approach.

In the past few years, the New Age movement has grown from a fervently supported countercultural underground to yet one more social force blanched into uniform inanity by the mass media. Those grim, mesmerizing faces of earlier occult leaders have been replaced by the hyperavailable grins of Shirley MacLaine. In short, what used to be called "the occult"—which means *hidden*—is occult no longer. This exposure has encouraged millions to check out nontraditional spiritual beliefs and alternative healing practices, but too, too few to critically examine these beliefs and practices. Indeed, since Prometheus Books commissioned this collection, literally hundreds of books have been published on New Age thinking; almost none have been skeptical; and none, until *Not Necessarily the New Age*, has offered a thorough, rigorous, and fair analysis of the movement as a whole.

* * *

It was Andrew Greeley's widely publicized survey in *American Health* magazine that alerted the country that some kind of "spiritual revolution" was going on. Greeley, in collaboration with the University of Chicago's National Opinion Research Council, reported that 67 percent of those surveyed had "experienced ESP," 31 percent had "experienced clairvoyance," 29 percent "had visions," and 42 percent had "had contact with the dead."[1] He wrote: "Our studies show that people who've tasted the paranormal, whether they accept it intellectually or not, are anything but religious nuts or psychiatric cases. They are, for the most part, ordinary Americans, somewhat above the norm in education and intelligence and somewhat less than average in religious involvement."

Because so many people have admitted having (or trying to have) experiences uncorroborated by science or attacked by traditional Western religion, it is hardly possible to describe them as a "fringe group." They have become *the* major alternative in America's spiritual life. Indeed, Greeley's survey became a kind of official announcement to entrepreneurs that there was a vast "target audience" for New Age books, magazines, catalogues, audiotapes, videotapes, yellow pages, seminars, physical and mental therapies, crystals, music, cosmetics, singles clubs, "transformational" vacation packages, Eastern gurus, channeled entities, graduate schools, "socially conscious" investment services, and spiritual "supplies."[2]

Despite its pervasive use now, the genesis of the term "New Age" is murky. It can be traced back as far as the 1920s in the writings of Alice A. Bailey.[3] But it is the term's more recent manifestations that concern us here. The current New Age movement has its origins in the counterculture of the 1960s. Twenty years ago a common phrase was the "Age of Aquarius," which according to astrological lore was to be a period of peace and enlightenment. Perhaps the word "Aquarius" has been dropped by most people to widen the movement's appeal and disguise its origin in pagan superstition. According to James Webb, author of *The Occult Establishment*: "The idea of the Age of Aquarius is simply a statement of astrological fact. That is, a subscriber to astrology believes not only in the links between the heavenly bodies and life on earth but also in an elaborate superstructure of periods. . . . The Aquarian characteristics were thought to be diametrically opposed to those of the preceding (Piscean) age—for confusion, harmony; for pursuit of material profit, the brotherhood of man."[4]

Those Christian critics who believe that the New Age is a "conspiracy" like to focus on the way the New Age movement hides this connection to religion and astrology. One such writer has commented: "The spiritual dimensions of the New Age enterprise are concealed in secular rhetoric. This is to some extent intentional. But it is also an inevitable result of occult mysticism's collision with Western culture. That collision has set in motion a process of secularization, yielding, among other things, a distinctive areligious vocabulary that has been infused with spiritual meaning. *Holistic, holographic, synergistic, unity, oneness, transformation, per-*

sonal growth, human potential, awakening, networking, energy, conscious-
ness—such words occur with predictable regularity in New Age writings.["]5

Appearing at least as regularly are promises that we are just a short
time away from the dawn of a new consciousness, the creation of a new
and peaceful society—in a word, the *millennium*. Promises of the millennium
have been made, of course, for millennia—they are not new with the New
Age movement. According to the Gospel writers, Jesus told his disciples
that they would live to see the millennium: "There are some standing here
who will not taste death before they see the Son of man coming in His
kingdom . . ." (Matt. 16:28). And the Jehovah's Witnesses have been preach-
ing the imminence of the Apocalypse since the early 1800s—continually
revising their predictions as the promised dates have come and passed.

The apocalyptic expectations of the New Age reached a kind of a
peak in August 1987 with the heavily publicized (but less heavily attended)
Harmonic Convergence—which consolidated under one rubric the bewilderingly diverse array of practices and beliefs that comprise the movement.

The Millennium

For a student of culture, the Harmonic Convergence was worth attending
for a lot of reasons. Books, magazines, and television often don't convey
how people actually experience a movement on a local level. Ideas can be
presented systematically; people, happily, can't. Almost by definition, a true
grassroots movement is populated by people who contradict each other,
who don't follow the party line, or who don't even know what the party
line is. If the people I interviewed at the Niagara Falls "sacred site" are
at all representative of others around the country, the New Age is a true
grassroots movement: passionate in its hope, but incoherent in its vision.

I made it to Niagara Falls about an hour before dawn. I was surprised
by the large number of elderly people there; I had believed that New Agers
were all reinvented hippies. I went up to one white-haired couple and asked
what they thought was going to happen.

"I don't know. But I do know that the world can't be the way it
is. It has to change," answered the man. "Otherwise, we will have nothing
in the future, nothing for the kids. Also, I'm curious about these things,
spirituality. And I've read books on the Far East."

"He does all the reading on it and then tells me," his wife said, looking
over her shoulder at a young woman who was passing out small quartz
crystals and telling people to bury them or hurl them into the rapids once
the sun comes up. "I want one," said the woman with a sigh, interrupting
the conversation to point at the crystals.

When the bank clock across the river read 5:45—fifteen minutes before sunrise—about three hundred people had gathered. While wandering through the crowd, I ran into a long-haired one-time campus radical whom I used to avoid in my college days. "We've got nothing to lose coming here," said Mike, whose attitude surprisingly was one of guarded skepticism. "If it's real, it's real, and that's great. At worst, it's just another day. What the hell, I've never seen the sunrise at Niagara Falls, and I hardly ever wake up at five o'clock in the morning. In fact, this thing might be nothing more than an excuse to get a good start on a nice summer's day. At worst, that's what it is. *At worst*. Lots of sand-flies, though."

Then I met a barefoot woman wearing a yellow cotton dress. On her lap was a copy of *The Mayan Factor: The Path Beyond Technology*.[6] This book, written by José Arguelles, an art historian with a doctorate from the University of Chicago, is credited with introducing the idea of the Harmonic Convergence. It was Arguelles's contention that the Mayans were not naive Central Americans but *extraterrestrials* whose complex calendar was a blueprint predicting—if you "interpret" it right—the millennium, which was to start that very morning above the Falls.

"I think it's possible," the woman said. "I'm really open to hearing about earth changes. Look at where we are, we're in big trouble, we're helpless. Why? Our technology has betrayed us; poisonous chemicals flood the land; nuclear weapons threaten to extinguish all human and, minus roaches, all animal life; computer technology degrades our dignity, makes us superfluous, meaningless." This disaffection with technocratic society is certainly one prominent theme of the New Age movement, and this is how Arguelles puts it:

> What makes us so sure that scientific materialism is the best technique to wrench answers from a cosmos infinitely more vast and mysterious than the rationalist mind can comprehend? . . . The spectre of technological crisis invokes . . . a paradigm shift of a genuinely radical nature. Such a shift has been in the air for a long time, thanks to pioneering research in quantum physics, but has needed [the] experiential jolt [provided by the space shuttle Challenger's fateful explosion] to get it grounded.[7]

Up to a point, I concurred with the woman: It's hard not to believe that, since humanity's technological inventions have brought us the means of our own extinction, a fundamental change in the way our society lives and regards the world is essential. New Agers' disgust with our world's predicament is extreme, and because many just cannot continue to imagine the extent of their impotence as individuals, they are tempted to avert their stares from the real world—which is ruled by governments and "covert actions" and run by technology sped by computers—to a supernatural world, where they can paint their own skies with astral colors; they are even tempted to dismiss human beings in favor of "spiritual entities" and semi-divine extraterrestrials who will, they hope, come and save us. This hope, for an alternative to a future that seems more and more to be an irrevocable destiny, is epitomized by a promise that is ubiquitous in New Age writings: "You can create your own reality."

Arguelles made an exact prophecy. This August morning, he wrote, would inaugurate one final twenty-five-year earth-cycle, which would culminate in a new "beam of energy." The language Arguelles employs to describe these last days is an urgent mixture of mystic hyperbole and high-tech bombast:

> The final five year period, A.D. 2007–2012, will be singularly directed to the emplacement of galactic synchronization crews at all the planetary light-body grid-nodes. . . .
>
> Then it shall be ready. The unique moment, the moment of total planetary synchronization, 13.0.0.0.0. on the beam, will arrive—the closing out not only of the Great Cycle, but of the evolutionary interim called homo sapiens. Amidst festive preparation and awesome galactic-solar songs psychically received, the human race, in harmony with the animal and other kingdoms and taking its rightful place in the great electromagnetic sea, will unify as a single circuit. . . .
>
> Then, as if a switch were being thrown, a great voltage will race through this finally synchronized and integrated circuit called humanity. The Earth itself will be illumined. A current charging both poles will race across the skies, connecting the polar auroras in a single brilliant flash. Like an iridescent rainbow, this circumpolar energy uniting the planetary antipodes will be instantaneously understood as the external projecting of the unification of the collective mind of humanity. In that moment of understanding, we shall be collectively projected into an evolutionary domain that is presently inconceivable.[8]

Arguelles doesn't go out of his way to be clear. His intention, I suppose, is not to instruct. His intention is *to delight*, in a bold euphoria of undefined terms arranged in a pattern so baroque and so frantic that it is impossible not to be jarred. His earlier writings on art, far easier to read, prefigure his current New Age propagandizing. Arguelles's essay "Art as Internal Technology," published in 1975, echoes the twin themes of *The Mayan Factor*: horror at technology, and the necessity to rip our culture up and start again:

> It is curious how history and the myth of progress distort our perceptions, so that we think of alchemy, shamanism, and yoga, for instance, as things

of the distant past, while in fact all of the mystical techniques that were relegated to the past in the European cultural continuum have continued to exist side by side with history. The endurance of the archaic is all the more astonishing, given the merciless willingness of technological civilization to uproot, desecrate, and where necessary, even to commit genocide in order that the progressive forces of history could prevail. But as the inner psychic house of history begins to collapse, suddenly appearing through the debris are the glints and glimmers of an eternal magic.[9]

A few years later, however, Arguelles came to feel that the world needed more than "the glints and glimmers of an eternal magic." The passages in *The Mayan Factor* in which Arguelles depicts the dawn of this realization are remarkably moving. As is the case in so many "conversion narratives," Arguelles's millennial vision was born in a time of personal horror. He had come to believe that the extraterrestrial Mayans had abandoned Earth because they knew that humanity was doomed:

> Such, at least, were my reasonings by the late 1970s when I entered my own hell realm of personal crisis and alcoholic breakdown. When I emerged from this dislocation of the self in 1981 and looked around, it appeared that the global crisis of the 1960s had now become endemic, so much so that it was taken for granted. My own researches had taken me to a place of synthesis, of seeing the Earth as a whole organism. Yet my inner feeling was that the thrust of modern civilization was taking things to the point where either the divine intervenes or extinction becomes our legacy. For me, the situation meant taking a leap, plunging off the edge as it were, into mental territory that had been declared extinct or tabu by the prevailing cultural standards.[10]

Arguelles's millenarian vision has not appealed to all New Age writers. Sy Safronsky, who edits *The Sun* magazine, complained: "Arguelles seems not so different from the politicians who promise change without hinting at the cost. 'Cleansing' the earth sounds messy to me. 'Full-scale de-industrialization' suggests tremendous suffering, unimaginable loss. Prophecies such as these go against the real spirit of change; they impose the future on the present, burden the blessed ordinariness of our day-to-day existence with someone else's dark view of life." His opinion of the Harmonic Convergence was even more bitter. Nothing more than a "pseudo-event," "it represented the worst kind of spiritual showmanship. Elitist, flamboyant, bewitchingly unreal, it parodied the New Age better than any satirist."[11]

At the Niagara Falls "grid node," however, all was not apocalypse and doom. I saw some light wit. One man I met was wearing a T-shirt that read "Awareness Is A Bitch." He was a computer programmer for a big bank in Toronto. "Yes, I'm a New Ager. I accept reincarnation, that you keep coming back until you get it right, that there's help elsewhere for you and your spiritual growth here on Earth.

"I was raised a Christian," he said. "But Christianity was too narrow-minded. New Agers go beyond that whole thing. Christianity has fixated on one very evolved being, Jesus, and forgets all the other examples we have of self-actualization." Mixing Maslow with Army advertising, he continued: "Christ was all he could be; but *we* can be all *we* can be, too."

This remark brought frightening howls from a group of people who were sitting on a blanket in back of him. At first I couldn't understand what they were saying, and I thought they were from some foreign land, having come here to contribute their own spiritual exotica to the Harmonic Convergence. But then I realized they were "speaking in tongues," one woman with especially unnerving fervor:

"Open their eyes to this deception, in Jesus' name! Oh Lord, have mercy on them, oh Lord oh Lord, b-b-[she breaks into glossalalia] . . . manabuddamanamana—MERCY, have mercy on their soul. . . . You'll not come against them, you'll NOT, in Jesus' name you'll NOT, Satan. . . . Open their eyes, Father, open their ears. Put a conviction upon them of Godly sorrow for repentance in Jesus' name, let them see the error of their ways, let them see that this is just a ploy of the DEVIL!"

They were Pentecostal Christians who had come to protest. Introducing myself, I safely noted, "You don't like what's happening here this morning."

"No, it's our Lord who doesn't like it," she said, handing me a bunch of cartoon tracts. "Have you read the Bible's attack on the New Age? Several thousand years ago the Apostle Paul by the spirit of God prophesied that a time was going to come when everybody's going to be crying 'peace' and 'safety' and then sudden destruction's gonna come upon them."

"But these people all look so peaceful and reverent," I said. "They talk about love. And they have nice complexions. How are you going to convince them that they've been led into sin?"

"We are not here to convince them. Paul talks about not wrestling with flesh and blood. Know this: The Bible warned that Satan would come as an angel of light to deceive the hearts of the unsuspecting. That's what everybody's into, 'the light,' the spiritual aspects of life, this meditation thing, this karma noise, all this 'absorption of energy.' But what they call 'energy' is nothing short of demonic powers manifesting themselves to their senses. All these people"—by this time, there were more than a thousand gathered, and the sky was filled by powerful pink light—"these people are *out of their minds.*"

I found out later that orthodox Christians have known for years that the New Age movement directly challenges the authority of the Bible and

Christian tradition. Indeed, until very recently, the only thorough critiques of New Age spirituality have come from Christian fundamentalist writers. The basis of their critiques, of course, is biblical. They see television images of Shirley MacLaine running into the Pacific Ocean yelling "I am God! I am God!" and it takes them two seconds to see that she's succumbed to Satan's first temptation: "For God knows that when you eat of the tree, your eyes will be opened and you will be like God . . ." (Gen. 3:5).

According to Robert Burrows, a member of the Spiritual Counterfeits Project, "The New Age phenomenon presents a sincere and impassioned response to the crisis and evils of our contemporary world. But from our perspective it is fundamentally misguided and unwittingly aggravates the very conditions it attempts to redress."[12] To Elliot Miller, editor of the *Christian Research Journal,* the New Age

> offers a spiritual view of life. Unlike atheistic humanism, it emphasizes a spiritual dimension. That is, we are not just evolved apes, but potential gods. But the New Age shakes hands with secular humanism in its belief that people have the answers within. It shouts "amen" to the ancient lie that "man is the measure of all things."
>
> Still, as Christians resist New Age activism, we can also learn something from it. In some ways, the rise of the New Age movement is a reproof to the undiscerning way the Western church has identified with society's status quo and generally neglected social matters. New Agers are far more inclined to develop creative alternatives for meeting people's needs. They have been at the forefront in creating food co-ops, hospices for the dying, bartering systems, the women's health agencies. Therefore, people in need must often look to New Agers for help. . . .
>
> Secularists cannot get an objective perspective of New Agers because, to a great extent, New Agers are secular humanists who recognized that the void in their lives is inescapably spiritual in nature. Thus, while secularism persists in its war with the Moral Majority, it is being co-opted by the New Age movement unawares. This is possible because it is more than just a movement. It is a massive cultural trend—a revolt against the spiritual void that secularism created by supposedly disproving Christianity.[13]

Which is a *nice* way of saying that New Agers will join secular humanists and other non-Christians in Hell. Not all Christian critics of the New Age are so decorous. Constance Cumbey, for instance, holds in *The Hidden Dangers of the Rainbow* that New Agers are latter-day Nazi conspirators who have infiltrated every major government and corporation in the world. "These people," she has said, "are advocating wholesale slaughter of fundamentalists and other Christians." Their influence is everywhere, *everywhere.*

Those rainbow stickers you put on your car's back window are really secret signs New Agers use so they can identify one another. Those supermarket bar-codes? Invented by "people who are deeply into . . . the occult . . . in response to instructions they believed they were receiving from superior intelligences, which we know of course to be nothing more than demons." One of the marvels of extreme paranoia is how coherent it makes the world appear. All technology, to Cumbey, is devil's work; anything so damn complex cannot possibly be made by humankind or ordained by God. The number 666, she claims, is routinely inserted into computer programs by teckies who share their souls with Satan.[14]

The Amorphous Appeal

Where did Cumbey get this stuff? No doubt, the title of Marilyn Ferguson's influential book, *The Aquarian Conspiracy*, pushed her alarm button. Even Ferguson's book-jacket, Cumbey exclaims, sports "a nice big fat triple six!" (I find it difficult to see.) An examination of the book's insides does nothing to assuage her, because this is how Ferguson opens: "A leaderless but powerful network is working to bring radical change in the United States. Its members have broken with certain elements of Western thought, and they may even have broken continuity with history. . . ."

Ferguson says that the "scientific paradigm" has reached a dead end because of its limited view of human potential. A new science, which encourages the human mind to reinvent reality, is on the verge of being born. You can help usher in this new science by taking part in any one of an offputtingly eclectic array of activities: Sensory isolation and overload, biofeedback, autogenic training, music, improvisational theater, consciousness-raising strategies, self-help networks, hypnosis, meditation, sufi stories, koans and dervish dancing, Est, dream journals, Theosophy and Gurdjieffian systems, Course in Miracles, yoga, sports.[16] Ferguson, like the Christian Fundamentalists who warn against her, is an ardent believer in the paranormal.[17] "There is a mounting body of evidence," she writes, "that [psychic and occult] phenomena irrefutably occur and that they can be facilitated by the psychotechnologies."[18]

Ferguson enthusiastically endorsed the Harmonic Convergence, seeing it as a kind of world-wide festival that would promote the "paradigm shift" she champions. Indeed, she wrote a blurb—a rather opaque one—for Arguelles's book: "Arguelles sees a coming moment of profound discontinuity. History has been an ordering principle, encoding information into the psi bank. We are now at the end of history. The psi bank itself— our accumulated knowledge—is about to become consciously articulated."

But it's doubtful that she buys the Mayan Calendar theory. For her, as for many other New Agers, it hardly matters whether Arguelles's theory describes reality. What matters instead is that the theory has a poetic, *personal* value. Anything that makes you more spiritually inclined, that helps you consider "alternative realities," is okay.

Many other New Age writers repeat: *It does not matter whether New Age staples are literally true.* Just thinking that they are literally true, or hoping that they could be, improves a person's behavior and a community's outlook. To be skeptical, New Agers claim, is to be *without hope.* Worse, not only do skeptics deny themselves access to spiritual and paranormal reality, they say, but by their suspicion they also hurt the whole world's spiritual evolution.

It is for this reason that the execrable idea of population "cleansing" is a common feature in New Age writing. Jack Underhill writes, for example, in a recent editorial in *Life Times: Forum for a New Age*, that "We are all either expressions of love or expressions of its opposite, and as we continue to further polarize into these two camps, the conflict of the two energies will find its release in physical expression, in both brother against brother, sister against sister and earth against, though ultimately *for*, us all." With bizarre nonchalance, he continues: "It is nothing to fear, for it is our way of cleaning things up and moving closer together. But it is really going to be quite a show. We are all so very fortunate to be alive right now— to be a part of the greatest show on earth."[19]

A kind of spiritual Machiavellianism is at work here. The ends (a more positive opinion of one's life) are justified by the means (population cleansing, pseudoscience, and bogus gurus). Interestingly, this Machiavellianism mirrors the age-old postulate, stated and restated by Christian apologists, that equates morality with belief in God. And, like these Christian claims, the New Age stress on faith in various "metaphysical" claims falls apart at both ends: evidence for UFOs, "psychic" powers, reincarnation, telekinesis, trance-channeling, and so forth is weak indeed, certainly no more conclusive than the evidence for Jesus' bodily resurrection; New Age belief grows from faith, not from evidence that the world at large can witness and replicate. Furthermore, nowhere has it been shown that people who adhere to New Age faith are any more moral than nonbelievers—just as few would argue that the history of Christian men and women shows them to be more ethical than non-Christians.

To skeptics, then, the reasons New Agers give for refusing to bother with the difference between the literal and the imaginary are wholly unconvincing. Their philosophical sloppiness occasionally even irks New Age advocates. For example, although Marilyn Ferguson was initially a big supporter of the Harmonic Convergence,[20] the media hoopla and the silly comments made by other supporters embarrassed her. "For future reference," she wrote in her *Brain/Mind Bulletin*,

> it might be wiser to emphasize creative possibilities for action rather than doomsday scenarios, Utopia, or extraterrestrial intervention. . . . Many more citizens can get behind the idea of celebration and cooperation than will align behind a particular ideology or mythology. . . . In view of the rising popular and even intellectual curiosity about the "New Age," proponents should take themselves seriously enough to respect the many ways in which their message might be misunderstood.[21]

Regarded superficially, Ferguson's mild reproval comes out like a dose of common sense. Yet is it? What, after all, was Arguelles's mistake? He made specific claims, claims that can be subsequently *tested*. Really, I cannot help but be impressed by how exactly Arguelles describes what will happen and when. Most other New Age writers aren't so forthcoming. Ferguson's worry—that the New Age "message might be misunderstood"—is odd, for in fact her criticism of the Harmonic Convergence is really that its message has been understood all too well—and it was found to be ludicrous. Her approach is intellectually cowardly. We better not make any testable claims, she seems to be saying—so let's proceed instead by offering appeals that are more amorphous.

In this vein, it is interesting to note exactly where Ferguson jumped on the "trance-channeling" bandwagon. Not with Kevin Ryerson, one of whose channeled entities hails from Elizabethan England; or J. Z. Knight, whose Ramtha became a god on the mythological continent of Atlantis 35,000 years ago; but with Jack Pursel, "exclusive channel of Lazaris"—pronounced *Luh-ZAR-us*—"a highly evolved entity who has never been incarnated on Earth." The entities emanating from Ryerson and Knight can be examined—against their will, of course. (In one recent session, for example, before he went into his trance Ryerson warned the audience that his entities would never answer questions regarding their existence.) We might ask Ryerson's "Tom MacPherson," for example, to describe his clothes and his diet, or to name the governors whom Queen Elizabeth appointed during her reign. And, because we know quite a bit about the physical set-up of the Earth of 35,000 years ago, we might ask Ramtha what fauna and flora flourished in Atlantis then. No such questions can be demanded of Lazaris, however; because his origin is obscure, he can more easily slide by skeptical investigation.[22]

We must wait until 2012 to verify or falsify Arguelles's major claims, but his preliminary forecast seems to have been incorrect. He promised that during the Harmonic Convergence UFOs would swarm through the skies[23]; there were none. He said there would be a great surge in telepathy; people would no longer need spoken words! But not even committed psychics reported any such surge. What did happen was this: The sun came up and made the day clear and bright. Nobody's mood seemed darkened by the absence of telepathic communion and extraterrestrial rescue. In fact, most of the people I have talked to like to be "open" to the idea of the paranormal, but they don't embrace it, if only because they have rarely—if ever—experienced it. Holding hands, singing, hoping together—that seemed to be the key offering that morning. More generally, Christopher Lasch writes, "The intuition underlying New Age movements, the bedrock feeling, hard to put into words but scarcely inchoate or confused, deserves better than ridicule: that mankind has lost the collective knowledge of how to live with dignity and grace; that this knowledge includes a respect not just for nature but for the nurturant activities our society holds in such low esteem; and that man's future depends on a renewal of prematurely discarded traditions of thought and practice."[24]

Lasch nonetheless attacks what he calls "the West Coast's latest contribution to our long history of bizarre spiritual fads and panaceas." He writes, "not just the degradation of piety but [the New Age's] blatant commercialization prompts suspicions of large-scale religious fraud."

> The New Age movement tries to combine meditation, positive thinking, faith-healing, rolfing, dietary reform, environmentalism, mysticism, yoga, water cures, acupuncture, incense, astrology, Jungian psychology, biofeedback, extrasensory perception, spiritualism, vegetarianism, organic gardening, the theory of evolution, Reichian sex therapy, ancient mythologies, archaic nature cults, Sufism, Freemasonry, Cabalistic lore, Chiropractic, herbal medicine, hypnosis, and any number of other techniques designed to heighten awareness, including elements borrowed from the major religious traditions. But the concoction, though it can sometimes furnish temporary relief of the symptoms of spiritual distress, cannot bring about the equivalent of a religious conversion, a real change of heart, nor can it bring about even an intellectual conversion to a new point of view capable of standing up against rigorous questioning.[25]

Why on earth is the movement thriving, then? Perhaps because it has succeeded where mainline religious institutions have failed—in convincing its adherents that they are included in the cosmos and are necessary participants in spiritual ritual. Much of Christianity—excepting, importantly, the charismatic movement—has largely excluded the laity from thrilling religious experience and, in its place, has subjected them to dogma and the weight of church history. New Agers don't even trust the word *God*—as a term it has become the property of the churches—so many turn to the Eastern religions, which instead of *God* use *âtman* or *nirvana* or *satori*; or they come up with their own terms, *the Light*, *the energy beams*, or *the higher worlds*. Those elements of the New Age that do embrace Christianity usually avoid conventional services and liturgies, and they tend to valorize the Gnostic Gospels and Dead Sea Scrolls as a way of challenging the canonical biblical texts. The New Age vaunts "holism" over Christian dualism—connection *with* the divine, not obedience *to* it.

It's not hard, therefore, to see why the movement is so attractive: solace appeals more than fear and loathing, community more than anonymity and separation. Nonetheless, the community that's formed around New Age ideas seems blind and naive. Who are these people, anyway? Mark Mayell, editor of *East West*, one of the largest New Age magazines, has written frankly about his own audience:

> Seems to me it's mostly a pretty flaky, if well-intentioned, bunch of people who believe in a fast-approaching millennium in which everybody will be vegetarians, conflict will be resolved through peaceful means; disease, suicide, and murder will be a thin ghost of the past; human potential will be maximized; we'll be in touch (psychically or otherwise) with civilizations from outer space; healing will be accomplished without drugs or surgery; energy sources will be renewable; the world's wealth will be justly distributed; and so forth.
>
> Is such a New Age upon us? Obviously not. Obtainable with the next century or two? I doubt it. Desirable? Probably, though I have my reservations about certain aspects. . . . I've met or read about too many self-professed New Agers who were total space cadets, naive airheads, ego-obsessed gurus, health junkies, or brainwashed zombies to be able to identify with the term. They suffer from delusions—that the self and society are perfectible, that world health necessarily leads to world peace, that political and economic forces are inconsequential when compared to the "power of love," and that we're on the verge of a massive "change of consciousness."[26]

The New Age and Science

Although the New Age movement likes to give itself the veneer of precision by using scientific terms, it in fact represents a large-scale renunciation of science. Brad Steiger, who has cranked out more than one hundred books on UFOs, astral projection, psychic powers, trance-channeling, and far-out religion, begins his credo this way, "I believe that man's one truly essential factor, his spirituality, may never be fully susceptible to scientific elucidation. I believe that the artificial words to which man has given the designation of science are no truer than the dreams, visions, or inspirations. Since all thought is subjective, man-made criteria may never be objective."[27] Because the movement begins with a flight from the premises of science and materialism, it asserts that primary reality is "indestructibly spiritual." The leap to beliefs in reincarnation, telepathy, psychokinesis, and "beings from other dimensions" is a short one.

The New Age continues with a second renunciation, which we have already touched upon: Traditional, institutional religion is no longer an adequate guide for one's spiritual quest. In a sense, the movement is a kind of neo-Reformation. The early Protestants rejected mediators like the pope, the clergy, and the weight of church tradition, which were established to separate men and women from a sense of immediate experience of the divine. But now, of course, for many people the Bible and Christian myth have also become illegitimate mediators between the temporal and the divine; they too must go. God is no longer separated from us; He is inside us all. The historical Jesus, severed from us by nearly two thousand years and the Higher Biblical Criticism, is out; Christ-consciousness, which we can all cultivate by imagining that we are as wise as the man we think Christ was, and which is much harder to criticize, is in.

Indeed, the question of what's inside you and what isn't is one of the most intriguing paradoxes of New Age thinking—perhaps nowhere more so than in the drama of trance-channeling. Channelers like J. Z. Knight, the late Jane Roberts, and Jack Pursel all claim to give, from within them, voices to divine or semi-divine beings. By being able to channel such beings, they represent human empowerment, our direct connection to higher powers. But they also highlight our distance from the divine, our human limits, our reliance on outside entities—after all, J. Z. Knight is not "Ramtha," Jane Roberts is not "Seth," Pursel, not "Lazaris." This problem is not lost on many channelers—so you see a lot of waffling. Jane Roberts, for example, was never able to figure out whether "Seth" was an individual entity or "a higher voice" emanating from her own subconscious. To her credit, Roberts frankly admitted that she was perplexed by this.

Many channelers simply gloss over the problem. About the spirit-guide Emmanuel (channeled by Pat Rodegast), Ram Dass writes, "From my point of view as a psychologist, I allow for the theoretical possibility that Emmanuel is a deeper part of Pat. However, experientially, I know Emmanuel as quite separate in personality, language, style and vibration from the way in which I know Pat. In the final analysis, what difference does it really make? What I treasure is the wisdom Emmanuel conveys as an essence spiritual friend. Beyond this his identity doesn't really matter."[28]

And Jack Underhill, editor of *Life Times: Forum for a New Age,* introduces his section on channeling this way: "Whether [channels] are tapping into higher realms of their superconsciousness, or allowing [*sic*] through spirit guides of one sort or another, is not very important, since we are all interconnected, since we all share this same 'knowledge' or 'nonsense,' through the communal mind of all life. . . . I believe that every one of them is providing knowledge and wisdom that bears consideration, no matter where its's coming from."[29] Underhill proceeds to introduce six trance channelers, two of whom claim to channel Jesus Christ. Needless to say, none is convincing.

Channelers who have tried to remain within the framework of Christianity have looked less silly channeling the Holy Ghost—perhaps because we don't have so many direct quotes from Him in the canon. The most successful attempt has been *A Course in Miracles,* published by the Foundation for Inner Peace, which has sold more than 150,000 copies and has spawned study groups all over the United States. The work was "channeled" by Helen Schucman with the "assistance" of William Thetford, who were professors of Medical Psychology at Columbia University's College of Physicians and Surgeons in New York City at the time. For most of their lives, they were "anything but spiritual. Their relationship with each other was difficult and often strained, and they were concerned with personal and professional acceptance and status." Until their dramatic contact with the "Holy Spirit," their lives "were hardly in accord with anything that the Course advocates." Schucman narrates her conversion:

> Psychologist, educator, conservative in theory and atheistic in belief, I was working in a prestigious and highly academic setting. And then something happened that triggered a chain of events I could never have predicted. . . . The head of my department . . . unexpectedly announced that he was tired of the angry and aggressive feelings our attitudes reflected, and concluded that, "there must be another way." As if on cue I agreed to help him find it. Apparently this Course is the other way.[30]

Thetford encouraged Schucman to write down her "highly symbolic dreams," which she did for several months. Then: *the Voice.*

> Although I had grown more accustomed to the unexpected . . . I was still very surprised when I wrote, "This is a course in miracles. . . ." . . . [The voice] made no sound, but seemed to be giving me a kind of rapid, inner dictation which I took down in a shorthand notebook. The writing was never automatic. It could be interrupted at any time and later picked up again. It made me very uncomfortable, but it never seriously occurred to me to stop. It seemed to be a special assignment I had somehow, somewhere to complete.[31]

They completed their assignment—1,188 pages, three books, and seven years later. Their theology, however, is actually quite simple. Drawing much from the Manichean tradition, the *Course* holds that the physical world is an illusion. It "makes a fundamental distinction between the real and the unreal; between knowledge and perception. Knowledge is truly, under one law, the law of love or God. Truth is unalterable, eternal and unambiguous. It can be unrecognized, but it cannot be changed. . . . The world of perception, on the other hand, is the world of time, or change, or beginnings and endings." Sideswiping Neitzsche's famous dictum, they go on to say that the world of time "is based on interpretation, not on facts. It is a world of birth and death, founded on the belief in scarcity, loss, separation, and death. It is learned rather than given, selective in its perceptual emphases, unstable in its functioning, and inaccurate in its interpretations."[32]

The two professors, though jolted by their conversion, didn't leave their academic or medical interests behind—although neither seems really aware of this fact. Their channeled text is, after all, a *course*. Moreover, their chief concern is with the cause of sickness. "All sickness," they write, "comes from separation. When separation is denied, it goes. For it is gone as soon as the idea that brought it has been healed, and been replaced by sanity. Sickness and sin are seen as consequence and cause, in a relationship kept hidden from awareness that it may be carefully preserved from reason's light. Guilt asks for punishment, and its request is granted."[33] But, one must ask, who does *not* die of sickness? That we can control and eliminate sickness from our lives by the powers of our mind—this seems to be a positive approach. In practice, however, this approach makes sick people— everyone, sooner or later—experience their sickness not only as physical pain and humiliation but as separation from the divine, a separation the divine damns as wilful! I am reminded of the sad, crippled children and elderly folk ripped off by evangelical faith-healers like Peter Popoff and W. V. Grant—not called from their wheelchairs, they must return home in despair; not only are they crippled, but by their apparent lack of faith in the power of God they now believe they are going to Hell.

One imagines these two doctors, admittedly cantankerous and more than likely unable to help a good number of their patients, giving in to that deep, subconscious malice that pervades medicine, which better doctors manage to fight off: the suspicion that patients not only cause but *deserve* their own sickness. This is an ugly and immoral idea, the more so as it is presented without medical evidence, given as the Voice of God and dolled up by obscure promises of love and forgiveness.

How can so many people find this message inspiring? We are part of the divine, says the Course, but what is that? Hardly more than death, it is what extinguishes all our particularity, our memory, and our accomplishments. The book ends barely able to hide its fundamental nihilism:

> And you will be with [the Holy Spirit] when time is over and no trace remains of dreams of spite in which you dance to death's thin melody. For in its place the hymn to God is heard a little while. And then the Voice is gone, no longer to take form but to return to the eternal Formlessness of God.[34]

In the past two years, the number of channelers has quickly multiplied. And, with the double forces of media attention and channeler competition, some of the groundbreakers have come in for nasty criticism, even from their own.[35] J. Z. Knight/Ramtha, for example, has been rightly attacked for her self-serving doomsday prophecies. At the very least, however, Ramtha will hold your attention. Some of the more recent channelers seem afraid to go out on a limb. They dish out advice so sane it's banal. In her book *Personal Power for Awareness*, Sanaya Roman, channeler for "Orin, a wise and loving spirit teacher," tells us that we should "know when to pay attention to [our] own needs and when to be selfless" and that it's better to "spend time thinking of what you want rather than what you don't want." These precepts are good to know, and I wish I followed them more often. Less appealing, though, is some of Orin's other practical advice. With $15.00 plus $2.50 postage, for example, you can get his 106-page spiral-bound book *Creating Money: The Spiritual Laws of Prosperity and Abundance*—which features lessons on "the advanced laws of manifesting." How vulgar! You awaken to "higher spiritual realms," make direct contact with your own guardian angel—and for what? To learn how to grub money better?[36]

This bland, ordinary acquisitiveness has now begun to pervade the movement. Perhaps this evolution was inevitable. In the essay published in this volume, Jay Rosen argues that a key feature in New Age thinking is the "fluid" and "formless" way in which it defines the self and the world. Rosen likens this to the "goal of marketing," which "is to erase the boundary between the product and the consumer, so that the consumer sees the product, not as an object worth owning, but as a piece of his subjectivity floating by." Goal number one of marketing, of course, is not to offend. In his book *Your Past Lives: A Reincarnation Handbook,* Michael Talbott writes that, "If you find that the picture of reality you discover in states of past-life awareness is different from the one you have grown accustomed to in your waking state, do not be too disturbed that you cannot hammer the two together. Parts of them may overlap, and other parts may not. Accept only the useful parts of each and don't worry about the rest."[37]

In other words, you can inure yourself against any information that truly challenges you, and what begins as a revolutionary technique for completely altering your vision of the world becomes a supernatural imprimatur of the status quo. That past-life regressionists and other New Age "practitioners" have sought the run-of-the-mill respectability of the "professional association" is both revealing and comic.

> The best way to find a good psychic, [Talbott writes], as with finding other professionals, is through the recommendation of a friend, or even better, through the recommendation of a past-life psychologist or other New Age Professional. Another possibility is to contact one of several professional organizations for psychics that have sprouted up around the country. One such organization is the Association of Psychic Practitioners in San Jose, California. Designed both as a professional organization and a sort of Better Business Bureau for psychics, the APP was founded by psychic Mary Palermo in 1980 because, as a practicing psychic consultant for more than twenty years, she was tired of being lumped in the same category as gypsy fortune-tellers and other so-called psychics of dubious ethics.[38]

How can they tell who the really good psychics are? The APP "offers a certification process to honest and sincere psychics. To qualify, a psychic practitioner must sign a statement of ethics, furnish letters of reference and 'self-definition,' and pass an oral evaluation conducted by a panel of volunteer psychologists, professors, and other related professionals." I find this hilarious. The "certification process" doesn't even attempt to measure psychic ability, only "sincerity," which is no guarantee, we know, against being sincerely *wrong* or *deluded*. You would imagine that a room full of professional psychics could claim to verify psychic ability as well.

Are channelers authentic? For someone who takes reincarnation, channeling, and past-life regression hypnosis as facts of physical reality so demonstrable that he can write something as mundane as a "handbook," Talbott's credence seems porous. "Although it is obvious that further research is required to determine authenticity of trance information sources, at the very least the pronouncements of discarnate entities provide interesting working hypotheses for some of the greatest mystical questions of all time. Similarly, if research shows that discarnate entities are nothing more than manifestations of the unconscious minds of their channelers, the data we gather on this phenomenon cannot help but teach us more about ourselves and the mysterious workings of the human brain."[39]

That ain't saying much, but it's said a lot throughout New Age apologetics. Here, for example, is the *International UFO Reporter* attempting to refute Philip Klass's criticism of "UFO abductions":

Klass chides ufologists for becoming progressively credulous toward abductions, but in fact they have only responded to accumulating evidence that something unusual is going on and needs investigation. They may be incautious and they may be wrong, but they have made a more genuine effort first to meet the evidence on its own terms and then to decide what it means than the members of CSICOP [The Committee for the Scientific Investigation of Claims of the Paranormal], who start out with a litany of reasons why such evidence cannot exist. Who follows the spirit of science and who the letter?

Whatever abductions prove to be, they offer an opportunity for new knowledge, if not about aliens than about mental processes, the origin of cultural traditions, and the social development of beliefs. [40]

That UFOlogists have to defend their practice as the study of social pathology is as pathetic as it is sophistic.

Where It Is Fitting In

Critics and adherents of the New Age both trace the movement to the counterculture of the 1960s. There are, however, two key differences. The 1960s counterculture was a drug-culture—and, as such, it has been totally discredited; because too many heroes have died, few dare sing the praises of lysergic acid anymore. Ram Dass is a notable exception. [41] So is Marilyn Ferguson. In *The Aquarian Conspiracy,* she writes, "It is impossible to overestimate the historic role of psychedelics as an entry point drawing people into other transformative technologies. For tens of thousands of 'left-brained' engineers, chemists, psychologists, and medical students who never before understood their more spontaneous, imaginative right-brained brethren, the drugs were a pass to Xanadu. . . . The annals of the Aquarian Conspiracy are full of accounts of passages: LSD to Zen, LSD to India, psilocybin to Psychosynthesis."[42]

Today, however, the key to enlightenment isn't dope—according to many New Age magazines, such a key is more likely to be raw vegetables. Although there were more than a thousand people at Niagara Falls' Harmonic Convergence, for instance, I smelled no pot, only incense. Neither, for that matter, did I spot any political banners—that other symbol of the sixties counterculture. To be sure, New Agers have abandoned politics, at least partisan politics. The career of Shirley MacLaine is instructive in this respect: An ardent campaigner for George McGovern in 1972, her new-found spirituality, she says, has made politics and public affairs largely irrelevant. Why vote, or why march, when all suffering serves good karmic purpose, when we'll all be reincarnated, when supernatural entities are coming to rescue us?

Having repudiated drugs and politics, the New Age is much less defined than the counterculture—it lacks a so-called "core philosophy." But the movement's amorphousness is the reason it is more, not less, powerful than earlier countercultures were. Slippery and insistent, the movement can coopt and disown single-issue movements easily; it can disguise itself in order to insinuate itself into mainstream institutions. Indeed, it is this successful slipperiness that has scared some critics into believing that the New Agers are going to take over the world. Fundamentalist Christians have brought suits against large corporations that have required managers to attend "motivational training" programs—programs, they correctly observe, that are shot through with New Age "psychobabble." These programs use meditation, "guided visualization," relaxation techniques, and good old-fashioned positive thinking—all of which subvert the traditional Christian's world-view. In one case, the California Public Utilities Commission chastised Pacific Bell, the state's largest utility, because many employees complained that they were required to attend seminars based largely (and surreptitiously) on the teachings of mystic G. I. Gurdjieff. In another case, a man fired from Firestone Tire and Rubber Company for refusing to attend a similar motivational program got a huge out-of-court settlement from the company.[43]

The Next Step

The scientific and academic communities, mocked and despised in New Age circles, are only now beginning to explore this fascinating religio-cultural movement seriously. Dismissing it as nonsense hasn't converted many away from the movement, and it hasn't added anything to our knowledge of New Age practice. To assert, for example, that channelers suffer from extreme disassociation of personality or that in their trance-states they find access to deeply subconscious material only transposes the mystery from spiritual to psychological language. Such a transposition might allow some of us to feel as though we have adequately described these bizarre phenomena. But more and more of us are not convinced that the work is done.

And, certainly, it *should* be done. But how? In *The Psychology of Transcendence,* Andrew Neher writes:

> Although it is true that our understanding of transcendental experiences has increased significantly in recent times, understanding is not the same as experiencing, and experience is the essence of transcendence. Although as we have seen, people who interpret their transcendental experience as paranormal sometimes pay dearly for their belief, they *do* experience transcendental states. On the other hand, people who debunk transcendental experience may do

so partly because such experience is foreign to them. Ideally, understanding and experience reinforce each other. . . .

[Many] creative geniuses have been able to repeat the benefits of transcendental experiences that are latent in all of us. Generally speaking, these remarkable people who have benefited so greatly from transcendental experience are found neither in the camp of those who mystify such experience nor in the camp of those who debunk it. Maybe we can learn from their example.[44]

I see no other way to bring the two camps together. New Agers believe that it is the goal of science to explain away their experience. Our goal instead should be to find explanations that retain the experiences, incorporating them in a mutually acceptable, open-ended world-view.

The essays that comprise this volume were written precisely to that end.

Notes

1. Andrew Greeley, "Mysticism Goes Mainstream," *American Health* (January/February 1987), 47–49.

2. See *Publisher's Weekly,* September 25, 1987, for a partial listing of titles. The Christian critiques discussed below were virtually the only ones to question the merits of the New Age trend. For scientific appraisals of the paranormal side of the New Age, the magazine *Skeptical Inquirer* remains *the* valuable resource; see also Martin Gardner's *The New Age: Notes of a Fringe-Watcher* (Buffalo, N.Y.: Prometheus Books, 1988). While the national media have for the most part eschewed helpful analysis of the movement, some local groups of scientists and skeptics have published excellent work. See especially *The Rocky Mountain Skeptic* (Box 7277, Boulder, CO 80306).

3. Alice A. Bailey, an admirer of Madame Blavatsky, claimed to "receive" her spiritual information telepathically from a mysterious "Tibetan," Master Dhwhal Khul. Among her numerous books were *A Treatise on White Magic, Discipleship in the New Age, Education in the New Age,* and *Letters on Occult Meditation,* all published by Lucis Publishing Company, New York.

4. James Webb, *The Occult Establishment* (Peru, Ill.: Open Court, 1980), 453–454.

5. Robert Burrows, "Buzzwords and World-View," *Spiritual Counterfeits Newsletter,* Winter 1984–85, 5.

6. José Arguelles, *The Mayan Factor: The Path Beyond Technology* (Santa Fe, New Mexico: Bear & Company, 1987).

7. Arguelles, 15.

8. Arguelles, 194–196.

9. José Arguelles, "Art as Internal Technology: The Return of the Shaman—The Descent of the Goddess," in *Esthetics Contemporary,* Richard Kostelanetz, ed.

(Buffalo, N.Y.: Prometheus Books, 1978). Originally published in *The Transformative Vision,* by José A. Arguelles (Berkeley, Calif.: Shambhala Publications, Inc., 1975).

10. Arguelles, *The Mayan Factor,* 36.

11. Sy Safransky, *The Sun,* October 1987 (Issue 143), 4.

12. Robert Burrows, correspondence with author, July 17, 1987. Burrows has edited and written for a number of issues of the *Spiritual Counterfeits Project Newsletter* that focus on the New Age movement. See especially Vol. 10, No. 5 (Winter 1985–86), "New Age Movement: Self Deification in a Secular Culture."

13. Elliot Miller, correspondence with author, July 31, 1987. See Miller's four-part series on the New Age movement in *Forward,* Winter 1986, Spring/Summer 1986, Fall 1986, and the *Christian Research Journal,* Winter/Spring 1987. See also Douglas R. Groothuis, *Unmasking the New Age* (Downer's Grove, Ill.: InterVarsity Press, 1986), for a phlegmatic summary of Christian objections to the New Age. Constance Cumbey in *Hidden Dangers of the Rainbow* (Shreveport, La.: Huntington House, 1983) ably represents the alarmist approach taken by so many other Christian critics.

14. Constance Cumbey, "Is the Antichrist in the World Today? An Interview with Constance Cumbey" (Oklahoma City, Okla.: Southwest Radio Church, 1982). See also p. 9: "Psychic powers are not to be underestimated. I can show you incredible diagrams with charts in scientific magazines. I don't have the scientific education to read these because they are so detailed. Those plans could have only been conceived by demons. There are horrible weapons that can be used in the 'New Age.' "

15. Marilyn Ferguson, *The Aquarian Conspiracy: Personal and Social Transformation in the 1980s* (Los Angeles: J. P. Tarcher, 1980), 23.

16. Ferguson, 84–86.

17. For an especially explicit discussion of fundamentalist views of the occult, see Johanna Michaelsen, "Psychic Influence in Contemporary Society," in *The New Age and the Occult: The Tie That Binds* (Oklahoma City, Okla.: Southwest Radio Church, 1984), 1–17. Michaelsen, who is the author of a book called *The Beautiful Side of Evil,* says: "If you fall into the category of a psychic, a medium with ESP and similar abilities, or use ouija boards, palm reading, tea leaf reading, or anything else that falls into the category of occultism, IT IS NOT FROM GOD. I don't care how holy it feels to you; I don't care how many people are healed and how many children are walking. It is still an abomination. Satan can and does work miracles; Revelation 16 tells us of spirits of devils working miracles," 8.

18. Ferguson, 174–75.

19. Jack Underhill, ". . . on Earth Changes," *Life Times: Forum for a New Age* (Vol. 1, No. 4), 1.

20. See Marilyn Ferguson, "August Sacred Sites Festival Keyed to Ancient Prophecies," *Brain/Mind Bulletin,* 3, June 1987, and "The Revolution of Respect: A Fable for Our Times," *Brain/Mind Bulletin,* 3, August 1987.

21. Marilyn Ferguson, "Commentary: Debriefing Harmonic Convergence," *Brain/Mind Bulletin,* 5, September 1987.

22. See *Brain/Mind Bulletin,* 3, October 1987. In this odd interview, the editors

ask Pursel/Lazaris about "a recent finding that some multiply allergic people are sensitive to electricity and electrical equipment." Responds Pursel/Lazaris: "These people are allergic to the 20th Century." Ouch! What can be done? "People can . . . set quartz crystals on top of a monitor. You can wear a copper coil—not closed—within a quarter inch of the points' touching."

23. See Meg Sullivan, "New Age to Dawn in August, Seers Say, and Malibu is Ready," *Wall Street Journal* (June 23, 1987), 1.

24. Christopher Lasch, "Soul of a New Age," *Omni* (October 1987, Vol. 10, No. 1), 82.

25. Lasch, 81–82.

26. Mark Mayell, editor of *East West: The Journal of Natural Health & Living*, correspondence with author, July 14, 1987.

27. Brad Steiger, "What I Believe," an undated brochure.

28. See Pat Rodegast and Judith Stanton, *Emmanuel's Book: A Manual for Living Comfortably in the Cosmos* (New York: Bantam, 1985), introduction by Ram Dass, xvii.

29. Jack Underhill, *Life Times: Forum for A New Age* (Vol. 1, No. 3), 82.

30. Helen Schucman, "Preface," *A Course in Miracles* (Tiburon, Calif.: Foundation for Inner Peace, 1976). The *Course* was originally published in three volumes. The edition cited here combines the three but retains the original pagination. The "preface" is unpaginated.

31. Schucman, "Preface."

32. Schucman, "Preface."

33. Schucman, "Text," 514–15.

34. Schucman, "Manual for Teachers," 86.

35. Like the Mafia, channelers are especially unforgiving toward their own. In a channeling session transcribed for *New Realities* magazine (July/August 1987), Lazaris takes thinly disguised swipes at two of his biggest competitors, the late Alice A. Bailey—who claimed to channel information imparted by a mysterious Tibetan—and J. Z. Knight—who claims to channel a semidivine being from Atlantis, Ramtha. "Now," says Lazaris (who refers to himself in the first person plural), "we realize it would be easier for us to say we lived in Atlantis some thousands of years ago, or perhaps we were a monk high in the Himalayas or a great guru or teacher, for there would be no way of confirming or denying the truth of these statements. We understand that perhaps more people would more easily be able to comprehend our existence. But, in fact, we've never been physical and we feel this particular need to tell the truth even though it's difficult for some people to understand that a consciousness of intelligence, personality, and identity can exist without ever having had a body," 28.

J. Z. Knight, meanwhile, has complained about "spiritual bashing." According to an April 15, 1988, Associated Press story, Knight has accused rival channelers of spreading the following awful rumors about her: Knight's marriage is on the rocks, she is nearly bankrupt, she's about to be committed to a mental institution, and she has faked Ramtha's "appearances." Her former business manager, Les Sinclair, accused Purcell of spreading the rumor—a charge one of Purcell's spokespeople denied.

36. See Sanaya Roman, *Personal Power through Awareness* (Tiburon, Calif.: H. J. Kramer, 1986). Roman is also coauthor, with Duane Packer, of *Opening to Channel: How to Connect with Your Guide* (Tiburon, Calif.: H. J. Kramer, 1987). Both books are unintentionally frightening, in that the higher spiritual worlds they describe are as featureless as the New Age music they recommend to accompany you on your way into them.

37. Michael Talbott, *Your Past Lives: The Reincarnation Handbook* (New York: Harmony Books, 1987), 181.

38. Talbott, 154.

39. Talbott, 171–172.

40. Thomas E. Bullard,. "Klass Takes on Abductions; Abductions Win," *International UFO Reporter* (November/December 1987), 20.

41. In a recent interview in *The Sun* (February 1987, Issue 135), Ram Dass says, "I've taken MDMA three times this year. I took acid last year. I've smoked marijuana two times in the last six months." Asked by the editor, "Have you ever taken a drug, believing it was the best way to achieve a certain state of awareness, and then concluded, after the experience was over, that taking the drug wasn't necessary at all?" Ram Dass responded, "Yes, that's exactly the way I've felt. But I won't make any general conclusion about it. Because now and then, when I take a drug, I get some direct experience that's worth something to me," 17.

42. Ferguson, *The Aquarian Conspiracy*, 89–90.

43. See Robert Lindsey, "Gurus Hired to Motivate Workers Are Raising Fears of 'Mind Control,' " *New York Times* (April 17, 1987).

44. Andrew Neher, *The Psychology of Transcendence* (Englewood Cliffs, N.J.: Prentice-Hall, 1980), 8–9.

THE HISTORY

T he New Age is not really "new," as J. Gordon Melton and
James Webb coolly observe here. The beliefs and practices that
characterize this quickly growing movement have been culled
from ancient oriental religions as well as from nineteenth-century American-
prairie spiritualism—a fact often obscured by the movement's tendency
to describe itself with scientific and technological language. Yet even
this habit of appropriating the latest scientific jargon has ample precedent,
beginning, perhaps, with Emanuel Swedenborg—the first great occultist
of the modern era, who was a highly respected scientist before he set
aside the material world in favor of conversations with angels and astral
journeys beyond the solar system. Swedenborg, writes Melton, "suggested
that the world he explored in his dreamlike states had greater metaphysical
reality than the visible world more properly explored by science, which
he considered an inferior, shadowlike realm." This devaluation of the
material world has remained postulate number one of the New Age
movement.

Postulate number two? A vision of transformation inspired by the
example of higher spiritual reality. This vision, writes Melton, is especially
appealing to single, young, upwardly mobile urban adults: "Such upwardly
mobile persons are most accepting of processes of transformation, which
they know naturally accompany increasing career success. At their youthful
age, they tend still to believe that utopian social visions can be realized."

While Melton's essay gives us the large historical sweep—showing
how J. Z. Knight/Ramtha can be logically traced through an American
visionary tradition grandly begun by Emerson and Thoreau—James Webb's
essay homes in on the New Age movement's most recent, previous incarnation: the 1960s hippie counterculture. Steeped in a bohemian tradition borrowed from turn-of-the-century Europe, American counterculture
seemed, for a year or two, actually to take center stage, synthesizing
aspirations for political reform with religious questing and LSD-induced

ecstasy. We meet many champions of such a synthesis—Alan Watts, Ken Kesey, Henry Miller, Allen Ginsberg, Timothy Leary, Aldous Huxley, and Jack Kerouac—which Webb sees as a logical, natural one: "Because the leading gurus of LSD identified the drug-induced experience with the mystical experience of saints and ecstatics, those who used the drug did so in an atmosphere that was likely to put them in contact with theories of the occult or the unorthodoxly religious."

Webb's essay—adapted from his classic *Occult Establishment*—is packed with period detail. We hear the voices of the time as preserved in raucous underground magazines like the *Berkeley Barb*, the *Buddhist Oracle*, and *Modern Utopian*. In tracing the bloodline of our culture and counterculture, Webb affirms that what we are seeing, as the 1980s come to a close, is the perennial appeal to rejected, visionary knowledge. The present incarnation of this quest, however, is not as happily, discombobulatingly bizarre as our previous one. The hippie counterculture was wrong about drugs, and it was naive about politics—but, when placed beside its blander progeny, one finds it hard to ward off the fatigue nostalgia brings.

A HISTORY OF THE NEW AGE MOVEMENT

J. Gordon Melton

Over the past few years, a new popular religious movement forced the awareness of its existence upon the general public. Those who did not see the prime-time televised account of actress Shirley MacLaine's pilgrimage from mild interest in things occult to leadership in this new movement, saw the numerous magazine and newspaper feature stories or one of the dozens of talk shows featuring the movement's ardent proponents and equally intense critics. The sudden emergence of this movement was surprising to many, especially those unaware of the long tradition of occult/metaphysical religion in North America. In the face of often severe cultural disdain during the last two centuries, occult/metaphysical religion, having jettisoned most of its older supernatural trappings and wed itself to newer models derived from science, has made a steady return to a place of prominence in Western culture, from which it seemed destined to disappear, buried under the combined weight of Enlightenment skepticism and Protestant iconoclasm.[1]

While calling itself "new" and dating itself only to the early 1970s, the New Age Movement in fact has deep roots in Western culture. It emerged out of the longstanding Western occult/metaphysical tradition and differs only by its appropriation of several new scientific concepts, derived primarily from transpersonal psychology, and recently arrived religious ideas and practices, derived primarily from the Eastern religions, which began a new wave of influx into the West in 1965. The often contradictory mixtures of science, religion, and the occult within the movement have taken on a bewildering array of forms and emphases. That is to say, the New Age Movement is a genuine *movement*—it has no central headquarters, and its adherents hold widely varying opinions concerning its exact nature and

---

Dr. J. Gordon Melton is the director of the Institute for the Study of American Religion and the author of *The Encyclopedia of American Religion* and *The Encyclopedic Handbook of Cults in America*.

goals. While members share a repudiation of the orthodoxies they have left behind, the movement is, however loosely, held together by its very real transformative vision of a new world and of new people who will transcend the limitations of narrowly chauvinistic cultures, religions, and political systems, and will surpass the outmoded thought-forms of "old age" theologies and beliefs. That transformative vision of a New Age both unifies the more visible diversity and gives the movement its name. By looking at the movement's historical predecessors, its own very brief history, and its major ideological components, I will draw some inferences as to its possible future.

Historic Background and Origin

The New Age Movement can best be dated from around 1971. By that year, Eastern religion and transpersonal psychology (the key new elements needed to create the distinctive synthesis) had achieved a high level of popularity, and metaphysical leaders could begin to articulate the New Age vision. *East-West Journal* became the first national periodical to focus the issues of the new movement, and Baba Ram Dass, a transformed refugee from the psychedelic age, emerged as its first national prophet. Early exponents created the typical organizational form of the new movement: networks so loosely tied together as to exist merely as mailing lists. By 1972, the first national network directories were published: Ira Friedlander's *Year One Catalog* and the first edition of the *Spiritual Community Guide*.

Despite its relatively recent appearance, the movement should not be viewed as a startlingly new phenomenon in Western culture. Rather, it is more adequately seen as the latest phase in occult/metaphysical religion, a persistent tradition that has been the constant companion of Christianity through the centuries and has blossomed heartily as a product of the Eighteenth-Century Enlightenment. The occult, largely destroyed by Protestantism and the first major waves of religious skeptical thinking represented in such movements as Deism, needed a new vehicle to replace the outmoded supernaturalism of medieval magic and alchemy. It found that vehicle in the new science of the eighteenth and nineteenth century. Indeed, one cannot understand the New Age Movement without recognizing its full acceptance of science and its subsequent use of science as a major vehicle for expressing its perspective. Thus, as science has grown, so has the metaphysical/ occult community. Metaphysicians rejoiced in science's critique of Christianity, celebrated its dominant ideas of natural law and evolution, and from scientific affirmations built a new alternative spiritual vision capable of interacting, and even contributing, to the fullness (from the occultists' viewpoint) of scientific knowledge. Thus one constantly encounters meta-physicians whose pilgrimage through life has led them from more traditional Western religious beliefs to the critiques of religion by natural scientists, social scientists, and historical researchers, to a state of dissatisfaction (even crisis) at science's inability to answer for them life's ultimate questions of human origins, meaning, and destiny, to the personal reconstruction of a new religious vision in an occult/metaphysical mode.

Certainly that pilgrimage was evident at the beginning of the modern metaphysical tradition, which is usually traced to one of the leading scientists of Sweden and a young physician fresh from the completion of his doctoral work at the University of Leipzig. Emanuel Swedenborg would likely be lauded today for his scientific accomplishments had his name not been deleted from the history of science after he left that career to become a "seer." During the several decades of his scientific endeavors, Swedenborg became the first to state the nebular hypothesis of the origin of the universe, and, as a metallurgist, he pioneered the development of crystallography and mineralogy. But he turned his back on his scientific pursuits to spend the last decades of his life in intimate communion with what he claimed were angels. One can ask hard factual questions about the adequacy of Swedenborg's metaphysical claims. For example, he claimed to have been taken astrally on a tour of the solar system, to its outer edge and beyond. Yet, strangely enough, on his trip he passed only the commonly known planets of his day, zooming past Uranus, Neptune, and Pluto but taking no notice of them. However, such obvious errors have had far less influence on subsequent generations of occultists than have the ideas and practices he popularized, which have became standard elements of the occult world-view. In the face of growing materialism, he championed *the primacy of the invisible spiritual world.* He suggested that the world he explored in his dreamlike states had greater metaphysical reality than the visible world more properly explored by science, which he considered an inferior, shadow-like realm. But Swedenborg stated his conclusions in such a way that the science of his day was neither contradicted nor discounted, merely put in its proper secondary place. This world was the product of the *divine influx*, the ultimate origin of power and life.

Swedenborg analyzed the relation between the two worlds in his treatment of the "scientific" *law of correspondences.* Everything in the visible material world corresponded to the spiritual world, though as a lesser reality. Disposing of the outmoded three-story universe, his correspondence theory gave the metaphysical community a modern scientific restatement of the old Hermetic principle, "As above, so below."

The idea of "influx" was given a more precise and "scientific" formulation by Franz Anton Mesmer, the Viennese physician, who proposed the existence of what he termed "universal magnetic fluid." Though rebuffed by the French Academy of Science, his disciples experienced the mysterious flow of energy of which he spoke and some, like Karl von Reichenbach, devised numerous experiments to prove its existence. That the experiments proved unconvincing to the larger scientific community became less important than Mesmer's articulation of a quasiscientific model in which to restate old claims about a magical power or a healing power or a sacred spiritual energy. In the nineteenth century it became known as *animal magnetism, astral light, odic force,* and *psychic energy.* Possessed states became *mesmeric sleep* and then *hypnotism* and the *mediumistic trance.*

In America in the early nineteenth century, Swedenborgianism and mesmerism as popular movements stood beside the third major building block of the metaphysical world—Transcendentalism. The pilgrimage of Trancendentalism's major spokesperson, Ralph Waldo Emerson, took him from Christian orthodoxy to Unitarianism to a new religious vision that brought angry responses from even his most liberal colleagues. Enthused with the new translations of the holy books of Hinduism, especially the *Bhagavad Gita,* Emerson created a uniquely American form of what might best be seen as a pagan nature mysticism. It was the first substantive religious movement in North America with a prominent Asian component (though totally derived from a few books). Emerson successfully integrated the Eastern idealistic metaphysics with more popular American values such as individualism, personal responsibility, and the drive to get ahead in life. In his writings (which were never particularly bound by that old bug-a-boo, consistency), Emerson left behind a workable mysticism to compete with both dualistic Christianity and materialistic nineteenth-century science.

By the 1850s, the first popular form of the metaphysical tradition to draw upon and synthesize Swedenborg, Mesmer, and Emerson reached its first peak of popularity. Largely superseding and sapping the strength of both Swedenborgianism and the popular magnetist movement, Spiritualism accepted the task of speaking in an acceptable scientific manner about cosmology and healing. But further, it proposed that, quite apart from traditional religious faith, Spiritualism could *scientifically demonstrate the survival of individual humans after death.* Not content to talk to angels, the Spiritualists talked to the spirits of the so-called dead, among the first being no less than Swedenborg himself. The means of intercourse between the living and dead was *trance mediumship,* a self-induced trance state. The entranced could, of course, heal, and not a few did. But the new emphasis creating Spiritualism's popularitry was spirit contact through living mediums.

Orthodox Christians were as horrified by the Spirtualists' rejection of their supernatural world-view (in favor of then-current theories of natural law and Darwinian evolution) as they were by their ignoring biblical injunctions against conversing with spirits. At the same time, the Free Thought Movement quickly perceived emerging battle lines, and responded by making common cause with their occult allies against their mutual enemy: religious superstition. Other scientists, unable to reconcile the faith of their childhood with the new discoveries they were making, devoted their life to researching the claims of the Spiritualist.

As Spiritualism spread across North America and around the world, the metaphysical community broadened its perspectives with new variations on the spiritual ideal. Mary Baker Eddy, with students like Emma Curtis Hopkins, attempted to combine the monist vision introduced by Emerson with the healing imperative of mesmerism. Rejecting the magnetic power as evil, or at best a lesser material force, these metaphysical healing groups developed a thoroughgoing idealism that quickly directed itself toward practical application. As naturally as science led to technology, so Christian Science and its stepchild New Thought moved to apply the principles they discovered to problems of health and then to poverty and unhappiness. And success came in demonstration of scientific principles. Metaphysical science did *seem* to produce healings, some rather spectacular, to the consternation of what passed for medicine in the late-nineteenth century.

Strictly applied metaphysics also produced business success. The early metaphysicians had discerned many of the rules of corporate social life, and to this day successful businessmen tend to follow those rules either consciously or intuitively.[2]

But, if people can contact the dead, utilize the healing power, and know the metaphysical world enough to use it for health, wealth, and happiness, then occult metaphysicians should be able to fill in *all* the pieces of our missing knowledge. Inner exploration should reveal the structures and powers of the spiritual universe and detail the great panorama of life and history, even provide a picture of the future. Arriving in the last quarter of the nineteenth century, the Theosophical Society saw its purpose in exactly those terms. It took the affirmations of the metaphysical movement and the latest findings of science (for example, the hypothesized lost continent of Lemuria— originally proposed by biologists), added its unique picture of the evolution of the race, and produced a vast panoramic vision of the cosmos. Key items in its new vision were the *Masters*, the "ruling spiritual elite." The Masters were the ones who really controlled the cosmos. From their lofty realms they constantly seeded society with new scientific ideas, and they periodically called humanity to higher levels of moral and spiritual attainment by sending one of their number to walk among the merely mortal. The belief in the Masters led the Society to mobilize hope in the appearance of a savior figure in the near future. According to many of the members of the early theosophical movement, its real occult purpose was to prepare the way for a *coming world teacher,* who embarrassingly made his initial appearance through a young Indian boy, Jiddu Krishnamurti, who later renounced his role in the endeavor—to the chagrin of his worshipers.

By the end of the nineteenth century, all of the major components of the metaphysical/occult tradition—Swedenborgianism, Spiritualism, Christian Science, New Thought, and Theosophy—found organizational stability. In the new century, each group—but especially Theosophy—divided and subdivided, producing literally hundreds of new organizations, a number of which became national in scope.

Theosophy became the seedbed that nurtured the important new movements that would emerge so forcefully in the twentieth century. Several hundred new occult organizations can be traced directly to the Society. For example, drawing upon the esoteric work initiated by Theosophy, ritual magicians developed high magic as almost a separate discipline. Ritual magicians have attempted to attain the mastery of the world through occult means in a measure only hinted at in theosophical circles. Whereas theosophists preferred a rather passive approach to inner exploration, thus allowing the gentle appropriation of the inner life, magicians tended to operate like spiritual stormtroopers, pushing their way into the inner world, invoking, confronting, and, if successful, subduing the forces they found there.

Theosophy also nurtured a reborn *astrology,* reconstructed with Swedenborg's "law of correspondences" and new discoveries about light waves and electromagnetic radiation. Beginning with minuscule astrological groups in the late nineteenth century, astrology made an astounding comeback to become the most pervasive popular occult practice in the latter part of the twentieth century.

Theosophy also provided the prime channel through which Hinduism and Buddhism reached out to claim non-Asian converts. Through theosophical literature, leaders, and centers, Eastern religious ideas flowed into the West. The first English-language Hindu book designed not merely to inform but to "convert" Westerners, *Nature's Finer Forces* by Rama Prasad, was published in 1890 by the Theosophical Publishing House. It was, during its early years, most conducive to the growth of Buddhism, to which its first international president had converted. Many of the early Buddhist groups in the West began in theosophical lodges. Ultimately, however, Theosophy proved itself more akin to Hinduism, and the new Hinduism of the Indian Renaissance of the nineteenth century used Theosophy effectively in its movement to Europe and North America. Theosophical founder Helena P. Blavatsky assisted this process immeasurably by her standardization of the term *reincarnation*. Her initial introduction of the concept in the West divided many in the older metaphysical churches, but finally through the success of Theosophical disciples such as the late Edgar Cayce, reincarnation reached a popular audience beyond the Society and earned the acceptance of the vast majority in the metaphysical community, a fact amply demonstrated in recent polls that show the high percentage of Americans who have accepted the idea.

Other groups, like the Arcane Society of Alice Bailey, popularized the practice of what today is called *channeling*. Bailey broke with the Theosophical Society in America because she was channeling material from the Masters. Her books found a devoted audience, and, in the years since her death, others have discovered their ability to channel from either the Masters of Blavatsky's hierarchy or other exalted beings—God, disembodied spirits, the collective subconscious, or flying-saucer entities.

Another Theosophical offshoot, the I AM Religious Movement, emphasized the importance of *light* (a common element in many reports of mystical experience) and added an emphasis upon the spiritual (occult) significance of *color*. The attention paid to color, especially as experienced in the light of gems, underlies the love of crystals in recent decades.

Throughout the twentieth century the occult/metaphysical tradition became even more firmly entrenched as an element in Western culture. The ever-growing number and variety of organizations provided more-or-less stable structures for passing on the teachings from one generation to the next. By the time the vision of the New Age began to be announced in the early 1970s, the occult/metaphysical community, consisting of the members and constituencies of several hundred alternative metaphysical religions (from the Rosicrucian Fellowship to the Unity School of Christianity), formed a large pre-existing potential audience. And, of course, the membership of these metaphysical groups became the first to be told of the New Age and the first to become enthused about the movement's vision. That initial support given the movement by the many older Spiritualist, Theosophical, and New Thought groups explains the seeming quickness of the movement's emergence and spread. The older community also provided the host of additional ideas and practices that gave the new movement increasing substance.

During the twentieth century the community continued its early love of science. Even a cursory examination of their literature manifests this devotion to scientific ideas and popular technology. Metaphysicians celebrated each new finding that they saw as providing them with another new metaphor for ultimate reality. Most enthusiastically received was the new science of psychology. Its emergence out of physiology as a discipline in its own right provided the occult/metaphysical community with rich intellectual support. Even though both the behaviorist and Freudian schools were extremely hostile to religion, defining much religious phenomena in pathological terms, psychology gave metaphysicians symbolic structures for mapping the inner territory about which each had been most concerned. And those few psychologists who had studied the occult, like Carl Jung, readily gave occultists credit as pioneers in psychological theory.

Equally important, psychology nurtured psychical research and its laboratory-oriented branch, *parapsychology*. As questionable as the accomplishments of these two subdisciplines within psychology have been, they supplied a unique seedbed out of which new crops of speculations could regularly emerge. The admission of the Parapsychological Association into membership in the American Academy for the Advancement of Science served to further the process of legitimization of "scientific" metaphysical thought.

The latest appropriation of psychology, a necessary step in the formation of the New Age, followed the emergence of humanistic psychology and its derivative, transpersonal psychology. Humanistic psychology projected a much more positive approach to religious phenomena, while transpersonal psychology went even further, to concentrate its study upon "religious" states of mind and to utilize the spiritual disciplines (from meditation to magic) most advocated by the metaphysical practitioners as primary research tools. In their attempts to isolate the effects of various spiritual disciplines, the transpersonal psychologists accomplished one unplanned but important task. Their methodologies separated particular practices (for example, a meditation or yoga technique) from the religious ideological context in which they had been developed and justified their free movement from one group to another. One now could do Zen meditation without becoming a Buddhist or chant mantras without becoming a Hindu. Concurrently, transpersonal psychology lent scientific respectability to a new language of *consciousness*, *creativity*, and *personal transformation* to explain the observed changes accompanying the use of the spiritual techniques, a language eagerly adopted by the emerging movement in the 1970s.

While science provided new data and new language upon which the New Age could build, the actual catalyst for its formation came in an unheralded action of the government, which, in 1965, for reasons completely unrelated to any matters metaphysical, rescinded the Asian Exclusion Act and in effect opened the dams of Asian teachings established at the beginning of the century. Most importantly, the new immigration law allowed teachers of Asian spiritual practices to come to America and share them with a popular Western audience. At the very beginning of the movement, one observer noted:

> A Great Spiritual energy has been moved to this country and holy men of the East are following it, and, of course, they bring the Light within them to become our mirrors. They establish centers or ashrams and reconfirm the spiritual centers within ourselves. They plant the seed of inner peace within the divine grace, which remains and nourishes like a good rain that falls on fertile soil; long after the rain has gone, the seed in the soil continues to grow.[3]

New teachers came intentionally to spread their ideas and practices among Westerners. The last days of the 1960s saw the launching of a major missionary thrust by the Eastern religions toward the West. Though not centrally coordinated, its various elements agreed on one point: The West is ready for the wisdom the East possesses, and it needs this wisdom now more than ever.

The Networks

Once the idea of the New Age was articulated, early exponents began to build the networks of those groups and organizations that seemed to be aligned either ideologically or practically. Early directories included centers of the various occult, Eastern, and mystical religions; health-food stores; metaphysical book stores; antivivisection societies; yoga teachers; parapsychology research organizations; psychic-development interest groups; communes; and alternative health-care facilities. The directories showed little discrimination and tended to include listings of any group that appeared to offer an alternative spirituality, even traditional Christian groups if they carried an unusual name.

As the community that accepted the basic vision of the movement evolved, service organizations sprouted up to facilitate its development. Most important in any decentralized movement, periodicals tied the diverse groups and individuals together and kept the movement informed. Early significant periodicals included the *New Age Journal* (created by former staff members of *East-West Journal*), *New Realities*, *New Directions*, and *Yoga Journal*. To these were added the many periodicals serving particular Eastern and occult groups, and local newsletters whose circulation was limited to a single metropolitan area or one organization's membership. In the early 1970s in San Francisco, *Common Ground* appeared as a directory of local New Age activities and services. Its format has been copied in other cities by periodicals that go under names like *New Age Chicago, Free Spirit* (New

York City), *New Frontier* (Philadelphia), and *New Texas* (Austin). *Whole Life Times,* which has emulated *Common Ground*'s format but is primarily concerned with alternative health networks, appears in several local editions and has spurred similar periodicals, such as *Alternative Health* (in Fort Lauderdale) and the *Holistic Learning Quarterly* (Pittsburgh).

Through the 1970s, the leading theoreticians appeared one by one. Baba Ram Dass was the first recognized national exponent of New Age consciousness. A former professor of psychology at Harvard, the Jewish-born Richard Alpert accompanied his colleague Timothy Leary through a period of experimentation with psychedelic drugs before going to India and finding his guru. He reappeared as Baba Ram Dass, a guru in his own right, just as the New Age was being announced. The excellent Western academic background transformed by his new-found Eastern faith made him the perfect symbol of the New Age. The movement consumed his popular books: *The Only Dance There Is* (1973), *Grist for the Mill* (1977), *Journey of Awakening* (1978), and *Miracle of Love* (1979). He was joined by other popular figures, some of whom were, like himself, leaders of their own alternative religious movements: Kirpal Singh, Yogi Bhajan, Pir Vilayat Khan, Swami Rama, Reb Zalman Schlachter-Shalomi, Swami Kriyananda, Sun Bear, Swami Muktananda, and Rabbi Joseph Gelberman, to mention a few.

The most important architects of the movement, however, were not those teachers of older traditions who happened to accept the ideals of the New Age, but those who possessed primary commitment to the New Age. Most prominent among these is Marilyn Ferguson of Interface Press, editor of *Brain/Mind Bulletin* and (the recently defunct) *Leading Edge Bulletin.* Ferguson jumped into prominence with her optimistic survey of the movement, *The Aquarian Conspiracy* (1980), which remains the most commonly accepted statement of the movement's ideals and goals. Possibly second only to Baba Ram Dass and Marilyn Ferguson as a spokesperson of the New Age Movement is David Spangler. After three years as codirector of the Scottish community at Findhorn, he returned to the United States and founded the Lorian Association, a New Age community now located in Washington state. His early volume, *Revelation, the Birth of a New Age* (1976), has been a major popular statement of New Age perspectives.

The 1975 publication of *A Course in Miracles* by the newly formed Foundation for Inner Peace thrust Judith Skutch, an early New Age advocate in New York City and president of the Foundation for Inner Peace, into the spotlight. The multivolume *Course,* channeled by a professor of Medical Psychology at Columbia University, restated more traditional New Thought metaphysics using the metaphor of "miracles" and became a very popular study book throughout New Age circles; several hundred groups were founded across North America during its first decade in print. Other popular New Age teachers include Patricia Sun, George Leonard, Jean Houston, Norman Shealy, Irving Oyle, and Sam Keen.

Admiring cooperation over competition, New Age exponents have tried several social structures to embody their ideals. Communes were a natural option, and some older communes were among the first groups to identify with the New Age perspective. Prominent among these communes are the Lama Foundation in New Mexico, the Renassiance Community in Massachusetts, and the Stelle Community in Illinois. Many of the Eastern teachers promoted communal living among their followers, and some nurtured communes within their organizations. Prominent among these communes are the Abode of the Message, founded by Pir Vilayat Khan of the Sufi Order, the Ananda Cooperative Community of Swami Kriyananda, and New Vrindaban, the community of the International Society of Krishna Consciousness in West Virginia.

The most important element in the New Age Movement are the many organizations and businesses that have arisen to facilitate the process of transformation at the heart of the New Age vision. Every metropolitan area has scores of individuals who teach transformational techniques—from meditation to the martial arts—or who practice the various forms of alternative medicine, "body work" therapies, and psychological processes. Organizations, primarily of a local and frequently ephemeral nature, support the practitioners and provide a point of contact between those seeking and those providing services. Particularly in the field of health, national professional and referral associations have been founded to bring some order to the competition between numerous forms of therapy (some of dubious value) being offered by individuals with highly varying qualifications. Among the most prominent are the American Holistic Medical Association (Washington, D.C.) and the Association for Holistic Health (San Diego). Numerous businesses have also been founded to serve the New Age community through their distribution of a wide range of New Age products—from yoga mats and meditation cushions to macrobiotic cookwear, health foods, natural vitamins, oriental art, and incense. Many of these businesses are also trying to be a model of the New Age for the business community and embody New Age principles in their organization.

The New Age Vision

The ideas of the New Age Movement are difficult for many to grasp, as they grow more out of intuition and experience than doctrines or logical reasoning. Moreover, the movement tends to embrace mutually contradictory ideas, and among its more important spokespersons are people who voice opinions completely unacceptable to the movement as a whole. Thus, it is easier to understand the New Age in terms of its ideals and goals rather than a set of beliefs to which it gives assent.

The central vision and experience of the New Age is one of radical transformation. On an individual level that experience is very personal and mystical. It involves an awakening to a new reality of self—such as a discovery of psychic abilities, the experience of a physical or psychological healing, the emergence of new potentials within oneself, an intimate experience within a community, or the acceptance of a new picture of the universe. However, the essence of the New Age is the imposition of that vision of personal transformation onto society and the world. Thus the New Age is ultimately a *social* vision of a world transformed, a heaven on earth, a society in which the problems of today are overcome and a new existence emerges. There is a wide range of opinion about the nature of that New Age and the means of bringing it about, but all adherents accept that this New Age will be grounded in the individual's experience of transformation. It is this focus on the personal that gives the movement its vitality and appeal.

The power to bring about the necessary transformation of both individuals and society comes from "universal energy," according to New Age thinking. Members of the New Age Movement assume the existence of a basic energy that is different from the more recognized forms of energy (heat, light, electromagnetism, gravity, etc.), which undergirds and permeates all of existence. This energy goes by many names—*prana, mana, odic force, orgone energy, holy spirit, the ch'i, mind, the healing force*. It is the force believed to cause psychic healing to occur. It is the force released in various forms of meditation and body therapies that energizes the individual mentally and physically. It is the force passed between individuals in the expressions of love. It is the underlying reality of the universe encountered in mystical states of consciousness.

That the movement is built around the experience of radical transformation and universal energy does not deny the presence of concepts and ideas that members of the movement affirm. Rather, it emphasizes the secondary role such ideas have and the nondoctrinaire approach taken toward the ideological framework of the movement. Affirmation of particular propositions or beliefs is not a criterion for participation in or acceptance by the movement, and members in good standing may vocally disagree with popular concepts without fear of chastisement or alienation.

Within the variety of ideals and goals that exist in the movement, some have found the greatest appeal. First, in the New Age, it is believed, *people will recognize one universal religion*. While that one religion will assume many different forms and draw from all the present religious traditions, the same mystical faith will underlie each grouping no matter what label (be it Christian or Buddhist) it chooses. This faith finds inspiration in nature, the changing seasons, and the growth and development of individuals through the common cycles of life. It also places great emphasis upon self-knowledge, inner exploration, and the participation in a continual transformative process only begun in that intitial transformation that led the individual to identify him- or herself as a New Age person in the first place.

The emphasis upon continual transformation will lead New Age persons on a *sadhana,* a spiritual path. For some that will mean commitment for a period or a lifetime to the practices taught by a single spiritual teacher. Others will continually sample transformative practices, picking and choosing from them, and thus develop a very individualized and constantly changing sadhana.

Since few individuals complete their sadhana in one lifetime, the commonly accepted belief of *reincarnation* and *karma* provides a longterm framework in which to view individual spiritual progression. Individuals will accomplish their moral and spiritual development as they live out the consequences of prior actions, from this life and previous ones, over a period of successive lifetimes in a physical body. The law of karma, the rule by which the universe returns rewards and punishment, provides the authority for moral action. Immoral action produces unpleasant consequences on its perpetrator (i.e., bad karma).

The sadhana will have as its goal the production of a mystical consciousness or awareness (frequently called by such names as *higher consciousness, self-realization, Christ consciousness, or New Age awareness*). To have a consciousness that transcends mundane reality is to be aware of the universal energy that undergirds existence and of the metaphysical unity that underlies the appearance of diversity. Most (but not all) New Agers identify God with that *ultimate unifying principle* that binds the whole together and the power that gives it a dynamic. Thus some New Agers are pantheists, identifying God and the world as one reality. Using metaphysical speculations derived from Einstein's identification of matter with energy, they will occasionally reduce all reality to "energy." Others tend toward a form of dualism that sees spiritual reality as ultimately good and real, but matter as an evil that must be left behind.

People participate in God as individualized manifestations of that ultimate unifying principle and as channels of the universal energy to the world. Jesus, and the other significant religious teachers like Buddha or Krishna, were particularly transparent bearers of the Divine, or Christ Principle. Such teachers appear regularly throughout history to illustrate the aware (fully realized) life, to teach individuals the goal of awareness, and to train them in particular techniques (the elements of the sadhana) that facilitate self-awareness of one's inherent divinity. Some New Age people see the need to find a living guru who is a fully-realized teacher. When such is found, he or she will be judged upon his or her perceived awareness (enlightenment) rather than by more mundane questions—like religious tradition, personal behavior (until it becomes scandalous or outrageous), or teaching idiosyncrasies.

Based upon their idealistic understanding of the nature of the universe, the devotees of the New Age frequently affirm their own Godhood. As a primary effect of such an affirmation, New Agers frequently report a sense of release from guilt and an acceptance of life. Carried into the ethical realm, New Agers often affirm that all is God, hence *all is good.* Evil is usually tied to ignorance—i.e., lack of enlightenment. The transformation from an ignorant state to an enlightened one releases the individual from the consequences (karma) of ignorance and brings forgiveness and/or understanding of the former experience of unpleasantness, what the mundane world calls evil. The enlightened being lives *beyond* good and evil.

Worship within the New Age Movement finds its typical expression in meditation and various transformative practices taught by the different spiritual teachers or gurus (to whom followers and critics will ascribe various levels of self-awareness). On the social level it is most clearly expressed in the Universal Worship of the Sufi Order, which honors all religions while seeking to find the consciousness and understanding of the cosmos underlying each one, and in the celebrations of those times all religions seem to commemorate. Many people within the New Age Movement, primarily those with a theosophical background, see the necessity of a particular person, a world teacher, a new avatar of the status of Jesus or Gautama Buddha, who will be a catalyst to bring about the New Age. The students of Alice Bailey have been energetic advocates of this position and have circulated uncounted thousands of copies of a prayer, "The Great Invocation," which calls for this avatar's appearance. It is frequently heard in New Age gatherings:

> From the point of Light within the Mind of God
> Let light stream forth into the minds of men.
> Let light descend on Earth.

> From the point of Love within the Heart of God
> Let love stream forth into the hearts of men.
> May Christ return to Earth.

From the center where the will of God is known
Let purpose guide the little wills of men—
The purpose which the Masters know and serve.
From the center which we call the race of men
Let the plan of Love and Light work out.
And may it seal the door where evil dwells.

Let Light and Love and Power restore the Plan to Earth.

Not only will there be one universal religion recognized in the New Age, but there will be *an allegiance to the planet and the human race that will supersede loyalties to the more limited groupings of clan, nation, race, or region.* This commitment to One World finds a typical expression in communes. Just as personal transformation is the symbol of social transformation, communes are the models of the new planetary society. They demonstrate the values of cooperation and sharing and the possibility of individual acceptance within an artificially created community.

Allegiance to the planet undergirds many new concerns (concerns also shared by many people in no way connected with the movement): ecology, peace, natural foods and healing processes, humanizing technology, cooperative models of living, overcoming hunger, and global politics. While some leaders within the New Age community hold well-known and definite opinions on these issues, the movement as a whole can be said only to share a focus and concern for these issues, which they see as planetary problems to be overcome in the transformation into the New Age. The concern with the planet and the development of networks to engage in social change have become significant factors separating New Age people from more traditional occultists, who tended to avoid social activism as irrelevant to spiritual development.

While separating themselves from what is termed "fortune-telling," the trivialization of various occult techniques to catch a glimpse of the mundane future, many traditional occult practices are accepted and used by New Age people as tools in the acquisition of greater awareness of themselves and the world. In this context, most New Agers have no hesitancy to consult astrologers, tarot card readers, and professional psychics. They will tend to avoid spiritualist mediums who primarily consult the dead, though they have little difficulty with mediumistic persons who channel higher spiritual teachers from a spiritual realm. Channeled entities may be pictured as ascended masters, the great white brotherhood, an ancient teacher, space beings, the divine (God), or just the medium's own higher self. Such channels do not as a rule establish contact with deceased loved ones or conduct traditional seances. They limit their channeling to religious-metaphysical teachings delivered by an evolved soul. They will occasionally venture into future prophecies, often with disastrous results.

It should be noted that acceptance of the separate metaphysical reality of a channeled entity, such as Seth or Ramtha or Mafu, is not integral to the acceptance of either the activity of channeling or the teachings of the channeled entity. From transpersonal psychology, New Agers have accepted the notion of a *higher self,* a part of the subconscious that might best be termed a *superconscious* or *transcendental* self. Channeling is thought by many, if not most, New Agers to originate in this very natural part of each human being, often dramatized as a spirit entity. Any teachings must stand on their own, apart from any "paranormal" credentials of their source.

What of the Future?

It is difficult to measure the extent of the New Age Movement. There is no central organization to which New Age people adhere and whose membership can be counted. It is a large movement, but hardly as large as some of the directories of New Age networks would suggest. Such directories typically contain a small number of people and organizations with a primary commitment to the New Age vision; a far larger number who share one or more New Age concerns (personal transformation, ecology, peace, cooperative models for living), but would otherwise not consider themselves New Agers; and many who, as entrepreneurs, provide services and products to the New Age community (like health services and natural food products) but may or may not have any personal commitment to the New Age. On the other hand, the movement has become visible in every major metropolitan center in the United States and has shown itself capable of supporting several national mass periodicals. Several annual gatherings—like the Human Unity Conference and the Whole Life Expo— have been able to draw attendance in the tens of thousands. National support for the New Age vision is estimated to number in the hundreds of thousands of individuals (in a land of 250 million).

Insofar as the New Age Movement represents primarily an updating of the long-standing occult and metaphysical tradition in American life, it has a bright future. This metaphysical community has been present in North America for at least a century and a half, and the number of people attracted to it has grown measurably decade by decade and at a heightened pace for the past two decades. The continued influx of Asians into the United States is giving the whole tradition the strong support in the larger culture heretofore denied it. Unlike the older forms of the community in previous decades, the movement has been able to penetrate and even develop its largest constituency from single young upwardly mobile urban adults, people who are most accepting of processes of transformation, which they know naturally accompany increasing career success. At their youthful age, they tend still to believe that utopian social visions can be realized. The density of population in the urban centers where they dwell allows the freedom to develop their own particular variation of the New Age in the company of others of similar vision. New Agers are, as an affluent social group, among the most capable of (1) providing firm support for a growing movement, (2) passing it along to the next generation, as yet unborn, and (3) spreading the movement among cultural influentials.

But as a movement, I believe, the days of the New Age are numbered. Why? The New Age has relied heavily upon contemporary science in its new synthesis of traditional occult/metaphysical teachings. But science has continued to revise itself at a tremendous pace—its ideas are always more or less ephemeral. It is already moving beyond concepts from which the New Age Movement has constructed its world-view. The very activity of science tends to undercut any metaphysics drawing heavily upon it. Once given religious meaning, words and models have difficulty changing and developing with the demands of science. As science continues to change, the New Age synthesis will simply fall apart. There are already strong indications that the New Age synthesis is crumbling.

Second, the success of the New Age in opening a new religious market in the 1970s has been followed by a fragmentation of that market in the 1980s. Simply put, some elements within the movement have been more successful in attracting continued support than others. Organizations that best program means to implement movement ideals, that provide the context for long-term meaningful relationships, and that support the most mature leaders, those who supply the most sophisticated teachings, are taking the primary religious commitments of large segments of the movement away from the movement as a whole. People will eventually find means to search for realization of the inherently religious ideals of the New Age Movement in very definite structured patterns. Those groups that supply those patterns will survive to become long-term religious institutions. Other, more-limited organizations will fall by the wayside.

Third, the movement has welcomed a large number of entrepreneurs— alternative health practitioners (from chiropractors to masseurs), publishers, organizers of retreat centers, independent writers and teachers, health-food storeowners, etc. In providing for their own economic needs, such independent service and product providers must enter the world of cut-throat competition, a world wholly at odds with the cooperative, one-world ideal espoused by the movement. The most successful of the providers have claimed a particular market; but, in their efforts to best the competition, they have further weakened the movement.

Finally, it should be noted that a concerted attack from both the conservative evangelical Christian perspective and the skeptical, nonreligious scientific community has been launched against the New Age Movement. To date, neither has had a measurable effect in detering the movement's growth. Members of the movement tend not to read anti-New Age material, and many are quite unaware of its existence (having as its main circulation evangelical Christians and scientific skeptics rather than its intended target audience). Having already seen how little effect the attack upon astrology in the 1970s has had upon the future course of the astrological community, there is little reason to believe that the very similar forces arrayed against the New Age will be able to effect any significant change in the movement, beyond encouraging the disintegrating forces already at work within it.

Notes

1. This paper has attempted to synthesize a host of materials—both those produced by the New Age Movement and those written by outside observers. These materials are located in the collection of the Institute for the Study of American Religion, which has been compiling New Age material since the early 1970s. The collection, now housed at the University of California, Santa Barbara, numbers in the thousands of pieces. Besides the written material, there is also a significant portion of essential New Age material to be found on video and cassette tapes, especially the work of the major New Age channelers. Except in the case of direct quotations, no attempt has been made to provide detailed references.

A good book-length, historical treatment of the metaphysical tradition is found in J. Stillson Judah, *The History and Philosophy of the Metaphysical Movements in America* (Philadelphia: Westminster Press, 1967), with important supplementary material appearing in this author's two books, *The Encyclopedia of American Religions* (Detroit: Gale Research, 1987) and the *Encyclopedic Handbook of Cults in America* (New York: Garland, 1987).

Important books summarizing the major ideas of the movement can be found in such volumes as Marilyn Ferguson, *The Aquarian Conspiracy* (Los Angeles: J. P. Tarcher, 1980); David Spangler, *Towards a Planetary Vision* (Findhorn, Scotland: Findhorn Foundation, 1977); Alan Cohen, *The Healing of Planet Earth* (Atlanta, Ga.: New Leaf, 1987); and John White, ed., *What Is Enlightenment?* (Los Angeles: J. P. Tarcher, 1984).

2. Metaphysical thought moved into business through the conversion of O. S. Marden, who in the 1890s became the first successful merchant of techniques for success to entry-level corporate executives on their way to the top. He—with

successors such as Napoleon Hill, Dale Carnegie, W. Clement Stone, Earl Nighten-gale, and Catherine Ponder—developed contemporary "prosperity consciousness" ideology. Discerning the frequent gap between such traditional values as hard work and native ability and any assurance of success, they attempted to discern rules for success, which they presented as universal metaphysical laws. They were the first to note that upward mobility demanded such things as self-confidence, enthu-siasm, the use of mentors, goal-setting, self-discipline, intuition, and the ability to manipulate money without feelings of guilt. The presentation of these "rules" for success is now integral to the training for most salesmen and young executives, and many corporate training programs unabashedly retain the heavy metaphysical overlay.

For treatments of "success consciousness" in the business setting, see Orison Swett Marden, *Prosperity—How to Attract It* (New York: Success Magazine Cor-poration, 1922); Napoleon Hill, *The Laws of Success* (Cleveland, Ohio: Ralston Publishing Co., 1960); and Napoleon Hill and W. Clement Stone, *Success through a Positive Mental Attitude* (Englewood Cliffs, N.J.: Prentice-Hall, 1960).

3. Ira Friedlander, *Year One Catalog* (New York: Harper & Row, 1972).

THE OCCULT ESTABLISHMENT
James Webb

The idea of "freedom" often has most tangible associations—let me out of here, give me enough to eat, create the opportunities for me to use my abilities to benefit myself or others. Always beside these easily understood demands has run another. It is an apocalyptic definition of freedom, which has its roots in various pre-Christian religious conceptions. And in this century it owes direct allegiance to the irrationalist reaction and the occult revival of the 1890s. It is notorious that no two men will ever agree on what "freedom" is: For the anarchist of the turn of the century it signified the dissolution of all legal and social bonds, but for the believer in Hitler's Germany, it meant a liberation from the vagaries of fate augmented by the anarchic and profiteering systems of Western liberalism. Each definition represents "freedom"; and each embodies definitions of what "unfreedom" is. It is the purpose of this chapter to imply that in many such definitions of free and unfree, the tangible meaning of the word "freedom" has its inevitable corollary in a conception of personal "liberation" from *the condition of being human*—a rejection of the helplessness, mutual isolation, and mortality of man.

This liberation is liberation of a mystical or occult nature. In its Western form it is to be found in the Gnostic systems. The cardinal tenet is that man contains God, a spark of the divine somehow entrapped in matter—and that he can only effect his salvation by realizing and rejoining the Godhead from which he sprang. This is also the position at the root of the most serious occult systems. It may be that there is an innate Gnosticism in humanity, which throws up the idea of man's divine origins from time to time in different forms to provide a consoling myth for an intolerable

The late James Webb was the author of *The Occult Underground, The Occult Establishment,* and a memorable biography of G. I. Gurdjieff, *The Harmonious Circle.* This essay is adapted from *The Occult Establishment* and is reprinted with permission from Open Court Press.

predicament. The idea is even found in orthodox Christianity—all myths of the Fall from grace embody some idea of a possible return to Heaven. In this century, with the presentation of traditional religious positions in secular form, there has emerged a secular Gnosticism beside the other great secular religions—the mystical union of Fascism, the apocalypse of Marxist dialectic, the Earthly City of social democracy. The secular Gnosticism is almost never recognized for what it is, and it can exist alongside other convictions almost unperceived. Thus, the Fascist or the Communist or the anarchist may cherish unknown to himself a vision of personal liberation, which in imagination fuses with the communal definition of "freedom" to which he nominally subscribes. It was the characteristic of the Sixties, however, to produce a form of secular Gnosticism, which took on a relatively independent existence and which defined "liberation" in terms that without a doubt derived directly from the occult revival or its influence.

This "pure" form of secular Gnosticism is found among the "Counter-culture," the "Youth movement," and parts of the "New Left."

So far we have discussed the coincidence of occultism and politics in terms of "illuminated politics," implying a politics that has a religious complexion and obeys a transcendental scale of values. The counterculture was packed full to bursting with the occult and mystical elements that indicate the illuminated attitude, and certain of its most cherished and supposedly "relevant" theories—the term of the self-proclaimed pragmatic wing of the movement in opposition to the out-and-out mystics—derived directly from the secularized Gnosticism of the occult revival. These concepts had been floating around for at least a century. But not until the 1960s did the Gnosticism become sufficiently secularized to provide the motor force for a widespread theory of everyday living. The Underground of the Sixties was often concerned with illuminated politics of a particular— Gnostic—form, whereas the illuminated politicians of the first half of this century more often put their idealism at the service of a political cause that made more concessions toward the aspirations of society at large.

Present-day illuminates are the obvious heirs of earlier illuminated politicians. We have already examined almost every tenet cultivated among the contemporary Underground. Insistence on a "natural" way of living, anti-industrialism, vegetarianism, protection of the environment, "organic" community, and spiritual evolution—all combine with occult enthusiasms and the political cause of the movement. The specific political objectives of any given time account for most of the differences between the later Underground and that of the 1890s—and in what follows some obvious differences are taken for granted. My concern is to point out the similarities and to argue that the Gnostic-occult idea of "liberation" is one common denominator of Underground groups. The Progressive Underground of the 1890s—equally concerned with spiritual evolution and spiritual revolution—was also the habitat of occultists and practitioners of strange religions like those from which the Underground of the 1960s derived its fundamental illuminism and much of its ideology. Because the Underground of the 1960s was a development from earlier Bohemias, those earlier Bohemias are important as a source of inspiration for contemporary idealists. Both the myth of Bohemia and the real configurations of that landscape have played a part in the growth of the modern Underground, and the occult has formed part both of the legend and the reality. The societies on which the Underground of the last decade were based had their own ideas of "liberation," and the occult preoccupations of Eckstein's Vienna, Symbolist Paris, or the Munich of the Cosmic Circle have had an inevitable effect on their spiritual descendants. "Modern" culture as a whole is so indebted to artists and writers who found their inspiration in the turn-of-the-century Occult Revival that the avant-garde of today necessarily makes use of "esoteric" ideas without realizing their nature.

*   *   *

American esotericism does not appear to have had much connection with illuminated politics until the past decade, and the most obvious reason is that the funds, organization, and drive needed to initiate any orthodox "political" movement in the United States have proved prohibitive for illuminated politicians. But the same rules of like-calling-to-like apply to the American situation; and one very good reason for the lack of occult groups in Progressive circles was the lack of such Bohemian political circles altogether. There was no lack of occultists. America had given birth to many of the movements that played a part in the nineteenth century occult revival—Spiritualism, Christian Science, innumerable cults of Christian derivation had arrived in Europe from America. The Theosophical Society in America broke off from the Annie Besant-dominated European and Asian group and established itself in California. Initiates from various magical orders had returned across the Atlantic ever since S. L. Macgregor Mathers of the Golden Dawn had started to initiate Americans for fees in Paris. During the 1930s and 1940s followers of Aleister Crowley began to build up support of Crowley's brand of magic. When Progressive circles did begin to develop in the 1920s and 1930s, the esotericists found their natural place. Thus the doctrines of Georgei Gurdjieff and P. D. Ouspensky penetrated the avant-garde. Margaret Anderson and Jane Heap of the *Little Review* left for France and the master himself, while others gathered around Gurdjieff acolyte A. R. Orage in New York. The potential for illuminated politics was there. For example, there was Alfred William Lawson (born 1869), who was a typical exponent of rejected knowledge—in this case of an individualistic "physics," which Lawson claimed governed the universe according to laws of suction and pressure—and he sprang into the public eye in the 1930s with an economic doctrine known as "Direct Credit," which resembled the theories of Major Douglas. Lawson did manage to whip up a remarkable amount of support—16,000 people attended a parade he held in 1933 in Detroit. This points to the moral that another essential factor for the fusion of pure irrationalism with political or social thinking is a sufficient anxiety level. Lawson found his hour—as (John) Hargrave did in England—with the Depression.

For America to display the patterns of behavior that we have observed in Europe, three factors were necessary. There must be a high level of anxiety to induce the crisis of consciousness, which in Europe had been kept at an extreme of tension since the end of the last century. There must be a broadening of Bohemian culture to provide the natural launching pad for the exploration of other realities. And for irrationalist views of politics or society to obtain a wide hearing some way must be found to overcome the obstacles to political organization in the United States. With the momentary fusion of all anti-establishment forces in the late 1960s, all these conditions were fulfilled. Anxiety had been mounting since the immediate postwar era. Bohemia had become the myth it had been so long in Europe and was at last based on a sufficient material reality. And the solution to the political problem was found by a new sort of political grouping—*around the myth itself.* Through the publicity of the mass media and particularly of television, the infinite desirability of Bohemia was projected as it had never been in Europe. And the rebellion against the established, materialist, rationalist order of things in America took the form of an extension of the Bohemian life-style and an application of the Bohemian critique of society to the political situation as a whole. This critique has always been powerful and has been adopted by *Realpolitik* revolutionaries for their own ends since the middle of the last century. In essence it is the creed of spiritual revolution, a *unio mystica* of humanity and a liberation from the flesh. . . .

One writer who ended up on the West Coast contributed as much as any of the East Coast refugees from Hitler's Europe toward introducing a sense of the magical into American Bohemia. This was Henry Miller. Miller became interested in the occult in the mid-1930s, and his later interest extended to announcing that he would hang framed photographs of Gurdjieff and Hermann Hesse beside each other on the wall. Around 1935 Miller was reading Rudolf Steiner, Eliphas Lévi, Madame Blavatsky, and the Tibetan series of Evans-Wentz. He met Count Hermann Keyserling, Dane Rudhyar, and the extraordinary astrologer Conrad Moricand (who became a good friend). In a number of *View* in early 1942, Miller told how after an evening with Moricand he had fallen through a glass door and gone to the hospital. The next day Moricand had appeared with Miller's horoscope, announcing that the indications had been for death, not injury. After the war, Miller had Moricand as a guest in his home in California, a disastrous episode, which he has fully described.[1]

Neither the occultism of the *View* group nor that of Henry Miller can be seen as having a direct effect on the hospitality of American artists to the miraculous. Yet artists of the postwar generation necessarily absorbed the occult preoccupations of their predecessors as part of their education. The accumulated traditions of European Bohemia meant not only that the occult was a subject that fascinated some of the more influential artists but that the philosophies that informed their work were based on esoteric ideas. We have seen how occult ideas of liberation and spiritual revolution permeated the artistic movements to which the postwar generation looked. Both in the myth of the *vie de Bohème* and the reality, the topics had a recognized place. But the place they had was a place in an imported European fashion. And when America began to originate its own distinctive forms of Bohemianism instead of being content to play host to the foreign avant-garde, the fashion was transformed. Despite this transformation, the Bohemia of the "beatniks" could not escape the influence of earlier Bohemias.

Two factors about the Beat Underground are important from the point of view of this inquiry. First, unlike that of American Bohemians of the 1920s and 1930s, the political stance of the more intellectual Beat could be expressed simply by a rejection of "square society" and an identification with the socially rejected—an attitude made famous by Norman Mailer in his essay "The White Negro." Any political commitment by the Bohemians of the 1930s was liable to have been to the Communist party.[2] Secondly, although a mutual dissatisfaction with established society had sometimes sent the denizens of the traditional Bohemias of Europe into the company of semicriminal elements, European Bohemia was permissive and accepting but intellectually fastidious. Partly because of the attitude exemplified by Mailer's "White Negro," but mostly because of the central position occupied by marijuana in the beatnik culture (and the consequent interest of semi-criminal drug dealers), the Beat Bohemia may have incorporated—although there is no means of being statistically certain—a larger proportion of un-motivated hangers-on than Bohemias of the traditional pattern. This resulted in a fairly large Beat "proletariat," who might conform to the expected patterns of behavior, make all the right noises, but fail to understand the language. Thus, in the summer of 1960, one estimate of the Beats in Greenwich Village made only one sixth "habituated to reading (none seem addicted)" and guessed that at least as many in this particular Bohemia were writing as in earlier artists' colonies.[3] It would be unwise to make too much of this, for lack of solid evidence. But it is quite certain that with the development of the Beatnik culture into that of the Hippies, the huge publicity given to this colorful Bohemia drew in many more existential window shoppers than did the traditional European Bohemias or Greenwich Village of the 1930s. The process seems to have begun with the Beats. From the point of view of the developing Bohemian critique of society, it had one important result: the use of language, inherited from earlier Bohemias, that dealt with highly sophisticated and esoteric concepts of "liberation," but with the meaning of the language forgotten, conventionalized, or misapplied, by a considerable number of camp followers or hangers-on.

At the same time as the American Beat culture developed an inchoate Bohemian critique of society—untied to Party lines—a particular Beatnik form of illuminism emerged in the adoption of Zen.[4] The romanticized use of Zen in the novels of Jack Kerouac created what was for America a new figure: the wandering scholar with religious leanings, more vagabond than academic. He had long been known in the literature of Europe, where he appeared in novels like Hesse's *Narziss und Goldmund,* and had found particular favor with the *Wandervögel.* Kerouac converted the character into a "Dharma Bum," who rode freight trains across the continent seeking enlightenment. The moving spirit of American Zen seems to have been the West Coast poet Gary Snyder, who passed his interest on to Kerouac and Allen Ginsberg in San Francisco in the 1950s. Kerouac describes Snyder as embodying both the inherited traditions of 1930s protest and the new vision of Zen. He was

a kid from eastern Oregon brought up in a log cabin deep in the woods with his father and mother and sister, from the beginning a woods boy, an axman, farmer, interested in animals and Indian lore so that when he finally got to college by hook or crook he was already well equipped for his early studies in anthropology and later in Indian myth and in the actual texts of Indian mythology. Finally he learned Chinese and Japanese and became an Oriental scholar and discovered the greatest Dharma Bums of them all, the Zen Lunatics of China and Japan. At the same time, being a Northwest boy with idealistic tendencies, he got interested in oldfashioned I.W.W. anarchism and learned to play the guitar and sing old-worker songs to go with his Indian songs and general folksong interests.[5]

In this portrait, Kerouac identifies a type who was to become more and more familiar to Americans: the rebel who combined a detestation of social ills with a religious search. Sometime after this description, Snyder himself left for Japan to study Zen with the leading practitioners of the discipline. But it is more the Zen-and-rosewater marketed by Kerouac that influenced Bohemia than serious religious study. The other chief figure in arousing interest in Zen in the United States was Alan Watts, who has deplored the shallowness of the Zen commitment of many camp followers in an essay "Beat Zen, Square Zen and Zen," which has become as celebrated as Mailer's "White Negro." Watts is a product of the European occult revival, and it is worth noticing that even in the creation of the "typically American" version of Bohemia by the Beatniks, neither the occult revival nor the inherited traditions of Bohemia could be excluded. Even Kerouac, the "creator" of the Beat legend, felt keenly his French-Canadian roots, and his novels—particularly the later ones—are studded with references to the archetypal Bohemians of Paris. In Watts—who appears, incongruously besuited, at a Beat party in *The Dharma Bums*—the emerging counterculture of California discovered a popularizer of Zen who had emerged indirectly from the Theosophical Society.

In 1903 an International Buddhist Society had been founded, following the period spent in the East by Allan Bennett, alias the "Bikkhu Ananda Metteya," who had passed into Buddhism from the magical activities of the Golden Dawn. An English Buddhist Society was formed in 1907, but by 1924 the chief association for the dissemination of Buddhist doctrine in England was the Buddhist Lodge of the Theosophical Society, founded by the eminent lawyer and judge Christmas Humphreys. In 1936 Alan Watts took over the editorship of the Buddhist Lodge's magazine, *Buddhism in England,* at the age of sixteen, and the same year, he published his *Spirit of Zen.* The father of this prodigy, L. W. Watts, was the treasurer and vice-president of the Buddhist Lodge;[6] and Alan Watts also sat at the feet of Dmitrije Mitrinović. In 1938 the younger Watts left for the United States and became a doctor of theology and an Anglican counselor at Northwestern University. Then he moved to San Francisco, from where his influence spread first throughout the Beatnik, then throughout the Hippie world. As has been rightly pointed out,[7] it is more the influence of Watts than the more learned message of the leading Zen authority for the West, D. T. Suzuki—whose second wife was American—that has been responsible for spreading Zen ideas. Watts by no means confined himself to Zen and was himself the modern representative of those "mediators between East and West" who first became prominent in Europe and America in the middle of the last century.[8]

If this were in any sense a thorough survey of Bohemian characteristics or even of the development of Bohemian ideas, much more attention would have to be paid to the political causes adopted by Bohemia at any given time, statistical evidence produced for the composition of the disaffiliated community, very many writers and artists more than mentioned. Here it is only necessary to note that by the time of the hippie explosion, American Bohemia had developed into an independent culture superficially unlike its European predecessors, yet inevitably owing allegiance to their achievements. Occult and religious elements occupied the place they have held in every Bohemia; and the specific political causes of previous generations of intellectuals were replaced by the general opposition of way-of-life to way-of-life that had also been traditional in Bohemian Europe.

By the end of the 1950s the Beats were moving out of their headquarters in North Beach, San Francisco, into New York's Greenwich Village and out again into the Lower East Side. In San Francisco itself they made for the area around Haight-Ashbury, a traditional low-rent area favored by San Francisco State students and conveniently located next to the "panhandle" of Golden Gate Park. With a further increase in the burden of anxiety, increased publicity for an "alternative" way of life, and the emergence of a vast semi-educated group of school leavers and dropouts whose opportunities for romanticism had been nourished as never before—a generation was produced that was devoted to the *image* through television, cinema, and large and uncritical reading while shielded from the strong winds of reality. The stage was set for the deposition of the kings of Bohemia and the proclamation of the republic of the Woodstock Nation.

With a suitable change of key, the Progressive Underground of the 1890s might have been quite at home in Beatnik California: exchanging the vegetarian restaurants and cafés of Paris, Munich, and Vienna for the Chinese cooking of San Francisco and the cellars of North Beach; listening to records of Charlie Parker rather than concert performances of Wagner. But, if the inhabitants of Monte Verita could have fitted with ease into the pads of Venice West, they would have been even more familiar with the society of Haight-Ashbury, where a resurrected form of Christian Socialism combined with every form of mysticism under the sun. Familiar, that is, except for one aspect, certainly the most distinctive: the economy based on the new drug LSD.

Norman Cohn has suggested that certain medieval movements that combined revolutionary millennarianism with mystical anarchism are, in a secularized form, "with us still."[9] In the last five years of the 1960s, a form of illuminated politics developed among the young, which gives more insight into the state of mind of a mystical revolutionary than has been possible at any earlier date, because its viewpoints were expressed in direct and unambiguous language. Detailed examination of Hippies, Yippies, and variations on the theme of rebellious youth proves Professor Cohn extraordinarily accurate in his assessment. Reading the underground newspapers of 1966 and 1967, in which the story of the movement is buried, nothing is so striking as the overwhelming impression of joy and hopefulness, the real sense of "liberation" achieved or about to be achieved. Whatever the political activists have subsequently written, the main factor in inducing this unparalleled euphoria was without a doubt LSD. Although the gurus of the "consciousness-expanding" drug were not by any means the sole instigators of the hippie revolt—as simplified accounts once made them seem—they were certainly very influential.

Drugs have been used in most cultures to dislocate man's sense of ordinary reality, or at least to give relief from the humdrum world. Frequently the strange effects of such substances have been associated with the divine. Visions, dreams, and prophecies can be ascribed to the effects of drug-induced consciousness. The occult revival knew all about drugs, and marijuana was a recognized weapon in the "sorcerer's armory" of Stanislas de Guaita or Baudelaire.[10] The chief aspect of drug action examined during the occult revival was the effect of ether or nitrous oxide, which was widely thought to induce mystical experiences and earned the name of the "anesthetic revelation." John Addington Symonds experimented with chloroform, and the prophet of esoteric Christianity, Anna Kingsford, experienced her visions under the influence of the same drug. In 1880 Professor William Ramsay (a fellow of the Royal Society who was subsequently knighted) carried out experiments in which he anesthetized himself at least fifty times. They induced in him a condition of rather disappointing mystical insight—that is, Ramsay did not find his Berkeleyan revelation to his liking. In June 1893 he read a paper on his experiences to the Society for Psychical Research and was followed by Edward Maitland, who recounted the visions of Anna Kingsford. Those stimulated to try the effects of ether for themselves were sufficiently numerous to hold a symposium of the topic in 1904.[11]

The most prominent supporters of the "anesthetic revelation," however, were to be found in America. These were William James of Harvard and the inventor of the term "anesthetic revelation," Benjamin Paul Blood. Blood was born in the 1820s and spent most of his life in New York State, where he died at the age of 86. In 1860 he had a revelation under anesthetics, which he describes as "an *initiation* historically realized as such, into the oldest and most intimate and ultimate truth. Whoever attains and remembers it, or remembers of it, is graduated beyond instruction in spiritual things." After repeating the experience at intervals, Blood produced a pamphlet on *The Anaesthetic Revelation* in 1874, which attracted many correspondents with corroborative evidence (including the poet Alfred Lord Tennyson). Blood was emphatic that his insight had nothing to do with philosophy. The basis was simply that one's self existed, nothing more. He wrote in 1910: "Sinai and Calvary were but sacred stepping-stones to this secular revelation." On the appearance of Blood's pamphlet, William James reviewed it very favorably and began a correspondence with the author. By 1896 James was writing to Blood that he had distributed copies of one of his pamphlets after a seminar in "speculative psychology." The last article James was to publish during his lifetime dealt with Blood, and the psychologist admitted that *The Anaesthetic Revelation* "fascinated me so 'weirdly' that I am conscious of its having been one of the stepping-stones of my thinking ever since."[12] Apart from their influence on James's thought, the visions of Blood stimulated the Harvard professor to try for himself the effects of nitrous oxide. His own mystical insight was embodied in the influential *Varieties of Religious Experience* (1902), and James's conclusion has served ever since as a text for those in search of "other realities."

> It is that our normal waking consciousness, rational consciousness as we call it, is but one special type of consciousness, whilst all about it, parted from it by the filmiest of screens, there lie potential forms of consciousness entirely different.[13]

Aleister Crowley, as the chief inheritor of the traditions of Symbolist Magery, was rather more indiscriminately concerned with drugs. Opium, cocaine, heroin, ether—he indulged and overindulged. Crowley's interest in drugs went further than simple dissipation, and his magical experiments were paralleled by those he undertook with drugs, notably what was then called *Anhalonium Lewinii*. This name for peyote, or mescaline, commemorates Ludwig Lewin, the first investigator of the Mexican cactus from which the drug is derived. After Lewin published his first study of this strange agent of visions in 1886, others (most notably Havelock Ellis) experimented with its effects, and Crowley followed suit. When in the U.S.A. during the First World War, Crowley visited the Parke-Davis factory in Detroit. He noted in his *Confessions:* "They were kind enough to interest themselves in my researches in *Anhalonium Lewinii* and made me some special preparations on the lines indicated by my experience which proved greatly superior to previous preparations."[14] There is firsthand evidence that Crowley introduced Aldous Huxley to mescaline in pre-1933 Berlin.[15] This is interesting and significant; for it indicates that Huxley's wide reading in mystical matters was supplemented by practical experience before he arrived in the United States in 1937—that yet another link with the occult revival can be made. (The more accepted story—that Huxley started experimenting with mescaline in 1953 under the supervision of Dr. Humphrey Osmond—may of course be true, without affecting the present argument.) It is certain that Huxley's book *The Doors of Perception,* which resulted from his later experience, had more effect than almost any other element in stimulating interest in what Osmond later called "pyschedelics."[16]

In the spring of 1943, Dr. Albert Hofmann, working in his laboratories at the Sandoz Corporation in Basel, accidentally absorbed a small quantity of lysergic acid diethylamide, a substance that he had synthesized while researching into the chemical constituents of the fungus ergot. Hofmann experienced hallucinatory effects and experimented on himself with a larger dose of LSD. Through Hofmann and Sandoz yet further hallucinogens were located. An American couple penetrated a Mexican Indian ceremony in which a hallucinogenic mushroom was used. On a second expedition the pair took an expert on fungi, who identified and afterward grew a culture of the mushrooms in his Paris laboratory. Some of these mushrooms he sent to Hofmann, who again experimented on himself and eventually synthesized the active constituent of psylocibin. He also discovered the hallucinatory properties of the morning glory seed. It was LSD, however, as manufactured primarily by Sandoz, which was responsible for the epidemic of mysticism that broke out on the American West Coast. According to John Wilcock's column, *Other Scenes,* most of the LSD reaching California in the spring of 1966 was made at the Sandoz plant in Switzerland, sold to buyers in Czechoslovakia, and delivered to the United States through Mexico. At this time there was no law against the use of LSD, and the drug naturally gravitated into the hands of the religiously inclined and the innumerable cults that have made California their headquarters since the end of the last century. It was also natural that the apparently mystical experiences produced by the drug should themselves generate religious aspirations in official researchers. Thus, in December 1966, in the issue that announced the celebratory dedication of Haight-Ashbury by Diggers and hippies, the *Berkeley Barb* carried an article by Thaddeus and Rita Ashby, who had been responsible for research carried out by Sandoz in Mexico into problems of LSD and creativity. Their article, entitled "Did Jesus Turn On?", argued that Christ *did* turn on, that much biblical poetry was produced by psychedelics, and announced that "Paradise must always be recreated." "The young people we meet in the LSD 'underground' seem to be groping towards such a renewal of religion." The Ashbys' own version of religious renewal ideally involved living in a house with a "tree-room" open to light and air, and a "womb-room" packed with psychedelic equipment for visionary experiences.[17]

From one relatively early survey of LSD use, a good idea can be gained of how the drug originally became diffused. LSD was at first thought to produce a "model psychosis": that is, to duplicate the effects of schizophrenia. Accordingly, it was to psychiatrists and medical men that the drug was of greatest interest. In the particular survey in question, three groups of LSD users were examined: an "informal professional" sample, over one-third of whom were initiated by a single psychiatrist member of the group; a group around a "religious-medical center" of a sort similar to Timothy Leary's; and a black-market sample, all of whom had been introduced to the drug by a single person, himself in touch with people who fitted into one of the other two categories examined. Although research workers had the opportunity to try LSD as early as 1950, in this particular survey the first LSD use occurred in 1956. The next year the drug began to be used in clinical study on patients, and the group that obtained its LSD on the black market first used it in 1959. The religious-medical center had LSD available in 1960. A single survey, of course, proves nothing about the general pattern, but there is little to show that this sample cannot be taken as typical for the beginnings of the cult of LSD. One interesting aspect is that despite the relatively early opportunity to take LSD, the first use even among the "professional" group did not take place until 1956. It is possible that this may have been linked with the publication in 1956 of Huxley's sequel to *The Doors of Perception,* entitled *Heaven and Hell.* This is reinforced by the survey's conclusion that even a sample of private patients introduced to LSD by their psychiatrists developed the characteristics of an "in-group" after having read Huxley, Alan Watts, or other theorists of mystical experience.[18]

Timothy Leary was the moving force behind the popular LSD movement. Leary (born 1920) has dated the beginnings of his religious quest to January 1959. He was living in Spain, having resigned from his university job and in a state of disillusionment. He contracted a veneral disease and, during the ensuing illness, decided that he had undergone a process of mystical rebirth. In August 1960 he ate several hallucinogenic mushrooms in Cuernavaca in Mexico and returned to his offices in the Center for Personality Research at Harvard—the university of William James—with a new conception of what his work should be. Leary knew all about the anaesthetic revelation of William James, "who had mystic experiences using nitrous oxide and saw God and scandalized people by running drug parties in Boston's scruffy Back Bay."[19] At this point, Leary had not yet read Huxley's accounts of his visions under mescaline, although two of his graduate students had been running tests with the chemical. One of these introduced him to *The Doors of Perception* and *Heaven and Hell.* During October and November

1960, Leary planned a series of experiments in conjunction with Huxley himself, who, by a strange coincidence, was staying in Boston. It is quite obvious that two factors conditioned the subsequent experiments: Leary's already-formed idea of "the possibilities of mind-free consciousness" and the influence of Huxley during the planning stage.

> We were not to be limited by the pathological point of view. We were not to interpret ecstasy as mania, or calm serenity as catatonia; we were not to diagnose Buddha as a detached schizoid; nor Christ as an exhibitionist masochist nor the mystic experience as a symptom; nor the visionary state as a model psychosis. Aldous Huxley chuckling away with compassionate humor at human folly.
>
> And with such erudition! Moving back and forth in history, quoting the mystics, Wordsworth, Plotinus, The Areopagite, William James. Ranging from the esoteric past, back into the biochemical present.[20]

In other words, Leary absorbed Huxley's own view of the significance of drug-induced experiences and took good note of his sources, those of Romanticism, Neo-Platonism, and the occult revival. His program expanded to include treatment of prisoners with a view to rehabilitation. But alongside the research arose a determination to *turn people on.*

The beginnings of the Bohemian use of hallucinogens probably date from Leary's initiation of Allen Ginsberg in December 1960. This produced in Ginsberg a determination to proselytize. Shortly afterward, Leary gave his magic mushrooms to another hero of the Beatnik era, the poet Charles Olson. Marijuana had been the drug of the Beatnik culture, and even then it had acquired religious connotations from its association with the Buddhism of Kerouac, Snyder, and Ginsberg. But the real eminence of the Beatnik drug world was William Burroughs, the son of the calculating-machine dynasty whose powerful book *Junky* had described his adventures with drugs much more potent than marijuana. Burroughs had taken up residence in Tangier, which became a place of pilgrimage for Beats like Kerouac on their way to Europe. It was logical that Leary and his new convert Ginsberg would approach the Grand Panjandrum of Junk, who was already experimenting with flickering and flashing lights to achieve "druglike" effects, which were to become familiar. In the summer of 1961, Leary, his colleague Richard Alpert, later known as Ram Dass, Ginsberg, and Gregory Corso held a mushroom session in Tangier. This was followed by an unsuccessful trip made by Burroughs to America and his rejection of the Harvard group's psychedelics. But contact with the leaders of the Beat Bohemia had been made, and it symbolized the directions that the drug religion was to follow.

Ginsberg left for India and the ashrams of the Ganges.

In November 1961 Leary was given LSD by an academic dropout called Michael Holingshead, who had taken the drug while working with a New York doctor. Soon afterward, the Harvard experimenters tried another chemical that produced visions, DMT. Both of these drugs resulted in experiences that were far more vivid and ecstatic than those caused by the magic mushroom. At Easter 1962, Leary and a Harvard Ph.D. student called Walter Pahnke gave a group of experimenters psylocibin in the chapel of Boston University and precipitated mystical experiences. Gerald Heard and Alan Watts arrived at Harvard, told Leary of the traditions of European occultism, of Madame Blavatsky, of Gurdjieff and Ouspensky. They all warned Leary that the classic technique of the occultist was the only one to ensure survial. Those who know, don't speak. Leary, on the other hand, felt the mantle of the guru clasped around his shoulders. "I found myself getting poetic and dogmatic. I know it is a real reality! I know it is the Divine message." He took to frequenting a Hindu ashram in Boston. Then he was asked to give LSD to Hindu devotees; and, during the course of the session, Leary became convinced that "we are all Hindus in our essence." A process of mutual conversion began between him and the inmates of the ashram. Leary's growing respect for Hindu mythology was accompanied by the growing respect of the Vedantists for Leary. When their guru was away they would visit him for advice, and gradually he accumulated a following of those searching for a spiritual leader.

> The slow, invisible process of becoming a guru, a holy man, had begun. It would be four years before I could openly admit to it. Accept my divinity, my divine election. . . . How ironic and ludicrous that an American Irishman should be forced into sainthood!

In the summer of 1962 he left once more for Mexico, and next year he was sacked from Harvard, whose authorities found it dangerous to have a valuable mystic on the staff. In succession he established the "Castalia Foundation"—named after the Order imagined by his hero Hermann Hesse, the "International Foundation for Internal Freedom," and the "League for Spiritual Discovery," with its headquarters at Millbrook, New York, where Leary and his followers were living at the time of the great drug explosion. There was time after the disruption of his Castalia Foundation for a trip to India, where he went to study under Sri Krishna Prem. "Relax," he told his colleague Richard Alpert, "sit back, have a ball. . . . It's done now: watch it happen."[21]

What was "done" was the broadcasting of LSD to the four winds.

Leary claims that Albert Hofmann, the synthesizer of the chemical, had at once realized the spiritual implications of his discovery. Concealing himself under the guise of a scientific researcher he had "initiated a high-level, ethical, gentleman's conspiracy of philosophically minded scientists to disseminate LSD for the benefit of the human race." Leary himself and Alan Watts—whose *Joyous Cosmology* (1962) proved to be the LSD equivalent to Huxley's propaganda for mescaline—joined with other semiacademics to provide the publicity. The chemical itself was the chief problem. Whether or not Hofmann himself was ever involved, some scientists fairly certainly did cooperate. The most influential evangelist of LSD was one Al Hubbard, who had made a fortune from uranium and planned to set up a network of medically approved LSD clinics around the country. He was responsible for converting Humphrey Osmond to the religious interpretation of the LSD experience. Hubbard's pilot project at Menlo Park, California, which (according to Leary) "turned on several hundred of the most influential people in the San Francisco Bay Area," was closed; and Leary himself failed to persuade Sandoz to put an "ecstasy pill" on the market. By 1962 he had, nevertheless, contrived to set up "a loose but effective" distribution system for free LSD. Then he met a distinguished scientist, whom he calls "Dr. Spaulding" and describes as "one of the ten leading chemists in the country," who claimed to be part of a well-established conspiracy that had been stockpiling LSD. "Spaulding" then sent Leary enough of the chemical to last four years.[22]

Partly through the efforts of Hubbard, partly through the natural receptivity of California, partly through the Beatnik preparation, LSD took its greatest toll in San Francisco. With the question of LSD supply so paramount, the activities of private "chemists" came to be of increasing importance, and San Francisco possessed the most important private manufacturer of LSD in America. This legendary figure, known as Owsley and rumored to possess the full name of "Augustus Owsley Stanley III," produced a fair proportion of the LSD used in the Haight-Ashbury culture. Leary has recorded a monologue by Owsley in which the Underground supplier expressed his belief that the Van Allen Belt was "the higher intelligence protecting earth from lethal solar radiation" and that LSD had been activated by this supreme intelligence as the counterforce to nuclear fission.[23] Owsley was also responsible for some of the public success of the Acid Tests conducted in San Francisco in 1965 and 1966 by Ken Kesey, the most remarkable of all LSD gurus.

Kesey (born 1936) attracted public notice in 1962 with his first novel, *One Flew over the Cuckoo's Nest*. Before that, he had been a schoolboy hero and a college athlete. He arrived at Stanford University, California, on a creative writing fellowship in 1958.[24] At Stanford, Kesey met a young psychologist with whom he volunteered to take part in experiments with the newly discovered psychedelics—then called psychomimetics because of the theory that they mimicked schizophrenic states. Kesey was among the first to be turned on, and soon the Bohemian community in Stanford was ordering peyote from Mexico and trying out the strange chemicals Kesey smuggled out of the hospital. Bohemia became Cockaigne. Richard Alpert arrived after he had begun to work with Leary; and equally important, Neal Cassady joined the circle. Cassady was the original Beat, the hero, "Dean Moriarty," of Kerouac's *On the Road:* the model for the Bohemia that was ending and a main protagonist of that which was to begin. In 1963 Kesey moved to LaHonda near Palo Alto, California, and early the next year the legendary adventure began.

From the bare description of what Kesey and his Merry Pranksters did, it is difficult to make the point that what developed was—far more than in the case of Leary with his explicit reliance on the traditions of the Orient and European occultism—a 1960s, Americanized version of the perennial occultist dream of a forcing house for souls. In the spring of 1964, Kesey and his friends crammed themselves, a jungle of electronic equipment and film cameras, and a quantity of LSD, marijuana, and whatever else they could lay their hands on, into a pre-war schoolbus painted with Day-Glo and bearing a sign on the front reading *"Furthur."* They set off across the continent for New York. During the trip, if we are to believe Tom Wolfe—and if we disbelieve him there is much in the whole hippie episode which makes no sense at all—the Merry Pranksters subtly changed in their conception of themselves. They became a band of truth-seekers bent on extending their own consciousness with the help of drugs and a perpetual surrealism, and bent on turning others on. Back in California after their strange expedition, Kesey formed a curious alliance with the Hell's Angels—and, even more significantly, a radical faction of Unitarians tried to form one with him. Owsley turned up, with his vast resources of LSD and a passion for electronics that was as great as the Pranksters' own.[25] Ginsberg had already become part of the group with a newly acquired Hinduism, which included chanting the *Hare Krishna* mantram. All the elements that go into the popular conception of the "hippie" had coalesced around Kesey.

In December 1965, Kesey began his series of "acid tests." They used his particular notion of "expanding consciousness"—LSD, provided by Owsley, music by an Owsley-sponsored rock group called the Grateful Dead, and Kesey's electronic gadgetry and stroboscopes—in an attempt to put the message of consciousness expansion over to the greatest number of people. The greatest result of these experiments was to start a new fashion in a decoration for discothèques and dances, and it becomes increasingly difficult to analyze who did and who did not believe in the grand metaphysics of the enterprise. The climax of the attempt at proselytizing, turning on, (and partly just having a ball) came at the end of January 1966. Kesey, the Grateful Dead, and Rock's number-one impresario, named Bill Graham, staged a three-day "Trips Festival"—LSD was still not illegal—which attracted large numbers of people and sparked off the high period of "hippie" culture in Haight-Ashbury.[26]

The widespread use of LSD was inextricably associated with occult and mystical groups through a two-way process. Because the leading gurus of LSD identified the drug-induced experience with the mystical experience of saints and ecstatics, those who used the drug did so in an atmosphere that was likely to put them in contact with theories of the occult or the unorthodoxly religious. And, because the traditional irrationalist Underground has naturally been concerned with mystical experience, some of its members jumped at what appeared to be the chance to induce the vision of truth that years of unassisted meditation had not brought them. The result was that the components of the late nineteenth-century occult revival—which provided the most accessible range of mystical goods on offer—pervaded certain sections of the hippie Underground. It was by no means universal, but it formed a substantial element present from the beginning. Thus Timothy Leary wrote a tongue-in-cheek article on the responsibility of Englishmen for the psychedelic revolution, which embodies a high proportion of truth: But this is because most of the Englishmen he mentions who are not contemporary gurus were leading figures of the occult revival. It is quite possible to agree with Leary's judgment when he writes that "the English in India got turned on" or thanks "William Blake and A. R. Orage for Alan Watts."[27] If "turning on" is made equivalent to a state of mystical consciousness, and occult interpreters are invoked to the adept's aid, Leary's position is perfectly clear.

The occult factor became p ominent throughout the underground press and particularly in papers in any way concerned with events in the Haight-Ashbury. Messiahs of every description combined with earnest seekers of liberation and syncretisms more bizarre than any yet devised. As John Wilcock noted in April 1966, California "is a renowned haven for faddists, individualists and nuts of every kind. . . . There's always some screwball out here who's got some new cult or ism working and a band of happily unrealistic acolytes around him who are now convinced that they've discovered the True Path to everlasting health, wealth and satisfactory orgasm."[28] The traditional hospitality of Bohemia to occultism was extended as the vision of Haight-Ashbury spread over America from the West Coast and eventually to Europe.

The spectrum of hippie irrationalism stretched from revamped fundamentalist Christianity to detailed knowledge of the works of Jung. The *Los Angeles Free Press* printed in March 1965, at the very beginning of the restive stirrings in Bohemia, a letter from Sam Shapira, "The Living World Messiah," who declared the existing American order to be "corrupt, criminal, diabolical from late John F. Kennedy and present Lyndon Johnson down." The Living World Messiah denied any identity with Jesus but claimed "to be heaven's called and anointed world Messiah or Christ by direct descending speech from the canopy of heaven witnessed" and demanded that in his honor all other religions cease to function. Sporadic items of metaphysical interest on the West Coast included the Church of the Awakening founded by Doctors John and Luisa Aiken in 1963, which was based in New Mexico and used psychedelics; and "Charlie Brown," otherwise known as Charles Artman, and "Little Eagle," who claimed to be a member of the Native American Church and kept its (legal) sacrament of peyote in a locket around his neck. Charlie Brown Artman was a figure of note in the first issue of the *Berkeley Barb* of August 1965—when the *Barb* was almost exclusively concerned with the student revolution in progress on the university campus. He was the son of an Iowa miner, and he believed in the advent of the New Age and the dawning of a state of "Christ-awareness." His arrests range from that of February 1966 for living in a tepee on Berkeley Heights displaying a sign reading "Impeach Lyndon Johnson" to that of two years later for a traffic offense in Salt Lake City. During the latter proceedings, Charlie Brown demanded solitary confinement in order to meditate, and his supporters expected "another out-of-sight, turned-on trial." Heroes from the worlds of pop, protest, and the church testified to the occult significance of the New Age. In September 1967 Bishop James Pike agreed that mystical experience and psychedelic initiation were identical. In November of the same year the folk singer Buffy Sainte-Marie—who has a degree in the history of religions—proclaimed in Jungian terms: "I'm dedicated to Satan and Jehovah—my God is Abraxas, the god of evil and of good."[29]

With the burgeoning of the underground press in 1967, occult and mystical attitudes found further outlets of expression. For example, in August 1967 the paper *Indian Head* of Santa Ana, California, published articles on Bhakti Yoga, Alan Watts, and Velikovsky's cosmology. The next issue was chiefly concerned with the economic-political analyses of Dr. Marcuse and Professor J. K. Galbraith; but by three numbers further on, the accent had shifted again to occultism and psychedelia, with discussions of Atlantis and the problems of taking LSD on a surfboard. The same year saw the beginning of the gloriously zany *Buddhist Oracle*—full title: the *Buddhist Third Class Junkmail Oracle*—of Cleveland, Ohio, which carried advertising for all manner of esoteric literature, such as Crowley's *Book of the Law*. The sanest magazines of reform could be invaded by weird and dubious cults. Thus, the usually practical *Modern Utopian* could consider the antics of the "Church of the Virgin Mother," which involved widespread transvestitism and claimed to explore the possibilities of parthenogenesis. In the late summer of 1967, the London *International Times* published an eccentric letter in which the writer claimed that Arnold Bennett—he meant Allan Bennett—had "invented methedrine."[30] The classical aims of the occultists' quest were bent into the oddest forms and overlaid with a heavy aroma of whatever drug might suit the fancy. The Montreal paper *Logos* printed an article describing its author's journey to the East, which culminated in three weeks in a South Indian ashram, where he was physically mauled by his guru. The next issue included a "Letter from Katmandu," which concentrated exclusively on the "heavy drug scene." "Hash, grass are sold in government shops. Meth and other things can be had at the pharmacy and the 'Doc' is always willing to shoot you up with morphine or heroin. In addition there is opium, bhang, acid, mescaline, psylocybine, STP and some other way out things. There are many worlds just here." Although drugs may have been the principal route by which the occult entered Bohemia, once the mystical had become an accepted part of the scene, it was not necessarily connected with drugs or improbable extravagance. Thus, the clear-headed occult column begun in 1969 by Elfrida Rivers in the New York *East Village Other* was adept at knocking dangerous lunacies on the head. How necessary this approach was is shown by the columnist's weary resignation in the face of letters asking for the name and address of "an experienced witch": Some version of this petition arrived almost every week.[31]

Whether in traditional or modernized form, with or without drugs, the occult has remained a consistent part of the modern Underground. Both the Leary and the Kesey experiments produced yet further esoteric organizations. Leary's base at Millbrook, the headquarters of the "League for Spiritual Discovery," was set cheek by jowl with the Sri Ram Ashram and the Neo-American Church of Art Kleps, whose surrealistic figure had lurched into Millbrook in 1963.

Kleps (born 1928) had been an educational psychologist and, according to the various reports of his activities to appear in the underground press, seems to have spent most of his time at Millbrook in an inebriated state. Leary described him as "a clumsy manipulator, a blatant flatterer, a bully to the willingly weak, the world's most incompetent con-man. He is in short a sodden disgrace to the movement." The object of the Neo-American Church was to have LSD accepted as a sacrament. Its members would thus be given comparable legal status with the Native American Church, whose Indian peyote religion was sanctioned by law. Kleps named his "priests" Boo-Hoos and issued a paper called *Divine Toad Sweat*—the sweat of a toad was supposed to contain some psychedelic chemical. On one level he declared that "the discovery of LSD may be taken as the intervention of God in human history"; and, on another, he offered to seal for $1,000 a certificate stating that "the chief Boo-Hoo never heard of you and regards you with indifference." The antics of Kleps introduced a welcome note of hilarity into psychedelic evangelizing. Once when he was in jail he contrived to make a Boo-Hoo of the son of a judge then occupied in trying to chase the Learyites out of the country. To Kleps also belongs the reputed distinction of having the Kleenex on which he had just blown his nose scooped up by narcotics agents for analysis.[32]

After the Trips Festival of January 1966, Ken Kesey had himself smuggled over the Mexican border, while his group continued the explosive Acid Tests that he had devised. One of the acquisitions to the Pranksters in this period was Hugh Romney, a former actor and inhabitant of the Beatnik world who had dropped out of the New York scene and met Kesey during the first Acid Tests. From this point, Romney says, he "went to work for the pudding"—the pudding being the Intergalactic World Brain (or any other new term for God that happens to appeal). Romney ended up in the hills with a commune called the Hog Farm. He developed an elaborated version of Kesey's techniques. His "original Tarot on wheels" first set out at the end of 1968. Romney described it as "a group mind-bank" designed to produce children with universal capacities. What appeared to be a combination of group therapy, communal living, spiritual forcing house, and experiment in cooperative education had an eclectic selection of courses among which the occult revival is prominent. In 1967 Romney marveled at the books which "keep appearing, like the *I Ching* and the Bible, the *Wind in the Willows*, the *Book of the Hopi*, the *Secret of the Golden Flower*, *Stranger in a Strange Land*, and *Siddartha* and the rest of Hesse and the last of Jung and all of Evans-Wentz and *Mount Analogue*, the Urantia Song, consummate *All and Everything* and still they keep coming."[33] Even more than Kesey's Pranksters, the Hog Farm represented an updated version of the occult quest, and their debts to Jung and Gurdjieff are especially obvious. In method the Hog Farm may have been following Gurdjieff; in theory, Jung.

Other groups coalesced round figures who had little to do with the

LSD-inspired cults but still became pivotal points of the Underground. An example is the group that published the Boston *Avatar* from June 1967. The *Avatar* ran a regular astrology column and another called "The Aquarian Age." It attracted contributions like that from one reader who decided that "An area designated for para-psychological and occult study coupled with programs designed to bring together factions now split over psychedelics, socio-economic trend interpretation, theological re-assessment of spiritual experience in a natural setting such as Colorado or Montana would be a groovy thing, I think." The center of this enterprise was Mel Lyman, the author of the *Autobiography of a World Savior* and producer of apocalyptic utterances on current problems. Lyman's pronouncements were completely unlike anything published on the West Coast; this World Savior had pronounced himself all in favor of "hard work" against occult trends. Nevertheless, his ideas of mission were intriguing: "sometimes I'm the AVATAR, sometimes I'm asleep," he announced; and in March 1968 the Avatar circle declared, "Today we simply incorporate ourselves as Mel Lyman." In answer to a correspondent who challenged him to explain his mission he replied: "I know God's plan, and I will reveal it to mankind, step by step, as God reveals it to me. That makes me a world savior." It is unsurprising that when the savior left AVATAR there was wailing among his devoted readership. A tragic letter from "Kathy" began, "Mel! I love you! I need you so bad! In 3 days I'll be 17 (yes, only a mere child). Maybe I don't matter to you, but I've always felt that you loved us all, no matter what. I may not have made it this far if not for you." Lyman's reply is explicit enough: "You have to lose me to find me in YOU."[34]

The center in which all such apocalyptic aspirations fused and from which they radiated, combined with politics and rearranged as a potent myth, was Haight-Ashbury. From the turn of the year 1965-66, when Kesey's Acid Tests became the Trips Festival, this San Francisco Bohemia gradually developed the characteristics that marked the image of "hippie" in the eyes of the public and of countless imitators. The term *hippie* was coined by Herb Caen, the columnist on the *San Francisco Chronicle,* from "hippy-dippy," otherwise "bebopping jerk." It is strange that Caen, who also named the Beatniks—from "beatitude"—should have pounced on the hippie style of dancing as the distinguishing characteristic and ignored the related search for enlightenment.[35] Apart from the use of drugs and exotic clothing, the characteristics of hippie culture with which people are most familiar—through the musical *Hair* if in no other way—seem to involve much chanting of *Hare Krishna* and mutterings about being in the Aquarian age. It is worth recording how these catchphrases passed into Bohemia.

When Allen Ginsberg was given psylocibin by Timothy Leary in 1960, it marked a turning point in his life. One of the results was that he stopped writing for publication. In 1966, as he confessed: "I took a lot of LSD and psylocibin previous to leaving for India and, well, I was in a slightly disordered state of mind. I thought it was absolutely necessary for me to drop dead in order to obtain complete enlightenment—for my ego to vanish entirely and for my person to vanish entirely and everything about me to vanish entirely in order to be perfect." He left with his companion Peter Orlovsky and Gary Synder on his own journey to the East and wandered around India meeting gurus and smoking marijuana. He visited the Dalai Lama and the Swami Shivananda of Rishikesh. It was Shivananda who recommended the chanting of the *Hare Krishna* mantra as an exercise, and Ginsberg was later impressed by hearing the same phrase on the lips of a woman saint on the banks of the Ganges.[36]

The real importer of the chant into the United States was Swami Bhaktivedanta (born 1897), who arrived in America in 1965 on a missionary expedition and started to give lectures on "Krishna Consciousness" in the Lower East Side of New York. He met Howard Wheeler, a teacher of English at Indiana State University, who introduced Ginsberg to the circle. Bhaktivedanta gradually acquired popularity among the New York Bohemians, and Ginsberg suggested that the fifteen "initiated disciples" of the Swami begin chanting in Tompkins Square, which the New York hippies had selected as their open-air meeting place. Wheeler distributed leaflets:

STAY HIGHER FOR EVER
No More Coming Down
Practice KRISHNA CONSCIOUSNESS
Expand your consciousness by chanting
the
TRANSCENDENTAL SOUND VIBRATION

During the Peace Parade of 5 November 1966, Ginsberg and Wheeler led the chanting of the mantra and distributed leaflets to thousands. Krishna Consciousness had arrived; and in January 1967 its missionaries came to Haight-Ashbury, which had been expectantly waiting for them.[37] Wheeler wrote:

> During the spring and early summer of '67, Haight culture was at its peak. We were flying high with mantra, and thousands opened up to us. We splashed in the Haight pond with a mammoth mantra-rock dance at the Avalon. Swamiji and Ginsberg danced on the stage with upraised hands. Multicolored lights swirled across huge wall slides of Krishna and Rama. The Grateful Dead,

Moby Grape and Big Brother blared away. Even Tim Leary garlanded one of us and salaamed, "A beautiful night, a beautiful night." Five thousand hippies, teenie-boppers and Hell's Angels stood reverently when Swamiji entered and listened attentively while he talked.

Every Sunday we chanted in Golden Gate Park and hundreds joined, holding hands and dancing in a ring. At any time of day I could walk down Haight Street playing cymbals and chanting and pick up at least a dozen enthusiasts. People were also attracted by our free prasadam [food] program and we would feed dozens daily. The Rhada Krishna Temple quickly became a dynamic influence in Haight-Ashbury life.[38]

From this success, the Krishna Consciousness movement expanded until it had centers in eight cities on the North American continent and four in Europe; and this rapid diffusion of the doctrine was an indication of how swiftly other related ideas might spread. To American Bohemia, such as it was, Hinduism *seemed* new; and, in the precise form of "Krishna Consciousness," indeed it was new. But it was the recurrence of a phenomenon that had been in progress ever since the end of the nineteenth century.[39]

The idea of the age of Aquarius is simply a statement of astrological fact. That is, a subscriber to astrology believes not only in the links between the heavenly bodies and life on earth but also in an elaborate superstructure of periods, including that of a "master period" of the Great Year, which is generally thought to last for about 36,000 ordinary years. The earth is at present at the end of the Great Year governed by the astrological sign Pisces, and due to begin the next Great Year, dominated by the characteristics of Aquarius. The precise dating of the change-over varies considerably with the individual astrologer and the system of calculation he employs. But the fact that the earth is due to enter a new astrological eon is not at all the invention of the hippies and could well have been calculated in the sixteenth century—or in ancient Chaldea well before the birth of Christ. To say that the change is due in "about the year two thousand" means little; for variations of a few hundred years count for nothing in the calculation of a Great Year. In the more esoteric sections of the nineteenth-century Progressive Underground, the calculations were naturally biased toward an earlier advent of the New Age; in pre-Nazi Germany the age of Aquarius was sometimes timed to coincide with the arrival of the Thousand Year Reich. In all cases the Aquarian characteristics were thought to be diametrically opposed to those of the preceding age— for confusion, harmony; for the pursuit of material profit, the brotherhood of man.

The occultism of Haight-Ashbury might well merely have produced a consensus of opinion among the astrologically inclined indicating the arrival of the Aquarian Age. In fact, one particular astrologer who lived in the Haight seems to have been chiefly responsible for popularizing the idea. His name was Gavin Arthur, otherwise Chester Alan Arthur III. He was the great-grandson of a United States president and a direct link with the European astrological revival. Arthur (born 1902) had passed through a varied career, which included gold mining in Alaska, the world of American high society, and Paris in the 1920s before he came to live in Haight-Ashbury. He had been given Edouard Schuré's *Great Initiates* at the age of nineteen and had dabbled in astrology for thirty years before a Jungian psychiatrist in San Francisco persuaded him to cast her patients' horoscopes as an aid to analysis. Gavin Arthur was at this time a counselor at San Quentin prison, and he began to use astrology in his prison work. His astrological book, *The Circle of Sex,* was less his claim to fame than the fact that he had predicted the death of President John F. Kennedy before the elections sent him to Washington and Dallas.[40]

Arthur saw himself as a Jungian astrologer and foretold the arrival of the Aquarian age for the year 2260. The earth had, nevertheless, entered a "new age of culture" in 1940. To this quite orthodox astrological tenet, Arthur added the equally orthodox belief in spiritual evolution, a doctrine that he supported by a conflation of R. D. Bucke's *Cosmic Consciousness*—a well-known text of the nineteenth-century occult revival, which owed much to the New England Transcendentalists and Walt Whitman—and the theories of Count Alfred Korzybsky's General Semantics. These theories he adapted to term minerals as one-dimensional, plants as two-dimensional, animals as three-dimensional, and humans as four-dimensional modes of being. By implication, a new five-dimensional form of life for the New Age was evolving. Arthur vaunted his intellectual ancestry: He had "sat at the feet of Edward Carpenter, who sat at the feet of Whitman."[41]

It was to the theories of Gavin Arthur that the enthusiast in the *San Francisco Oracle* was indebted when he watched the "be-in" of 14 January 1967. "Not since the vast empire-armies of old Persia has there been such an exotic massing for a common purpose," he wrote. "Not since the last day of the Christ has the purpose been so gentle and so strong. Not in the 26,000 years have the aborigines of a new mankind gathered in recognition of their heritage and their gig."[42] The mood of apocalypse—as well as the success of the idea of Haight-Ashbury—also derived from the Diggers, but the occult and religious factors that came together at one place and time were at least as responsible; and the apocalyptic feelings generated by other causes reactivated interest in the occult. Before considering the Diggers and the social-political aspects of the Hippie Myth, some further results of the combination of LSD-cults, occultism, and Oriental religion should be noticed.

Gavin Arthur was by no means the only guru to pronounce for the idea of spiritual evolution. It was a cardinal tenet of those who followed Timothy Leary. How far anyone followed Leary completely is an open question, but his ideas could not help but be influential. Some six months after Kesey began his Acid Tests, LSD was declared illegal in the State of California—on 6 June 1966—and soon afterward, Leary and Alpert delivered a "manifesto for an inner revolution" to an enthusiastic crowd. In October a writer in the *Berkeley Barb* wrote that "Timothy Leary comes to us as apostle and martyr of the new religion. Let us respect him, but let us take Spartacus, not Christ, as our model." The split between the political activists and the mystical drop-outs was obviously present from the start; but the important thing about Haight-Ashbury was the temporary fusion of ideas. A moving spirit behind the Haight's vision of itself was Ron Thelin, the owner of the Psychedelic Shop on Haight Street, a center of the new culture. Thelin was behind the most distinctively "hippie" paper to emerge from the Underground, the *San Francisco Oracle*, and he was far from an opponent of Leary.[43] In the pages of the *Oracle* the rationale of a new "mutant consciousness," which might be produced by LSD, was elaborated together with the idea that Haight-Ashbury was the center of the new developments. Was LSD producing a new subspecies? To some it seemed like it:

> *Mutants! Know now that you exist!*
> *They have hid you in cities*
> *And clothed you in fools' clothes*
> *Know now that you are free![44]*

Richard Alpert called the Haight-Ashbury a "very high energy center" and "the purest reflection of what is happening in consciousness, at the leading edge in the society." The *Oracle*'s column, "Gossiping Guru," thought it apparent that "a real and viable synthesis of Eastern and Western modes of consciousness is taking place and the result is sure to be the most powerful cognitive tool ever to fall into the hands of men of good will." Astrology not only predicted the New Age, but possibly an avatar. In early 1967 the *Oracle* carried a request for further information about "Him who was born on February 5th, 1962, when 7 planets were in Aquarius." According to some sections of opinion there had been a great convocation of adepts on the inner planes to prepare for this Messiah![45] The triumph of the new consciousness was seen in the "gathering of the tribes" (14 January 1967) for the Human Be-In in Golden Gate Park. By this point, the hippie culture had become defined and could do nothing but expand or decline. In fact it did both.

From the point of view of the individual's role in society, this new Bohemia produced a new version of the dream of the nineteenth-century occult revival: "liberation," "spiritual evolution," "expanded consciousness." It did this partly by using something of its Bohemian inheritance, partly by absorbing the occult tradition, mostly by adapting such ideas into a new form. It was nonetheless the Progressive Underground—spattered with Day-Glo paint, stoned out of its mind, dancing with a frenzy that some have compared to the outbreaks of dancing mania in the Middle Ages— but recognizably the same creature. Its critique of society was derived from sources similar to those of earlier undergrounds of opposition to materialist establishments. Because of this, the junction between the representatives of the new consciousness and the radicals who demanded a less materialist, less individualist society was made on the basis which our story has identified again and again: a common idealism, a common pursuit of cities not of this world, a community of the implicitly "spiritual" against the legions of Mammon. The union of all such elements took place in San Francisco, and Haight-Ashbury possessed a particular kind of illuminated politics in the shape of the Diggers.

The Diggers were responsible for the "love" part of Haight-Ashbury, just as the occult and drugs were responsible for ideas of an emergent new consciousness. The hippie culture based on drugs and a new Bohemianism flourished during 1966. But it was only recognized in December of that year when the Diggers staged a ceremony to mark the "Death of the old Haight and the Birth of the New Haight." A step further was the Be-In of 14 January, and the idea that the whole ethos would flower in the "Summer of Love." The mass media moved in, and the myth of the hippie was born. The anticipated influx of teenagers and summer hippies exceeded all expectations. Tourists began to frequent Haight-Ashbury, where gentleness quickly evaporated under the pressure of too many people and a shortage of marijuana, which gave criminal groups and pushers of horror-drugs like methedrine the chance to infiltrate. In October 1967, Thelin closed his Psychedelic Shop, and the Diggers held another ceremony designed to mark the death of "Hippie, son of Mass Media," and the birth of the "Free Man." This was also the month of the antiwar demonstration against the Pentagon.

The Haight was never to be resurrected, but what there was of value had by this time been grafted on to a zany version of *Realpolitik* and developed into a new idealistic critique of society. By the time most of the world had heard of hippies, the species was transmogrified, but the myth was spread abroad. It should be emphasized that the *vision* of Haight-Ashbury has been much more influential than the *reality*, which by the summer of 1967 had degenerated into a state which, by all reports, was more like the rotting of the old society than the incubation of the new.[46]

Notes

1. George Wickes (ed.), *Lawrence Durrell-Henry Miller: A Private Correspondence* (London, 1963), 347; Sidney Omar, *Henry Miller: His World of Urania* (London and California, 1968), 63; Alfred Perles, *My Friend, Henry Miller* (London, 1955), 132; Henry Miller, *Big Sur and the Oranges of Hieronymus Bosch* (London, 1958), 45 ff., 260; Henry Miller, "A Night with Jupiter," in *View* (February-March 1942), 5.

2. For a comparison between the Beats and their predecessors, see Lawrence Lipton, *The Holy Barbarians* (London, 1960), 263 ff.

3. Ned Polsky, "The Village Beat Scene, in *Hustlers, Beats and Others* (London, paperback ed. 1971), 173-74, 176 ff.

4. Polsky, *Hustlers, Beats and Others,* 174; Lipton, *Barbarians,* 244 ff.

5. Jack Kerouac, *The Dharma Bums* (orig. 1958, paperback ed. London, 1969), 11.

6. Christmas Humphreys, *Sixty Years of Buddhism in England* (London, 1968), 20-40. Other heroes of Kerouac—for example, Dwight Godard, compiler of *A Buddhist Bible*, published in the United States in 1928—are also the heroes of the European Buddhists.

7. Theodore Roszack, *The Making of a Counter-Culture* (London, 1970), 132.

8. An additional factor in spreading consciousness of Zen in America was undoubtedly the occupation of Japan. After 1945 there was a great increase in East Asian studies, and it is interesting that Zen properly entered England after the Second World War, when Christmas Humphreys—who had been sent as a counsel to the War Crimes Trials in Tokyo—visited Suzuki. It is symptomatic of the close links between the Occult Revival and the coming of Zen to the West that at the time of his trip Humphreys was preparing a new edition of the *Mahatma Letters to H. P. Blavatsky*, and that his journey included a visit to the headquarters of the Theosophical Society at Adyar near Madras. See Humphreys, *Via Tokyo* (London, 1948).

9. Norman Cohn, *The Pursuit of the Millennium* (London, paperback ed., 1970), 286.

10. See *The Occult Underground* (Peru, Ill., 1974).

11. For Symonds, see William James, *The Varieties of Religious Experience* (paperback ed., London, 1968), 367-77. For Anna Kingsford and others, see *The*

Occult Underground; B. P.Blood, *Pluriverse* (London, n.d.), 217–25. CF. *Journal of SPR* June 1893, 94–96.

12. Blood, *Pluriverse*, vii; for Tennyson's letter to Blood, see 215–17, and Hallam, Lord Tennyson, *Tennyson, a Memoir*, vol. II, 158–59; Blood, *Pluriverse*, xxiv; *Letters of William James* (London, 1926), vol. II, 39; William James, "A Pluralistic Mystic" reprinted in *Memoirs and Studies* (London, 1911), 373.

13. James, *Varieties of Religious Experience*, 373–74.

14. See, e.g., Symonds, *Beast*, pp. 160 ff.; *The Confessions of Aleister Crowley* (ed. Symonds and Kenneth Grant, London, 1969), 768. The editors note (934, note 4) that Crowley had been taking the drug "for some years."

15. The source is a former disciple of Crowley.

16. As his correspondence shows, Huxley kept in touch with almost every prominent member of the mystical underground. At first there were Gerald Heard and Christopher Isherwood, later Alan Watts and Timothy Leary. Huxley himself was prone to accepting every chance-blown scrap of rejected knowledge: for example, the Bates system of sight-training and Dianetics. See *The Letters of Aldous Huxley* (ed. Grover Smith, London, 1969) and Laura Huxley, *This Timeless Moment* (London, 1969).

17. Sidney Cohen, *Drugs of Hallucination* (paperback ed., London, 1970), 26–27, 32–35; John Wilcock, "Other Scenes," in *Berkeley Barb* (22 April, 1966), 7; Thadeus and Rita Ashby,"Did Jesus Turn On?," *Berkeley Barb* (23 December 1966); Thadeus and Rita Ashby, "Ecstatic Living" in *The Alchemist* (Manhattan, Kansas) vol. I, no. 3 (December 1968), reprinted from San Francisco *Oracle*.

18. Richard Blum, Eva Blum, and Mary Lou Funkhauser, "The Natural History of LSD Use" in *Utopiates* (ed. Blum, London, 1965), 23–38, 55–56.

19. See Timothy Leary, *High Priest* (New York, 1968), 2–60 (p. 60 quoted).

20. Leary, *High Priest*, 66.

21. For Ginsberg, see Leary, *High Priest*, 110 ff.; for Olson, 143 ff.; for Burroughs, 214 ff.; for the "Good Friday Experiment," 304 ff.; for Watts and Heard, 288; quote on 300; see Leary and Ralph Metzner, "Poet of the Interior Journey," in Leary, *The Politics of Ecstasy* (London, 1970), 146 ff.; Norman Hartweg, interview with Richard Alpert in *Berkeley Barb* (3 September 1965), 9.

22. Leary, *High Priest*, 110–12; "God's Secret Agent AOS 3" in *Politics*, 225 ff.

23. Leary, "God's Secret Agent."

24. The main source for information on Kesey is Tom Wolfe, *The Electric Kool-Aid Acid Test* (paperback ed., New York, 1969). This book needs no recommendation to its already large public, and only those who have had anything to do with Kesey-type experiments can judge whether the atmosphere it creates is authentic. However, from the point of view of a student of strange religions, Wolfe has conveyed better than any other writer the sense of living within another order of experience induced by a novel scale of values. Ouspensky's *In Search of the Miraculous* has something of the same atmosphere, but is primarily concerned with exposition. There are one or two novels of the nineteenth-century Occult

Revival that induce the claustrophobia and even the aspiration. But Wolfe's head-over-heels prose shows something that is surely important for a twentieth-century historian to understand—how people still believe in miracles.

25. For Owsley and Kesey, see Wolf, *Acid Test*, 188–89.

26. Wolfe, *Acid Test*, 222 ff., and Ralph J. Gleason, *The Jefferson Airplane and the San Francisco Sound* (New York, 1969).

27. Leary, "The Magical Mystery Trip" in *Politics of Ecstasy*, 88, 96.

28. Wilcock, in *Barb*, 22 April 1966, 7.

29. "The Messiah Speaks," *Los Angeles Free Press*, vol. 2, no. 11; *Berkeley Barb*, vol. 3, no. 11, 6; on Charlie Brown Artman, see *Barb*, 1/1 (August 13, 1965) and 2/20 (20 May 1966); and *Electric News* (Salt Lake City) 1/3,51; *Helix* (Seattle, Wash.), 2/2/ (29 September 1967); *Distant Drummer* (Philadelphia) vol. 1, no. 1 (November 1967), 2.

30. See *Indian Head* (Santa Ana, Calif.) vol. I, nos. 4, 5, 8; *Modern Utopian*,vol. I, no. 3, 29 ff.; *International Times*, no. 18 (13 August-13 September), 2.

31. David Ryan in *Logos*, vol. II, no. 2 (July 1969); reprinted from *International Times*; also "Letter from Katmandu" (August 1969), 2; Elfrida Rivers, "Emanations," *East Village Other*, vol. IV, no. 39 (27 August 1969), 13.

32. Leary, Review of the Neo-American Church Catechism and Handbook in *East Village Other*, vol. II, no. 19, (19 August-1 September 1967), 9; Walter Bowart in *Berkeley Barb* (17 June 1967), 9 (reprinted from *EVO*), "The Way to God" in *Modern Utopian* vol. I, no. 1, and *EVO* vol. III, no. 4 (1–15 January 1968), 5.

33. Wolfe, *Acid Test*, 241 ff., and Richard Strauss, "A strrool trooomnmn down Memory Lane with Hugh Romney" in *Oracle of Southern California* (January 1968), 6 ff.; Al Katzman, "Hog Farm in Open Celebration" in *Logos* (April 1969), 7A and 14A; Hugh Romney in *EVO* (week ending 17 August 1967), 10.

34. *Avatar*, vol. I, no. 3 (7 July 1967); see *Avatar*, nos. 18–24 (February-May 1968).

35. On Caen and his terms, see *EVO*, vol. II, no. 22 (1–15 October 1967), 3.

36. Ginsberg in *Los Angeles Free Press*, vol. III, no. 3 (21 January 1966); "Reflections on the Mantra," in *The Alchemist* (November 1968), 19 (reprinted from *Fifth Estate*).

37. Howard Wheeler, "The Hare Krishna Explosion," in *The Alchemist* (March 1968); Makunduh Das Adhikary in *San Francisco Oracle*, 8.

38. Wheeler, "Hare Krishna," 10.

39. See Wendell Thomas, *Hinduism Invades America* (New York, 1930).

40. *L. A. Free Press*, vol. IV, no. 33 (8–24 August 1967), 16, and *San Francisco Oracle* (January 1967), 4.

41. *Oracle* and Arthur, "Evolution and Cosmic Consciousness," reprinted from *Oracle* in *The Alchemist*, vol. I, no. 2 (November 1968). On Alfred Korzybsky, see Martin Gardner, *Fads and Fallacies*, 281 ff. Gardner's arguments here should be watched as carefully as Korzybsky's own.

42. *S. F. Oracle* (January 1967), 7.

43. *Berkeley Barb*, vol. III, no. 14, and vol. II, no. 25, vol. III, no. 11 (16 September 1966), and Leary, *Politics*, 301.

44. Ted Berk, "Manifesto for Mutants" in *S. F. Oracle* (January 1967).

45. *S. F. Oracle* (5–15 November 1966) for Alpert, 3, 10–11; and "Gossiping Guru," "The Stoned Age," 6. See January numbers for the idea of Avatar.

46. For a description of what happened during the "summer of love" see Nicholas von Hoffman, *We Are the People Our Parents Warned Us Against* (paperback ed., New York, 1969), and Helen Perry, *The Human Be-In* (London, 1970). Hoffman, while not unsympathetic, concentrates on Haight-Ashbury as a culture based on a drug-economy. It is an excellent antidote to the naïve enthusiasm of Helen Perry, who does show what was expected of the hippie ethic and makes the interesting point that Haight-Ashbury to some extent acted as a sort of "automatic psychotherapy" for people out of control. Perry also compares the hippies to the New England Transcendentalists. The much-praised account by Joan Didion, "Slouching towards Bethlehem," in the book of the same title (London, 1969), is quite useful, but lacks perspective. The best sources are, of course, the Underground Press—*Barb*, *Oracle*, *East Village Other*, *Fifth Estate*—and they should be compared with more jaundiced accounts like Didion's or Hoffman's. There is an anthology of the early underground press heavily edited by Jesse Kornbluth, *Notes from the New Underground* (New York, 1968), in which see 284–300 for the decline of Haight-Ashbury.

THE IDEAS

The concepts of karma and reincarnation are the New Age movement's basic staples. Borrowed from Hinduism and Buddhism, the Western versions are often spruced up by the addition of "human potential" concepts and instant, high-tech access to past centuries. But the core remains: After we die, we are born into another body in order to answer karma accumulated in past lives. The attraction of karma and reincarnation is clear: They pump meaning into the senselessness and horror of the human condition; accidents don't just happen, *they are deserved.* Many New Age authors, including Shirley MacLaine, ascribe bad karma to innocent infants who suffer from painful diseases or tragic misfortune: "As hard as it is to accept," writes one popular author, "a child too has a long history of past lifetimes, and has reincarnated to resolve his karma and fulfill his dharma. If, in a past life, he has mistreated, abandoned or molested children, karma must be balanced."

Paul Edwards dismantles this kind of rhetorical turpitude with immaculate rigor. In what is certainly the most powerful critique of karma and reincarnation ever written, Edwards finds them empirically unverifiable, logically untenable, and morally insulting.

If Edwards goes after New Age thinking with the mind of a fine philosopher, Melvin Harris enters the fray as a resourceful investigator, a private eye of ideas. Here, Harris takes his magnifying glass to "hypnotic regression," the technique by which we allegedly can learn of our past lives. He looks at what have been considered the most convincing cases of remembering past lives and comes up with explanations that don't rely on supernatural agencies but which are fascinating nonetheless— locating these memories not in past lives but in a kind of "unconscious plagiarism." Put simply: We don't remember what we remember.

Such underestimation, writes Susan Blackmore, is the main reason people give occult explanations to strange memories and experiences. Blackmore, a researcher whose interest in the paranormal was sparked by her own out-of-body experience, became a skeptic after her many tests failed to turn up any evidence of "psi." Her conversion was not taken too kindly by believers in the paranormal, one of whom pronounced her a "psi inhibitor"! But Blackmore has found that by abandoning the paranormal hypothesis one can make great scientific progress in understanding people's "strange experiences."

It might seem odd that the program of science needs to be defended from many college-trained critics who have taken hold of the New Age movement. Maureen O'Hara writes: "I frequently find myself having to explain to the New Age contingent of my humanistic brethren what 'science' really is. The image of the mainstream scientist held by most New Agers is of a person, usually a white male, with no feelings and no spiritual yearnings, who is probably oblivious to both the darker applications of his craft and to the magical possibilities of the human mind." O'Hara proposes that the open-mindedness of New Agers can make for a wonderful environment for "trial balloons"—but that "without reliable, agreed-upon criteria with which to test and evaluate these trial balloons, potentially valuable ideas and innovations cannot be sorted out from those without merit."

An essential element of scientific investigation, then, is *agreement*: A fact that's true for you should be true for me, too. Such objective standards are commonly pooh-poohed by New Age leaders, who stress that truth is a personal opinion, that you can "create your own reality." Martin Gardner shows us a Ramtha and a Shirley MacLaine so beholden to solipsism that they cannot even bring themselves to condemn murder. "Murder is not a sin to be expiated, it is a teaching experience. You never have to *pay* for anything," claims MacLaine.

Brad Steiger, one of the New Age's most ubiquitous entrepreneurs, also downplays the issue of scientific fact: The "spiritual" or "internal validity" of paranormal claims is what counts, not whether the claims are literally true. While this approach doesn't do a whole lot to improve our understanding of the world, it does afford writer-businessmen like Steiger the opportunity to cash in on the wishes, dreams, and fears of a benighted culture.

New Age music has also become big business—but has it become music? It's hard to tell at this point, writes *Village Voice* critic Leslie Berman, when some fine, quiet jazz is often squished beneath the same label as the worst of Muzak. Berman's description of a musical movement that is trying to define itself can also, in large measure, apply to the movement from which the music takes its name.

THE CASE AGAINST
KARMA AND REINCARNATION
Paul Edwards

The beliefs in reincarnation or rebirth and in the Law of Karma are generally held together, but they are logically distinct theories. There are numerous arguments which, if they were valid, would prove reincarnation without proving Karma, and conversely there are objections to the doctrine of Karma that do not automatically refute reincarnation. In this article I will examine the main arguments in support of both theories, showing their fatal flaws, and then offer a number of reasons for rejecting both of them.

Reincarnation may be defined as the view that human beings do not, as most of us assume, live only once, but on the contrary live many, perhaps an infinite number of times, acquiring a new body for each incarnation. Belief in reincarnation comes in many forms. According to several Eastern versions the body into which a person migrates is not necessarily another human body: it can be that of an animal or a plant or even an inanimate object. According to a well-known story, Pythagoras stopped someone from beating a dog, on the ground that he had recognized the voice of a friend in the yelping of the dog. In the *Brihadaranyaka Upanishad* it is taught that some wicked human beings are reborn as insects—wasps, gnats, and mosquitoes. The Harvard anthropologist Oscar Lewis, who studied the behavior and beliefs of peasants in an Indian village, was told that people guilty of serious crimes may in a future life sink so low as to become jars. Presumably it is believed that such jars have an inner life. They cannot

This selection consists of the first two installments of a four-part series on "The Case Against Reincarnation" published in *Free Inquiry* in four successive issues, starting in the Fall of 1986. Part 3 (Spring 1987) deals with the dependence of consciousness on the brain and how this undermines reincarnation. Part 4 (Summer 1987) discusses the difficulties stemming from the "interregnum," the period between incarnations. It also shows in some detail the flaws in the research of Ian Stevenson. This four-part article earned Professor Edwards the Selma V. Forkosch prize as the best article to appear in *Free Inquiry* during 1986 and 1987. This selection is reprinted here with the permission of Paul Edwards.

communicate with anybody but they realize their fate as a dreadful deprivation. Among recent Western converts and also among the more philosophically articulate Eastern supporters of the theory, rebirth is believed to occur only in human bodies. For obvious reasons this is a much more defensible position.

An important difference between reincarnation and Western beliefs in survival is the view that human beings, or rather the souls that inhabit their bodies, did not have a beginning. Incarnations stretch infinitely into the past. In the *Bhagavad Gita,* which dates back to about 500 B.C. and thus precedes the rise of Buddhism, Krishna, the god of love, assures his as yet unenlightened companion Sanjaya that grief and sorrow are quite inappropriate emotions in relation to the death of somebody we loved. The reason is that a human being will live forever and that "the eternal in man cannot die." A person's birth is not the beginning of his existence and his death is not the end:

> We have all been for all time: I, and thou, and those kings of men. And we all shall be for all time, we all for ever and ever. [II/12–13]

The last sentence of this passage must not be misunderstood to mean that the series of incarnations will also stretch into the future without limit. Eventually those who have lived sufficiently good lives will attain a state of enlightenment and reach Nirvana, which is not, as is frequently supposed, the absence of all consciousness, but a kind of Absolute or Cosmic Consciousness. Recent Western converts to reincarnation who have been brought up in a Judeo-Christian environment have great difficulties with the notion of an infinite past and in most cases they simply ignore this question. They also do not seem to concern themselves with the question of the "ultimate" fate of the soul. Their main concern seems to be that death, i.e., the death after the present life, should not be the end, and a few additional lives would probably be quite sufficient to appease their longings.

It is not easy to find a clear and unambiguous statement of the Law of Karma. However, insofar at least as it concerns the immediate human scene, the basic idea is quite straightforward. The doctrine maintains that the world is just and justice is equated with retribution. Everything good that happens to a human being is a reward for some previous good deed, and everything bad that happens to him is punishment for an evil deed. As we shall see later, far larger claims are also made, but for the time being it will be convenient to ignore them. It should also be mentioned that, although many supporters of Karma, especially Hindus, believe in gods or a God, many others do not. In the West reincarnation and Karma are frequently offered as an alternative philosophy to those of theism and deism.

It is clear that somebody can believe in reincarnation without believing in Karma but that the converse does not hold. To say that a human being will live again in other bodies does not by itself imply anything whatever about rewards and punishments. On the other hand, if somebody believes in Karma he must believe in reincarnation, unless he takes the absurd position that all the good and bad things happening to people are just rewards and punishments for deeds they performed in this life. It would be difficult to find an Eastern believer who accepts reincarnation without also accepting Karma, but some of the best-known Western philosophers who have advocated reincarnation have not also endorsed the karmic theory as *true,* although they usually regard it as an admirable idea.

It is evident that reincarnationism makes several huge assumptions that have been the target of severe criticisms by Western philosophers in recent decades and, in some instances, for many centuries. To begin with, reincarnation logically presupposes an extreme form of dualism. If we include as dualists all those who agree that mental events and processes cannot be identified either with actual and possible behavior or with any bodily states or processes, then we may distinguish the more moderate variety, which holds that a person is *both* a mind and a body, from the extreme form, which maintains that a person *is* his mind and that the body is simply one of his possessions. It is clear that reincarnationists are committed to the latter of these views. A person's body is different in every incarnation, but he is the same since it is the same mind that animates all the different bodies. In the words of the *Bhavagad Gita:*

> As a man leaves an old garment and puts on one that is new, the Spirit leaves his mortal body and then puts on one that is new. [II/22]

To refute reincarnationism it is quite sufficient to show that the extreme form of dualism is untenable; and I think that the great majority of contemporary philosophers—reductive materialists, identity-theorists, and moderate dualists (including epiphenomenalists among the last group)—would unhesitatingly agree that the extreme form of dualism *is* quite indefensible.

Not only is reincarnation opposed to all of the most widely held views on the mind-body problem. It also follows from what has been said that it is opposed to one of the major current theories about personal identity. This is the view that holds that, however much more than a body a human being may be, personal identity involves bodily continuity. If we refer to this view as "corporealism" it should be emphasized that it is not the same as either reductive materialism or the identity theory. These do indeed presuppose corporealism, but the reverse is not true. What concerns us here is that, unless corporealism can be shown to be false, reincarnation is ruled out from the start.

Finally, although a reincarnationist need not hold the view that the mind can or ever does exist without a bodily foundation or concomitant, he *is* committed to the assumption that a person's mind does not require the *particular* body or brain with which it is connected in the present life. This follows from the claim that in other lives the mind will be tied to different bodies and brains. I shall try to show in some detail later on that this assumption of the causal independence of the mind from the person's present body and brain is more than a little doubtful.[1]

The Logical Advantages of Reincarnation Over Other Forms of Survival

The question is often asked why reincarnation should have become such an attractive theory to large numbers of people in Western countries in recent years. This is no doubt an interesting question, which receives ample analysis elsewhere in this book. I prefer to say something about the related question of why reincarnation might appear logically superior to other forms of survival. Although I don't believe that reason and evidence have much to do with the current vogue of reincarnation, some of its new-found friends may have been partly influenced by certain of these advantages. Some of the advantages we shall find to be illusory, but others are quite real.

In the first place, although many Eastern reincarnationists do believe in a "higher region," this is not an essential part of the theory, and it is quite consistent for a reincarnationist to rule out any kind of "Beyond." This means that reincarnationists can dispense with anything like heaven and hell. Survival is said to take place right here on earth and not in a mysterious realm whose location cannot be specified and which has never been seen or otherwise observed by anybody. Next, reincarnationism seems to be able to dispense with the notion of the disembodied mind as the vehicle of survival. Many liberal Protestants are stuck with this view and, although believers who follow Aquinas take the position that the soul will eventually be united with a resurrected body, they too are committed to a disembodied mind at least for the period between death and the availability of the resurrected body. Now, the notion of a disembodied mind seems to many philosophers quite incoherent; but even if it is not incoherent, it seems incompatible with the evidence from neurology concerning the dependence of consciousness on the brain. The other main form of survival believed in the West involves the notion, mentioned a little earlier, that after we die our bodies will be resurrected. Except for a small number of professional theologians, this view seems nowadays as incredible to educated believers as to unbelievers. Reincarnationists have not been slow to heap scorn on it. Thus Professor C. J. Ducasse, the leading philosophical supporter of reincarnation in recent decades, protests that nothing in the position of reincarnationists is remotely as paradoxical as belief in the "resurrection of the flesh," which is or was accepted by many Christians "notwithstanding the dispersion of the dead body's material by cremation or by incorporation of its particles into the living bodies of worms, sharks, or vultures." Ducasse does not address himself to the more sophisticated version of resurrectionism that teaches that somehow, somewhere replicas of our original bodies will be created that will serve as the physical under-pinning of our conscious lives. Aside from presenting serious problems concerning personal identity, such a claim strikes most sane people as utterly fantastic, no less fantastic than the literal resurrection of the flesh.

Another advantage or apparent advantage of reincarnation may be described as its "symmetry" as opposed to the "asymmetry" of Western beliefs in survival. In *Reason in Religion,* Santayana observed that "the fact of having been born is a bad augury for immortality" (p. 165). Santayana was only concerned to point out the antecedent implausibility of Western beliefs in survival. Schopenhauer and Hume made similar remarks with the explicit purpose of showing the logical superiority of reincarnation or, as Hume preferred to call it, "metempsychosis." "Judaism," Schopenhauer wrote, "together with the two religions which sprang from it, teaches the creation of man out of nothing." It then becomes a "hard task" to "link on" to beings with a finite past, "an endless existence *a parte post*" (*The World As Will and Idea,* vol. 3, p. 305). Unlike Schopenhauer Hume did not believe in reincarnation, but he also regarded it as logically superior to the Christian view. "Reasoning from the common course of nature," he observes in a passage that has frequently been quoted by reincarnationists, we must hold that *"what is incorruptible must also be ingenerable,"* and hence that "the soul, if immortal, existed before our birth" ("On the Im-mortality of the Soul," in Antony Flew, ed., *Body, Mind and Death,* p. 182, Hume's italics). A little later he adds that "the metempsychosis is the only system of this kind that philosophy can harken to" (p. 186).

Emphasis on the superiority of reincarnation because of its avoidance of the asymmetry of the Western view is usually accompanied in the writings of reincarnationists by scornful comments about the absurdity and in-credibility of the Christian doctrine of "special creation," which holds that at conception God infuses a soul into the newly formed embryo. "If we claim that some divine power creates the soul," writes Irving S. Cooper, one of my favorite theosophists, "it is rather difficult to explain why the exercise of that power is dependent upon the sexual passion of man" (*Reincarnation: A Hope of the World,* p. 58). Similarly, Professor Ducasse speaks of "the shocking supposition, among Christians" that when two human beings mate, "be it in wedlock or in wanton debauche," an infinitely loving God creates "outright from nothing an immortal human soul and that arbitrarily with a particular one out of many possible sets of latent capacities and incapacities" (*A Critical Examination of the Belief in Life After Death,* p. 210). I may observe in passing that I unreservedly endorse these criticisms of the Christian position. It seems ludicrous that something as important as the creation of a soul that is going to exist forever should be tied to such accidents as the failure of a birth control appliance. It is safe to say that in practice educated Christians and Jews do not believe in the special creation of the soul any more than atheists and agnostics and that they adopt a completely naturalistic view concerning the origin of human beings, their psychological no less than their physical attributes.

The Evidence for Reincarnation

I now proceed to a discussion of the various kinds of evidence that have been adduced in support of reincarnation and Karma. I believe that I have not left out anything of significance, but in two cases, for reasons to be explained, my discussion will be somewhat sketchy.

1. *The Moral Argument.* This argument, which is also called "the argument from justice," though it could just as appropriately be called "the argument from *in*justice," is used by the great majority of the defenders of reincarnation, the more articulate and educated writers as well as the more primitive believers. It closely resembles the "moral" arguments for the existence of God and life after death found in Kant and numerous Christian and Jewish apologists. To many of its supporters the argument seems so overwhelmingly plausible that they find it difficult to conceive how anybody could fail to see its cogency. Unlike most of the other arguments to be considered, the moral argument would, if valid, prove Karma as well as reincarnation.

The first step in the argument is a declaration that the world as we know it contains a vast amount of injustice. It will be helpful to distinguish three kinds of injustice. To begin with, there is the undeniable fact that human beings are born with very unequal endowments and into environments offering very unequal opportunities. Some are born intelligent, with healthy and handsome bodies; others are born with less intelligence and sickly or even crippled. Some are born to parents who are affectionate and well-to-do; others into families that are unloving, uneducated, and poor and into a society in which the prospects for happiness are exceedingly slim. Next, there is the suffering later in life resulting from illnesses, accidents, and natural disasters like floods, fires, and earthquakes, which are not in any obvious way due to voluntary human actions. Finally, there is the injustice inflicted by other human beings.

I will follow Dr. Raynor Johnson, a Christian reincarnationist, in stating the remainder of the argument. Dr. Johnson was for many years the Master of Queens College of the University of Melbourne. In addition to his theology degree he also holds one in physics; and he is frequently cited by other reincarnationists as one of their foremost spokesmen. After listing numerous instances of injustice, he mentions "mere chance" and God's plan as two ways of explaining the facts. Chance is no explanation of anything, and it would be highly paradoxical to saddle a good God with the responsibility for the world's injustice. He then asks this question:

> If neither of these alternatives is acceptable, what explanation have we to offer which carries with it the reasonable assurance that we live in a just world? [*The Imprisoned Splendour,* p. 376]

Fortunately there is a third alternative. We can discover it if we have the courage to extend the "Law of Cause and Effect" from the physical domain to the "levels of desire and thought" and to human behavior and consciousness generally, even if in doing so we endanger the freedom of the will. Surely it is "most improbable" that mental phenomena are any less subject to cause and effect than those that are purely material.

Now, if we extend the Law of Cause and Effect to the mental domain we have to maintain "that the grossly unequal conditions of birth and childhood," to confine ourselves to one form of injustice, "are the result of prior causes." Since, however, such causes are "not by any means apparent in the present life," we must "as a logical necessity" affirm "the pre-existence of souls." We must affirm that "we are the product of self-generated forces in states of prior existence" (ibid.). In this way we arrive at "the great Law of Karma," which teaches that

> Whatsoever a man sows, whether in the field of action or thought, sometime and somewhere the fruits of it will be reaped by him. [p. 377]

It is a "reasonable law of justice which runs through the world on all levels" and applies "equally to good things and evil things." We have thus explained human suffering and inequality as not being due to chance or the will of God but to our own deeds in previous lives.

It is amazing that an argument that is so transparently fallacious should have gained such widespread support. First of all, Dr. Johnson and all the other reincarnationist writers who argue along the same lines are grossly confused about what extending the "Law of Cosmic Effect" to mental phenomena involves. It involves the search and, where one succeeds, the discovery of causal explanations. It most emphatically does not involve the demonstration that justice in the karmic or any other familiar sense prevails. If we show that a given mental phenomenon is the result of certain conditions or factors, we *have* causally explained it regardless of whether it has thereby been shown to be a just reward or punishment. Indeed, finding the causal explanation of a certain act may at the same time show it to be just. If we find that certain individuals are engaging in revolutionary activity because they have been viciously mistreated by the rulers whom they are attempting to overthrow, we have found the cause of their activity and also exhibited its justification. However, much more often, finding the cause does not at the same time show the act in question to be just. If we discover that the tortures inflicted on a political prisoner by his guard during the recent military regime in Argentina were the result of the guard's sadistic impulses coupled with a fanatical hatred of liberals and radicals, then we have found the cause of the guard's conduct, but we have in no way shown it to be just. The confusion involved here is facilitated by a certain ambiguity in the word *rational* and other cognate expressions. It is sometimes said that causal explanations show the rationality of the world and this is true in the sense that they show it, at least in the area in question, to be orderly or law-governed. However, causal explanations do not by themselves show the world to be "morally" rational, i.e., to conform to our moral demands or sentiments. If we use terminology made familiar by the existentialists, we might say that showing that physical as well as mental phenomena can be subsumed under laws in no way shows that the world is not morally "absurd."

Reincarnationists habitually state the available alternatives inadequately. We saw that Dr. Johnson presents us with the three alternatives of "mere chance," God's plan, and reincarnation. This simply ignores the theory known as "naturalism," which holds that all phenomena, if they are caused at all, are the result of natural causes. Needless to say, a naturalist regards the hereditary inequalities of individuals as resulting from purely biological factors. Since he does not go beyond natural phenomena, a naturalist cannot escape the conclusion that the world is not just. Reincarnationists are so wedded to their position that they seem quite incapable of stating naturalism fairly and they also have a tendency to beg crucial issues by the very way in which they formulate their questions. One of the few American philosophers during the period between the two world wars who championed reincarnation was A. G. Widgery, who taught at Duke University for many years. In an article on "Reincarnation and Karma" in *The Aryan Path* of October 1936 he poses the apparently innocuous question: "Why is an individual born with this or that kind of body?" He complains that "occidental thought" ignores this "problem," but that the "doctrine of reincarnation" gives an answer to it. It is evident that Widgery will not accept the usual occidental answer in terms of biological causes. He thereby assumes at once, in the very act of raising the question, that there must be a "moral" justification for hereditary endowments and this by the usual route leads to good and bad deeds in previous lives.

It should be emphasized that a naturalist is not committed to the view that the hereditary endowment of human beings is a matter of "mere chance," at least in one important sense of the word. If *chance* means absence of causation then the naturalist does not maintain that hereditary inequalities or any of the other instances of injustice in the world occur by chance. He *is* committed to the view that they are instances of chance only if *chance* means absence of design or of moral significance in the karmic sense. While it would indeed be absurd to maintain that hereditary inequalities and human misfortunes are uncaused, it is not at all obvious that they are designed or that they have karmic significance. The latter is what the reincarnationist is supposed to show. In ignoring the naturalist view the reincarnationist in effect assumes that the world is just. It would be difficult to find a more flagrant instance of a question-begging procedure.

It should be added that the moral argument proceeds in a counter-inductive fashion that in any everyday situation would be dismissed as totally perverse. Let us suppose that in a course of weekly lectures the instructor has been excruciatingly boring the first ten times. It is not impossible that on the eleventh occasion he will have an off-day and surprise everybody by being lively and interesting. This is not impossible, but we have no right whatever to infer it from the ten preceding performances. If anything, we have reason to believe that on the eleventh occasion he will be tedious once again. To argue that *since* the lecturer was boring in all the ten previous classes he will be interesting during the eleventh class is altogether perverse. In the absence of proof that the universe *is* just, the reasoning of reincarnationists is just as perverse. From the undisputed fact that we have observed vast amounts of injustice in the past, it most certainly *cannot* be inferred that in the future, here or anywhere else, everything will be perfectly just.

Ultimately the only reason naturalism and its consequence that the world is not just are rejected is that they are emotionally unsatisfying. Reincarnationists and also many of the defenders of Western religions cannot bear the thought that good people should suffer and that death should be the end for them. Some of the Eastern defenders of reincarnation are quite open here. Thus Swami Nikhilananda, the very able editor of an abridged edition of *The Upanishads,* maintains that "the theory of total annihilation is not satisfactory," and prominent among the reasons is the fact that "it is inconsistent with the self love we all possess." Such an outlook is understandable, but it is logically indefensible. It does not follow from the fact that something is "inconsistent with our self-love" that it therefore cannot be real.

2. *Otherwise Inexplicable Empirical Facts.* The next argument or set of arguments is of a quasi-scientific kind. Various empirical facts are enumerated, and it is claimed that they cannot be adequately explained in terms of natural or, more specifically, biological causes. Only an explanation along reincarnationist lines is plausible. Existence in one or more previous lives is here advanced as an explanatory hypothesis. Since the structure of these arguments resembles that of many arguments in the sciences, it is tempting to call them "scientific." Among the facts frequently mentioned in this connection, both by Western and Eastern believers, are "infant geniuses" and remarkable precocious performances generally, the so-called déjà vu experience, love at first sight, striking differences between children of the same parents, and many more.

The prize case of Western reincarnationists is that of the Irish mathematician Sir William Hamilton (1805-1865) who, in addition to remarkable mathematical feats at a very early age, had mastered no less than thirteen languages by the time he reached adolescence. These included not only modern languages like French, German, Italian, and Spanish but also Persian, Arabic, Sanskrit, Hindustani, and Malay. There are also of course the cases of musical geniuses like Mozart, Schubert, and Mendelssohn who composed some of the world's greatest music at a very early age. Referring to a girl who, although coming from a quite unremarkable family, conducted the London Philharmonic Orchestra in a difficult program at the age of eight, Leslie Weatherhead, a prominent Christian reincarnationist, asks the question:

> Is it an accidental group of genes that makes a little girl of eight a musician far in advance of grown men and women, who have slaved for many years in that field? [*The Christian Agnostic,* p. 300]

Returning to Sir William Hamilton, he asks if it is nothing more than "a piece of luck that a boy of fourteen can write perfect Persian?" If the answer is in the affirmative then life is "unjust as well as chancy." Fortunately the answer is not in the affirmative. It seems evident to Weatherhead that these child prodigies acquired their skills and knowledge in a previous life, and he quotes Plato's *Meno* as supporting this conclusion.

It must not be thought that great artistic gifts are invariably the result of the acquisition of certain skills by the person in previous *human* incarnations. According to *The Tomorrow of Death,* a book published in Boston in 1888, "the soul of a musically inclined child" may not have come from a human being at all but from "the nightingale, the sweet singer of our woods." As for children with a talent for architecture, it only stands to reason that they should have inherited "the soul of a beaver, the architect of the woods and waters" (p. 247). The author of this charming work does not express any opinion about how some New York City landlords and physicians acquired their blackmailing proclivities. I have no doubt that in a previous life they were sharks.

Homosexuality is not usually regarded as requiring an explanation in reincarnationist terms, but at least one writer, and this is a very famous one, was convinced that no other explanation is adequate. In E. D. Walker's *Reincarnation, A Study of Forgotten Truth,* which was published in 1888 and has frequently been reprinted since then, Louisa M. Alcott, the author of *Little Women,* is quoted as saying, "I must have been masculine [in my previous life] because my love is all for girls." I am not aware that any male homosexual has offered this kind of explanation for his sexual orientation, but if it is true for lesbians there seems to be no reason why it should not equally hold for their male counterparts.

Many other puzzling facts seem to lend themselves to the same treatment. How are we to explain the characteristic differences between the English and the French? Of the English people, my favorite theosophist, Irving S. Cooper, writes, we notice a "tendency toward colonization," a "lawmaking instinct," a thoroughness in every undertaking, and a "massive style of architecture." These admirable characteristics, it must be noted with regret, are accompanied by a "sacrificing of beauty to utility and strength" and a "lack of imagination in art, religion and philosophy." In France it is just the opposite. There is very little interest in colonization and no lawmaking instinct worth mentioning. However, the French have an "imaginative touch," a love of beauty, a "worship of form and expression," and a special "intellectual keenness." There is only one way of accounting for these differences in "racial" characteristics. May it not be, writes Cooper, in what is a purely rhetorical question, "that in a mass the egos of Greece have taken incarnation in France, the egos of

Rome in England?" (*Reincarnation—A Hope of the World,* p. 67).

There are many other pearls in Cooper's remarkable book. He calls attention to the fact that great painters, composers, and writers frequently come in clusters. It is surely significant that "the founders of music" lived around the same time, an idea that Cooper obscurely expresses by telling us that all of them were "born in a singular way." He then enumerates the founders of modern music:

> First came Handel and Bach, then Mendelssohn, Mozart and Beethoven, and lastly, in quick succession, a large group composed of Schubert, Chopin, Schumann, Liszt, Wagner, Rubenstein, Brahms, and Grieg. [p. 68]

Cooper's chronology is slightly off in the case of Mendelssohn, and there is much else about his list that is defective. Be this as it may, another "suggestive" phenomenon that cries out for explanation is the "appearance of an isolated group of American poets and philosophers" all of whom were "born together in one section of the United States, and many of them, later on, became intimate friends" (pp. 68-69). The most important members of this group were Bryant, Emerson, Longfellow, Whittier, Poe, Thoreau, Whitman, and Lowell. These remarkable clusters suggest the thought that "life after life, groups of intimate friends and co-workers incarnate together to continue their activities." For all we can tell such group incarnations of composers and writers are going on right now. How can we be sure, for example, that Norman Mailer is not Charles Dickens, Saul Bellow William Thackeray, Phillip Roth Henry James, and Susan Sontag George Eliot? The possibilities are endless.

It is doubtful that Cooper ever read Schopenhauer, but, if he had, he might have stressed the superior consoling power of reincarnation over that of traditional Christianity. Christians console themselves, wrote Schopenhauer, "with the thought of meeting again in another world." Reincarnation teaches that "the meeting is already going on now," to which Schopenhauer adds the qualification that it is occurring "incognito." He grants that recognition is limited to an "obscure intimation," but if one contemplates the history of mankind in a "purely objective manner," the conviction is forced on one that "the present generation, in its true inner nature, is precisely and substantially identical with every generation that has been before it" (*The World As Will and Idea,* vol. 3, p. 303).

Some of the writers just quoted are a delight, but their arguments are incredibly flimsy. Most reincarnationists know absolutely nothing about science and they do not show the slightest interest in remedying their ignorance. The authors of the quasi-scientific arguments evidently work with a pre-Mendelian, "common sense" theory of genetics that holds that all features in an offspring must have been exhibited in one or both parents. It appears that they have heard neither of recessive genes nor of mutations. The differences between siblings are in part due to differences in the environment (no two children are treated exactly alike by their parents or by other people), but they are undoubtedly in large measure genetic. There is nothing here the least inconsistent with contemporary genetic theory. Love at first sight and instant or almost instant likes and dislikes have not been studied in any systematic way by psychologists, but I think few people cannot give at least a partial account of what draws them to or repels them from certain individuals. Those familiar with Reichian psychiatry know that deeply rooted emotional attitudes like contempt, disgust, sadism, and many more are revealed by various chronic muscle-tensions, some of them in the face, especially in the eyes, the chin, and the mouth. People who know nothing about psychiatry nevertheless perceive these chronic expressions; and this at least in part accounts for their instantaneous reactions. As for déjà vu experiences, psychologists have done some research on this subject. One theory reported by Arthur Reber in the Penguin *Dictionary of Psychology* (1985) maintains that these experiences are "due to a kind of momentary neural 'short circuit' so that the impression of the scene arrives at the memory store (metaphorically speaking) before it registers in the sensorium" (p. 183). Reber adds that there is some evidence for this view since déjà vu experiences are known to be symptomatic of certain kinds of brain damage. I do not profess to know whether this theory is true, but it seems a good starting point for further research; and there is every reason to suppose that eventually a fully satisfactory account will be worked out involving solely physiological and psychological factors. Reincarnationists never show the slightest interest in such theories when they are mentioned to them.

The case for reincarnation may appear to be strongest when we come to child prodigies. For here it must be admitted that so far genetics and psychology have told us very little that is specific. Nevertheless the reincarnationist argument is also quite worthless in this case. There is not the slightest reason to suppose that in order to explain the extraordinary gifts of men like Mozart or William Hamilton we have to go outside a study of the human brain. It should be remembered that in spite of the impressive progress of recent years, brain research is still in its infancy. I think very few brain researchers have any serious doubts that with further improvements in our instruments we will be able to shed much light on these problems. It seems entirely plausible, for example, that Mozart's auditory cortex was in certain ways significantly different from that of people lacking his gifts.

To foreclose further research in this area would be an utterly defeatist procedure. To substitute an explanation in terms of the acquisition of musical skill in an earlier life (for which there is not the slightest positive evidence) would be like abandoning medical research into the causes of cancer and substituting theological speculation on the ground that medical science has so far provided us with only a very limited understanding of cancer. Even if a thousand or ten thousand years from now researchers have not come up with a satisfactory theory this would in no way support a reincarnationist explanation. It would only show that up to then no naturalistic explanation had been discovered. It would not and could not show that none is possible.

The preceding remarks naturally lead to what I think is the most basic objection to reincarnationist attempts to explain infant prodigies or any of the other phenomena under discussion. Reincarnation is put forward in this context as a scientific hypothesis, but it can be shown that it is nothing of the kind.[2] In the formulation of various of its key assertions, concrete words associated with certain observable processes are employed and this suggests that we have a theory with empirical content. It is said that the soul "enters" or "invades" the womb of the prospective mother where it "merges" or "combines" with the embryo. It is also constantly asserted that the soul at the moment of death or else during the interval between incarnations "chooses" its new parents. In normal contexts these words refer to certain observable processes but, as I shall show, in the present context they do not. If this is so and if reincarnation is not an empirical or scientific hypothesis but a metaphysical theory, then, whatever value it may have, it *cannot* be a competitor of genuinely scientific hypotheses and it cannot explain empirical facts in the sense that is relevant here. A simple illustration will make this clear. X, a notoriously vicious person, suddenly collapses and dies. We want to find out why he died. Somebody answers that he was a sinner, that God was fed up with him and that he therefore eliminated him from the world. Let us grant that this is true. It still does not explain X's death in a scientific way. We are inquiring into the medical cause of his death: Did he die of a cerebral hemorrhage or a sudden heart attack or perhaps an overdose of cocaine, or did he take Tylenol capsules laced with cyanide? To our *empirical* question concerning X's death, the statement about God's decision to eliminate the malefactor is no answer at all. A coroner who happens to be a religious man and who in fact believes in this theological claim would not enter such a nonempirical explanation into his report. It is exactly the same with questions about the cause of genius, déjà vu experiences, love at first sight, and all of the other phenomena for which reincarnation is supposed to be the best explanation. Reincarnation may or may not have value as a metaphysical theory, but it cannot compete with physiological, genetic, and psychological theories as a scientific explanation of *any* facts.

Perhaps one further observation on the origin of the special skills and aptitudes of a child genius like Mozart may help to clarify the issues. Reincarnationists are in the habit of talking very vaguely about the soul's acquiring skills and knowledge in a previous life and taking these along into the next incarnation. One must pin them down and inquire about the "mechanics" of this transmission. Let us assume that, before it came to inhabit the body of Wolfgang Amadeus, the soul of Mozart lived in the body of Heinrich Hanauer and that it was during that incarnation that it acquired the knowledge passed on to the Mozart body. I think that reincarnationists who are not altogether lost to some fantastic form of occultism will admit that the transmission from the Hanauer to the Mozart body occurred via the brain and nervous system of the new embryo. If they admit this they have tacitly admitted that Mozart's special ability is due to certain features of his brain that are not present in the brains of other human beings. Reincarnation has in a sense become redundant. It will no doubt be replied that reincarnation is still necessary to account for the special features of Mozart's brain. However, if we have reason to believe in what I call the "sufficiency" of genetics and embryology, this will take care of the last reincarnationists. I will discuss this issue in a later section.

3. *Past-life Regressions.* The general public is probably not familiar with any alleged evidence for reincarnation except the recollection of previous lives by hypnotized subjects. The most famous case of this kind in America is that of Virginia Tighe, whose apparent memories of a life in Ireland at the end of the eighteenth and the first half of the nineteenth centuries are the subject of Morey Bernstein's *The Search for Bridey Murphy* (1956). This topic is handled so expertly by Melvin Harris in an article adapted for this volume that it is unnecessary for me to say more than a few words. Mr. Harris deserves special admiration for his expert detective work in tracking down the source of the "remarkable" information displayed by Jane Evans, the most impressive of the Bloxham cases.

I should like to supplement Mr. Harris's remarks by mentioning some examples of the transparently bad faith of past-life regressionists. At the time of the publication of *The Search for Bridey Murphy* it was already well known that by rehypnotizing a subject and asking direct questions one could usually obtain the source of her information concerning historical facts of which she pleaded total ignorance in her waking consciousness. The Summer 1956 issue of *Tomorrow,* a popular quarterly review of psychic research that often allowed space to complete skeptics, was entirely devoted to the Bridey Murphy case. Dr. Eric Dingwall, a British investigator who started his professional life as an assistant to Houdini and who has spent many years exposing fraud and unscientific practices among psychical researchers, contributed a devastating analysis entitled "The Woman Who Never Was." Dr. Dingwall concluded his article with the remark that, if Virginia Tighe were asked under hypnosis where she had obtained the story of Bridey Murphy, the source might be given. "It is curious," he adds, "that this was not tried at the time." *Life* magazine, which at first had been extremely sympathetic, featured a critical study of the case when it was beginning to fall apart. Among those interviewed were two leading medical hypnotists of the time, Drs. Jerome Schneck and Lewis Wolberg. Both expressed the opinion that questioning Virginia under hypnosis about her early life would have revealed the source of her Irish recollections. Bernstein was an expert hypnotist when he undertook the sessions with Virginia Tighe, and in the book he showed an intimate familiarity with the literature of hypnosis. He quotes from the publications of Dr. Wolberg and refers to him as "the famous medical hypnotist." Throughout the book he speaks of an unnamed "keen thinker" of "national prominence" with whom he discussed the Bridey Murphy tapes and who persuaded him that reincarnation was the only plausible hypothesis to account for Virginia's recollections. I might mention in passing that thirty years later this "keen thinker of national prominence" has still not been identified and I have always suspected that he is none other than Bernstein himself. The keen thinker is quoted as saying that "if she had read or heard all of this, your subject could easily explain that fact under hypnosis." Very possibly Virginia could have done so if Bernstein had asked a few questions about the source of her recollections. To bring up the fact that Virginia did not reveal the source of her recollection as evidence favoring reincarnation is surely a brazen coverup of Bernstein's failure to ask her about it. If, as an experienced hypnotist, he did not know that such questions frequently reveal the source of the subject's information, his ignorance was culpable. If, what is far more likely, he did know about the need for such questioning and nevertheless failed to engage in it, one can only wonder about his motives: was it the fear on the part of an ardent reincarnationist of losing a good case or were perhaps visions of a potential best-seller already crossing his mind during the sessions? I should add that although later editions of Bernstein's book are advertised as reprinting the original text without alteration this is not true. Some passages whose inaccuracies had been exposed by Dr. Dingwall were simply eliminated or changed without one word of explanation. In *Fads and Fallacies* Martin Gardner described *The Search for Bridey Murphy* as an "utterly worthless book designed to exploit a mass hunger for scientific evidence for life after death" (p. 316). This seems a fair verdict and it equally applies to dozens of books published since then, including Raymond Moody's *Life After Life,* which, to the shame of the American public, also became a best-seller.

In recent years past-life regressionists have extended their activities to exploration of future lives. It is reasoned that, if hypnosis can regress a person to a period before he was born, it should also "progress" him to a period after his death. In their future lives the subjects would of course be familiar with the state of the world at that time and all kinds of interesting things might be learned that cannot be learned by ordinary means. There is just one catch. The "progressionists" never show any interest in the near future. People are always progressed to future centuries when all of us, including all the skeptics, will be safely dead. One of the leading past-life regressionists, Dr. Helen Wambach, author of two widely circulated books, *Reliving Past Lives* and *Life Before Life,* a star of the tabloids and one of the "authorities" to whom Shirley MacLaine appeals for a scientific underpinning of her investigation, has in recent years concentrated on mass-progressions. Her findings were published in the *National Examiner* in May 1982. "Amazingly," we were told, all subjects progressed into future lives between 2100 and 2300 agreed on what they saw, "a frightening world devastated by a nuclear holocaust and pollution, and devoid of vegetation." How they survived is not clear, but perhaps they had taken sufficient provisions into their space vehicles since half of Wambach's subjects were "inside space colonies orbiting around the earth." Fortunately after 2300 conditions on the earth "had" greatly improved. Nevertheless, many of those progressed were by then living on other planets. "Amazingly," we are also informed, "people from outer space had been helping in the evacuation of the earth."

One of my favorite progressionists is Dr. Bruce Goldberg, a Baltimore comedian who earns his living as a dentist and who also has a practice in past-life therapy. In his *Past Lives, Future Lives* (1982), a book that easily answers all the most difficult metaphysical problems, he presents numerous progressions. He admits that progressing a person is much more difficult than regressing him and explains this as due to the fact that all of us have been "programmed to believe that the future hasn't occurred yet." This is evidently a serious error. In spite of this widespread prejudice, Dr. Goldberg frequently succeeds in progressing his subjects into distant centuries. He reveals in some detail what life will be like in the year 2542. Some altogether remarkable changes will have taken place by then, especially in such areas as transportation, farming, and the dissemination of information. Dr. Goldberg made his discoveries by progressing a young man from

Baltimore by the name of Larry who in his future life became Zeku, the son of a scientist by the name of Lus-Lu who was in charge of constructing an underwater city. The progression gets really exciting when Dr. Goldberg asks Zeku how people moved around in 2542. The answer, to use *National Enquirer* terminology, was "startling": "You could be beamed from one place to another, which consisted of disassembling the molecules of your body and reassembling them at the other transportation center at your destination" (pp. 163-164). Unfortunately the technique of "disassembling" and "reassembling" the molecules of the body is not described. I hope that mistakes were not frequent at the destination, especially as far as brain-molecules were concerned. Zeku had equally "amazing" information about the size of fruits:

> Farming had undergone tremendous change. Very large forms of vegetation were developed by geneticists, resulting in fruits the size of cars. Lasers were used to divide and process the foodstuff. [p. 164]

What is not explained is how these giant fruits were delivered or stored. No doubt there were by then refrigerators the size of baseball stadiums to accommodate the new giant apples, peaches, and strawberries. As for transportation, perhaps the fruits were temporarily shrunk to the familiar size in the store and then returned to their real size upon reaching the customer's home. Undoubtedly, however, the highlight of technological improvement concerned the new methods of transmitting information to the public. Newpapers disappeared. Instead there was the "information pill." This timesaving device "contained all the new scientific achievements, new items of general interest, and all of the latest advancements" (p. 165). New information pills were available every day and my guess is that, in addition to the scientific information, they also contained all the latest gossip. The information pills were swallowed just like other pills, and here for once one could be sure that all the new ideas were really digested.

Dr. Goldberg in his modesty has not realized that he himself constitutes the best evidence for reincarnation. His comic gifts are quite in the same league as those of Fatty Arbuckle and Ben Turpin. I do not for a moment believe that such a stupendous talent can be explained by ordinary genetics. The only adequate explanation would be in terms of one or more previous lives of assiduous labor or else the hand of God.

Much as I admire Drs. Wambach and Goldberg, I must register one complaint. I wish that they would give us information about the near future, perhaps the next two decades or even the next two years, expecially in such matters as nuclear disasters and the conquest of disease. Stock-market quotations would also be welcome. I venture the guess that they and other hypnotic explorers of the future will not comply and that they will continue to confine their progressions to distant centuries.

4. *Spontaneous Memories of Past Incarnations.* Throughout the ages claims have been made by or on behalf of certain individuals that they could recall previous lives. These memories or ostensible memories differ from hypnotic regressions in that they occur to the person in his waking life and, furthermore, they are not provoked by an artificial stimulus. "I have been born many times, Arjuna," says Krishna in the *Bhagavad Gita,*

> and many times hast thou been born. But I remember my past lives and thou hast forgotten thine. [IV, 5]

It is widely believed by Buddhists that yogis have the power to remember entire past lives, and not only recent ones, but all those in which they inhabited a human body. In his Preface to the fourth edition of the *Tibetan Book of the Dead,* the editor, an American anthropologist by the name of W. Y. Evans-Wentz, who was a convert to Buddhism, insists that the belief in reincarnation need not be taken on faith. On the contrary, it has a "sound basis" in the "unequivocal testimony of yogis who claim to have died and reentered the human womb consciously" (p. v). Similarly, Swami Nikhilananda, the editor of the abbreviated version of the *Upanishads* whom I quoted earlier, rejects the theory of annihilation partly because it is inconsistent with "the intuitive and direct experience of the seers regarding the indestructibility of the soul" (p. 58).

In Buddhist scriptures the Buddha is frequently credited with remembering an unlimited number of his own earlier lives and also with the power to intuit the details of the past and future incarnations of other human beings. In the *Sanyutta-Nikaya* the Buddha is reported to have made the following claim:

> I, brethren, according as I desire, can remember my divers former lives, that is to say, one birth, or two, or three, or four, or five births, or ten, twenty, thirty, forty, fifty births, or a hundred, a thousand, or even a hundred thousand, or even more. . . .

John Hick, whose *Death and Eternal Life* contains much interesting information about the Buddha's alleged recollections, points out that there is no credible historical evidence that the real Buddha ever made such claims and he adds that details of his past incarnations "belong to the rhetoric of fairytale rather than to historical reality" (p. 390).

Reincarnationists habitually list numerous famous men and women in history who supposedly had spontaneous recollections of earlier lives. The list usually includes Pythagoras, Empedocles, Ovid, the emperor Julian the Apostate, Swedenborg, Goethe, and Alexander Dumas fils. They also include in their list the somewhat less famous Madame Blavatsky and Annie Besant, the first two leaders of the Theosophical Society. Empedocles, Swedenborg, Dumas, and the two theosophist ladies really belong on this list, but in the case of the others the evidence is either dubious or nonexistent. Pythagoras did believe in reincarnation and he may well have claimed to recall previous lives, but the only evidence for this are two paragraphs in Diogenes Laertius, a notoriously unreliable purveyor of gossip and hearsay, and one of Ovid's poems in which Pythagoras is made to recall his participation in the battle of Troy as a brave soldier by the name of Euphorbus. Julian the Apostate (331-363) is invariably said to have remembered being Alexander the Great. Julian was raised as a Christian but abandoned Christianity as a result of his philosophical studies. He was a just and noble ruler who tried to return the Empire to the practice of religious toleration. His early death proved a boon to the persecuting Christians, and I would not at all be surprised if the rumor about his "recollection" was started by Julian's Christian enemies in order to suggest that he was mad. In any event, even reincarnationists admit that it is nothing more than a story. Goethe did on several occasions express sympathy for "metempsychosis," but the only evidence that he claimed to remember having lived before is the following statement: "Surely, I must have lived already before the Emperor Hadrian, for everything Roman attracts me with inexpressible force." Paul Siwek, a Catholic opponent of reincarnation, devotes a chapter of his *The Enigma of the Hereafter* (New York, 1952) to these "memories of the initiated." Siwek rightly ignores the claims about Ovid and Julian but he takes all the others very seriously and tries to discredit the value of their ostensible memories on the ground that these persons were known to be either psychotic or else exceedingly unbalanced. This seems to me a misguided approach for the simple reason that, as C. D. Broad remarked in a different context, showing that a person is "cracked" does not by itself provide a good reason for supposing that what he claims is false. I should also remark in passing that Siwek fails to show in some cases, especially those of Empedocles and Goethe, that the individuals were either mad or highly disturbed. There are much better strategies of dealing with the reincarnationist appeal to spontaneous memories.

The occultist literature of the late nineteenth and early twentieth centuries is filled with accounts of memories for which "remarkable" independent corroboration is claimed. However, it is only with the arrival of Ian Stevenson on the scene that this kind of evidence has acquired an investigator and spokesman whose presentations deserve to be taken seriously. Born in Montreal in 1918, Stevenson obtained his medical degree at McGill University. He eventually specialized in psychiatry and at the age of thirty-nine obtained an appointment as professor of psychiatry and neurology at the University of Virginia Medical School in Charlottesville. As the Carlson Professor of Psychiatry, a post to which he moved some years later, he founded the Division of Parapsychology, whose director he has been ever since. Stevenson is distrustful of hypnotic regressions and all the cases he has studied are of the spontaneous variety. He has also been interested in other areas of parapsychology, but his fame rests exclusively on work bearing on reincarnation. In his early publications he did not take a definite stand, but in more recent years he has come out as a very ardent supporter of reincarnation. It should be remarked that he is an excellent writer and that the presentation of his cases is always lucid, systematic, and extremely detailed. Ian Wilson, one of his critics, acknowledges that Stevenson has brought "a new professionalism into a hitherto crank-prone field" (*Mind Out of Time*, p. 48). It will hardly come as a surprise that he has become a hero to believers in reincarnation all over the world. It is difficult to pick up a book or pamphlet defending reincarnation that has been published in the last fifteen years or so and that does not refer admiringly to Stevenson's work.

Stevenson got involved with one adult spontaneous-recollection case that caused something of a stir in England in the early 1970s and to which I will turn shortly. However, the bulk of his cases concern small children, and they have a fairly uniform pattern. These children usually begin making statements between the ages of two and four about coming from a home and place different from those in which they are living. They recall altogether different parents and most of them speak of having lived as adolescents and adults. Some also recall their death, often a violent one, in their preceding life. Children vary greatly in the quantity of their utterances and the richness of the details they recall. The volume and clarity of the statements usually increase until the age of between five and six. After that there is less and less mention of a previous life and by the age of eight the memories have in most cases faded completely. During the period when the child remembers his earlier life he often behaves in strange ways. The strange behavior, Stevenson notes, is consistent with the character and occupation of the remembered person. However, none of this would be particularly impressive and even begin to be evidence of reincarnation if the children's recollections could not be corroborated. Often indeed they cannot be, and Stevenson dismisses such cases as not deserving further consideration. However, in several cases, which form the subject matter of his books, there has been extensive corroboration. Research shows that the person the child remembers to have been did in fact exist and many, though usually not all, descriptions of the experiences, acts, and relationships turn out to be correct. This at least is what Stevenson maintains; and if one reads his books and articles without knowing what the critics have to say, one can hardly fail to be impressed.

The adult case in which Stevenson became prominently involved concerned an elderly Englishman by the name of Edward Ryall, who wrote a letter to the *Daily Express* in May 1970 saying that he had clear and extensive memories of a life in the seventeenth century as a West Country farmer by the name of John Fletcher. The letter was published and came to Stevenson's attention. Stevenson corresponded with Ryall and paid two visits to his home. He became convinced of the authenticity of Ryall's recollections and encouraged him to write a book about his previous life. Ryall's book, *Second Time Around,* appeared in 1974, with an introduction and supplementary notes by Stevenson. The case caused so much interest that in 1976 the British Broadcasting Corporation devoted a program to it. Participating in the program, the bulk of which was reprinted in *The Listener* of June 3, 1976, were Ryall himself, Stevenson, and two skeptics—John Taylor, professor of mathematics at London University, and John Cohen, professor of psychology at Manchester. Ryall came off very well, parrying all the hostile questions, though he quite expectedly failed to convince the skeptics of the genuineness of his recollections.

What are we to make of Stevenson's work? I will discuss the cases of the children in my fourth article.[3] There are certain general reasons for rejecting them as evidence for reincarnation that equally apply to all cases of ostensible memories of past lives. These general reasons cannot be adequately stated until the arguments against reincarnation have been discussed. However, aside from these general reasons, there are also more specific, and extremely damaging, objections to Stevenson's investigative methods. Here I wish to say a few words about the denouement of the the Ryall case.

Ryall was eventually exposed as either a hoaxer or the victim of delusions, or, very possibly, a combination of the two. Credit for his exposure belongs to Michael Green, an architectural historian whose role will be explained in a moment, Renée Haynes, editor for the British Society for Psychical Research and an Oxford history graduate, and to Ian Wilson, whose *Mind Out of Time* (1981), a book I quoted previously, presented the full details of the story for the first time. I should remark in passing that *Mind Out of Time,* a book hardly known in the United States, is far and wide the best work on reincarnation I have seen. All the most famous reincarnation cases are minutely examined and on the basis of meticulous research all of them are found wanting.

From the start, Ryall's book failed to convince most readers. It simply did not have the ring of truth. It did not read like a series of recollections but rather like erotic fiction embellished by some period details. Renée Haynes in her book *The Seeing Eye* (1976) and in several subsequent articles pointed out numerous anachronisms. She and Ian Wilson found that while some of Ryall's recollections did check out, others of a crucial character did not. The main of these was that the parish records of Weston Zoyland do not list any John Fletcher for the period of Ryall's story. They do not record his marriage to a Cecily Fuller or the death of his father or his mother or of Fletcher himself or the baptism of his two sons, all these being events mentioned in Ryall's book. What finally proved the undoing of Ryall's claims were the investigations by Michael Green, who is Inspector of Ancient Monuments and Historic Buildings for the Department of Environment in London. Green found Ryall's statements about his house and farmlands extremely vague. He began corresponding with Ryall, who displayed great uneasiness at having his claims for the first time submitted to a real expert. After much evasion and prevarication he finally answered Green's request to mark on a large-scale map that Green had sent to him the location of his lands and to supply details about the construction of his house. It should be mentioned parenthetically that Ryall claimed to have had recollections of his earlier existence throughout his life and they were not only not fading but becoming clearer and more specific. When Ryall finally replied, he placed the farmlands on a location that had been open marshland until 1800, and the house he described was not a type or made of material found in that part of England in the seventeenth century. Ryall died in 1978, and Stevenson went on defending him for a number of years, but in the end he admitted, somewhat grudgingly, that the case was not as strong as he had originally thought. In an interview in the September-October 1986 issue of *Venture Inward*, a periodical published by the Association for Research and Enlightenment, the organization that promotes the ideas and writings of Edgar Cayce, Stevenson remarks that he does not now regard the case as "enthusiastically" as he had ten years earlier. He concedes that the absence of any John Fletcher in the parish records is damaging, but he does not refer to Michael Green's exposure, which seems quite decisive to anyone without an axe to grind. Stevenson's surrender is in fact far from total. "What we may be dealing with," he tells the interviewer, "are perhaps some real memories of a previous life which Ryall then . . . embellished rather like a historical novel." Some people never give up!

In the BBC discussion of the Ryall case there occurred the following exchange:

Cohen: ". . . memories are tied to a particular brain tissue. If you take away the brain, there is no memory."

Stevenson: "I think that's an assumption. Memories may exist in the brain and exist elsewhere also."

Cohen: "But we have not the slightest evidence, even a single case, of a memory existing without a brain. We have plenty of slight damage to a brain which destroys memory, but not the other way round."

Stevenson: "I feel that's one of the issues here—whether memories can, in fact, survive the destruction of the brain."

Taylor: "Professor Stevenson, do you have any evidence, other than these reincarnation cases, that memories can survive the destruction of physical tissue?"

Stevenson: "No. I think the best evidence comes from the reincarnation cases."

We have here a very clear statement of one of the basic issues dividing unbelievers from believers in most forms of survival, including reincarnation. The question is whether memories can continue without the brain and more generally whether the consciousness of a person can continue to exist without its bodily foundation.

The Pseudo-empirical Nature of the Law of Karma

I have so far concentrated on pointing out the flaws in the arguments commonly advanced in support of reincarnation and Karma. I now proceed to give reasons why these theories should be rejected. I will begin with Karma. It is clear, for reasons stated earlier, that a rejection of Karma does not by itself require abandonment of belief in reincarnation.

In familiar formulations the Law of Karma appears to be an empirical claim. It asserts a causal connection in both directions between two classes of observable phenomena. Suffering and happiness are, at least in a broad sense, observable, and so are sinful and meritorious actions. There is admittedly some difficulty about getting a consensus as to what counts as sinful and meritorious behavior, but we may here ignore all problems of this kind. Except for its vastly greater significance, the Law of Karma is regarded by its proponents as entirely comparable to "natural" or scientific laws. Karma, writes Annie Besant, is a "natural law" and as such it "is no more sacred than any other natural law" (*Karma Once More*, p. 6). "The sins of the previous life of the Ego," writes Madame Blavatsky, are punished by "this mysterious, inexorable, but in the equity and wisdom of its decrees infallible law" (quoted in R. W. Neufeldt, *Karma and Rebirth,* p. 243).

Now, a little reflection shows that the Law of Karma is not an empirical statement and that it is wholly unlike "natural" laws. To begin with, the Law of Karma has no predictive value whatsoever. A simple example will make this clear. Let us suppose that a plane takes off in which all the crew and passengers are, as far as we can tell, thoroughly decent people. The believer in Karma cannot predict any more or less confidently than the unbeliever that the plane will not crash. The best he can do is offer a statistical prediction based not on Karma but on data concerning the safety of airplanes or, perhaps more specifically, of the kind of plane in which these people are flying. Let us now suppose that a madman or a terrorist planted a time-bomb on the plane and, furthermore, that it is a very efficiently constructed time-bomb. The lunatic, because of his empirical information, can predict with high probability that the plane is going to crash.

It may be argued that the lack of predictive content of Karma is not a serious matter since some scientific laws, notably Darwin's theory of natural selection, also lack predictive content. I do not think that this comparison is sound, but I will not press the point and will concentrate on a more basic consideration that incorporates whatever is significant in the observation that the Karmic law is devoid of predictive value. Scientific laws and indeed all statements that are not empty are *not* compatible with anything that may happen. All of them exclude some conceivable state of affairs: If such an excluded state of affairs were to obtain, the statement would be false. Just like Boyle's law or the second law of thermodynamics, Darwin's theory of natural selection is *not* compatible with anything.

The Law of Karma on the other hand *is* compatible with anything. The emptiness of the Karmic theory can be seen most clearly if we compare it to another pseudoscientific theory that on analysis turns out to be completely empty. I am thinking of social Darwinism as advocated, for example, by the American sociologist William Graham Sumner. Sumner was a militant opponent of any kind of social legislation that might help the poor, the sick, or even the unemployed, and he justified his stand by reference to the principle that those who are successful have thereby proven their fitness while those who are downtrodden have thereby proven their unfitness and inferiority. The following is a report provided by one of Sumner's admirers of a conversation between Sumner and a student dissenter:

"Professor, don't you believe in any government aid to industries?"
"No! it's root, hog, or die."

"Yes, but hasn't the hog got a right to root?"

"There are no rights. The world owes nobody a living."

"You believe then, Professor, in only one system, the contract-competitive system?"

"That's the only sound economic system. All others are fallacies."

"Well, suppose some professor of political economy came along and took your job away from you. Wouldn't you be sore?"

"Any other professor is welcome to try. If he gets my job, it is my fault. My business is to teach the subject so well that no one can take the job away from me." [Quoted in Richard Hofstadter, *Social Darwinism in American Thought*, p. 54]

There is some evasion in the last statement, in which Sumner talks about his teaching the subject so well that no one else can take the job away from him. Many people who, by all usual standards, are inferior teachers might take his job away from him—by intrigues, by spreading rumors about his private life, or perhaps by such drastic measures as poisoning him. However, what is relevant for our purposes is that Sumner does not know who is fittest until the outcome, until the competition has been resolved. He, Sumner, is the fittest if he keeps his job. If somebody else, X, gets the job in his place, then X has turned out to be the fittest in virtue of his success. It should be remarked parenthetically that in Darwinism or neo-Darwinian theory, as contrasted with social Darwinism, "fit" can be defined in such a way that it is *not* synonymous with "surviving" or "winning out," so that the statement "the fittest tend to win out in the competition for the means of survival" is a synthetic statement and not a tautology. In social Darwinism, at least in Sumner's version, the statement that the fittest succeed *is* a tautology. Sumner does not define "fittest" or "fit" independently of succeeding. We do *not* have a statement about the connection between two characteristics but two words for the same characteristic. The theory is empty and totally *post hoc*. We know who is fittest only after the issue has been resolved. Sumner's claim is consistent with anything whatever. Sumner himself had no doubt that socialist revolutionaries would never win out; but, if they had, they would automatically have shown themselves to be the fittest.

It is easy to see that the Law of Karma, too, is compatible with anything and hence totally empty. Let us suppose that a horrible criminal like Hitler is finally brought to justice. This of course confirms the principle since the criminal's suffering was the result of his evil deeds. Suppose, however, that a person who, according to all the best available information, is decent and kind comes to a bad end, as the result of being run over by a drunken driver, a judicial frameup, or perhaps because of some dreadful illness. Would this disconfirm the principle? Not at all. It only shows that in a previous life he committed evil deeds of which his present suffering is the just punishment. Let us suppose that we know that the next incarnation of this individual is going to be one long horrendous nightmare of torture and persecution. Would this show that the Law of Karma is not true? Not at all: It would only show that his sins in past lives were so enormous that the disasters of his present life were insufficient punishment.

In 1965 there was an instructive exchange in the *Philosophical Quarterly*, an Indian publication not to be confused with the Scottish journal of the same name, between Professor Warren E. Steinkraus, a liberal Christian with an interest in Oriental philosophy, and Professor G. R. Malkani, a Hindu believer in Karma. Professor Steinkraus expressed his consternation as to how the Law of Karma can be reconciled with the staggering sufferings experienced by a great many people:

> The punishments do not fit the crime. Some of the miseries of disease and the excruciating pains of injuries suffered by human beings would not be inflicted by the most vindictive of human judges for the most heinous crimes. [p. 151]

Steinkraus concludes by raising the question:

> Can the defender of *Karma* admit that some suffering is outrageously severe or must he say that all suffering is *a priori* just and necessarily derived merely because it occurs? [p. 151]

Professor Steinkraus was firmly put in his place by Professor Malkani, who, as the editor of the *Philosophical Quarterly,* saw to it that he had the last word. After remarking, quite irrelevantly, that any explanation of evil and injustice in the world must leave God "blameless," Malkani insisted that there are certain ultimate mysteries that we must "not seek to probe any further." One of these is the question of "what punishment is appropriate for what sin or accumulation of sins." We are not gods and cannot know the answer to the question of why there is "so much punishment and for what." This unavoidable human ignorance is not, it appears, incompatible with total assurance that the world is just and that what may appear to be excessive punishment is not in fact excessive at all:

> It should suffice to console us that there is no limit to the enormity of the errors of omission and commission which an individual might have committed in his countless past lives. [p. 45]

It should be emphasized that, when the partisans of Karma "explain" the misfortunes that befall apparently decent human beings by telling us that they sinned in a previous life, their pronouncements are just like Sumner's claims about who is fittest, *totally post hoc*. Sumner could not identify an individual as "the fittest" until he was sure that he had won out, and the Karmic theorists cannot say anything about past misdeeds until suffering and misfortune have befallen a human being. To this it must be added that the "wisdom after the event" possessed by Sumner and by the Karmic believer is radically different from the real wisdom after the event that we often possess as the result of causal investigations. All of us are often wise only after the event, but we are *really* "wise" if we can offer a retrodictive explanation that is supported by adequate evidence. A plane crashes on takeoff at the Miami airport. It was not predicted, but we find evidence that a certain defect in the engine caused the crash. The Karmic procedure is also *post hoc* but it does not provide any genuine wisdom after the event. After a person who was a fine human being is run over by a drunken driver the Karmic theorist tells us that this happened because of his sin in a previous life. Unlike the investigators of the plane crash, he is *not* wise after the event. For he cannot tell us how and where the person had sinned. He does not have any information corresponding to the information obtained by the crash investigators about the engine defect. He makes a retrodictive claim; but, unlike the retrodictive statement about the cause of the crash, his claim is pure dogmatism.

To avoid unfairness to certain reincarnationists, the above remarks require one qualification. Some Karmic theorists who also believe in Nirvana or a superhuman Absolute Mind maintain that after his last incarnation the individual will be able to review in one glance the infinite number of lives he has lived. Reincarnationists holding this view could consistently allow that *their* Karmic theory is falsifiable by a review that showed the absence of any dependable moral pattern. Their position is thus not compatible with any conceivable state of affairs and hence it is not open to the charge that it is empty. However, one cannot help wondering how a human being could "in one glance" or for that matter in more than one glance survey an infinite number of past lives; and, furthermore, all the pronouncements about misdeeds in past lives are just as *post hoc* and just as much pure *ipse dixits* as those of Karmic believers who do not allow a final review.

Karmic Administration Problems

Anybody not intimidated by the virulence with which the champions of Karma brush off objections to their theory will want to raise a very simple and, as it seems to me, utterly devastating question about the execution and more generally the "administration" of Karmic ordinances. It should here be emphasized that many of the believers in Karma do not believe in a god and that those who do nevertheless maintain that the Law of Karma operates autonomously. Professor Malkani combines belief in the Karmic law with "the best form of theism," but he does not maintain that God is in any way involved in the administration of Karma. On the inexorable and autonomous operation of Karma Malkani, who here fairly represents the Hindu position, is in complete agreement with the atheist and agnostic supporters of Karma. Karma, he writes, "automatically produces the appropriate results like any other law in the natural domain. Nobody can cheat the law. It is as inexorable as any natural law."

The claim that Karma operates autonomously invites the following questions: How, to begin with, are good and bad deeds registered? Is there some cosmic repository like a huge central social security office in which the relevant information is recorded and translated into some kind of "balance"? Next, how and where is it decided what will happen to a person in his next incarnation as a result of the balance of his acts in a given life? How and where, for example, is it decided that in the next life he will become a human being rather than a roach, a man rather than a woman, an American rather than an Indian, white rather than black or yellow, physically well formed rather than crippled, intelligent rather than retarded, sane rather than insane? Finally, there is still the problem of how such decisions are translated into reality. As an illustration I will use a natural disaster, the famous Lisbon earthquake of 1755. A large number of people perished as a result of it. An even larger number were injured and also lost their possessions; and a large number of people indirectly benefited because of the death and injury of others. Somebody who does not believe in Karma and who also does not believe that the earthquake was a special intervention on the part of the Deity would of course regard it as a purely natural phenomenon that is entirely explicable in terms of natural, in this instance geological, causes. The believer in Karma, by contrast, must be prepared to claim that the earthquake was brought about in order to punish or reward the various people who suffered or benefited from the earthquake. How and where were the bad deeds of those killed and injured and the good deeds of those spared registered? How and where were the penalties and rewards decided? And just how did Karma determine the geological conditions whose existence is not disputed as the "natural" or at least the "immediate" cause of the disaster? Surely, if ever intelligent planning was needed, this is a case in point. Let us assume that the chief of a terrorist organization is about to send his forces into a town in which there are 5,000 houses. His instructions are to burn down all but the hundred that belong to secret supporters of his cause. Let us also suppose that these hundred houses are spread all over the town. Such an operation obviously requires a great deal of careful planning and a high level of intelligence on the part of the planners. Even then it is entirely possible that mistakes will be made so that some houses of the sympathizers will be destroyed while some belonging to the enemy will be spared. The Law of Karma by contrast is infallible. It never punishes the innocent and never spares the guilty; and it does so although it is not an intelligent person or principle. To rephrase our earlier question: Just how did this nonintelligent principle set up the geological forces in the present case so as to achieve the desired results with complete precision?

In this connection even the otherwise so confident Professor Malkani is almost reduced to silence. All he can offer is the following lame response:

> Does the law of Karma act upon the forces of nature and bring about cyclones, earthquakes, floods, etc., which in their turn cause wide-spread havoc and destruction of both life and property affecting millions? But if a metaphysical law, like the law of Karma, cannot do that, can it do anything whatsoever? Is it a law only in name? A powerless law is as good as no law. [p. 43]

This bluff and bluster answers nothing. If defenders of Karma cannot do better they should surely adopt the alternative mentioned in a tone of horror at the end of Malkani's outburst and admit that Karma "is as good as no law."

Unlike the more sophisticated champions of Karma, Mrs. Besant saw the need for introducing divine Karmic administrators. In *The Ancient Wisdom,* her best-known work, she first insists that "in no case can a man suffer that which he has not deserved" (p. 293). She then speaks of the "Lords of Karma" who are "great spiritual intelligences" keeping "the karmic records" and adjusting "the complicated workings of karmic law." They know the Karmic record of every man and with their "omniscient wisdom" they "select and combine portions of that record to form a plan of a single life" (pp. 293–294). This means primarily that they select the race, the country, and the parents of the soul or Ego in its next incarnation. Thus an Ego with highly developed musical faculties will be "guided to take its physical body in a musical family"; an Ego of "very evil type" will be guided "to a coarse and vicious family, whose bodies were built of the coarsest combination"; while an Ego who yields to drunkenness will be led to a "family whose nervous systems were weakened by excess," and he will be born from "drunken parents who would supply diseased materials for his physical envelope" (p. 295). It is in this way that the lords of Karma "adjust means to ends," ensure the doing of justice, and see to it that the Ego can carry his "karmic possessions and faculties" into his next life.

This solution of the "administration" problem calls for two comments. In the first place, the lords of Karma have not been seen by anybody recently and, even during the decades when Mrs. Besant flourished, they were, as far as I know, not perceived by anybody other than Mrs. Besant, not even by Madame Blavatsky. Second, Mrs. Besant did not have an adequate grasp of the scope of the problem. To solve it we not only need an explanation of how the lords of Karma secure appropriate bodies for Egos in subsequent incarnations, we also need to be told how they affect natural objects and forces so as to bring about events like the Lisbon earthquake that in one swoop punish thousands of the wicked and reward large numbers of the good. To this question Mrs. Besant totally failed to address herself.

The Emptiness of Karmic Directives

So, far from providing moral guidance, the doctrine of Karma is bound to lead to perplexity, and it is hence apt to paralyze action. The ordinary person who does not believe in Karma usually has no difficulty in deciding whether it is right to help people who are ill, who have been the victims of accidents, or who are in various other kinds of difficulties. Things are not so easy for the believer in Karma. The suffering individual in his view *deserves* to suffer because he committed evil acts in this or else in a previous life. It is not only not our duty to help him but it would seem on Karmic principles that it is our duty *not* to help him. "It would be impossible," wrote Madame Blavatsky, "either to delay or to hasten the Karma in the fulfillment of justice," and in order to expiate one's sins fully it is necessary "to suffer all the consequences to the bitter end, to exhaust all the defects until they have reached their plenitude" (quoted by Siwek, op. cit., p. 122). Mrs. Besant, who started her career as a radical, apparently had not lost all her humanity after she succeeded Madame Blavatsky as leader of the theosophists. She reports "some members saying: I cannot help this man since what he is suffering is his karma." She thought them cruel and wrong-headed and compared them to somebody who says, "I cannot pick up this child who just fell, since the law of gravitation is opposed to it" (*Popular Lectures on Theosophy*, p. 67).

I do not think that this is a fair analogy and it does not answer the members who refuse to help people in need. The law of gravitation is not a moral law and the fact that the child fell down does not, without bringing in Karmic morality, imply that it is now being punished for an earlier sin. As far as I can see, no prescription of any kind can be derived from the Law of Karma for this situation or for any other; and, if this is so, Karma is completely vacuous as a principle of moral guidance. No matter what we do, whether we help the individual or whether we refuse to help him, we will be doing the right thing. If we help him cut short his suffering, this means that his earlier deed did not require more severe punishment than what he suffered until we brought relief. If on the other hand we ignore him and let him continue in his misery, this shows that his sin was so great as to deserve the total amount of his suffering—what he suffered before we could have intervened as well as what he suffered afterward when we failed to come to his assistance. Believers in Karma constantly and emphatically insist that their theory does not imply fatalism, that, quite on the contrary, it is entirely compatible with belief in human freedom, understood as our ability to shape our lives, within limits, in accordance with our desires and choices, and that our efforts frequently do make a great deal of difference to what happens. I see no reason to dispute this claim, but it in no way answers the challenge of vacuousness. The vacuousness, as far as moral prescriptions are concerned, follows from the Karmic doctrine that the world is just. A Karmic believer's commitment to this proposition is unqualified—it is categorical and not merely hypothetical. He does not maintain that the world would be just if we did certain things. He maintains that the world *is* just regardless of what in fact we do. No matter what happens, whether we help the underdog or not, whether our efforts at making lives less full of suffering and sorrow succeed or not, the ultimate outcome will be just, in the sense that every human being will be getting exactly—no more and no less than—what he deserves.

This is as good a place as any to point out that believers in Karma, especially those in the West, are careful not to spell out certain of the implications of their theory that would strike most people as appalling. It follows from their principle that Abraham Lincoln, Jean Jaurès, the two Kennedy brothers, and Martin Luther King got no more than they deserved when they were assassinated. It equally follows that the six million Jews exterminated by the Nazis deserved their fate. I will add one more of the morally outrageous consequences of Karma. Contrary to what almost everybody believed and believes, the seven *Challenger* astronauts who perished in 1986 were entirely responsible for their deaths, and the grief felt by millions of people all over the world was quite out of place. The reckless NASA officials whom the Rogers Commission found to be responsible for the *Challenger* explosion were in fact (not consciously, of course) only executing the ordinances of Karma. The case of the astronauts illustrates particularly well the completely *post hoc* procedure of the Karmic theorists. Is there the slightest empirical evidence that the seven astronauts who died were morally any worse than the astronauts who did not participate in the mission of January 28 and were thus spared? Of course there is no such evidence. The only reason a Karmic theorist would or could give is that they in fact died while the others are alive. Returning to the Jews and their Nazi exterminators, it would seem that, since the Jews deserved extinction, the Nazis were not really criminals and should not have been prosecuted. I assume that Eichmann deserved to be hanged since he *was* hanged, but the many Nazis who escaped deserved to escape. Speaking of executions, the main argument against the death penalty evidently collapses if the Law of Karma is true. For in that case no innocent man can ever be executed. People may indeed be innocent of the crime with which they are charged, but if they are executed this is what they deserved. It makes one dizzy.

"Cosmic" Claims

This discussion of Karma would be incomplete without saying a few words about certain "cosmic" claims found in the writings of reincarnationists. It is commonly asserted that all lawful connections in the universe are really "nothing more" than instances of Karma. Dr. Rayner Johnson, the Christian reincarnationist mentioned earlier, writes that "the Laws of Cause and Effect, as we know it in the material world," are really "nothing more than a special case" of the Law of Karma (*The Imprisoned Splendour,* p. 338). Again, it has been claimed—and perhaps this is what Dr. Johnson had in mind—that the same tendency to restore balance or equilibrium that appropriate punishments and rewards exemplify is found throughout the universe. Thus in a rather haughty note in the *Aryan Review* of October 1936, in which the editor offers advice to the author of the preceding article, the author being none other than A. J. Ayer, we are assured that "Karma is an undeviating and unerring tendency in the universe to restore equilibrium." It "operates incessantly" and, what is more, "it operates on all things and beings from the minutest conceivable atom to the highest of human souls." All such claims are open to the criticism that, if they are interpreted in a fairly straightforward way, they are simply absurd and, if they are interpreted in such a way as to avoid absurdity, they say absolutely nothing. If it is maintained that the lawful behavior of molecules or mountains or planets are instances of rewards and punishments, this is plainly absurd, since molecules, planets, and mountains cannot perform good and evil deeds.

If, to avoid this absurdity, "Karma" is taken in a broader sense in which it is simply a synonym for "lawfulness" or "regularity," then calling the various laws of nature instances of Karma is saying nothing at all. It is plain that we do not understand the regularities of the world any better and nothing whatever has been added to the content of any known law. Calling natural regularities instances of Karma is about as enlightening as describing them as manifestations of the Absolute Mind or as instances of the dialectical interplay of Being and Non-Being.

I now turn to the objections to reincarnation itself. Each of those I will discuss seems to me decisive against one or in some instances all versions of the theory. Some of the objections are of great philosophical interest, and these I will discuss most fully.[4] There is, however, one important objection, briefly mentioned at the beginning, which cannot be adequately considered here. This is the objection based on the view that an essential part of what we mean when we say that a person at time T_x is the same as somebody at an earlier time T_1 is that he has the same body. If this view is correct then none of the facts presented by writers like Ian Stevenson, even if they were fully authenticated, could possibly be evidence for reincarnation, though they might call for a revision of other generally accepted beliefs. If Edward Ryall remembered fighting and dying as John Fletcher at the battle of Sedgemoor in 1645 and if it could be shown that there really was a John Fletcher who fought at the battle, that all the events Edward Ryall remembered really occurred, and if we could know that Ryall did not obtain any of his information by normal channels, he would still not be the same person as John Fletcher, simply because the bodies are not identical. We might then abandon the view that people can have accurate first-person recollections only about their own past, but we would not allow the conclusion that the same person lived two lives. An adequate discussion of this objection would involve a consideration of the arguments for and against what I earlier called "corporealism," and the present article is not the place for this. I will therefore not say anything more about this objection and, although I believe that corporealism is substantially correct, I will proceed on the assumption that it can somehow be answered.

Tertullian's Objection

The first objection is a very simple and obvious one. It has been stated concisely and forcefully by the early church father Tertullian (c. 160-c. 220), in Chapter 31 of his *Treatise on the Soul*. "How happens it," he asks there, "that a man who dies in old age returns to life as an infant?" Whoever continues life in a new body might be expected to "return with the age he had attained at his death, that he might resume the precise life which he had relinquished." If "souls depart at different ages of human life," Tertullian continues, "how is it that they come back again at one uniform age?" (A. Roberts and J. Donaldson, eds., *Ante-Nicene Fathers,* vol. 3, p. 211). John Hick, who endorses this objection, points out that babies are not born with adult egos "as they would be if they were direct continuations of egos which had died at the end of a normal lifespan" (*Death and Eternal Life,* p. 363).

Although several of the more scholarly reincarnationists show familiarity with Tertullian's writings I am not aware that any of them has so much as attempted a rebuttal. Hick suggests that it might be possible to build an answer on the distinction between the empirical ego and the metaphysical soul. The empirical ego is what Kant called the "phenomenal" self. It is, in Hick's words, "the conscious, remembering, anticipating, choosing, acting self." The metaphysical soul on the other hand is an entity "lying behind or beneath or above the conscious self." Once this distinction is made, the defender of reincarnation could meet Tertullian's objection by maintaining that what survives in a new body is not the empirical ego, which perishes with the death of the old body, but the metaphysical soul that is manifested in successive empirical egos each of which has to begin as a baby. To make this rejoinder more convincing a reincarnationist could refer to the difference between the age of an actor in a play and his age in real life. In a play an actor may age from eighteen to eighty, but although he himself ages between performances, every time he plays the same part he starts once again at the age of eighteen. In much the same way the metaphysical soul grows older with every incarnation although it starts as a baby in all its empirical manifestations. It should be pointed out that this answer to Tertullian is open to Hindus and other "metaphysical" supporters of reincarnation who believe that what survives is "Atman," a transcendent principle, but that it is not available to Buddhists or Western sympathizers with Buddhism whose "Anatta" has often been compared to Hume's "bundle of impressions and ideas" and which is in effect the empirical ego.

Everything in this reply hinges on the plausibility and relevance of the distinction between the empirical ego and the metaphysical soul. If the notion of the metaphysical soul is unintelligible, as many philosophers hold, or if it is not unintelligible but if there is no reason to suppose that there are such metaphysical souls, or if there are such souls but if they are not what we refer to by the word "I," the rejoinder collapses. I will discuss this distinction in some detail in the section on the dependence of the mind on the body. Here I will merely observe that quite plainly we do not mean anything as abstruse as the metaphysical soul when we use the word *I*. Aside from the body, what we refer to *is* the empirical ego; and it is this empirical ego that reincarnationists like other believers in immortality would like to survive. This is as true of Hindus as it is of Buddhists, whatever they say in their more "philosophical" moments. As for the analogy with the actor and the part he portrays, it should be remembered that a part or character in a play is not a human being living in the actual world. If it were then it *would* be older at every new performance. The analogy also breaks down at the other end. We have ways of determining the age of an actor, but since it is a transcendent principle that is not accessible to any kind of observation, we have no means of determining the age of the metaphysical soul. In fairness I want to stress that reincarnationists are not responsible for this analogy. It is my work—I introduced it in order to give some semblance of content to the otherwise totally obscure assertion that the metaphysical soul ages from life to life although the empirical ego always starts as a baby.

Evolution and the Recency of Life

The next two objections are based on scientific findings that were of course not available to the individuals who first thought up the idea of reincarnation. Confining ourselves for the moment to the version that maintains that human beings can be incarnated only in human bodies, it seems clear that such a theory is inconsistent with evolution. In the first place, evolution teaches that the human race descends from nonhuman species and that there was a time when human bodies did not exist. The reincarnationist, however, is committed to an infinite series of past incarnations in *human* bodies. Furthermore, as we observed a little while ago, whatever believers in reincarnation may say in their more theoretical moments, in practice they refer to the empirical ego when they use the word *soul,* and the empirical ego is the most highly developed form of consciousness. Now, evolution teaches that our consciousness developed gradually along with the development of the brain and the nervous system. The reincarnationist is committed to holding that no such development occurred since it is the same soul that migrated from body to body. He may indeed concede that there has been *some* development—that some souls have gradually grown kinder and wiser and better informed. However, this is not the kind of development postulated by evolutionary theory. It may be thought that the wilder form of reincarnation that holds that human souls may have been incarnated in animal bodies escapes this objection. This is not so. Reincarnationists defending this version do *not* teach that the sequence of bodies in which a soul is incarnated is in any way parallel to the sequence postulated by evolutionists. A human being, as we saw, can become a dog or a gnat and, at the other end, the soul may most recently have been in the body of a nightingale or a beaver.

In any event, both versions are defeated by what science has discovered about the relative recency of life. It is now generally accepted that for many billions of years after the Big Bang the universe contained no life at all. Reincarnation in all forms postulates a series of incarnations stretching back into the past without limit; and this is clearly inconsistent with the facts. Pythagoras and the founders of Eastern religions can hardly be blamed for not knowing these facts, but this does not make the objection any less cogent. As for contemporary Western believers, I have already noted that they usually are not the least bit interested in the findings of science.

It should be pointed out that in reincarnationist publications of the twentieth century, especially those by theosophists, the word *evolution* is constantly used in a highly eulogistic fashion. It is suggested that reincarnation is not only consistent with evolution but that it is in fact its completion and logical extension into the spiritual realm. In every reincarnation we are slightly better and wiser than in the one before and eventually we will attain perfection. Whatever may be thought about such a view, it clearly has nothing to do with evolution as this term is understood in biology. Let us grant for the sake of argument that the human race will develop into a "higher" species, whatever that may mean, and this higher species into a still higher one, and so on. Such a development in no way implies that the bodies of the members of those higher species are inhabited by souls that once lived in human bodies.

The Population Problem

The next objection is based on the well-established fact that the human population of the earth has shown enormous increases throughout recorded history. In an article published in the July-August 1981 issue of *BioScience,* Professor Arthur H. Westing of Amherst summarized the best available information about the number of human beings alive at various times. At the time at which he wrote, the population was estimated at 4.4 billion. In 1945 it had been 2.3 billion, in 1850 1 billion, in 1650 500 million, at the time of Christ 200 million, and in 800 B.C., approximately 5 million. Among other interesting calculations Professor Westing estimated that the 1981 population of 4.4 billion amounted to 9 percent of all human beings who ever lived and that it was greater than the number of people who lived through the entire Paleolithic age, a period accounting for 86 percent of the duration of human life. It should be added that in spite of famines and wars the same trend has continued since 1981. According to figures supplied by the United Nations the earth's population reached 4.8 billion at the end of 1985, and just a few weeks prior to my writing these words, on July 7, 1986, it passed the 5-billion mark. If current trends continue the total human population will be 10 billion by the year 2016.

These facts are incompatible with the less fanciful version of the reincarnation theory according to which human souls can occupy only human bodies. As we saw earlier, reincarnationism is opposed to any doctrine of "special creation" of souls. It denies that "new souls" are ever added to the world. All souls have always existed. Every birth is a *rebirth*—the rebirth of a soul that has already existed. All this clearly rules out any population increase. Reincarnationists who maintain that some souls are eventually allowed to give up their earthly existence and merge into the Absolute or Nirvana are committed to the view that in the long run the population must *decrease*. Other reincarnationists imply that the total human population is stationary. In either case, whether committed to a stationary or decreasing population, reincarnationism appears to be refuted by the population statistics.

It is noteworthy that this argument has hardly ever been explicitly discussed by any of the academically respectable reincarnationists. I suspect that the reason for this is the great difficulty of finding an answer that would strike a sober person as even remotely credible. The less inhibited reincarnationists, however, have attacked the population argument with relish. Morey Bernstein, the author of *The Search for Bridey Murphy*, has an easy answer. We can dispose of the objection by bringing in the population of the astral world.

> The total number of entities in this and the afterworld can remain the same while the balance shifts between the numbers of entities on earth and the number in the unseen world. [p. 259]

If we refer to the human population on earth by the letter e and to the population of the astral or unseen world by the letter u we can answer the objection by simply maintaining that, although neither e or u are constant, the total of $e + u$ never varies.

Substantially the same answer is offered by numerous theosophists. Writing thirty years before Bernstein, Irving C. Cooper, my favorite theosophist, some of whose fascinating ideas I mentioned earlier, also maintains that every increase in the human population on earth can be explained as due to a corresponding decrease in the number of inhabitants of the astral plane. Cooper takes note of the fear in some quarters that the constant increase in the earth's population will eventually deplete the astral plane. He therefore assures his readers that no such dire fate is in store for the astral world. It can absorb mass emigrations without serious damage, much as a giant corporation can easily absorb losses by a subsidiary here and there. In view of "the length of periods between incarnations," which Cooper evidently considers very great, "the population of the unseen world at any time must be many times that of the earth" (op. cit., p. 57).

V. F. Gunaratna, a Buddhist philosopher whose slender volume *Rebirth Explained* (1971) comes recommended by the Venerable Narada Mahathera as the "profound treatise" of a "learned writer," fully endorses the Bernstein-Cooper view that we must not focus our attention exclusively on the earth and should remember that there are "countless other world systems of which the Buddhist texts speak." We must also remember that, just as human beings may turn into animals or gods, so earlier incarnations of a human being may well have been on a nonhuman plane." "An animal or a celestial being can be reborn as a human being" (p. 80). If, as before, we represent the human population on the earth as e and if we refer to the animal population by the letter a and to the totality of gods by g, reincarnationism is not committed to the view that e is unchanging. It is committed to the very different proposition that $e + a + g$ is the same at all times. The facts of population growth do not in any way conflict with this broader view.

Another Buddhist writer who has dealt with the population argument is K. N. Jayatilleke, who until his death in 1970 was professor of philosophy at the University of Ceylon. Jayatilleke held an M.A. from Cambridge and a Ph.D. from the University of London. Although he professed himself an admirer of A. J. Ayer and regarded himself as an empiricist, he swallowed even the most extravagant of the claims made by and on behalf of Edgar Cayce and he fully endorsed the Bridey Murphy case as evidence for reincarnation. Jayatilleke has a twofold answer to the population argument. Like Gunaratna, he appeals to the possibility that human beings were animals in previous incarnations. To this he adds that we must not rule out the possibility of the transmigration of souls from other planets. The Buddhist view of the cosmos holds that there are "hundreds of thousands of galaxies spread out in space" and that they include "thousands of inhabited spheres." It is entirely possible that some of the population increase on the earth is the result of invasions of human embryos by souls from these spheres. If, as before, we represent the human population of the earth as e, the animal population as a, and the souls living in human or nonhuman form on other planets as p, the unchanging totality is not e but $e + a + p$.

The second component of Jayatilleke's rejoinder has the wholehearted endorsement of Professor Geddes MacGregor, who is perhaps the most distinguished Christian theologian writing in defense of reincarnation at the present time. Holding degrees from Oxford, the Sorbonne, and Edinburgh, he is a Fellow of the Royal Society for Literature and taught for many years in the philosophy department of the University of Southern California. MacGregor admits that in Tertullian's time bringing up the population increase was "pardonable." However, now that we "know of the vastness of the galaxies and of the extreme likelihood that there are millions of inhabited planets besides our own" the objection no longer has "any force at all" (*Reincarnation As a Christian Hope*, p. 47).

The sufficient answer to all these rejoinders is that they involve what I call "noxious" *ad hoc* assumptions. Not all *ad hoc* assumptions are automatically objectionable, and it will be worthwhile to explain the distinction between those that are and those that are not. The difference is essentially the same as the one between the two kinds of *post hoc* pronouncements noted earlier when discussing Karmic assertions about sins committed in past lives. All of us make perfectly reasonable *ad hoc* assumptions in everyday life and occasionally *ad hoc* assumptions have proved highly fruitful in the history of science. The discovery of the planet Neptune provides a particularly instructive illustration of a reasonable and successful *ad hoc* assumption. Full details can be found in most histories of astronomy, but for our purposes the following brief summary will suffice. By the end of the eighteenth and the beginning of the nineteenth centuries Newtonian celestial mechanics enabled astronomers to calculate the orbits of most of the planets with very great accuracy. The orbits of two planets, however, those of Uranus and Mercury, defied all their calculations. To explain the discrepancy between the calculated and the observed orbits of Uranus, two astronomers, John Adams (1819–1892) and Urbain Leverrier (1811–1877), postulated the existence of a new planet having a certain size, shape, mass, and position in the sky. This was an *ad hoc* hypothesis in the sense that it was not based on any direct evidence and that its purpose was to "save" the Newtonian theory, i.e., to retain it in spite of observations that seemed to contradict it. In 1846 Leverrier requested the Berlin astronomer Johann Galle to carry out the appropriate telescopic observations, and the result was the discovery of Neptune, one of the so-called giant planets with a mean diameter of approximately 28,000 miles and a mass of 17.2 times that of Earth. The Adams-Leverrier hypothesis of a new planet was not "noxiously" *ad hoc* for two reasons: the theory that it was meant to save was itself powerfully supported by a vast array of observations and, although *ad hoc*, it was independently testable.

By contrast, the various rejoinders to the population argument are "noxiously" *ad hoc* because reincarnationism, unlike Newtonian mechanics, is not a theory for which there is powerful observational evidence—in fact of course there is none—and because the assumptions that are introduced are either, like mass immigrations from the astral world or from "other planes," not even in principle testable or, as in the case of population reductions on other planets, so vague as not to be testable in practice. It is perhaps of some interest to note that Leverrier later postulated the existence of a further planet he called Vulcan to explain the perturbations in the orbit of Mercury. However, astronomers have never been able to observe such a planet and the Vulcan hypothesis is now discredited. In the sense in which I am using the word here, the Vulcan hypothesis, although it turned out to be false, was not noxious because, like the Neptune hypothesis, its purpose was to save an empirically well-supported theory and because it was independently testable.

There is also something disingenuous in the appeal to the possible decrease in the number of animals (and gods) that is supposed to occur simultaneously with the increase in the human population. Let us suppose that we could obtain an absolutely reliable census of the animal and god populations of the universe during the period between 1900 and 1950 and that it revealed no such decrease as is required by the answer of the reincarnationists. I very much doubt that they would then abandon their belief. As for the constant influx of souls from other galaxies postulated by Professor MacGregor, would he abandon reincarnation if he could be shown that there is no life elsewhere in the universe, something that more and more astronomers have come to believe in recent years? In an article published in 1974 Ian Stevenson concedes that if "the recent increase in the world's population" continues, it would "bring difficulties for the reincarnation hypothesis." He adds that these difficulties "have not reached us yet" ("Some Questions Related to Cases of the Reincarnation Type," *Journal of the American Society for Psychical Research,* 1974, p. 400). Stevenson omits to tell us how great the population increase has to be before the difficulties do reach us. However, it is worth pointing out that since 1974 the increases have continued at an enormously accelerated pace and yet, so far from abandoning his belief or flirtation with reincarnation, Stevenson has become an ever more convinced and forthright supporter.

I have left to the end the rejoinder by Dr. Bruce Goldberg, the futurologist from Baltimore. Dr. Goldberg is up to form and, with his usual confidence, offers a theory that is as bold as it is ingenious. There is no reason to suppose that the same soul cannot occupy "more than one body at a time." If we modestly assume that one soul occupies three bodies, the population problem can easily be disposed of:

> If one soul occupied three bodies in the year 300 B.C., for example, and if each of these sub-souls occupied three additional bodies each, it would not be difficult to see how one soul could occupy one and a half million bodies in a matter of thirteen lifetimes. [op. cit., p. 181]

Unfortunately this soul-fission theory does not solve the problem. In the first place, the logic of personal identity make it impossible for a person to occupy more than one body. If two bodies, B_1 and B_2, were to behave in exceedingly similar ways and if we had reason to believe that their sensations, feelings, and thoughts were qualitatively similar in all respects, we would still not describe them as the bodies of the same person. If, for example, B_1 were Ronald Reagan's body, we would not say that Ronald Reagan also inhabited B_2, but rather that the mind associated with B_2 is Ronald Reagan's double. I do not wish to lay too much stress on this consideration here because to defend it fully would require a long discussion and also because some competent philosophers would not agree that a person cannot be in several bodies at the same time. However, allowing such multiple occupations as *logical* possibilities, the actual facts clearly defeat Dr. Goldberg's rejoinder. "Goldberg's Law," as we may call his fission theory, is presumably not confined to the future but has always operated in the past. If this is so, we should not find five billion separate souls but a handful, perhaps a few hundred souls, each occupying millions of bodies. Yet that is not at all what we find. There are not, sad to say, millions of Ronald Reagans, William Rehnquists, or for that matter, Bruce Goldbergs.

The population difficulties can be avoided by somebody who is prepared to offer a drastically modified version of reincarnationism. Professor Ducasse never discusses the population objection, but at the end of his article "Life After Death Conceived As Reincarnation" he refers to such a revised position. Speaking of the Bridey Murphy case (of which he was a vigorous champion) and the spontaneous recollection of earlier lives by certain children, he observes that, if these cases are as strong as their supporters maintain, they are evidence for the view that "reincarnation, whether general or not, occurs at least sometimes." Ducasse leaves this question open; but, according to Stevenson, some Turkish believers are quite definite that only those who die a violent death are reborn ("Characteristics of Cases of the Reincarnation Type in Turkey and Their Comparison with Cases in Two Other Cultures," *International Journal of Comparative Sociology,* 1970, p. 4). Somebody who holds the view that reincarnation occurs but that it is not general could quite consistently admit the population growth without invoking any of the noxious *ad hoc* assumptions. He would maintain that, while the origin of some human beings has to be explained in terms of the trans-migration of souls, the origin of many (perhaps most) human beings is of a natural kind. By this I mean that the latter sub-class of the human race is *entirely* the result of biological reproduction. Such a position could then also explain population growth in the usual way, by references to biological and social factors.

There is something appealing about the modesty of this revised position, but it is easy to see why it has not commended itself to most believers in reincarnation. It does seem more than an *a priori* prejudice to hold that all human beings have the same kind of origin: they are either all the result of a divine infusion of a soul into an embryo or they are all the result of transmigration or they are all produced in a purely biological fashion. Furthermore, many of the arguments for reincarnation, if they were valid, would show that *all* human beings are the reincarnation of previously existing souls. Finally, somebody taking this position is faced with the unenviable task of supplying criteria allowing us to tell who among human beings is naturally produced and who is the result of reincarnation.

Notes

1. See *Free Inquiry*, Spring 1987, 46–49.
2. See *Free Inquiry*, Summer 1987, 48–49.
3. See *Free Inquiry*, Summer 1987.
4. The reference is to the objections discussed in the third and fourth installments of the *Free Inquiry* series.

PAST-LIFE REGRESSION: THE GRAND ILLUSION

Melvin Harris

Carl Jung wrote: "With a free and open mind I listen attentively to the Indian doctrine of rebirth and look around in the world of my own experience to see whether somewhere and somehow there is some authentic sign pointing towards reincarnation." For many thousands in the Western world the signs have arrived. For them, hypnotic regressions have lifted the heavy veil that once shrouded the subject, and the domestic tape-recorder has become the great ally of Truth by capturing "authentic accounts" of long-forgotten life-cycles.

It all began with the Bridey Murphy case of 1952. "Ruth Simmons," an American housewife apparently regressed back to an earlier life in nineteenth-century Ireland. The book of the case topped the United States best-seller list and was translated into five languages. The book spawned a motion picture; a record of one of the sessions sold tens of thousands of copies; and all over the United States tape recorders began purring away at innumerable regression sessions.

Twenty years after the Bridey Murphy sensation a much more impressive group of "past lives" startled the public. The Bloxham Tapes were first presented as a BBC Television documentary produced by Jeffrey Iverson. Then they were included and enlarged on in Iverson's book *More Lives Than One?* They were regarded as "the most staggering evidence for reincarnation ever recorded . . . amazingly detailed accounts of past lives—accounts so authentic that they can only be explained by the certainty of reincarnation." Inevitably they achieved international renown.

The tapes themselves had been accumulated for years by an elderly

Melvin Harris is the author of many books, including *Investigating the Unexplained* (Prometheus Books, 1986). He is a writer, broadcaster, and researcher for the BBC, specializing in unexplained mysteries of all kinds.

Cardiff-based hypnotherapist, Arnall Bloxham. He was a lifelong believer in reincarnation, but his past-life regressions only emerged quite late in his career. Despite that, he managed to collect a cupboard full of past-life tapes drawn from his experiments with over four hundred people.

Jeffrey Iverson first heard about this collection casually at a party. As a producer with the BBC in Cardiff he was constantly on the lookout for program ideas, so in October 1974 he called at Bloxham's house. After listening to the calm old man's claims, Iverson concluded that if these claims were true then the recordings were possibly the largest investigation ever undertaken into this type of regression. If true, Iverson thought, "then that single famous case . . . the search for Bridey Murphy, was just a tune on an Irish fiddle compared to his symphony of voices."

Iverson began with a weeding-out process, discarding those tapes which he felt could not be researched and proved. Gradually he came to concentrate on a limited number of the tapes where it seemed to him that the details "coincided remarkably with known but quite obscure periods of history . . . in which people talked about cities and countries they had apparently never visited in their present lives."

Two oustanding cases resulted from all this weeding. In one, Graham Huxtable, a Swansea man, regressed to a squalid life aboard a Royal Navy frigate engaged in action against the French some two hundred years ago. But the most important case involved a Welsh housewife, Jane Evans.

Mrs. Evans produced a remarkable set of six "past lives." They were remarkable not so much for their number and diversity as for the sheer, almost overwhelming, amount of detail packed into three of them. In her minor "lives" she was first a London sewing girl named Anne Tasker living about 1702; then a lady-in-waiting to Catherine of Aragon two centuries earlier; and finally Sister Grace, an American nun living in Des Moines, Iowa, up until the 1920s.

Of the three major "lives" two center on the town of York. The earliest was set in the third century at the time of the rebellion of Carausius, the Roman Admiral who seized power in Britain and declared himself Emperor. Jane Evans was then Livonia, the wife of Titus, tutor to the young son of Constantius (Governor of Britian) and his wife Helena.

As Livonia, she describes how Constantius had to return to Rome and how the rebellion is engineered in his absence. As a consequence she and her husband and the rest of Constantius's household flee from Eboracum (York) to Verulam (St. Albans) where they live apprehensively until the rebel regime is overthrown by an army led by Constantius. Yet her husband's triumphant return only brings sadness for the Lady Helena. Roman power struggles have dictated that her husband has had to divorce her and contract a new marriage with Theodora, daughter of the Emperor Maximianus.

Helena, therefore, decides to stay in Verulam. There they are influenced by a Christian woodcarver, Albanus, and Titus becomes so zealous that he volunteers for the priesthood. On the eve of Titus's induction as a priest, Roman troops swoop on Christian houses and burn them. Titus dies in the melée and Livonia apparently dies in some terror a short while afterwards.

Her next life in York also ended tragically. It unfolded at the year 1189 in the north of the city where "most of the wealthy Jews live." Then, she was Rebecca, wife of Joseph, a rich Jewish moneylender. For her and the rest of the Jews, the times were troubled. Anti-Jewish risings had occurred in Lincoln, London, and Chester. In York they were subject to abuse and threats. One of their community, Isaac of Coney Street, was even murdered by a mob.

By the spring of the next year it was obvious that violence was inevitable. So Rebecca and her family prepared their flight from the city, but they left their move too late. An armed band broke into the next-door house, killed their inhabitants, looted the place, then set fire to it. Joseph, Rebecca, and her two children were able to run only as far as the castle of York. But even there they were unable to reach safe shelter. They finally found refuge of a sort when they entered a church, took the priest and his clerk captive, and hid down in the cellars.

Later, from the safety of the church roof, they could see flames and hear distant mobs screaming, "burn the Jews, burn the Jews!"

Their respite turned out to be short-lived. Their captives escaped and alerted the mob, and the soldiers came into the church to deal with the family. At this high point in the story Jane Evans became "almost incoherent with terror" as the soldiers took her daughter. Then, whispering "dark . . . dark," she presumably died.

Her other major "life" was lived in medieval France about 1450. At that time she was apparently a young Egyptian servant named Alison in the household of Jacques Coeur, the outstanding merchant prince of that period. She was able to talk at length and knowledgeably about Coeur's intrigues, about the kings's mistress, Agnes Sorel, and about the clash between the Dauphin Louis and King Charles VII. She knew a great deal about Coeur's possessions and his extraordinary house at Bourges. Her knowledge of the clothes worn by her master is accurate: "tunic edged with miniver, red hose . . . shoes of red Cordovan leather . . . a jewelled belt around his waist and a chain around his neck."

She is again accurate when she tells of Jacques Coeur's fall from favor. He was once close to the King, but after the death of Agnes Sorel rumors spread at the Court hinting that Coeur had poisoned Agnes. Coeur was arrested, tried on a number of charges, and imprisoned. But Alison knew only of the arrest. According to her, when the soldiers came for her master he gave her a poisoned draught to drink, and she ended her life by accepting it.

When television viewers saw Jane Evans under hypnosis and heard the astonishing stories come naturally from her, they were rightly impressed. Her narratives seemed completely free from any attempts at acting a part. When fear and anguish came into her voice, it was clear that she was racked with real emotions. And her easy grasp of often difficult names of people and places made it seem that she was indeed remembering things that she had once known about intimately. But Jane Evans in her unhypnotized state was adamant that she knew nothing of Jacques Coeur, nothing of Carausius and his times, and nothing of the massacre of the Jews at York.

Iverson's conclusion was that "the Bloxham Tapes have been researched and there is no evidence that they are fantasies. In our present state of knowledge about them, they appear to convey exactly what they claim: a genuine knowledge and experience of the past." But were these tapes ever researched as painstakingly as they should have been? And was the search for Bridey Murphy ever thorough enough? And is it possible that quite another phenomenon, rather than reincarnation, can account for these rich narratives?

Are past-life regressions really evidence for reincarnation? Or could they be glimpses of ancestral memories? Both theories have their followers. Yet rigorous research provides a distinctly different answer. These regressions are identified as fascinating examples of *cryptomnesia*.

To understand what cryptomnesia is, we have to think of the subconscious mind as a vast, muddled storehouse of information. This information comes from books, newspapers, and magazines; from lectures, films, television, and radio; from direct observation and even from overheard scraps of conversion.

Under everyday circumstances much of this knowledge is not subject to normal recall, but there are times when some of these deeply buried memories are spontaneously revived. Some of these revived memories re-emerge in a baffling form, since their origins are completely forgotten. This is cryptomnesia proper.

Because the origins are forgotten, the information can seem to have no ancestry and can be mistaken for something newly created. The late Helen Keller was tragically deceived by such a cryptomnesic caprice. In 1892 she wrote a charming tale called "The Frost King." It was published and applauded, but within a few months it was revealed that Helen's piece was simply a modified version of Margaret Canby's story "The Frost Fairies," published twenty-nine years earler.

Helen Keller had no conscious memory of ever having been told the story. She was blind and deaf, completely dependent on others for her knowledge. But inquiries revealed that a friend had in fact read a batch of Miss Canby's stories to her by touch in 1888. "The Frost Fairies" was among them.

When this was made plain, Helen was devastated. She wrote: "Joy deserted my heart . . . I had disgraced myself . . . yet how could it possibly have happened? I racked by brain until I was weary to recall anything about the frost that I had read before I wrote "The Frost King"; but I could remember nothing."

Other authors have been trapped in the same way, as Samuel Rosenberg has testified. Rosenberg worked for Warner Brothers pictures as a literary consultant on plagiarism cases. He records the valuable advice given him by his legal supervisor, who said: "Don't be fooled by the sometimes astonishing resemblances you will find when you compare any two films, plays, stories, books, or film scripts. During the past twenty-five years we have made hundreds of such comparisons in preparation for court trials, and in a great many cases we have found that both of the quarrelling authors—each convinced that he was honest and that the other writer was an idea-thief—had copied their plots, ideas, sequences from an earlier literary classic or from the Bible or some forgotten childhood story."

In a similar fashion a number of cases of automatic writings, supposed to be from discarnate spirits, have been traced to published works. For example, the famous "Oscar Wilde" scripts of the 1920s were gradually shown to be derived from many printed sources, including Wilde's own *De Profundis* and *The Decay of Lying*.

Dr. S. G. Soal, one of the writers of these automatic scripts, was led to remark: "The variety of sources from which the script is drawn is as amazing as the adroitness with which the knowledge is worked up into sentences conveying impressions of the different mannerisms of Wilde's literary style."

This is a significant verdict. But even so, could such unconscious plagiarism account for Bridey Murphy and her offspring? Were the "past existences" nothing but subconscious fantasies yielded up in order to please the hypnotist? Were they simply a pastiche of buried memories made gripping by the sincerity that accompanies cryptomnesia? In 1956 Dr. Edwin Zolik of Marquette University set out to answer these questions.

Once he had hypnotized his subjects he instructed them to "remember previous existences," and his subjects obliged by providing convincing accounts of "past lives." Everything was tape-recorded, preserving every sublety and nuance in the voice as the tales unfolded. The recordings were listened to by the subjects in their waking states. Their verdicts were clear— they knew nothing about these "past lifetimes."

Their disclaimers were obviously sincere. But, when he rehypnotized and re-examined his subjects, they were able to remember the fictitious sources they had used in constructing their past-life adventures. In brief, Zolik's detailed analysis showed that past-life memories could easily be nothing but a mixture of remembered tales and strong symbolically colored emotions.

Zolik's method of probing for the real-life origins of reincarnationist material was something he recommended to anyone seriously interested in the truth. Unfortunately few, if any, of the enthusiastic hypnoregressionists took any notice of his advice, and session after session was committed to tape and marvelled over without any effort being made to verify the origins or meaning of this material. Hypnotherapist Arnall Bloxham, for one, recorded over four hundred past-life regressions without ever once digging for the possibly mundane origins of these alleged "lives." On the other hand, the Finnish psychiatrist Dr. Reima Kampman devoted years to the systematic investigation of the cryptomnesic origins of past-life accounts.

Dr. Kampman of the Department of Psychiatry at the University of Oulu, Finland, began his work in the 1960s. He found his subjects among large groups of volunteers drawn from the three highest grades of the secondary schools of Oulu. All those who could enter a deep hypnotic state were selected for closer study. Kampman found it relatively easy to induce past-life recall as a response to his instruction: "Go back to an age before your birth, when you are somebody else, somewhere else."

His most amazing subject proved to be a girl who conjured up eight "past lives." In one "life" she lived in ancient Babylonia, her next "life" began in Nanking, then followed a "life" in Paris, another in England, and a final existence in revolutionary Russia.

One of her "past lives" was as Karin Bergstrom, a seven-year-old girl who had died in an air raid back in 1939. She was able to supply an address for her old home, and she knew the names and occupations of her former parents. Inquiries showed that indeed there had been an air raid on the exact date she had given. What is more, the addresses she had given had been hit. But the population records showed that neither a real Karin Bergstrom nor her relatives had died in the raid.

So the girl was asked to age-regress to the time when she first heard of the Bergstroms or the bombing, and she soon remembered herself as a little girl turning over the pages of a patriotic book. In that book were photographs of the streets and houses hit by the bombs, and something about the people made homeless. The exact date of the raid was given and one picture showed two of the victims killed that day—significantly a mother and her seven-year-old daughter. So, the complete regression was assembled from nothing more than the disjointed material found in this one book.

But the really exciting adventure involved her thirteenth-century "English life" as Dorothy, an inn-keeper's daughter. This brought to light a very explicit account of contemporary happenings. And she astonished everyone by singing a song that none of the listeners was familiar with. She called it the summer song.

The unusual language used in the song was later studied by a student with high honors in the English language. He had no difficulty in identifying the words as examples of an old-style English—possibly Middle English. But this meant nothing to the girl, who had no memory of ever having heard the words or music of the song before.

The solution to this riddle came during a later experiment. She was asked to go back to a time when she might have seen the words and music of the song, or even heard it sung. She then regressed to the age of thirteen and remembered taking a book from the shelves of a library.

This was a casual choice. She made no attempt to read and absorb its contents. She merely flicked through its pages. Yet she not only remembered its title, but was able to state just where in the book her "summer song" could be found.

The crucial book was *Musiikin Vaiheet,* a Finnish translation of *The History of Music* written by Benjamin Britten and Imogen Holst. And the mystery music was, of all things, the famous round "Sumer is Icumen In" with words rendered in a simplified medieval English.

A spate of similar successes led Kampman to conclude that he had demonstrated "that the experiences of the present personality were reflected in the secondary personalities, both in the form of realistic details and as emotional experiences. The recording of a song from a book simply by turning over the leaves of a book at the age of thirteen is an outstanding example of how very detailed information can be stored in our brain without any idea whatever of it in the conscious mind, and how it can be retrieved in deep hypnosis."

These findings allow us to look at the Bridey Murphy and Bloxham cases with extra understanding.

When the Bridey Murphy case first surfaced, it was greeted with naive enthusiasm, and this inevitably provoked a sour reaction. The *Chicago American* published a stinging "exposure" claiming that Ruth Simmons's

Bridey-knowledge came from her relatives and acquaintances in Chicago. The *Denver Post* countered by sending their man, William J. Barker, to Ireland in search of supporting material. The rival papers fought fiercely for their totally opposed viewpoints. Yet neither side produced a conclusive answer.

But in the end the onus of proof must always lie with the side that makes the positive claims. Regrettably, Bernstein and his friends were far too quick to make claims on the basis of slender research. And even this slender research is marred by flaws.

Let us note how they marvelled over Ruth's knowledge of the old custom of kissing the Blarney Stone yet failed to spot a complete work on the custom, written by John Hewlett and called *The Blarney Stone*. It was published in New York, of all places, in 1951. They were equally over-awed by her knowing about the Irish Uillean pipes, about Irish jigs, and about Irish customs and geography. She had never set foot in Ireland, they reasoned, and yet she knew all this fine detail concerning last-century Erin. But their skimpy research failed to uncover the fact that Americans had twice had the chance of delving deeply into Irish life and customs without moving a single inch out of the United States.

In 1893 The World's Columbian Exposition was staged in Chicago. Among the exhibits at this giant fair was an Irish village, the brain-child of Lady Aberdeen. Her original idea was modest—just a single Irish cabin. Yet by the opening day this had grown into a complete village of fifteen cottages. They were grouped around a green facing a full-sized replica of the tower of Blarney Castle.

To give the exhibit life, Ishbel Aberdeen traveled to the farthest corners of Kerry, Connemara, and Donegal and chose girls who could spin, sing, make butter, and dance jigs. The rose-cheeked colleens were then shipped, suitably chaperoned, over to the States to live and work in the Chicago village.

Every day for the six months of the fair visitors could hear the burbling Uillean pipes, listen to the songs of old Ireland, and see the traditional jigs danced on the green. A huge relief map of Ireland could be viewed from on high; books and souvenirs could be bought; and to crown it all, a replica Blarney Stone could be kissed in the traditional manner at the summit of the massive Blarney Castle tower.

On opening day some twenty thousand visitors paid their twenty-five cents to enter the Irish village. After that the crowd grew, the sales mounted, and the village became one of the three shows that made money. So, by the end of the fair, over three and a half million people had been brought into contact with all things Irish. And it did not end there! The whole venture was so wildly successful that an Irish village, complete with the full-size tower of Blarney Castle, was erected once more for the St. Louis Fair of 1904.

Now, Ruth Simmons (or rather Virginia Tighe) was born in 1923, so during her formative years there was still a veritable army of people around who had first-hand experiences of these Irish villages. The possibilities for gaining knowledge of Ireland in her home town of Chicago were obviously enormous.

Just as the possible sources were neglected, so was the tried and proven method of probing, under hypnosis, for the real-life origins of the Bridey saga. Perhaps it is still not too late. An independent hypnotist could still put the crucial questions to Virginia. Until she consents to this the case can only reasonably qualify as a famous curiosity—and no more.

It is very different, though, with the Bloxham Tapes. The extravagant claims made for these tapes impelled me to investigate them, even with the limited amount of time and funds at my disposal. The snags were great. Graham Huxtable proved unable to help in any constructive way, while Jane Evans flatly refused to cooperate. As a result the only course left open lay in a scrutiny of the texts and a laborious search for the probable origins of the previous "lives."

The Huxtable naval regression proved empty. Its verifiable content was nil. Even its period flavor was grossly overrated. I carefully listed every archaic and little-used word in this regression and found that there were only two of them that were not known to me as a schoolboy. And my own schoolboy memories reminded me that there were large numbers of historical novels and boys' adventures based on the Royal Navy of the relevant period. A check with publishers' lists showed that there were, indeed, scores of books falling into this category. Apart from that, there were innumerable magazine stories along the same lines.

The ship that the "seaman" Huxtable sailed in is clearly fictional. He calls it the *Aggie*. It has thirty-two guns. No ship of that description served in the Royal Navy at that period. Remember, we are not talking about an obscure period in British history, but one that is extremely well documented. For example, Captain Manning and Commander C. F. Walker's book *British Warship Names* (Putnam, 1959) lists the name of every warship of importance for centuries. A thirty-two gun frigate is automatically in this category. But you will not find an *Aggie*, or any name resembling this, in their listings.

Some people, as a last-ditch attempt to salvage this story, have nominated the *Agamemnon* as a possibility. But this is out of the question. The *Agamemnon* was a sixty-four gun giant.

Little need be said about Huxtable's voice transformation. It has been described as having "a much deeper tone and a strong South of England accent." In other words, a real-life character from the past has emerged. In reality, however, what we encounter is simply the easily assumed pantomine-style *Treasure Island* accent, with all its unsubtlety. As such it has no evidential value.

The six "past lives" of Jane Evans were obviously the real challenge. Iverson himself considers this to be "the most consistently astonishing case in Bloxham's collection." I agreed—hers was the case to concentrate on.

My reinvestigation soon showed that the claims made for the tapes were false and the result of misdirected and inadequate research. For example, one of Jane Evan's minor "lives" as a handmaiden to Catherine of Aragon could easily have been based, sequence for sequence, on Jean Plaidy's historical novel *Katherine, The Virgin Widow*.

But the three major "lives" proved to have the most illuminating ancestries. Her recital as Alison, a teenage servant to Jacques Coeur the fifteenth-century French merchant prince was said to prove that she "knew a remarkable amount about medieval French history." Yet in her waking state she said: "I have never read about Jacques Coeur. I have never heard the name."

Jeffrey Iverson even concluded that she could not have picked up her many facts through the standard sources. After all, she knew so much, including inside knowledge of the intrigue surrounding the King's mistress, Agnes Sorel. Among other things, she was able to describe fully the exteriors and interiors of Coeur's magnificent house, even giving details of the carvings over the fireplace in his main banquet hall. More surprisingly, she spoke of the carved tomb of Agnes Sorel that was housed in a church. According to Iverson, this tomb "had been cast away by French revolutionaries and spent a hundred and sixty five years, until its rediscovery in 1970, out of sight in a cellar." But—like a number of observations in the book *More Lives Than One?*—this does not stand up to scrutiny.

The truth is that the Sorel tomb was placed in its present setting in 1809. It has been a tourist attraction for the whole of this century, and it is described in detail in H. D. Sedgwick's *A Short History Of France*, published in 1930, a book popular for decades and often found in public and school libraries. Apart from that, the tomb has been referred to in many other books and photographed frequently.

It is very much the same with Jacques Coeur's house. In fact, this is one of the most photographed and filmed houses in all France. Fine, explicit photographs are included in Dame Joan Evans's book *Life in Medieval France*. There one can see the stone carvings over the fireplace and gain a sound idea of how the place looked, both inside and out. There is now little doubt that Jane Evans has seen these or similar pictures.

There is overwhelmingly strong evidence that the rest of Jane's material was drawn from a source not known to Iverson—a 1948 novel, *The Moneyman*, by C. B. Costain. This is based on Coeur's life and provides almost all of the flourishes and authentic-sounding touches included in her past-life memory.

In particular, the novel very neatly answers an important question raised by Iverson and other commentators, a question prompted by the curious fact that Alison does not know that her master is married! As Iverson puts it: "How is it that this girl can know Coeur had an Egyptian bodyslave and not be aware that he was married with five children—a fact published in every historical account of Coeur's life? If the explanation for the entire regression is a reading of history books in the twentieth century, then I cannot explain how Bloxham's subject would not know of the marriage."

Thomas Costain's short introduction to his novel clears up the mystery. He writes: "I have made no mention of Jacques Coeur's family for the reason that they played no real part in the events which brought his career to its climax. . . . When I attempted to introduce them into the story they got so much in the way that I decided finally it would be better to do without them."

Yet the view that her tapes were simply the result of cryptomnesia could still be contested, if it were not for the confirmation provided by the setting of her remaining two major "lives."

As Rebecca, the Jewess of York, she was supposed to have met her death during the massacre of 1190. At that time most of the Jewish community died in the York Castle Keep, but Rebecca's death came in the cellar of a church where she had taken refuge. Around this cellar episode a formidable legend has grown up. It is now asserted that the church was positively identified as St. Mary's Castlegate and that a crypt was actually discovered there after Jane's regression. The truth is that the original television program script stated that there were three possible churches that could qualify as the place of refuge.

St. Mary's was chosen to film in simply because it was the most convenient, since it was being converted into a museum. And it was this conversion that led to the uncovering of an aperture under the chancel. For believers, this was naturally a medieval crypt and proof of Rebecca's story.

For many of them it was joyfully received, almost as if it were some sign from heaven! It gave a fillip to their beliefs or yearnings, so it had to be true.

Writer after writer gloried in unravelling the tale of the wonderful evidential crypt. "This really makes the skeptics' doubts stick in their throats," wrote one, while Brian Inglis wrote: 'It is little touches of this kind which rule out cryptomnesia. . . . It is no longer possible, therefore, to maintain that cryptomnesia (or, for that matter, deliberate fraud—the pretense of remembering a past life) is an adequate explanation."

To add strength to their assertions the believers constantly cited Professor Barrie Dobson of the Department of History, University of York, as if he were a supporter and ally. In doing so they drew on phrases found in Iverson's book. But the point needs to be made, and made as strongly as possible, that some of the references to Professor Dobson in that book are misleading. They are based on informal correspondence never intended for publication. As such they are easily open to misinterpretation.

It is significant, though, and predictable that not one of the believers ever took the trouble to check things out with Professor Dobson. Had they done so, they would have found that his views on the crypt are as follows (I quote with his full permission from his helpful letter to me dated 15 January 1986): "There remains the issue of whether the 'cellars under the church' in which Rebecca alleges she is sheltering at the time of the massacre of the Jews at the castle of York can be proved to have existed in 1190. The answer to this can only be a definite negative, for it now seems overwhelmingly most likely that the chamber which workmen reported encountering when renovating St. Mary's Castlegate in 1975 was not an early medieval crypt at all but a post-medieval charnel vault. The Royal Commission on Historical Monuments' *Survey of York, Vol. V (The Central Area)* 1981 says of it on page 31: 'Beneath the east end of the chancel is a charnel vault with a barrel vault of stone rubble, probably a later insertion and now inaccessible.'

"The fact that this vault or chamber remains inaccessible in January 1986 must not, in my opinion, persuade anyone into believing that Rebecca's reference to cellars under a church adds any authenticity to her story. The evidence available is now revealed as so weak in this instance that it fails to support any thesis which suggests that Rebecca's regression contains within it genuine and direct memories of late twelfth-century York."

For all that, the furor over the crypt is meaningless, since the Rebecca regression is clearly a fantasy. It is an amalgamation of at least two different stories of persecution taken from widely separated centuries.

The proof that we are dealing with a fantasy lies in the historical absurdities found in the tale. Rebecca repeats four times that the Jewish community in York was forced to wear yellow badges ". . . Circles over our hearts." But the Jewish badge was not introduced until the following century, and even then the English pattern consisted of two oblong white strips of cloth, representing the tablets of Moses. The yellow circle was, in fact, the badge worn in France and Germany after 1215. This is one aspect of Jewish history over which there are no legitimate doubts whatsoever.

A group of further absurdities was discovered in passages from the tapes that were excluded from both the book and the film. In these revealing passages Rebecca repeatedly speaks of living in the ghetto in the north of York. This ghetto was a quarter without street names where only the rich Jews lived, and she pointedly mentioned a poor Jew who could only afford to live in ". . . the middle of York in a street called Coney Street."

There never was a special Jewish quarter in York. The Jews lived scattered among the Christians in places like Micklegate, Fosgate, Bretgate, Feltergayle, and near the center in Jewbury. And the idea that a Jew would live in Coney Street because of his poverty is ludicrous. Coney Street was in truth the choice place for many of the rich Jews to settle, including Josce, the wealthy head of the Jewish community!

As for the notion of the ghetto itself, this involved a leap in time of over three hundred years, since the first ghetto was not set up until 1516 in Venice. It was established on an old foundry site—and the very name is derived from the Italian *geto*, which means "foundry."

This indicates, inevitably, that Jane Evans has the ability to subconsciously store vivid accounts and combine and edit these creatively to the point where she becomes one of the characters involved. The clinching proof that this is so is provided by "the Roman wife" (or "Livonia") regression, for this is the purest of all, based on one source only.

This particular life involves a turbulent period in Britain's history, a time of rebellion and instability. At the opening of this period the name of the Roman Governor in Britain is unrecorded in existing historical records. The past-life memories seem to fill this gap for us by stating that Constantius, father of Constantine the Great, was in charge. After consulting his reference books Iverson was happy to conclude: "Nor can the regression be dismissed as a fiction built around a blank area of history. Livonia knows a considerable number of verifiable historical facts that fit perfectly into her vision of the missing years. No modern student of history could contradict the names and events she describes. . . ."

After hearing the tape Professor Brian Hartley, an authority on Roman Britain, seemed to agree, since he commented: "She knew some quite remarkable historical facts, and numerous published works would have to be consulted if anyone tried to prepare the outline of such a story."

Professor Hartley was right. Much painstaking research went into the making of Jane's story, but the research was undertaken by the late Louis De Wohl. In 1947 he wrote a best-selling novel, *The Living Wood*, and

Jane's life as Livonia is taken directly from the novel. Brief comparisons will show just how.

Livonia's tale opens in Britain during 286 A.D. She describes the garden of a house owned by the Legate Constantius. His wife is named as Lady Helena, his son as Constantine. The son is pictured being taught the use of shield, sword, and armor by his military tutor, Marcus Favonius Facilis. This entire sequence is taken from Chapter II, Book II of the novel, where Constantine trains in the use of arms and armor under Marcus Favonius, called "Facilis . . . because everything was easy to him." De Wohl based this character on a real-life centurion whose tombstone is now in Colchester Castle Museum. But his account of this centurion's life is pure fiction, since Facilis died in the first century A.D.

Livonia then describes a visit by the historical character Allectus. He brings Constantius an urgent message from Rome, but despite the urgency he had "stopped at Gessoriacum to see Carausius, who is in charge of the fleet." This section is drawn from the same section of the novel, where the visit leads up to the takeover of rule in Britain by the rebellious Carausius, aided by Allectus. Iverson writes: "Livonia gives a basically accurate picture of this quite obscure historical event." Quite so, but only because the whole of the material rests on De Wohl's research.

In the same way, every single piece of information given out by Jane Evans can be traced to De Wohl's fictional account. She uses his fictional sequences in exactly the same order and even speaks of his fictional characters, such as Curio and Valerius, as if they were real people.

There are two minor differences worth noticing, since these involve her editing faculty. In the first instance, she takes the slight character Titus Albus, a Christian soldier willing to die for his faith, and recasts him as a tutor to Constantine. But only the name itself is taken, for all of Titus's feelings and actions are those of De Wohl's character Hilary. Hilary is converted to Christianity by Albanus, ordained as a priest by Osius, and killed during a violent campaign against his faith. All these things happen in turn to Jane Evans's Titus!

In the second instance, she takes another insignificant character, Livonia, described as "a charming creature with pouting lips and smouldering eyes," and amalgamates her with Helena. A composite character recast as the wife of Titus emerges. This new character is able to act as both an observer and as someone who voices Helena's sentiments, thus making the story that much fuller and far easier to relate.

This feat of editing reveals a little of the psychology behind these fantasies. For Hilary is the eminently desirable male in the novel, described as having "a beautiful honest face with eyes of a dreamer." He is also secretly in love with Helena. As Titus, he becomes the lover of Livonia of the pouting lips and smouldering eyes—in other words, of Jane Evans herself. And there we have all the combustible material that warmed a young girl's daydreams. And all inspired by an exciting historical novel.

In conclusion, I should emphasize that in investigating regressionist claims I chose the most difficult and best-known cases available. They had remained unchallenged for years and were regarded as impregnable. A BBC documentary team had checked them out in every detail. They were triumphantly marketed as "the most staggering evidence for reincarnation ever recorded . . . accounts so authentic that they can only be explained by the certainty of reincarnation." Yet in the end they turned out to be nothing but fantasies, pure and simple.

SCIENCE, PSEUDOSCIENCE, AND MYTHMONGERING
Maureen O'Hara

It's a fine thing to have an open mind—but not so open so as your brains fall out—Episcopalian Bishop.

I first became involved with the whole question of the relationship between science and pseudoscience and New Age[1] thinking when I was researching an article for the *Journal of Humanistic Psychology* debunking the then-popular "Hundredth Monkey" story—the widely promoted New Age myth that if enough monkeys could be persuaded to wash their sweet potatoes something called a "critical mass" would be formed, which would result in mind-to-mind knowledge transfer wherein all monkeys in and around Koshima Island would instantaneously take up potato washing. In that article I tried to show how the so-called "Hundredth Monkey Phenomenon" was a myth and a cryptofascist myth at that.[2] In another article for *JHP*, I argued that another New Age notion, Rupert Sheldrake's hypothesis of "morphic resonance,"[3] was not a fine example of "real new age science" (whatever that is), as had been suggested by New Age writer Ken Wilbur. I had argued that it was, in fact, reductionist pseudoscientific clap-trap, which had nothing at all to offer real students of human nature.[4] In both these articles and in subsequent writings and presentations for similar audiences I have tried to explore what for me are the more interesting, and I believe ultimately more important, psychological, political, and philosophical questions that emerge when we look at stories like the "Hundredth Monkey," theories like "morphic resonance," and the whole cultural phenomenon of so-called New Age thinking. In particular, I have

Maureen O'Hara is a practicing psychotherapist and a professor of Women's Studies at San Diego State University. The ideas in this essay were first presented to the members of the Association for Humanistic Psychology at its annual meeting in 1986.

tried to understand what it is that makes members of professional organizations like the Association for Humanistic Psychology so vulnerable to pseudoscientific scams, paranormal claims, quantum flim-flam, and all manner of psychological ideas and ideologies that are often based on nothing more than popular acclaim and successful marketing. How do we account for the enormous fascination and gullibility of a broad spectrum of well-educated, well-meaning, largely middle-class Americans when presented with claims of the miraculous, magical, or paranormal? What are we to make of the obvious fact that rational people can be so easily conned by Shirley MacLaine's "trance-channelers" or be so willing to hand over a thousand or so dollars to walk over "hot" embers?

I ask these questions as an insider, sympathetic—even enthusiastic—to the broader aims of those involved with humanistic approaches in psychology and with the consciousness movements. I have experienced many of the spiritual longings—and satisfactions—spoken of by such denizens of the New Age as Jean Houston and Ken Wilbur. For the last seventeen years I have worked all over the world with psychologist Carl Rogers, trying to put many of the principles highly prized by New Age writers to the test of concrete action. We have done this in villages in the Third World and in elite universities in Europe, and Rogers himself has taken the work to Moscow and South Africa. I make my living as a humanistic psychologist, and I teach feminist studies at a university. I also serve on the board of the Association for Humanistic Psychology and as associate editor of its journal.

It is precisely because I have such a stake in humanistic psychology, in what truly is a worldwide network of committed folks working in widely ranging settings to further humanistic values, that I think it is worthwhile—indeed urgent—to try to tease out some of the nonsense that has crept (flooded?) into humanistic psychology in recent years.

What began twenty-five years ago as a serious and successful challenge to Freudian and behaviorist orthodoxy in psychology quickly blossomed into a broader social movement calling for a greater democratization of American life. Humanistic psychology and its applied wing, the "human potential" movement, invented techniques, theories, and attitudes that transformed the way we think of counseling, education, and even business management. It is doubtful whether these ideas could have been so phenomenally successful if its early leaders had not been superb scholars and thinkers dedicated to research excellence.

The Rogerian idea, for example, that a therapist's warmth, acceptance, genuineness, and willingness to listen were all that were necessary for effective psychotherapy was considered radical when first proposed. Now these ideas are taught to every mental-health professional as the *sine qua non* of good therapeutic practice. Rogers's work had credibility with practicing professionals and established academic psychologists because he was a brilliant thinker who based his claims on concrete, practical knowledge, and subjected his hypotheses to the most rigorous scientific evaluation.

The best of humanistic psychology is very good and offers, in my view, one of the only visions of human possibilities with the potential to guide us toward the next century and beyond. But, if we are to realize this potential and not become bogged down in ultimately empty—though perhaps deeply comforting—superstition, if we are not to be lured into a metaphysical dead-end by New Age Pied Pipers, we will need to take a hard look at our gullibility.

My intention here is to speak to people who are sympathetic to the humanistic vision, even in its New Age persona, and yet are willing to consider the movement with a critical eye.

Professional Authority—Professional Responsibility

Although I have aimed my arguments toward readers who would approve of the aims and methods of humanistic psychology, I must acknowledge that much of what I want to say is applicable not only to them. Obviously it takes more than the five thousand members of an organization like the Association for Humanistic Psychology, for example, to make best-sellers out of books like Marilyn Ferguson's *Aquarian Conspiracy*, Fritjof Capra's *Tao of Physics*, Lyall Watson's *Lifetide*, and Rupert Sheldrake's *A New Science of Life*. Nor are we the only people who have been fooled by scams like the hundredth-monkey story; firewalking; "Senoi Dreamwork"; spoon-bending psychics; Carlos Casteneda's fantastic fabrications; mediums who claim to communicate with animals, visitors from far-off galaxies, dead relatives, and spirits of all manner of departed sages; and quackery both physiological and psychological. In many respects, humanistic psychologists are no different from perhaps the majority of people in American society. We all have, as William James once observed, a strong "will to believe," but we seem to have neither the will nor the intellectual discipline to critique our beliefs.

Despite its small size, the Association for Humanistic Psychology and its publications have had a disproportionately large impact on the cultural picture of late twentieth-century America. Its members have included Abraham Maslow, Carl Rogers, Rollo May, Gregory Bateson—all founders—as well as Fritjof Capra, Marilyn Ferguson, Charles Hamden-Turner, Jean Houston, Walter Truitt Anderson, Frances Vaughan, Michael Marien,

Jim Bugenthall, Virginia Satir, who are all active members today.

Our association is composed of bright, committed seekers dedicated to the advancement of human life through knowledge. In all our publications and public statements it is clear that members wish to be taken seriously as professional scholars with the authority to advance human knowledge. We ask that our utterances be given credence, be considererd valid and duly established as "real" by the lay public in the way that the reports of scientists are. A large proportion of our association's membership also offers services for a fee. A recent National Research Council report estimates that American corporations spend at least $30 billion on these kinds of services.

In claiming professional authority for their statements and propositions, members of a scholarly community tacitly agree to hold themselves and each other to higher standards of thinking, scholarly research, critical judgment, and professional integrity than is incumbent on the general public. In other words, when an organization or profession claims its truths are "established" and offers them to the public so it can disseminate the "new reality," they have an obligation to offer the public more than they can get in the *National Enquirer*.

How then are we to account for such a willingness on the part of serious people who are genuinely dedicated to search for truth to accept all manner of extraordinary and bogus claims with such eager enthusiasm?

The simple answer is that people are people. There is a great deal of research that shows that all people, but especially highly intelligent people, are easily taken in by all kinds of illusions, hallucinations, self-deceptions, and outright bamboozles—all the more so when they have a high investment in the illusion being true.

Many writers and speakers popular with New Age audiences are describing wondrous new powers that they believe are emerging in the human psyche. They herald new consciousness, new ways of perceiving reality, and so on. This is heady stuff. It is the kind of optimistic dream-spinning that drew me, as a young college teacher, out of the biological sciences and into the humanistic science of persons. But, if this capacity for wonderment is not to lead to a fool's paradise, or worse, I think we need to remind ourselves and each other that such openness also has its pitfalls. A short review of some of what we know about ourselves psychologically might illustrate just how vulnerable to perceptive errors we really are.

If I Hadn't Believed It, I Wouldn't Have Seen It

Our experience of reality can never be entirely accounted for by stimulus alone. It is always a construction based on our perceptions and interpretations of things—not the things alone.

Probably everyone has had the auditory hallucination of hearing a phone ring while in the shower, for example. The components of this hallucination are twofold. One element is perceptual set—the web of memories, concepts of reality, imaginations, and expectations we bring to any experience—the other is the actual here-and-now sensory excitation due to the effect of sound vibrations on sense organs. Part of our perceptual set might be the belief that someone "always calls when we are in the shower."[5] It is created through a combination of folklore and a process of paying more attention to experiences that conform to our beliefs than those that do not. We register hits and ignore misses. (In science-dominated, technological societies like ours, for example, "folklore sets" are frequently solidified by claims that there is "scientific" evidence for the phenomenon.)

This is not carelessness. Our perceptual capacities are designed to single out what is interesting and to ignore what isn't. They are also designed to construct coherence, predictability, and reasonableness out of ambiguous or chaotic stimuli. The sound of running water has sufficient ambiguity that the mindset can prevail over the physical stimulus and can create a ringing out of the frequencies present in the sound of running water. If one's folk belief is influenced by Alfred Hitchcock, the mind has no difficulty creating the sound of approaching footsteps out of the same water!

I clearly remember once as a child, the whole of England agonized for almost two weeks over the fate of Captain Carlson on the bridge of his badly listing *S. S. Flying Enterprise*. One evening on the way home from school the cumulus clouds above me seemed to me to be an exact replica of the doomed ship. I watched it fascinated, and when the cloud slowly rolled over in the sky I wept, "knowing" that Captain Carlson had perished. I learned on the next newsreels that in fact he had been rescued, but my experience had been so strong that I was unwilling to believe this good news.

The perpetuation of the "Hundredth Monkey" phenomenon myth within the New Age community gives another wonderful illustration of this process. At the time the story first appeared there was already a widely held pre-existing folk-belief that we were witnessing the dawn of the new age of aquarius, in which minority ideas might become universally accepted once a certain number, called a "critical mass," had been converted.[6] Then along came Lyall Watson supposedly producing objective scientific evidence of such a phenomenon in monkeys. This "scientific data" was used to bolster the collective perceptual set. Wherever groups of folks with New Age inclinations met, whether at an est seminar, an encounter group, a New Age gathering of some sort, if those assembled came to a consensus (a highly prized situation for most of them) and began to feel or think the same way about something, someone in the group would likely recount the monkey story. The group would count a "hit" and believe they now had more evidence for the "reality" of the phenomenon. All counterexamples would be ignored or rationalized, and other ambiguous stimuli—i.e., situations that are complex enough to read *anything* into—would be interpreted as examples of the phenomenon.

It should be easy to see how, if you take as your "field of data" something as vast as "modern culture," and if you come at it with a strong mindset, you will be able to discern some kind of "new process paradigm" for which you can find "supporting evidence." Only of course you didn't find it—you produced it!

We are all aware of how eyewitness reports of accidents or crimes vary a good deal.[7] There is also evidence that what is remembered of an accident will be greatly influenced by subsequent suggestion. In one experiment, when an interviewer suggested to witnesses of an accident that a blue car had been present, subsequent eyewitness descriptions included the blue car. In another experiment, graduate students were shown videotapes of a group meeting in which participants appeared only in silhouette. When they thought participant "Lou" was the only black in an otherwise white group, raters said Lou was very active, almost to the point of domination; when observers believed the group to be racially balanced, however, nothing unusual was noticed about Lou. This kind of "singling out the token" has been confirmed for other minorities and women.[8] Observations are usually biased in the direction of whatever belief the observer has about the situation.

We are easily fooled both by others and by ourselves. Professional magicians will tell you that the more intelligent a person is the more easily he or she can be fooled. When you point your finger, for example, an adult will look away from the finger to the point indicated, but a child and a dog will look at your finger. The magician's ability to fool the spectator lies in "leading his audience down a (conceptual) path but not going there himself."[9]

Another well-documented characteristic of the human mind is that, if presented with a conceptual or perceptual field with gaps in it, we will fill in the missing elements and we will believe that we have seen them. This is especially true of bright and agile minds. An agile mind will make connections where none is actually given. This is, of course, the basis of all creativity. The artist and scientist may begin with only the rudiments of an idea and be able to see within it the reality of the finished work. It is also the basis of much psychotherapy. Therapists help clients pull out seemingly disconnected images and memories which, at a moment of insight, suddenly become reorganized and elaborated into enlightening new understandings about their whole life predicament.

If a mindset is very strong it may even prevail over contradicting information that is not at all ambiguous, as shown in a recent experiment with students at California State University at Long Beach. To examine the willingness of people to accept claims of paranormal or psychic powers, two researchers had a young amateur magician perform for their class a short magic routine containing some of the standard "psychic" illusions—metal bending by mind power ("telekinesis" in the psi world), reading numbers while blindfolded (clairvoyance), and materializing sacred ashes from the palms of a young woman. Half the classes were told the magician was a conjurer who was going to perform magic tricks and who wanted to get feedback on his act. The other half were told he was a psychic and wanted feedback about his psychic powers. Singer and Benassi were stunned to find 77 percent of the students believed the magician's claim to be psychic on the basis of three simple magic tricks. They were even more stunned to learn that 65 percent of those who had been told Craig was a stage magician doing conjuring tricks still were convinced he was psychic.[10]

In the success of charlatans, fakes, quacks, and conjurors—whether consciously perpetrated, as with professional con-artists and entertainers, or innocently promoted by people who genuinely believe they are in the possession of special powers or have witnessed or discovered new realities—the greatest ally is the fallibility of human consciousness itself.

Openness—The Good News and the Bad News

We have very strong social needs to trust other people. As children we must learn from others. Vulnerable creatures like us could never learn all we need to know quickly enough to survive in a hostile environment were it not for trusting others to pass on what they know and believe. We are, therefore, especially open to people who create an aura of trustworthiness. Psychotherapists, physicians, educators, and parents all rely on trust to do their work. Successful psychics, telepaths, mediums, pseudoscientists, magicians, and con-artists also present the appearance of being trustworthy. Many are also very bright, handsome, and charismatic. The air of trustworthiness is often bolstered by biographical material indicating altruistic motives, aligning themselves with "good works" and keeping a financially modest profile, at least at first.[11]

Folks who are drawn to New Age ideas are unusually trusting people. They have enormous good-will, believe themselves to be nonjudgmental, and express faith in the basic goodness of people.[12] Implicit in their positive regard of human nature is the obvious imperative to place a high value on acceptance, open-mindedness, and willingness to give others the benefit of the doubt, especially those who bring good news. This creates a wonderful environment for trial balloons, where new ideas—whimsical, serious, inspirational, foolish, trivial, and important—can be generated, entertained, and explored. New Age gatherings are hospitable to all kinds of new ideas. A list of conference speakers and workshops sponsored and promoted by the Association for Humanistic Psychology over the last twenty-five years, for example, will reveal just how hospitable.[13]

While acknowledging its positive aspects—who can say anything against tolerance?—there is a major problem in being so undiscriminating. Without reliable, agreed-upon criteria with which to test and evaluate these trial balloons, potentially valuable ideas and innovations cannot be sorted from those without merit. After a while, trial balloons become simply balloons— pretty but disposable. This puts anyone seriously interested in furthering studies in humanistic psychology between a rock and a hard place. Some choose to avoid the mess by invalidating the whole field, declaring humanistic psychology dead, killed off by the "New Age" fringe within it. This is the choice being made by more and more of the established graduate schools of psychology as they turn back to psychoanalysis and ego-psychology in the clinical schools and to cognitive and behavioral psychology in the research schools. But those who, like me, still believe humanistic scholarship has something significant and distinct to contribute to the search for under-standing and knowledge of the human condition and who wish to ask the kind of questions only the humanistic movement within psychology has addressed, there is no current alternative but to be willing to swallow an awful lot of chaff along with our whole-wheat.

Science and Certainty

When I speak at gatherings of humanistic psychologists, I usually encounter considerable anti- and pseudoscientific sentiments. I frequently find myself having to explain to the New Age contingent of my humanistic brethren what "science" really is. The image of the mainstream scientist held by most New Agers is of a person, usually a white male, with no feelings, no spiritual yearnings, and who is probably oblivious to both the darker applications of his craft and to the magical possibilities of the human mind. The image of "science" is of a completely rational, reductionistic power-trip where "linear or left-brained thinking" and closed-mindedness predominate. At times the New Age response to science can become downright hostile. On a telephone call recently one New Age advocate, wanting a place in a conference I was working on, called me a narrow-minded dogmatist; my attitudes, he felt, were divisive and demonstrated dangerous elitism.

Nothing could be further from the truth. Science, as a way of apprehending nature, was invented for people exactly like today's seekers by people like them. Folks who wish to understand their world, to look beyond the present limited visions, who wish to open themselves to novelty and to creative achievement, to dream of new worlds and then work to bring them about, need some kind of science. We humanistic psychologists and New Agers need it precisely because of our openness and because, like all agile-minded people, we can be so easily fooled. If we are not to exist in a confusing "Alice in Wonderland" world of uncertainty, where real and imagined are interchangeable, where we are, like the schizophrenic, at the mercy of our imaginations, prejudices, and ignorances—as well as of those who would bamboozle us for their own purposes—we need a way to separate what might "possibly be true from what is actually true."[14]

This problem of uncertainty as to what and what is not "real" has been with us since the dawn of culture, but before the rise of modern science the problem was taken care of for laypeople by varied priesthoods vested with the authority to speak for God and to declare truth for everyone else. Entry to a priest class was always closely restricted by the ruling classes, and access to their knowledge was jealously guarded. In Christian Europe, for example, where scholarship was restricted to monasteries and Christian-run universities, no infidels or women needed apply!

With the Copernican revolution this began to change. Over the three hundred or so years since the beginning of the scientific revolution there has been a steady erosion of priestly authority in matters of what is true, natural, preternatural, supernatural, and divine. We have seen in its place the rise in secular authority in general and of scientific authority in particular. The will and courage to doubt—often at great personal cost both social and psychological—that lies at the heart of the scientific quest led to the development of processes with which to systematically question and evaluate the grounds for beliefs, collect evidence, suspect one's prejudices, hypothesize, test and theorize, and so on, all the processes that we now recognize as comprising the scientific approach to the quest for knowledge.

Authority to name truth was wrested away from dogmatism and papal fiat with the hope that universal, impersonally derived, abstract principles—some kind of litmus test for truth—could be discovered that would on the one hand free us forever from the priestly tyranny of, say, an Inquisition, a Khomeini's Iran, or a Stalin's Soviet Union—worlds of "one truth"—and protect us on the other hand from the terrifying uncertainty of a world of hopeless subjectivity with authority vested nowhere.

This quest for a value-free science was so spectacularly productive for almost three centuries that by the late nineteenth century scientific truth was popularly considered to be synonymous with "reality." By the 1920s we had gone full circle from faith in papal infallibility to a hope of infallibility for scientific objectivity.

We are all now well aware that events in subsequent decades of this century have scuttled this positivist project, especially—but not only—in the social sciences. Undermined by discoveries in physics, mathematics, thinking in history, philosophy of science, and discoveries in the social sciences, especially psychology, claims that science can deliver absolute certainty have turned out to be overstated. We now know that there is no way to escape uncertainty in any fundamental sense. Having grown beyond childlike reliance on priestly guidance and reassurance, having discovered our hopes in positivist science were exaggerated, our vulnerability is once more exposed. Only this time it is worse, since not only do our ultimate questions remain unanswered but we have lost faith in our faith. Theodore Roszak has suggested that by its phenomenal success science robbed modern people of their age-old access to the sacred, via the great religions, but failed to fill the void as nineteenth century scientific optimism had promised. We hunger to feel at home in the universe and find that neither traditional religion nor modern science can help.[15]

Myth Mongering in Uncertain Times

It is in this abyss of uncertainty—which most of us find profoundly anxiety-provoking—that the pseudopriest and the pseudoscientist find a ready audience. It is no coincidence that within a community like the consciousness movement, which had its origins in a period of history in which all established authority was suspect and which elevated subjectivity almost to sacredness, that both pseudoscience and pseudoreligion flourish. Nor should it surprise us that within the movement and within the broader society in general the most successful delusions are those that claim to draw authority from both traditional religious and scientific sources. Parapsychologists, UFO believers, Scientologists, esties, spiritists, creationists, new-paradigmers, aquarian conspirators, and mythmongers of all stripes can be easily identified by their generous citation of scientific authorities—preferably physicists or Nobel Laureates—and of sacred texts—preferably oriental. They can also be identified by their wholesale disregard for the basic principles, tenets, disciplines, and axioms of the very traditions from which they borrow authority, and by their willingness to support their claims by selecting disembodied bits and pieces of evidence from very wide ranges of sources that neither they nor their audiences are in any position to evaluate. This form of intellectual sleight-of-hand identifies the "pseudo" status of many writers popular with New Age adherents.

In both science and established spiritual disciplines adepts rarely wander far from their own disciplinary neighborhood. They are too well aware of how hard it is to remain current in even a small area of study. The fabric of a broad discipline such as biology, for example, is made up of a patchwork of overlapping competencies with folks in neighboring patches *perhaps* able to engage in fruitful dialogue. Those in more distant areas have no choice but to take the pronouncements of other scientists on a kind of faith. For the whole thing to hold together and for real research to proceed, it must be possible to trust the integrity of countless unknown others. Unburdened by the disciplinary realities of ever doing any real research, pseudoscientists feel free to wander far and wide, to cite willy-nilly from fields as different as physics, astrology, and embryology. They strip knowledge of both its context and concreteness, turning it into "data" or bits of information that can be recombined without regard to any disciplinary integrity, rules of evidence, attention to questions of logical coherence, validity, or counter-evidence.

The work of New Age or "Aquarian" author Marilyn Ferguson is a good example of what mght be called "recombinant information." In her keynote speech at the San Diego conference of the Association for Humanistic Psychology she said that she doesn't take advice—she takes *information*. What she appears to mean by this is that she strips the statements others offer her of their moral and purposive contexts and transforms "advice"—a human value-ladened proposition—into "data." That was one of the scarier things I had heard in a long time! With this much freedom, creatures with minds like ours—who can make a telephone ring out of running water or a psychic out of an amateur stage magician—should be able to come up with any position we want. And, of course, we do. Ferguson's book, *The Aquarian Conspiracy*, and her magazine, *Brain-Mind Bulletin*, are nothing more than pastiches of such "data" arranged in accordance with whatever idea she wishes to promulgate.

It was Ferguson's *Brain-Mind Bulletin*, in fact, that brought wide New Age attention to Lyall Watson's story about the "Hundredth Monkey Phenomenon." The magazine's report referred to Watson as a biologist, when in fact he was known for his books on the occult. The *Brain-Mind Bulletin* writer also omitted, from an otherwise verbatim quote from *Lifetide*, a statement by Watson that he was basing his ideas on speculations and "piecing together stories that scientists are too afraid to publish." Ferguson is obviously more excited by bold ideas that can be fitted directly into her millennial vision than by scientific truths corroborated by careful lab work. She seems quite willing to erase the line between science and fiction and, what is worse, does not seem to recognize the sinister possibilities of such suspension of disciplined thought. Nor, it seems, do her enthusiastic audiences of New Agers who, in San Diego at least, roared their approval. In her disregard for traditional methods of inquiry and basing her assertions on some individualistic view of reality, Ferguson is clearly an heir to the antiauthoritarian push for the "personal" that has characterized at least some of the humanistic movement in psychology. This endears her to many in the consciousness movement who regard her confident self-assertion as a sign of intellectual courage and creativity.

Subjectivity and Power

In their legitimate rejection of the pursuit of a kind of dehumanized "objectivity" in the study of human beings, psychologists like Abraham Maslow and Carl Rogers stressed the crucial importance of phenomenological analysis of subjective experience—an "insider's view"—in what they hoped would be a "new science of persons." When they decided it was time to abandon their attempt to gain scientific legitimacy for psychological research by aping the methods of physics or biology, they embarked upon a radical project to create a whole new psychology based on holistic phenomenological studies capable of apprehending the glorious complexity of authentic human existence. They struck a culturewide nerve of alienation in the American psyche. Their bold, rebellious words and their antiauthoritarian methodologies were taken immediately to heart by a generation that was refusing to be "folded, spindled, or mutilated."

Discussion of the social and historical contexts of the campus movement in the Sixties are beyond the scope of this chapter, but we should remember here that a large proportion of the people who today strongly identify with New Age ideas were on college campuses during this time. At a stage in their lives when their minds were at their most awake, when the "learning curve" was at its peak, this generation was being urged by its leaders to "question authority," not to "trust anyone over thirty," to "lose their mind and come to their senses," and to "turn on, tune in, and drop out." They were told the only trustworthy authority was individual authority and the only reliable truth individual truth. They read books with titles like *If You Meet the Buddha on the Road, Kill Him, Burn This Book*, and *The Politics of Experience*. They were challenging (with justification) academic curricula that defended a world-view dominated by white middle-class males and pressuring colleges and universities to establish women's- and ethnic-studies departments.

There was much talk of "becoming a person," much experimentation with "peak experiences" as first college students, then others, hungrily gobbled up the outpourings of books, seminars, and workshops designed to realize human potential. The idea took hold in the popular psyche that we were all being held back from our true possibilities by oppressive systems of education, cultural practices, and mores, by sexism, racism, and "left-brained linear thinking" in the form of big science, big government, and militarism. And, since the whole established culture was deemed tainted by the vested interests of the "oppressor," the only standards upon which we felt we could base our sense of "truth" or "reality," or determine our decisions and actions, became our own, inner, private sense of rightness. This internal or (as it was called) "intuitive" sense of truth was no longer just an important source of data among many, but in a world in which every other authority had been discredited it had become the *only* source. Whether this source was reliable or not, and I hope I have shown that it often was not, was beside the point, since by this time no other acceptable basis for certainty existed.

What none of us foresaw in our enthusiasm to proclaim the personal, however, was that in a world where an insider's view becomes the *only* view, when each individual's private truth is considered to have the same status as everyone else's, when we ignore the problem of false consciousness, then there is, in fact, no truth at all. There is only *power*—power of the press, of persuasion, coercion, and ultimately of force.

To show what I mean, let's imagine a society where there was the kind of merging of science and religion hoped for by many New Age believers. How would such a community approach the problem of AIDS, for example? One person might promote the "virus" idea, another the "God's curse" idea. Someone else might learn in a dream that AIDS is caused by an energy imbalance, another that it was brought in from some other planet as a vehicle by which to learn something very profound about the relationship between human sexuality and "life beyond the body." If, in our mythical New Age community, everyone's individual truth is equally valid, how would the group go about deciding how limited resources would be spent in response to the epidemic? What would happen in such a community, of course, is that the idea with the most politically powerful adherents would prevail. So, let's say that in this community it is the "channelers" who have the most respected place. They have learned from their spirit sources on a far-off planet that AIDS symptoms occur only in those earthlings who have low consciousness and who are prone to "negative thoughts." The community resources are to be mobilized to provide "positive thinking" workshops for every man, woman, and child and to reprogram the sick. The "virus" proponents, in turn, would try to amass "evidence," but no one would know what to make of it. Who has ever seen a "virus"? How could something as cosmically beautiful as lovemaking be responsible? Eventually the virologists might become fanatical, take to the labs, and wait out the inevitable (in their superstitious eyes at least) demise of the channelers. They would teach scientific thinking and practice to their children and hope that one day they might be part of a "paradigm shift" in the direction of rational thought. They would probably dedicate themselves to finding ways to discredit the channelers and to weaken their power.

To some degree the modern world already shares some characteristics with our mythic community. The ideal of one absolute truth has given way to the idea that different spheres of life and different communities can base their understandings and explanations of things on differing "stories" that give coherence to their experience. But coherence is not the only necessity of a system of thought. At some point we need to be able to select from alternative stories, stories that—as far as we can tell—correspond to realities we have no part in creating. Call them "facts," call them "universal realities," call them "truth," call them what you like, but some realities exist outside of subjective experience and some stories are truer than others. We have no way of separating those independent realities upon which we can base public actions from private intuitions other than by a system of collective critical and public evaluation of all claims on our belief. If we want a world— as I do—in which we can all be open to the whole of creation, to let the universe speak to us directly, and in which each person can become a vehicle for truth, an ideal I also share with New Agers, then we will need to be able to separate mythic truth from scientific truth.

It is not at all clear that New Agers will be able to do this. The problem they face is that they have no obvious theoretical way to go about this, and the further away New Age thinking gets from its origins in philosophy and research-based psychology, the more difficult becomes the task.

In the early days of the human potential movement the individual and social levels of human life were examined together. Much energy was devoted to considering the personal effects on public life as well as the effects of larger social systems and structures on intrapsychic experience. The slogan of the times was "the personal is political." As early as 1972, however, when I was beginning my doctoral studies in clinical psychology, a schism was already appearing between "politicals"—those influenced by Marx and Hegel, who saw private consciousness as the product of social realities like sexism, racism, economics, and so on—and the "experientials"— influenced by Kierkegaard, Freud, Rogers, and Maslow—who felt that societies are reflective of the individual consciousness of their members. The "politicals" believed if we made laws that changed the structure of society so that the poor would be fed and the oppressed emancipated, a New Age would be upon us in which individual and collective consciousness could flower. The "experientials," on the other hand, believed that if we were all to resolve our internal conflicts, expand our consciousness through psychotherapy, meditation, or some other consciousness discipline, we could transcend fear and negativity. This approach would foster the growth of individuals who could parent better, teach better, manage better, and govern better, and reset social priorities so that the poor would be fed and the oppressed emancipated.

Yet another issue upon which people with a humanistic vision differed— and still do—is the question of whether or not human nature is essentially good. One view—represented in recent dialogues by Carl Rogers—holds that human nature is basically trustworthy. If left alone, the theory goes, humans will move towards health, growth, wholeness, and altruism. Evil, in this view, is seen as an unfortunate maladaptation to a society that fears human possibilities and so represses them. An opposing view, represented in the dialogue by Rollo May, argues that human nature is neither good nor bad *per se*. May's view follows more closely the existentialist position that human consciousness (as compared to nonhuman) implies free will and the necessity of consciously choosing good over evil, by embracing Being rather than nihilism. Combinations of these views can be summarized in the grid below.

"politicals"
focus on external forces

Revolutionary social activists suspicious of psychotherapy as "blaming the victim"	Social analysis and introspection. Criticizes social structures *and* self-deception.
positive nature	**existential choice**
trusts and accepts	**alert to false consciousness**
"New Age" consciousness movement	existential therapists

"experientials"
focus on inner experience

When the "essentially positive and trusting" view of human nature is held together with the inner directed "experiential" position, as is the case for most New Agers, the whole belief system folds in upon itself and ends up in a state of acritical solipsism. There is simply no need, if you are a believer, for any form of self-doubt, for external verification of personally held truth or for social structures and institutional practices that would contain, regulate, or arbitrate individual consciousness or actions based in it.

Within the Association for Humanistic Psychology in particular, and within the broader social movement it helped fuel, it seems the "experientials" have won out over the "politicals," and the "trust human nature" belief has won out over the position of existential choice. Certainly, if we look at who draws the biggest crowds at conferences and which books are the most widely read, it is clear that the New Age voices predominate. (The revolutionaries, by the way, have long since left for more fruitful fields, like Critical Theory, and are now nowhere to be seen or heard in humanistic psychological circles.)

Throwing out the Bathwater and Cleaning up the Baby

Is there any way the humanistic vision can be rescued from these built-in tendencies toward hopeless solipsism? By virtue of our human nature and the ideals of our culture we are prone to all manner of self-deception, illusion, and quackery; and we have been encouraged by history to look beyond traditional authorities and orthodoxies for knowledge. Does that leave us in such conceptual murkiness that we must finally admit, as many critics claim, that the humanistic vision has been irrevocably compromised by the New Age movement and is intellectually bankrupt? Should we follow the universities and return to the apparent solidity of psychoanalysis (despite its obvious theoretical difficulties for women) or to empiricism (despite its emphasis on behavioral control)? Should we accept that we are all individually lost and turn to those charismatic speakers and personalities among us who give the appearance of knowing what is going on? Or perhaps we should simply withdraw from philosophical discussions of truth and declare everything metaphor. If deception works to achieve the ends we want, shouldn't we use it?

No doubt some people will follow each of these options, but when we consider the example of our mythical New Age community facing its AIDS epidemic, it should become clear that not all of these options are equivalent and *none* of them would be much help in the face of a real problem like the one we consider. Our community needs some way for the truth about the epidemic and its viral origins to surface and prevail against majority prejudice and vested power. It needs to know—with as much confidence as possible—the basis upon which precious resources should be spent. It needs processes that can be seen to be more or less impartial—however imperfect that impartiality turns out to be in practice—and that can be seen to have validity outside of and across differing belief systems, so that even communities who base their world-view upon different articles of faith are willing to give them credence. In other words, *the community needs some form of established science.*[16] It also needs democratic institutional structures that can protect minority constituencies from groups with bigger sticks so that unpopular views can get a hearing.

A volume like this one may be part of such a path out of the murkiness, and in my view it offers a great deal to the cause of humanism. It represents a willingness on the part of the writers to seriously evaluate the claims and aspirations of all—including New Agers—who feel in their souls that something is very wrong with the world we have created and so explore new realms of consciousness and new possibilities for our global collective. But, at the same time it also recognizes that in a world in which the search for externally located absolute truth has given way to an intersubjective, cogenerated view, criticism and debate are perhaps the only ways we have to separate show from substance.

I have been a strong advocate for recommitment, in humanistic psychology, to an ideal of disciplined scholarship. While I agree with those who caution against reactionaryism and locking ourselves into an empty (and dehumanizing) search for scientific certainty, I nonetheless believe we need to cultivate what may best be described as a scientific attitude. In addition to our justified suspicion of reductionism, our prizing of openness, creativity, and curiosity, we must also develop competency in logic, criticism, and evaluation that are suitable for our field. Open-ended investigation of something like "channelling," for instance, may reveal unfamiliar dimensions of consciousness, altered states of awareness, or deep psychological realities. We might gain understanding of the phenomenon as a response to social pain, a legitimate (yet futile) revolt against nihilistic forces at large in mechanized society, as a symptom of alienation of people stripped of any other sources of self-affirmation. Whatever approach we choose—whether phenomenological, interpretive, or experimental—we need to ground our investigations in thoughtful and healthy skepticism.

I would like to see us rededicate ourselves to an unfinished task, one that is (however distorted and derailed it has become) at the heart not only of the New Age vision but of the American democratic ideal: the creation of a world in which individual persons can be nourished and cherished by a society whose basic sustaining beliefs, structures, and institutions strive to support its multiple and varied constituencies in ways that are just and nonexploitative with regard for both persons and nature and wherein—in the long run at least—the ideal of truth, however imperfect, will have a chance to prevail over prejudice, however comforting.

I firmly believe that progress will not come from as-yet-unknown magical powers, from messages "channelled" from dead people or extraterrestrials. If progress comes at all, it will come from the concerted actions of countless ordinary folks on this planet struggling together with the concrete dilemmas of existence.

From our deeper, perhaps inarticulate—some might say *religious*—selves may come visions of imaginary futures wherein suffering ends, death is conquered (or its sting soothed), joy and plenty are universal, and wherein each person born may live a fully human existence. But if we are to bring these imaginary worlds into reality, it will take more than visions—it will also take well-articulated ideas based in sound research. We would make a good start by telling the pseudoscientists, con-artists, mythmongers, and other silver-tongued snake-oil salesmen we don't need them and by bidding them a tolerant but firm *adieu*.

Notes

1. The term *New Age* is somewhat vague; but, since I use it throughout, I want at least to sketch a broad description if not a precise definition. New Age thinking is a fundamentally optimistic set of beliefs that focuses on such questions as expanded consciousness, human transcendence, ecological awareness, and global peace. It particularly emphasizes the possibility (some would claim *inevitability*) that human consciousness is in the process of undergoing a "paradigm shift," in which old ways of knowing—identified as rational, Newtonian, capitalistic, competitive, violent, left-brained, masculine, and materialistic—will give way to a new world where there is integration of masculine and feminine, which is cooperative, nonviolent, intuitive, Einsteinian, and spiritual. Its view of human nature is essentially positive, attributing evil deeds to maladaptive responses to an oppressive culture. People who hold New Age beliefs tend to be interested in extraordinary human capacities like ESP, psychic phenomena, and mediumship. They embrace and go far beyond Maslow's ideal of a fully actualized person, or Rogers' "person of tomorrow," believing that enormous new powers—especially of the mind—are about to become manifest as humankind makes a large evolutionary leap. New Agers tend to hold a combination of religious beliefs, such as reincarnation, karma, Taoism, Zen, spiritism, animism, and shamanism, yet they reject Christian fundamentalism, Catholicism, and Judaism. Books and authors recently influential among New Agers include Marilyn Ferguson's *The Aquarian Conspiracy*, Shirley MacLaine's *Out on a Limb*, Fritjof Capra's *Tao of Physics* and *The Turning Point*, Gary Zukav's *Dancing Wu Li Masters*, Ken Keyes's *The Hundredth Monkey*,

Rupert Sheldrake's *New Science of Life*, Ken Wilbur's *Up From Eden*, and Jean Houston's *The Possible Human*, among many others.

2. Maureen O'Hara, "Of Myths and Monkeys: A Critical Look at the Theory of Critical Mass," *Journal of Humanistic Psychology*, Vol. 25, No. 1, 61–78.

3. The main thrust of the hypothesis proposed that once "a form" (a term that for Sheldrake encompassed things as different as a five-digit vertebrate limb, an architectural design, a molecular structure, and an ideology) has occurred, it is more likely to occur again. This is due, according to Sheldrake, to subtle nonenergetic forces that he calls "morphogenetic fields" (after a concept in embryology), which directs nature down already trodden paths by a yet-to-be discovered process of resonance with forms already in existence.

4. Maureen O'Hara, "Reflections on Sheldrake, Wilbur, and New Science," *Journal of Humanistic Psychology*, Vol. 24, No. 2, 116–120.

5. J. W. Connor, "Misperception, Folk Belief, and the Occult: A Cognitive Guide to Understanding," *The Skeptical Inquirer*, 8 (Summer 1984): 344–354.

6. We had experienced the "Summer of Love" and the musical "Hair"; encounter groups were ubiquitous. The educated middle-class was flocking to Esalen, following the Maharishi, listening to John Lennon, and reading Carlos Casteneda. Marilyn Ferguson had published *The Aquarian Conspiracy*, in which she promoted the idea that there was a global movement of "New Age" consciousness. Baghwan Rajneesh was proclaiming the end of culture and the birth of an entirely new form of human. Werner Erhardt was promoting the idea of "critical mass" in est's "Hunger Project." Fritjof Capra, in *The Tao of Physics*, had suggested some kind of equivalence between subatomic physics and human consciousness, and Gary Zukav's *Dancing Wu-Li Masters* had given the general public the idea that Werner Heisenberg's principle of uncertainty implied that thought transfer across space and across time were within the realm of scientifically established possibilities. Terms like "critical mass" were taken out of the specialized language of nuclear weaponry and into the language of the "New Age." Thomas Kuhn had introduced the concept of "paradigm shift," supporting the idea that modern science of mind might be in a "pre-paradigmatic" state. All these cultural elements were quite familiar to those in the "consciousness movement." We were eagerly expecting news of a "paradigm shift."

7. See E. F. Loftus, *Eyewitness Testimony* (Cambridge, Mass.: Harvard University Press, 1979).

8. See Rosabeth M. Kanter, "Women and the Structure of Organizations: Explorations in Theory and Behavior," in *Another Voice*, Marcia Millman and Rosabeth M. Kanter, eds. (Garden City, N.Y.: Anchor/Doubleday, 1975).

9. H. W. Ganoe and J. Kirwan, "Magicians, Scientists, and Physics: The Foot is Quicker Than the Mouth," *The Skeptical Inquirer*, 8 (Winter 1984), 133–37.

10. B. Singer and V. A. Benassi, "Fooling Some of the People All of the Time," *The Skeptical Inquirer*, 5 (Winter 1980–81), 17–24.

11. This might be changing in the "go for it" eighties, where financial success

itself is often regarded as a sign of credibility. New Agers did not seem to begrudge Baghwan Rajneesh his Rolls Royces, and, recently, Shirley MacLaine has made it part of her pitch that in her personal struggle between spirituality and materialism she has come down on the side of materialism. This echoes the direction of the flock of New Age evangelist Terry Cole-Whittaker, who can be identified anywhere in San Diego county by their bumper stickers proclaiming "Prosperity—Your Divine Right."

12. Critics of the New Age often point out that this tolerance and faith does not seem to extend to scientists and technologists, militarists, Republicans, and the religious right.

13. Conferences have included Gestalt astrology, Scientology, "past-life regression," "Lunaception," "tantric medicine," a West African voodoo healer, rebirthing, spirit-painting through a medium, Rajneesh body-work, ARICA, "crystal healing," aura-reading, shamanism of all sorts, "trance-channeling," as well as work that, while on the fringe at the time it was first presented, has subsequently become integrated into more mainstream psychological and medical practice, such as bioenergetics, acupuncture, psychodrama, gestalt therapy, Tai Chi and Akido, humanistic education, relationship enrichment, stress reduction through meditation, and many health and nutrition approaches that have stood the test of subsequent scientific evaluation. In the early days, for instance, conferences like these were the only places to get a hearing for suggestions that mood and attitude may have clinical effects on the immune system.

14. See F. Jacob, *The Possible and the Actual* (New York: Pantheon, 1982).

15. See Theodore Roszak, "In Search of the Miraculous," *Harpers*, January 1981.

16. About the word *science*. I am aware that there are very good arguments for leaving the word to those disciplines and questions in which the ideals of objectivity, replicability, quantifiability, and predictability are appropriate and finding another word for the project of human inquiry. I personally lean towards this position, preferring words like "studies," "inquiry," or "scholarship." I leave this important discussion for some other occasion.

OUT OF THE BODY?

Susan Blackmore

People have strange experiences.

And people who work at developing their awareness and insight have experiences that can seem especially strange. Being human, we start to seek explanations. But experiences of *any* kind are private and hard to describe—and most explanations offered for them are pitifully inadequate. Our challenge, then, is to explain our strange experiences adequately, not to explain them away.

Two Traditional Traps

Strange experiences can be alluring and rewarded socially. Perhaps most alluring of all is the possibility of having inexplicable experiences and then being able to explain them. At the crudest, this could be finding that something is excitingly "inexplicable by science" (seeing "auras," for example) and then proceeding to offer "explanations" based on nebulous concepts like "energy fields," "vibrations," and so on. At its most sophisticated, there is parapsychology's concept of "the paranormal." Paranormal phenomena are defined negatively, as some kind of interchange with the environment that cannot be accounted for by the recognized senses and physics. This kind of explanation comes perilously close to defining the paranormal as inexplicability itself—and yet parapsychology *does* seek explanations for strange phenomena. While parapsychology is a scientific endeavor with an altogether more sophisticated approach than any of the popular cults, it shares with them the tension between inexplicability and explanation.

Susan Blackmore is the world's leading expert on out-of-body experiences. Her *Beyond the Body* and *Adventures of a Parapsychologist* are seminal works in the history of parapsychology, challenging the field itself with a high level of scientific rigor and psychological insight.

Strange experiences are also alluring as signs of "personal development." Such experiences may indeed occur during "spiritual progress," but it is all too easy to confuse the signs for the progress itself and end up trying to acquire strange experiences like cash. (Everybody knows that, when telling stories, the stranger the story the more impressed the audience.)

Numerous spiritual traditions have warned their adherents to avoid these two powerful traps—facile explanations and the allure of strange experience. To the Buddhist monk-in-training the danger is straying from the path to enlightenment. For Western Man in the 1990s the danger will be of becoming embroiled in pseudoscientific explanations and the quest for experiences that seem to confirm them. For the former it is a matter of faith and for the latter an empirical question, whether there is a path and whether special experiences lie along it. Perhaps both ways lead to the same place. Certainly both must avoid these traps.

Three Kinds of Explanation

In dealing with the occult and with inexplicable experience generally—three kinds of explanations (or nonexplanations) are typically used:

1. *Occult and pseudoscientific nonexplanations.* These range from the trivial (like "other dimensions" or "vibration rates") through the interestingly unworkable (like theosophy's "astral body"), to the almost convincing (like the "observational theories of psi"). These concepts are helpful to the extent that they attempt to provide detailed constructs to account for experience. Superficially at least, they *do* seem to explain some strange experiences; they can therefore be very satisfying to some people. However, occult and pseudoscientific nonexplanations usually assume that the phenomena are explicable only by positing a revolution in science or some totally new theory. Almost invariably they are couched in scientific terms and use lots of technical phrases; but they fail to do any real scientific work. Although sometimes these revolutionary concepts are testable, when tests fail they become highly flexible, eventually retreating to untestable positions. In other words, it is impossible to make any progress with them.

2. *Dismissive and unscientific explanations.* These are no more helpful than occult and pseudoscientific explanations, as they argue that the phenomena are not what they seem—they are "just" hallucinations, imagery, error, or fraud. At their worst these explanations say nothing at all. At their best they provide a starting point for something better. An example is the "theory" that near-death experiences are due to cerebral anoxia—that is, lack of oxygen to the brain. On the surface this statement sounds "scientific," but it explains nothing. It could, however, be the basis for explaining why

(for example) images of tunnels and not oceans emerge from oxygen-starved brains. With some important exceptions, such crudely skeptical approaches add little to our understanding. Indeed, to people familiar with the experiences, they miss the point entirely. They may be scientific in the limited sense that they relate to other areas of science, but often they, too, fail to provide testable predictions. Furthermore, they are no fun, lacking the curiosity so necessary to making real progress in the sciences.

3. *Constructive explanations—or real science.* A third kind of explanation, possible but rare, provides a constructive approach that demystifies strange experiences but does justice to their nature at the same time. From considering the previous kinds of nonexplanations we can see what the criteria for a truly valuable explanation should be. First, it should account for all the phenomenology of the experiences. That is, it should produce recognition in the people who have the experiences and help them to understand, accept, and possibly develop them. Second, it should succeed in accounting for the phenomena by building on (rather than rejecting) other areas of science. Third, it should provide testable predictions.

As we have seen, occult nonexplanations fail on the second and usually third counts. Skeptical nonexplanations fail on the first.

It is my contention that, in the end, a kind of complete explanation— an explanation whose understanding is equivalent to having the experience itself—is possible. This kind of understanding is not possible so long as one is bound by pseudoscientific notions such as "thought forms," "energy fields," "vibration rates," "magnetic influences," and others often found in New Age literature. Nor is it possible by dismissing the experiences and their effects as "just imagination." A constructive skepticism must be true to the phenomena as well as scientific.

It is not my purpose here to address directly the many kinds of explanations or theories proposed, although I shall do so incidentally. Nor shall I dwell on the nature of self-development. Instead, I wish to concentrate on the strange experiences themselves. It has long been believed, and there is now good reason to concur, that self-development naturally gives rise to a progression of ways of being and new kinds of experience (Wilber, Engler, and Brown 1986). What follows are just some of the many kinds of experiences that often occur along the way. They are roughly ordered, in that the earlier ones are accessible to most people who use simple procedures (like relaxation, hypnosis, or many other New Age techniques), while the later ones usually occur only after more extensive training. Having said that, however, I should add that any can arise spontaneously. Indeed, some of the later ones form the core of naturally occurring mystical experiences (James 1908). Others occur as part of the near-death experience (Lundahl 1982). So, the ordering is far from rigid.

Bright Lights, Big Tingles

It is easy to induce minor perceptual phenomena. The main requirements? Be relaxed and keep still. It is astounding how complex the procedures used by some psychic training systems are—often they serve only to conceal the very simplicity of what is needed. The very simplest (though not the quickest or easiest) way to induce such phenomena is by "open" meditations— that is, just sitting still with one's eyes open and "watching" one's breath. Within a short time, if the eyes are kept still, the visual world begins to change. The patterns on the carpet begin to dance. Colors suddenly flash before you, then they disappear. The whole room suddenly seems to blank out and then re-emerge; or objects within it come and go, sometimes even becoming transparent. Tinglings in the hands, feet, or base of the spine feel like currents of electricity. One's body can seem to shrink, grow, or start to float.

What are these sensations? In Zen they are referred to as *makyo*— which means *illusion*. They appear when the meditation is going well, but with more practice they disappear or they can be ignored. LeShan (1974) considers them one of many ways in which we avoid the hard discipline of meditation—just one more thing to distract the untrained mind from simply watching the breath. How can they be explained? As usual, there are three ways. First, it is easy to use cheap analogies to produce ridiculous theories. If a tingling feels like "a flow of energy," one can invent some "new" kind of energy and describe the purported paths along which it flows. From this beginning entire techniques can easily be built up to encourage this "new energy" to "flow." If these techniques stick to a few simple rules of imagery and relaxation, they will really work—in the sense that they *will* produce more tingles. To the unwary, this will seem to confirm the theory. These energies, however, have either evaded attempts at scientific detection or are *defined* as undetectable. Similarly, objects disappearing or becoming transparent can be "explained" in terms of gaining "new vision" or "true sight" into another world.

The second, dismissive approach is simply to call all the phenomena "imagination" and forget about them. This approach says nothing useful to people who have the experience, and it fails entirely to account for the experience's many odd particulars: Why, for example, do tingles occur more often in the classical "chakra" positions than elsewhere, or why do objects fade out but don't turn upsidedown?

The third, constructive approach is to hunt down the experiences' origin in the perceptual system. In the case just described, it is not hard. The visual phenomena arise out of how the visual system is constructed.

Vision requires rapidly changing stimuli. Receptor cells in the retina respond only to changes in brightness over a small area. If a constant input is received, adaptation rapidly sets in and the cells stop responding. A common instance of this phenomenon is the *after-image*. If you stare at a bright light for a few seconds and then move your eyes, you will see a dark shape in place of the object. The relevant receptor cells have become less responsive to light and, for a further few seconds, don't "fire" as much, thereby causing that area of your field of vision to look comparatively dark. The after-image wears off as the cells recover from adaptation. Because most cells in the retina are color-sensitive, they also produce colored after-images—in the color complementary to the original stimulus.

Normally the eyes are actively looking around and after-images do not have time to build up, so we are not very familiar with their behavior. Only rarely do people sit completely still and stare at the same spot of floor for half an hour. If we did so more often, we would not find it so surprising that the carpet begins to swim with color and objects acquire hazy glows. Experienced meditators have learned not to be surprised— or enthralled—by these trivia.

The disappearance or fading of objects is also predictable. As long ago as 1804 the "Troxler Effect" was known to occur with steady eye-fixation, especially for objects in the periphery. More recently it has been shown that, if an image is stabilized on the retina (by using special contact lenses for example), it is seen only for two or three seconds before it fades to gray or black. If it contains sharp boundaries, it may reappear intermittently; sometimes, parts come and go independently (Ditchburn 1973). Without a special apparatus it is very hard to hold one's eyes still enough to test this effect, and the natural reaction to its occurrence is to move one's eyes and so end it. In meditation, however, with a stable posture and relaxed muscles, it can be done. Objects in view then fade out or seem to be transparent as the nothingness in visual space is replaced by an assumed background. (If this sounds odd, remember that there is a blind spot in the retina, where the nerve fibers leave the eye to form the optic nerve. We are not aware of this blind spot because there is enough other visual information for our system to gloss over the gap, as it were.) With practice, we can make the whole room seem to disappear. Any remaining disjointed images can easily be intepreted as peeps into another world.

In this way, even something as apparently esoteric as transparency becomes explicable. Predictions (though not, perhaps, very exciting ones) are clearly possible. If a table leg becomes transparent, it should "solidify" again as soon as the eyes are moved. If an object is unexpectedly hidden behind the leg, it should not be correctly seen even when the leg looks transparent. If these predictions are not correct, the theory (simple as it is) needs revision.

These simple phenomena have often been glorified. The response in many ancient traditions was to teach people to ignore them rather than get embroiled in fanciful theories. However, this response requires strong discipline and does not make money. It was and is far easier to ignore the exhortations than the fascinating phenomena. Today, however, we have the further choice of developing workable physiological and psychological theories, setting the phenomena in perspective *and then* ignoring them.

The Tunnel Experience

The tunnel experience may sound esoteric, but in fact it is quite common. Under circumstances ranging from near-death, to severe stress, simple meditation, relaxation, or falling asleep, people report sensations of rushing or floating down some kind of tunnel. Often described as dark or dimly lit, the tunnel can be no more than a vague dark space, or it can be something specific like a pipe, tube, sewer, underground train, cave, or mine shaft. Usually the person seems to be moving through the tunnel towards a bright light at the far end (Drab 1981).

Hallucinogenic drugs like LSD and psilocybin often induce tunnel forms, as do migraine headaches, epilepsy, and entoptic stimulation (pressure on the eye-balls). It is commonly found as part of the near-death experience (NDE). For example, Moody (1975) in his classic description of the NDE described "moving very rapidly through a long tunnel," and Ring (1980) includes "entering the darkness" as one of the elements of the "core experience," after "peace" and "body separation." It is followed by seeing and then actually entering the light.

Drab (1981) analysed more than one thousand reports of unusual experiences (not necessarily near-death); just under 10 percent of them included the "tunnel." He quotes a 27-year-old Englishwoman whose heart failed:

> I became less and less able to see and feel. Presently I was going down a long black tunnel with a tremendous alive sort of light bursting in at the far end. I shot out of the tunnel into this light. I was in the light, I was part of it, and I knew everything—a most strange feeling. (Drab 1981)

The tunnel was usually the first element in the unusual experience; the only element that tended to precede it is the out-of-body experience (OBE). The tunnel was more common when the experience occurred with cardiopulmonary arrest than under stress or in normal conditions. Interestingly, no tunnel experiences were reported by stroke victims.

Explanations of the tunnel are diverse. Robert Crookall, famous for his books on astral projection, explains it as the shedding of various bodies (Crookall 1961). According to Crookall, there are at least three "deaths": First the physical body is shed, as one passes through one dark space or tunnel, then the soul body, and finally the spiritual body, unveiling the Eternal Self. According to this theory, the tunnel effect is produced because, in the interval during the shedding of bodies, consciousness is nearly blanked out

This is a fairly typical occult explanation. Consciousness is treated as some kind of "stuff" or "entity." (Entities, or bodies, are typically multiplied *ad hoc* to fit the reported experiences.) Since the experiences are not all the same, different bodies are invoked with different properties. Only one of the criteria for explanation discussed earlier is therefore met. That is, the fit is quite good, in the sense that much of the phenomenology is described. However, the theory does no useful scientific work; it neither relates to other areas of science nor makes any useful predictions. The predictions it does make—that other "bodies" are detectable, for example— have been tested and have so far failed (Blackmore 1982a).

Another theory is even more popular. Carl Sagan (1977) has argued that the universality of many experiences can be accounted for only by reference to our one shared experience—birth. According to this view, the tunnel is "really" the birth canal and the tunnel experience is a reliving of one's birth. This theory and its many relatives have given rise to an enormous enterprise of "hypnotic regressions" to birth, "rebirthing," and all kinds of techniques designed to recreate one's entry into life.

This theory, despite its popularity, presents enormous problems. What does it mean to "relive" something through hypnotic regression? Presumably, one can only "relive" by reconstructing on the basis of memory. Yet newborns have a very limited capacity for memory and, in any case, do not perceive the world as adults do. An adult human, with cognitive capacities trained and developed over many years, cannot easily reconstruct the very different capacities (and hence experiences) of the newborn. And even if adults could, many problems would remain. The birth canal in labor is nothing like a long tunnel. Moreover, babies do not "float" down it but are forced out by strong contractions. And babies rarely look into an "approaching light," because they are usually born with their eyes facing the womb, not the world outside. It may be an appealing idea that we die as we were born, but Becker (1982) has made it quite clear why birth models cannot account for near-death phenomena.

The only positive feature of birth theories is that they make some, if limited, predictions. For example, if they involved reliving one's birth, then those born by Caesarean section should have different experiences from those born normally. Indeed, one might expect that people born by Caesarean would not have tunnel experiences at all. To check this I gave a questionnaire to 254 people, thirty-six of whom had been born by Caesarean (Blackmore 1982b). Thirty-seven percent claimed to have had tunnel experiences, a percentage almost identical to that of the non-caesarean group.

The proportion of out-of-body experiences was also the same among both groups. Clearly, the type of one's birth does not predict future OBEs or tunnel experiences.

In defense of Sagan's thesis, it has been argued that the experience is based on the *idea of birth in general,* not one's own birth. This, of course, takes the theory a big step towards being untestable.

As an alternative it has been proposed that the tunnel is nothing more than a hallucination based on symbolic representations of the transition between altered states of consciousness. This theory belongs to the "skeptical nonexplanation" type, which I believe has no more use than the occult theories—even though it requires no great revision of science. Like them it makes no predictions and can do no scientific work. A hallucination it may be, but why the tunnel? Why not, let's say, a door, a gate, or the great river Styx as a symbol? And why *this* kind of tunnel, with a light at the end? Why at the beginning of other experiences and not the end? Why with certain drugs and not others? Why near death as well as in drug states? And why so apparently real?

It has long been known that the tunnel is just one of the forms taken by drug-induced visual hallucinations. In the 1930s Kluver (1967) listed four constants in mescaline-induced hallucinations: the grating or lattice, the tunnel, the spiral, and the cobweb. These forms are not after-images, because they move independently of eye movements. They can occur in total darkness and even in blind subjects. And they can be induced in many other ways, including by pressure on both eyes (not just one). This suggests that they are generated inside the brain rather than in the eye.

Why should they take this form? Cowan (1982) asks what patterns of activity in the visual cortex would correspond to the form constants in the visual world. The relevant mapping is well known. Retinal space (the visual world as represented on the retina) is mapped by a complex logarithmic function onto cortical space. The center of the retina takes up far more space in the cortex than do the areas around it. Cowan demonstrates that tunnels and spirals map onto stripes at right angles to the axes or obliques respectively. Dilations and rotations correspond to translations of such stripes at right angles to each other in the cortex.

Therefore, if there are stripes of activity occurring in the cortex, the impression given will be one of tunnels and spirals, and, if those stripes move, the tunnels or spirals will contract or shrink.

Cowan further argues, on an analogy with fluid mechanics or spontaneous symmetry breaking in elementary particle interactions, that an increase in cortical excitability (for example, by release of inhibition) destabilizes the uniform state and induces such stripes of activity. The result is that the visual world takes the form of a tunnel or spiral.

This fits well with what is known of drug actions. For example, LSD and psilocybin, which often induce tunnel experiences, suppress the action of the Raphe cells, which regulate activity in the visual cortex and other areas. In epilepsy, spontaneous activity occurs in the temporal lobe and other parts of the brain. A similar release of inhibition may also occur while falling asleep, giving rise to hypnagogic images in this form (Schacter 1976). The same mechanism could be at work during near-death experiences, when cortical control mechanisms must be greatly disturbed, and in other highly stressful situations or serious illnesses.

If this is the origin of the tunnel, it makes sense that it can be very bright. Uninhibited cortical activity might be stronger than any produced by actual stimulation of the eyes. It would have a light brighter at the center because of the denser representation of the fovea, and this could easily become the "bright light at the end of the tunnel" that is so common in near-death experiences (Moody 1975, Ring 1980, Lundahl 1982).

It also makes sense that it can take the form of a sewer pipe, stars in space, a tunnel of trees (Blackmore 1982a), or a tube full of television sets (Siegel 1977). There is increasing evidence that the same visual mechanisms are used in imagining as in perceiving (Finke 1980). If these mechanisms are distorted by tunnel-producing stripes, any other images being processed at the time might become incorporated into the tunnel.

Why does one seem to move forward and not backward along the tunnel? Perhaps because of the movement of the stripes of activity across the visual cortex. But why in one direction and not the other? It has been found that when patterns with equal components of movement in both directions (such as counterphase gratings) are presented in the periphery, they seem to move away from the center (Georgeson and Harris 1978). This effect, called foveofugal drift, implies an asymmetry in the visual system that might account for the direction of movement in tunnels.

To summarize, this approach is reasonably successful. It accounts for much of the specific phenomenology of the tunnel experience and fits with some otherwise odd findings. For example, that tunnels are less common during meditation (when no increase in cortical excitation is found), and near-death experiences are less common, or less complex, in people with brain damage. Most important, it leads to many predictions. For example, tunnels should be directly related to patterns of cortical excitation. Moreover, different kinds of brain damage should affect different aspects of the near-death experience. Furthermore, tunnels ought to be suppressed by drugs that inhibit cortical activity. The minor tranquilizers (like valium) act by potentiating the neurotransmitter GABA and increasing cortical inhibition. Tunnels ought therefore to be less common in people taking such drugs; and, if they are given to people near death, their near-death experiences ought less often to include the tunnel component. Moreover, while tunnels should not occur in people whose visual cortex is damaged, it should occur in people blind from deficiencies in the eyes rather than the cortex. There is plenty of research waiting to be done!

There are still many gaps in this account; but it seems reasonable to assume that with greater understanding of cortical mechanisms they will gradually be closed and a tighter theory will be constructed. The occult or "birth" theories never give us this hope.

For those who have been in such tunnels, one last question may be pressing. Why does the tunnel seem so real? As we move from simple visual phenomena to the more complex experiences of flying, leaving the body, and entering "other worlds," this question becomes ever more critical. So I shall deal with it separately now.

It Seems Real

Strange experiences often seem absolutely real. This fact alone causes many people to reject the kind of explanation I have offered for the tunnel experience. They say, in effect, "this tunnel was real. I know it because I was there. So there must be some actual tunnel somewhere, in another world, on another dimension, or out of space and time altogether."

I sympathize with the sentiment. The tunnels, the flying, the other worlds *do* seem real. But this fact should prompt us not to conclude that they *are* real (whatever that means) but to ask why and how *anything* ever seems real.

To start, we need to understand that perception is not a process of somehow copying a world of real objects onto corresponding mental objects, but one of using the input to the eyes, ears, and skin to construct a model of a "world out there." It is a model-building process whose end-result is coordinated behavior and the impression of a self perceiving a real world. Yet both the self and the world are no more and no less than constructs of the brain's information processing.

In this construction process, memory is used to model familiar objects and make assumptions about their behavior. So the "real" world consists of a model constructed from input and memory. So also do the models used in thinking, remembering, and imagining. Yet we do not usually confuse the two. Why not?

It seems unlikely that the system could label input as such; not only because stored information is incorporated but because the units modeled change from retina, to subcortical, to cortical structures. It seems more likely that the system decides, on a much higher level, just what is "real" or "out there," and what is not, by comparing highly processed models of the world (Blackmore 1984a, 1986a). For example, the choice might be between a model of a modern kitchen with a table and a bowl of soup, and a great medieval feast with hundreds of different dishes. One model is stable, coherent, detailed, and efficiently predicts the changing input. The other is fleeting, unstable, lacking in consistent detail, and does not predict input at all. The system has no trouble in concluding that one is "really" my lunch and the other is imagination. I suggest that as a useful heuristic the system at any time treats only the most stable model as representing the outside world. Other models are treated as "imagination" and are inhibited from interfering with "reality."

This normally works fine. Our perceptual system is sure what is "real" and what isn't—until, that is, something makes the decision harder. It is easy to imagine what that might be. Reduced, noisy, or unreliable input could easily threaten the input model; or a failure of inhibition could make other, normally less stable, models stronger. Then the system might not be so certain as to which model were real. If a predominantly imagined model were the most stable, it would take over and seem, at least temporarily, real.

These are the very conditions, of course, that typically induce our strange experiences. Near-death is the prototypical example, but stress, fear, epilepsy, migraine headaches, sensory deprivation, falling asleep, dreaming, and many other conditions are likely to make our determinations of the "real" harder. All can disrupt input-processing without shutting down the whole system.

Sleep is a particularly interesting example. During sleep most input is cut off. There is no (or a very poor) input-based model of reality from the real world. During deep sleep there is little if any modeling—and so little experience. But in dreaming sleep the cortex becomes more active and modeling starts up again. We might then expect that whatever is the best model the system has at any time will seem real. This is exactly what the experience of dreaming feels like—it seems quite real until you wake up and a much better model supervenes.

In lucid dreaming the dreamer realizes his dream is a dream and seems to be more awake, conscious, and able to control the dream (Gackenbach and LaBerge 1988). This occurs during periods of higher arousal in REM sleep, when presumably a reasonably good model of self can be constructed. Because the model is more similar to waking models of self, the experience seems more real to "me," and "I" seem to be more awake. Since "I" am precisely a model of self, I am indeed more awake (Blackmore 1988). So, this approach makes sense of lucid dreaming without invoking any special psychic aspects.

The key to this approach is this: Whichever model is best at any time seems real. To return now to the tunnel experience, we might expect that, if it is induced when there is plenty of input, it will not seem especially real. This is in fact the case with drug-induced tunnels, which typically are not thought real but described by the experiencers as hallucinations (Siegel 1977). On the other hand, in near-death experiences—in which there is little competing input, because the eyes are closed and much of the perceptual system is under stress—the tunnel is often the most stable structure in the system at that time. That is why it seems real.

Out of the Body Experiences (OBEs)

> An emergency gastrectomy was performed. On the fourth day following that operation I went into shock and became unconscious for several hours. . . . Although thought to be unconscious I remembered, for years afterwards, the entire, detailed conversation that passed between the surgeon and anesthetist present. . . . I was lying above my own body, totally free of pain, and looking down at my own self with compassion for the agony I could see on the face; I was floating peacefully. Then I sensed some despair as I became completely alienated from my husband and sons (close by) . . . I was going elsewhere, floating towards a dark, but not frightening, curtain-like area . . . then I felt total peace. . . .
>
> Suddenly it all changed—I was slammed back into my body again, very much aware of the agony again.

OBEs are surprisingly common. Many of the more dramatic ones tend to occur near death, like this one recounted by a woman from Cyprus, but they can also happen when a person is relaxing in bed, meditating, taking drugs, or just walking along the street (Blackmore 1982a, Green 1968). Numerous surveys have shown that anywhere between 10 and 30 percent of people surveyed report having had at least one OBE during their life (Blackmore 1984b, Palmer 1979). Some people have even learned how to induce the experience at will.

Early research failed to find any consistency in the type of people who reported OBEs. Age, sex, religious belief, and education all seem to be quite irrelevant (Green 1968). For those tempted to think that OBEs are pathological, I found that schizophrenics have neither more nor fewer OBEs than randomly selected subjects (Blackmore 1986b); and Gabbard and Twemlow (1984) have found that the typical OBEr is psychologically as healthy as the average American. People who have OBEs are, however, more likely to report a variety of other related experiences, like "psychic" episodes, mystical experiences, and lucid dreams (Blackmore 1984b, Kohr 1980, Palmer 1979).

OBEs are typically short, often lasting no longer than a few seconds, although they can last for many minutes or even (very rarely) hours. During an OBE, a person usually seems to float above the body and then either returns abruptly or goes on to fly around and observe things from a distance. Everything can look odd, transparent, lit by a curious light, or lacking in detail. Some of the more dramatic cases involve people claiming to see things they could not possibly have seen; but I have argued that the evidence for this kind of ESP during OBEs is very weak indeed (Blackmore 1982a). In fact, all sorts of visual errors can occur. The out-of-body world can often be manipulated by thought. Occultists actually call it a "thought-created world." Nevertheless, it seems perfectly real—a fact that has led people to conclude that it *is* real. From here it is a short step into the kind of occult non-explanation discussed earlier—the most popular of which is the doctrine of "astral projection," derived from the teachings of Theosophy (e.g., Crookall 1961). According to this theory, we all have many bodies that can act as "vehicles of consciousness." The physical body is only the "densest" one, and it is normally coincident with the others until death parts them. But, according to this view, there are occasions when the astral body can temporarily split off from the physical one and travel around on the astral planes.

The astral theory sports one big advantage: It *seems* to account for the facts. After all, it certainly does *feel* as though one has another body that can travel around somewhere. But the "astral projection" theory is fraught with problems. First, what are the astral plane and astral body made of? Two answers have been given. One is that they are immaterial substances of some kind unknown to science. Now, if this "substance" is immaterial, how can it interact with material things? And, if it cannot interact with the world, it cannot possibly be seen, because vision implies just such an interaction. So, the theory becomes vacuous because there is no reason why the astral world should resemble the physical world at all. Theosophists are clever, though, and have proposed ways around this problem—they have posited complete astral replicas of everything in the world, but this only shifts the problem of interaction back a stage, to interactions between the physical and its astral counterpart. Another alternative is that the astral plane does have physical properties. This makes the theory far more testable, because interactions between the two planes should be observable. But they are not. All the obvious experiments have been done. Experimenters since the last century have tried to weigh and photograph astral bodies, even setting up infrared and ultraviolet detectors, magnetometers, thermometers, and thermistors to try to trap them! But they have completely failed to find any reliable evidence of the astral body (see Blackmore 1982a, Morris et al. 1978).

Morever, if the astral body can see, then people having OBEs should be able to see targets concealed at a distance. This kind of experiment has also failed. Although there have been occasional successes (e.g., Tart 1968), experiments in which the conditions were well controlled have produced at best highly inaccurate "perception" (see Alvarado 1982, Blackmore 1982a for review).

Is the OBE just "imagination," no more?

This theory has been proposed often enough. For those who maintain that distant vision does in fact occur, there is also the "imagination plus ESP" theory. But these are typical pseudo-explanations. They do not account for the phenomenology of the experiences nor do they make any predictions about them.

We need a theory that will avoid all the problems of astral projection but also account for the nature of the experience and make clear why it seems so real.

Let's go back to models of reality and the conditions under which they break down. The very conditions in which the OBE occurs. Whether drugs, sensory deprivation, onset of sleep, or stress, they threaten the stability of the input-based "model of reality." It ceases to be the best model in the system, allowing doubt as to what is real. At this point any stable model can take over as "reality," anything from a tunnel (induced, perhaps, by cortical noise), to hallucinations of a medieval banquet, to going skiing. Clearly, such hallucinations are dangerous for the organism, so the system will try to get back to normality. But how?

One way is to try to reconstruct a new model of reality. If there is good input and the stress is over, this will succeed; otherwise, the system will have only memory and imagination to go on. Now we know something important about memory models. They are often constructed in a "bird's eye view," as though seen from above (Nigro and Neisser 1983). If such a model becomes the most stable in the system, it will take over and seem real.

And this is the OBE: A model of reality constructed from imagination and memory that has taken over as "reality." This explains why the OBE world is seen from above, is distorted, lacking in detail, and full of errors—*that is how our memories usually are*. It also explains why experiments searching for the astral body have failed—*there is no astral body*. One may ask why the woman in the example given above was able to hear the surgeons' conversation if not by astral ears. The answer is that hearing is the last sense to be lost in unconsciousness. Moreover, hearing is not as "directional" as vision and will not force a return to the normal view. When we listen to the radio, for example, we can imagine the characters as though we can see them. Similarly, in the OBE state the voices can be "seen" coming from people physically present—but seen, as from above, in the imagination. A very convincing picture is possible. In the case of our woman, the return to normal view would mean returning to the pain of the operating table—a good reason for prolonging the OBE experience.

This theory provides many testable predictions. For example, people who have OBEs should be those who are especially good at switching viewpoints in their imagination. This has been broadly confirmed in several experiments (Blackmore 1987, Irwin 1986). Furthermore, spontaneous OBEs (set off by a breakdown in the normal models of reality) should be quite different from deliberate OBEs, for which special imagery and relaxation skills are needed. This too has been confirmed (Blackmore 1986c).

This theory builds on other findings in psychology, is testable, and explains much of the phenomenology but is it also successful for the rest of my third criterion—in helping people who have OBEs understand their experiences better? That, I think, needs time to tell. One advantage it has right now, though, is that it can show people who have had OBEs that they are neither mad nor losing their grip on reality. The occurrence of convincingly real experiences that are clearly imaginary is something to be expected once we understand the human mind better. Nor should OBErs fear getting lost in the astral worlds and failing to "return"—for they never left.

Perhaps more important, my theory should help us see through the illusion that the out-of-body world is real. Only in this way is it possible to use the opportunity an OBE provides to step further into altered states.

Here the comparison with lucid dreams is interesting (Blackmore 1988). In the lucid dream one knows that everything is imaginary but is limited by being asleep. In the OBE one is awake but limited by thinking everything is real. Only the insight that the OBE is not "real" makes further progress possible.

Communication with Others

Nothing seems more superficially plausible than the idea that we can communicate directly with other people. When the vivid dream seems to come true, when the person mentally called for telephones a moment later, or when that dramatic feeling that something was wrong proves to coincide with a loved one's illness, it is easy to conclude "this cannot be a coincidence. *It must be psychic.*"

Surveys show that over half the population claims to have had some kind of psychic experience (Blackmore 1984, Kohr 1980, Palmer 1979). Just like the previous experiences we have considered, it is often the impression of "realness" that sticks. Sometimes the other person can confirm the message; often not. How are such experiences to be explained?

Psychical research and parapsychology have studied these and related experiences for over one hundred years. They have postulated basic phenomena such as telepathy, clairvoyance, precognition, and psychokinesis and underlying all of these, some general process or force referred to as "psi."

There are many useful surveys of the field of research (e.g., Krippner 1987), and it is not my intention even to summarize them. I would only suggest this: Although there have been advances in methodology, experimental design, and statistics, there has still been no real progress. After a hundred years the same basic question is being asked: "Can information be transmitted independently of the recognized senses?" No clear affirmative answer has been forthcoming.

The problem may be the whole idea of "psi." This is partly due to the asymmetry inherent in the way the terms are defined. Extrasensory perception and all its subtypes (telepathy, clairvoyance, and precognition) are defined *negatively*. If a repeatable experiment were devised, properties of ESP could be discovered and a positive definition constructed. Then there would no longer be any question of whether psi existed or not. No such experiment, however, has ever been found. From this one cannot conclude with certainty that psi does not exist. One can only conclude that we don't know it does. The negative case can never be established, not because "you can't prove a negative" (see Pasquarello 1984), but because you can't prove a double negative, like: "There is not something that is not 'normal.'" If something like ESP exists, we shall one day know a lot more about it and cease questioning its existence. If it doesn't, we shall never know for sure and can keep questioning forever.

Why, then, not forget all about it? Because people keep having apparently convincing experiences. It is just not enough to say "you must be deluded." What is needed is to set aside the idea of psi, which has so far totally failed, and replace it with attempts to understand the nature, reason for, and impact of the experiences.

One approach is to ask why, if there were no psi, people should think they have experienced it. Many of the experiences cited as evidence for psi involve judgments of probability. For example, the coincidence between the dream and what happened the next day was "too close to be chance." But who judged that it was, and were they right? If there is really no psi, we might expect the people who believe in psi and report "psychic" experiences most often to be those who underestimate the probabilities of unlikely coincidences. In a series of experiments, Troscianko and I (1985) showed that disbelievers do better at various probability-based tasks than believers.

Similarly, believers in psychokinesis might be those who suffer a greater "illusion of control" (Langer 1975) when trying to influence random events. This has also been confirmed.

What is needed now are constructive attempts to understand how and why these kinds of experiences come about and affect people so deeply. Only when people can understand their own minds well enough not to be fooled by chance events will they stop needing the unhelpful psi hypothesis to make sense of their worlds.

Finally we need to look again at the popular New Age idea that we and everything else are "all connected." In a sense we are. We are all parts of one system that can be treated, for certain purposes, as a whole. In some altered states this is clearly seen. The universe is modeled in a new way, and it can be an overwhelming experience. However, this does not imply that information can be transmitted from one part of the system to another by paranormal means. We, as conscious beings, are still just limited models constructed by information-processing. To see clearly the nature of the wholeness we first have to face up to our own utter aloneness.

Cosmic Consciousness

It is easy to laugh at the idea of "cosmic consciousness" or simply treat it as beneath contempt. This dismissal, like all the others I have mentioned, does not do justice to experience. I think it is clear that we don't yet have a psychology that can make sense of mystical experience, but the approach I outlined above might give a clue as to what is possible.

Let us accept the controversial idea that that consciousness is what it is like being a mental model (Blackmore 1986a). If so, all and any mental models are conscious, and humans (because their brains construct multiple models) are collections of consciousnesses. What gives us the illusion of being one continuous being is the fact that the brain constructs one overall coordinating model of self in the world. In fact, the people who experience things are only limited constructs within models of the world. According to this view, the way to understand strange experiences is to ask what models the system was constructing at the time.

Normally the model of self seems to observe things in an external world, but it doesn't have to be like this. It is possible (if difficult) for the system to construct self-less models. Obviously, the experience associated with such models is not one of "me" looking at anything. There is no separate me, and so everything is experienced "as one." To the self reconstructed afterwards this is hard to recall, let alone explain.

Alternatively, the system might be highly active and the brain aroused but fail to model anything at all. What would this be like?—a sense of everything being possible?—an experience of emptiness? We can then ask how meditation changes a person's models of reality. The usual techniques are well designed to let go of the normal model of self and allow more integrated, simpler ones to arise. For the long-term meditator, used to "emptiness," the world seems a very different place. To understand this, future research needs to concentrate on changing models of reality.

These are the sketchiest of suggestions, but I hope I have made the point that no experience is too weird to deserve serious attention; each experience requires its appropriate psychology.

I referred at the start to a kind of perfect explanation. Let us assume that models of the world underlie all experience. If so, we should be able to develop theoretical descriptions of possible models. If these are good enough, the person understanding (or conceiving of) such a model would naturally also be constructing it. In this way the experience itself would inevitably arise. Understanding and experience would no longer be separate. Whether or not this is possible, I believe the way forward lies neither in intellectual endeavor alone, nor in experience alone, but in a determined combination of both. Tart (1972) proposed "state specific sciences," in which scientists try to work and communicate within altered states. I am proposing something more like "trans-state sciences," in which we construct the models that underlie altered states so as to enter them, and then bring back the insights gained to the normal state in which they can be described to other people and related to the rest of psychology. This means accepting the illusory nature of constructed worlds and overcoming the limitations of state-specific memory, as well as breaking down the barriers between experience and description.

When our successors look back on the efforts of the twentieth century, I think they will see the battles between the proponents of the occult pseudo-explanations and the dismissive nonexplanations gradually giving way to the development of genuinely constructive explanations. They will see that astral projection, mystical insight, cosmic consciousness, and ineffable oneness are not ridiculous ideas to be laughed at but peoples' brave attempts to describe their experience.

References

Alvarado, C. 1982. "ESP During Out-of-Body Experience: A Review of Experimental Studies." *Journal of Parapsychology* 46:209–230.

Becker, C. B. 1982. "The Failure of Saganomics: Why Birth Models Cannot Explain Near-Death Phenomena." *Anabiosis* 2:102–109.

Blackmore, S. J. 1982a. *Beyond the Body*. London: Heinemann.

———. 1982b. "Birth and the OBE: An Unhelpful Analogy." *Journal of the American Society for Psychical Research* 77:229–238.

———. 1984a. "A Psychological Theory of the Out-of-Body Experience." *Journal of Parapsychology* 48:201–218.

———. 1984b. "A Postal Survey of OBEs and Other Experiences." *Journal of the Society for Psychical Research* 52:225–244.

———. 1986a. "Who am I? Changing Models of Reality in Meditation." In *Beyond Therapy*. Ed. G. Claxton. London: Wisdom: 71–85.

———. 1986b. "Out-of-Body Experiences in Schizophrenia: A Questionnaire Survey." *Journal of Nervous and Mental Disease* 174:615–619.

———. 1986c. "Spontaneous and Deliberate OBEs: A Questionnaire Survey." *Journal of the Society for Psychical Research* 53:218–224.

———. 1987. "Where am I? Perspectives in Imagery and the Out-of-Body Experience." *Journal of Mental Imagery* 11:53–66.

———. 1988. "A Theory of Lucid Dreams and OBEs." In *Conscious Mind, Sleeping Brain: Perspectives on Lucid Dreaming*. Ed. J. Gackenbach and S. LaBerge. New York: Plenum.

Blackmore, S. J., and T. S. Troscianko. 1985. "Belief in the Paranormal: Probability Judgements, Illusory Control, and the Chance Baseline Shift." *British Journal of Psychology* 76:459–468.

Cowan, J. D. 1982. "Spontaneous Symmetry Breaking in Large-Scale Nervous Activity." *International Journal of Quantum Chemistry* 22:1059–1082.

Crookall, R. 1961. *The Study and Practice of Astral Projection*. London: Aquarian Press.

Ditchburn, R. W. 1973. *Eye Movements and Visual Perception*. Oxford.

Drab, K. J. 1981. "The Tunnel Experience; Reality or Hallucination?" *Anabiosis* 1:126–152.

Finke, R. A. 1980. "Levels of Equivalence in Imagery and Perception." *Psychological Review* 87:113–132.

Gabbard, G. O., and S. W. Twemlow. 1984. *With the Eyes of the Mind*. New York: Praeger.

Gackenbach, J., and S. LaBerge. 1988. *Conscious Mind, Sleeping Brain: Perspectives on Lucid Dreaming.* New York: Plenum.

Georgeson, M. A., and M. G. Harris. 1978. "Apparent Foveofugal Drift of Counterphase Gratings." *Perception* 7:527–536.

Green, C. E. 1968. *Out-of-the-Body Experiences.* London: Hamish Hamilton.

Irwin, H. J. 1986. "Perceptual Perspectives of Visual Imagery in OBEs, Dreams, and Reminiscence." *Journal of the Society for Psychical Research* 53:210–217.

James, W. 1908. *The Varieties of Religious Experience.* London: Longmans, Green, and Co.

Kulver, H. 1967. *Mescal and Mechanisms of Hallucination.* Chicago: University of Chicago Press.

Kohr, R. L. 1980. "A Survey of Psi Experiences among Members of a Special Population." *Journal of the American Society for Psychical Research* 74:395–411.

Krippner, S. 1987. *Advances in Parapsychological Research.* Jefferson, N. C.: McFarland.

Langer, E. J. 1975. "The Illusion of Control." *Journal of Personality and Social Psychology* 32:311–328.

LeShan, L. 1974. *How to Meditate.* Boston: Little, Brown, and Co.

Lundahl, C. R., Ed. 1982. *A Collection of Near-Death Readings.* Chicago: Nelson-Hall.

Moody, R. A. 1975. *Life after Life.* Covinda, Ga.: Mockingbird.

Morris, R. L., S. B. Harary, J. Janis, J. Hartwell, and W. G. Roll. 1978. "Studies of Communication During Out-of-Body Experiences." *Journal of the American Society for Psychical Research* 72:1–22.

Nigro, G., and U. Neisser. 1983. "Point of View in Personal Memories." *Cognitive Psychology* 15:467–482.

Palmer, J. 1979. "A Community Mail Survey of Psychic Experiences." *Journal of the American Society for Psychical Research* 73:221–252.

Pasquarello, T. 1984. "Proving Negatives and the Paranormal." *Skeptical Inquirer* 8:259–270.

Ring, K. 1980. *Life at Death.* New York: Coward, McCann, and Geohegan.

Sagan, C. 1977. *Broca's Brain.* New York: Random House.

Schachter, D. L. 1976. "The Hypnagogic State: A Critical Review of the Literature." *Psychological Bulletin* 83:452–481.

Siegel, R. K. 1977. "Hallucinations." *Scientific American* 237:132–140.

Tart, C. T. 1968. "A Psychophysiological Study of Out-of-the-Body Experiences in a Selected Subject." *Journal of the American Society for Psychical Research* 62:3–27.

———. 1972. "States of Consciousness and State-Specific Sciences." *Science* 176:1203–1210.

Wilbur, K., J. Engler, and D. P. Brown, Eds. 1986. *Transformations of Consciousness: Conventional and Contemplative Perspectives on Development.* Boston: New

ISNESS IS HER BUSINESS: SHIRLEY MACLAINE

Martin Gardner

I.

In the halcyon days of spiritualism, psychics whose vocal chords were seized by a spirit, or in whose presence the dead were able to speak without using a live mouth—often by talking through a floating trumpet—were called "direct-voice" mediums. In the United States the most gifted direct voicer was George Valiantine, of Williamsport, Pennsylvania. His entities had more than a hundred different accents, and spoke in half a dozen languages. One of his "controls," as the directing spirit was called, was Confucius. Valiantine's followers were typically undismayed whenever he was caught in fraud. After a luminous trumpet was found warm on the side and moist at the mouthpiece, doubters were told that spirits couldn't use it without materializing warm hands and wet lips.

Today's direct-voice mediums, now called trance channelers, no longer float trumpets. Some even speak in their own voices without troubling to acquire strange accents or personality changes. For decades the occult shelves of bookstores have been crammed with volumes supposedly directed through channelers, notably the popular Seth books of the late Jane Roberts, of Elmira, New York. Jane liked to fling her thick glasses on the table when Seth, in a deep booming voice, took over her body. Tam Mossman, her editor at Prentice-Hall, edits a quarterly about channeling, and himself now "channels" an entity called James.

Martin Gardner was for many years author of the "Mathematical Games" column in *Scientific American*. He is the author of *Science: Good, Bad and Bogus*, *The Magic Numbers of Dr. Matrix*, and many other books on science, mathematics, and literature. This essay is adapted from his recent collection of essays *The New Age: Notes of a Fringe-Watcher* (Prometheus Books, 1988) and originally appeared in the *New York Review of Books* (April 19, 1987).

Among those who are into New Age trends, searching for occult alternatives to Judeo-Christian faiths, there is a growing hunger for evidence of reincarnation. In response to this demand, channelers are popping up all over the nation, especially on the West Coast. In California, a former lady singer of country-western, Jamie Sams, channels the entity Leah, who lives on Venus six hundred years in the future. In Malibu, Ron Scolastico channels a group called the Guides. In North Hollywood, Darryl Anka channels Bashar, from the planet Essassani. Jack Pursel, another California medium, channels Lazaris. Nobody knows how many hundreds of other mediums are now channeling here and there.

Trance chanelling got its biggest boost in 1983 when Shirley MacLaine's third autobiography, *Out on a Limb*, became a top seller. *Out on a Limb* has two startling main themes: Shirley's undercover romance with a married member of the British Parliament—she calls him Gerry Stamford—and her rapidly exploding enthusiasm for reincarnation and the paranormal.

Among dozens of eminent thinkers and writers cited by Miss MacLaine as believing that we lived before on Earth, many actually opposed this view—Kant and Milton for instance. John Dewey would be amazed to find himself among those who "deeply believed in metaphysical dimensions that would ultimately explain the mysteries of life." At the same time, Shirley missed philosophers who really did believe in reincarnation, such as F. C. S. Schiller and C. J. Ducasse, and writers like William Butler Yeats. Somehow she did discover Cambridge University's great eccentric John McTaggart Ellis McTaggart, a Hegelian of sorts who managed the extraordinary trick of combining reincarnation with outright atheism.

"Profound McTaggart," as Yeats called him in a poem, deserves a digression. Bertrand Russell recalls attending student breakfasts at McTaggart's gay bachelor lodgings where the food was so meager that guests took to bringing their own eggs. When Russell decided that stars existed even when no one looked at them, McTaggart asked him to stop coming. Shirley MacLaine has a long quote from McTaggart, rightly calling him the greatest philosopher of this century who defended reincarnation. If you're interested, there's a good section in Paul Levy's book *Moore* about McTaggart's curious crablike walk, his penchant for riding a large tricycle, his Tory opinions, and his inexplicable influence on the early views of G. E. Moore. It's hard to believe that this now forgotten sage was once so respected that his colleague C. D. Broad actually devoted two volumes (1,250 pages!) to refuting McTaggart's bizarre metaphysics.

In *Out on a Limb* it is David Manning, a young occultist, who initiates Shirley into a smorgasbord of fashionable paranormal beliefs. Shirley later disclosed that David is a composite of "four spiritual men," each claiming to have known extraterrestrials from the Pleiades. The book swarms with occult shibboleths: energy vibrations (of which love is the highest), karma, other dimensions, auras, OBEs (out-of-body experiences), synchronicity, ESP, precognition, holism, Atlantis, Lemuria, UFOs, the Shroud of Turin, and a hundred others. "Discarnates," disembodied spirits, who tell Shirley about her past lives, get their data from the Akashik records. These are archives, theosophists have long maintained, on which are stored the vibrations of every event that has occurred since the universe began. "Akasic records of all that ever anywhere wherever was" is how Stephen Dedalus puts it in Joyce's *Ulysses*.

Channeled entities, consulting the Akashik records, inform Shirley that she and Gerry had been married in a previous incarnation—a stormy marriage because Gerry was too preoccupied with "important work involving cultural exchanges with extraterrestrials." In his present body, Gerry is a socialist who wants to be England's prime minister. (After the book was published, Shirley revealed that he too is composite, a blend of two political leaders she knew.)

A film dramatization of *Out on a Limb*, in which Shirley plays herself, was shown on ABC-TV on January 18 and 19, 1987, as a two-part miniseries. Charles Dance took the role of Gerry, John Heard played David, and Anne Jackson was Shirley's longtime friend, the big-hatted Bella Abzug. Apart from the film's paranormal poppycock, its dialogue is hard to bear. Over and over again Shirley murmurs "I love you" or "I missed you" to Gerry, and he comes back with "I love you, too" or "I missed you, too." Twice Shirley says "I love you" to Bella. Bella responds with "I love you, too."

Other highlights:

Shirley: "Intelligence has become my new erogenous zone."
    In an occult bookstore a volume entitled *Dwellers on Two Planets* magically hops off a shelf into Shirley's hands.
    Shirley and David face the surf on a Malibu beach, arms outstretched like Jesus on the cross. They repeatedly shout in unison, "I am God!"

Miss MacLaine's first conversation with a spirit entity is through channeler Kevin Ryerson. As a youth in Sandusky, Ohio, Kevin steeped himself in occult literature, later studied at the Edgar Cayce Institute in Virginia Beach. He became a medium after he discovered that while he was meditating, entities from the astral plane would grab his body.

Kevin plays himself in Shirley MacLaine's miniseries. Both he and Miss MacLaine have since insisted that on the set he went into a genuine trance. Young, tall, with dark hair and blue eyes, handsomer than Uri Geller and, from my impression, twice as smart, Kevin shows up at Shirley's Malibu house wearing a slouched hat that makes him look like Humphrey Bogart. First he removes his jacket, loosens his tie, seats himself, and says, "I'll see you later." After several deep breaths and a few coughs he goes into a trance. John, a contemporary of Jesus, takes over. He speaks English, not Aramaic, in a slow, scholarly fashion, with lots of biblical ye's and thou's. "Ye are co-creator with God," he tells a wide-eyed Shirley, reminding her of the time on the beach when she shouted, "I am God!" Miss MacLaine is floored by this revelation. How could John possibly know? It never occurs to her that since Kevin is acquainted with many of her friends, he easily could have obtained this information.

After more coughing, John is replaced by Tom McPherson, an earthy Irish pickpocket from Elizabethan England. The light bothers McPherson, so he asks Shirley for something to cover Kevin's eyes. She finds a black cloth and Tom, or rather Kevin, ties it around his head like a blindfold. Kevin now goes into what magicians call an "eyeless vision" act. (If you want to know how they do it—by peeking down their noses—see the relevant chapter in my *Science: Good, Bad and Bogus*.) Kevin stands up blindfolded, gets a mug from the pantry, then returns to pour himself tea. Don't worry, he says in his Irish brogue, he won't spill any. Shirley is dumbfounded. How can Kevin's body do these things when his eyes are covered?

After the brief return of John, who tells Shirley about her life with Gerry in Atlantis, Kevin wakes up and asks, "How did it go?" (Channelers profess not to recall anything said while channeling.) When Shirley tells him about the blindfold bit, he is amazed. He didn't know, he says, that Tom could manipulate his body like that. Shirley feels herself "vibrating with a strange magnetic energy."

David, who has been painting pictures of UFOs, invites Shirley to go with him to Peru to look for some real flying disks. Shirley accepts. Unfortunately, the cameras were never able to photograph a single UFO while on location in Peru, but the natives assure MacLaine that flying saucers constantly land in the area.

Although the relationship between David and Shirley is platonic, they constantly bathe together nude in icy mineral-water pools. During one such immersion, Shirley stares at a candle flame until she feels she and the universe are one.

Observing Shirley's spiritual progress, Dave decides the time is ripe for some darker secrets. He tells about his "cosmic love affair" with Mayan, a small girl with big black eyes who was in Peru disguised as a geologist. The Earth, she told him, is close to self-destruction. Because our planet is "important to the cosmos," her mission is to give David "scientific information" to pass on to Shirley. After much prodding, Dave finally reveals the stupendous truth. Mayan came from another planet.

Shirley becomes furious at the news of this cosmic love affair and wants to go home. Has she been duped? The pair drive back to their lodgings in silence. Next morning Dave tells how Mayan once asked him to go to a foothill and observe a certain peak. He went. A flying saucer emerged and landed near him. It was so beautiful—all white and iridescent. Then it shot upward and vanished. "After that," David says, "I listened to Mayan."

The world awaits the truth, Dave rattles on, and you, Shirley, have been chosen to provide it. Miss MacLaine is angry again. She calls it all "metaphysical mumbo-jumbo" and accuses David of setting her up to write a book just so he'll be in it. "I was wrong about you. You're a nut."

David, who never gets mad, quotes Mayan as saying that if you want to get to the fruit on a tree, you have to go out on a limb. Gerry once made the same remark when he and Shirley were lovers. Shirley weeps while David slips on her wrist a metal bracelet Mayan had given him. In the book he says it amplifies one's thoughts by drawing on what Mayan called a third force.

Shirley, hopelessly confused, drives alone into the Andes mountains to think. Is David crazy or for real? Night falls. It grows freezing cold. Birds and animals make weird sounds. Winds blow. The car won't start. On the verge of total panic, MacLaine massages the magic bracelet and cries, "David, see me!"

Cut to a sleeping David. He suddenly awakes, rushes to his truck, and is there in a jiffy. He and Shirley embrace. How did he know where to find her? Mayan told him.

On the drive back, the film's most embarrassing episode now unrolls. Like Kevin's blindfold act, it's not in the book because, as Shirley has said on talk shows, her readers were not then prepared to believe it. Here's what happens. David asks Shirley not to touch the truck's steering wheel. He starts deep breathing, closes his eyes, and takes his hands off the wheel. The car speeds along the perilous road, making all the turns, while a frightened Shirley huddles on the seat. After moments of sheer terror, she starts to laugh. Then, so help me, she bursts into her most famous song, "If You Could See Me Now!" Next morning, in a bathing pool, David explains how the truck did it. Mayan put "an invisible force field" around it.

Suddenly, Shirley sees an aura enveloping a plant, then a brighter aura around David. This is followed by her first OBE. A thin silver cord keeps her soul linked to her body as she soars above the mountains and travels to the moon. Beyond the moon she glimpses a spiral nebula, no doubt the very galaxy where Mayan lives. The cord draws her back. Shirley awakes, kisses Dave's hand, says, "Thank you." Dave kisses her hand and says,"Thank yourself."

David has to stay in Peru to finish whatever mysterious thing he has to do, but Shirley must go home to write the book that may save our planet. She cries while she packs. "When will I see you again?" she asks. Dave doesn't answer. "Just remember that I love you," he says. Shirley: "I love you, too."

Back in the Big Apple, in a taxi with Bella Abzug, Shirley tells about asking Maria, a Peruvian psychic, whether Bella will get the Democratic nomination for mayor she is seeking. No, said Maria, it will go to a "tall man with no hair and long fingers." *Oy, vey!* Could this be Ed Koch? Up to now Bella has been a doubter, but now she phones her office to ask them to take another poll.

Gerry turns up in what Shirley, in the book, calls the "insane, sweet chaos that is Manhattan." She and Bella meet Gerry just before he is to give a speech. When Shirley tries to embrace him she is pushed away. Can they get together later? No, he has to catch a plane. The affair is at last kaput.

In 1984 Shirley won an Oscar for her brilliant portrayal of the mother in *Terms of Endearment*. A photo of her doing a high kick appeared on *Time's* May 14 cover. That same year Hunter College gave Miss MacLaine an honorary degree for, among other things, her "quest into philosophy and metaphysics." The following year Shirley hit the jackpot again with her best seller *Dancing in the Light*. This time the romantic centerpiece is her tempestuous love affair with a Russian film maker. She calls him Vasily Okhlopkhov-Medvedjatnikov, but everyone in Hollywood knows his real name, Andrei Mikhalkov-Konchalovsky. In the book she addresses him as Vassy or Honeybear. He calls her his Nif-Nif, a Russian name for a small, adorable pig.

Unlike Gerry, Vassy shares Shirley's views on reincarnation, but he has never escaped from his church's teachings about Satan and evil. He even thinks Shirley is influenced by Satan when she's angry. For Shirley, evil doesn't exist. It is nothing but "energy flying backward." Spell *live* backward, she writes, and you get *evil*.

Shirley's spirit guides, speaking through channelers, tell of many occasions when she and Vassy were together in previous lives. They were pals in ancient Greece—she a man, he a woman—studying to be oracles, the trance channelers of the time. In at least four incarnations Vassy was her son.

A new spirit guide called Ramtha, or the Ram, now joins Tom McPherson as one of Shirley's top spirit guides. Ramtha is the control of J. Z. Knight, currently one of the most fashionable channelers in the

United States. Mrs. Knight is a handsome, husky-voiced blonde, with an upturned nose, who lives in Yelm, Washington, a small farming town south of Seattle. My own opinion is that she's a reincarnation of Aimee Semple McPherson, in turn a descendant of Tom McPherson. Aimee died in 1944. That would be just right for her to be recycled as J. Z.

When J. Z. goes into a trance, Ramtha takes over to lecture for hours to guests in hotel ballrooms who pay $400 each, or $1500 if it's a weekend seminar. According to *The New York Times* (November 11, 1986), Mrs. Knight admits she earns millions every year from her Ramtha performances, from sales of Ramtha audio and videotapes, and from her books. In *Ramtha*, based on tape recordings and edited by Steven Lee Weinberg, Ph.D., we are told the Ram was born 35,000 years ago in the slums of Onai, the major port city of Atlantis. Using a mammoth magic sword given to him by a "wondrous woman," he assembled a vast army, invented war, and became the world's first conqueror. Slowly he came to realize that he himself was part of the God he hated. After sixty-three OBEs, his body vibrating faster than light, he became one with the wind. On the side of Mount Indus, in Tibet, free of weight, he ascended into the Seventh Heaven where he and God became one. He is now part of an "unseen brotherhood" of superbeings who love us and hear our prayers.

Ramtha's God is not "out there," like the transcendent God of Christianity. He is the impersonal pantheist deity of such "process" philosophers as Samuel Alexander, Alfred North Whitehead, and Charles Hartshorne. He is the Absolute of Hegel, the Tao of Taoism, the Brahman of Hinduism. God is simply Everything. All he "knows how to do is be." The Ram likes to tack "ness" on words, and his favorite word for God is *isness*. God is "The isness of All That Is." The word occurs hundreds of times in *Ramtha*, often accompanied by God's ongoingness and foreverness. God is the great I AM. He is pure thought, pure joy, and the "cosmic glue called love" that holds everything together.

God is neither good nor bad. He is entirely without morals and unjudgmental. There are no divine decrees. Isness is his only business. Hell and Satan are the "vile inventions" of Christianity, a product of "your insidious Book," which Ramtha advises his listeners *not* to read. There is no such thing as evil. Nothing you can do, not even murder, is wrong. The slain go on to better lives, but the slayers will endure remorse for eons. To all this God is totally indifferent. I AM never weeps. He "does not even have the *ability* to judge you." There is no forgiveness of sins because there are no sins to forgive.

"Every vile and wretched thing you do," says the Ram, "broadens your understanding." Everything we do is done because we needed to do it:

If you want to do any one thing, *regardless* of what it is, it would not be wise to go against that feeling; for there is an experience awaiting you and a grand adventure that will make your life sweeter.

Regardless? Suppose a man feels the need to rape and kill a child. You might expect Ramtha would invoke karma to explain how such crimes are punished, but no—he is down on karma. It no more exists than hell and Satan. Murder is not a sin to be expiated, it is a teaching experience. You never have to *pay* for anything. Why the guilt a murderer feels is not a payment, or how a deed can be called vile if there is no evil, are questions that Ramtha, at least in this book, leaves unanswered.

In light of the above sentiments, it is hardly surprising that the Ram has nothing to say about helping the poor and suffering, the starving millions in Africa, the wretched untouchables in India:

Everyone . . . whether he is starving, or crippled . . . has chosen his experience for the purpose of gaining from it. . . . When you become a master, you can walk in the murk and mire . . . and maintain your totality, because you understand the teeming masses and why they are the way they are.

To love the masses "does not mean you must go out and teach them or succor unto them. Simply leave them alone and allow them to evolve according to their own needs and designs."

This, together with belief in karma, is precisely how the rich and powerful, in countries where reincarnation flourishes, have tended to look upon the suffering masses. And why not? If a child is starving because of bad karma, or (as the Ram teaches) because its soul has chosen starvation as a teaching experience, why interfere?

Ramtha's main message is simple. You are God and therefore capable of creating any reality you desire, if not now, then in a later incarnation. To support this notion, Ramtha provides a mythology that comes straight out of the science-fiction fantasies of Scientology. God was originally a "void without form," but he wanted to experience all possible emotions and sensations. You can't smell a flower unless there is a flower and a nose. So what did the great Isness do? He "expanded himself into light," which in turn fractured into billions of "light beings" or gods. These spirits were all formed at the same time and endowed with a free will so that through them God could create a universe in which he could play endless games that would continue his "expansion into forever."

We are those gods. We created the universe. We made the stars. It is through us that God experiences the joys of creativity and adventure.

To play the games, we first had to make what Ramtha calls "electrum" (his neologism for electromagnetism). The electrum "coagulated" into matter, and the matter coagulated into the cells of living bodies. The great game of evolution was underway.

We now come to Ramtha's version of the Fall. After thousands and thousands of incarnations, we the great gods of light have forgotten who we are. We no longer remember that we created the universe, that we invented all our adventures and dreams. The Ram's mission is to ram us into remembering.

Once we realize who we are, we must stop worrying about right and wrong, relax, go with the flow, and love God by loving ourselves. Even now we have the power to reverse aging and live forever in our present bodies. We have the power now to heal any disease, even to grow a new limb if one is cut off. What prevents us from doing these things? It is our "altered ego," the "antichrist" within us who keeps telling us we are not God. In our present amnesiac state, most of us will have to die and go on to adventures in other bodies, but many enlightened souls will conquer their altered egos and ascend like Ramtha, Jesus, Buddha, and Osiris. Omeka, Yukadf, and Rackabia (whoever they are) are also ascended, as well as thousands more we never heard about.

Because of impending natural disasters predicted by Ramtha—quakes, floods, and so on—he has freqently recommended that everyone move to higher ground, especially to the mountains of the Pacific Northwest. According to *The New York Times* (cited above) up to fifteen hundred people have already moved to the Yelm region, something Knight hadn't anticipated. A "20/20" television show about J. Z. (January 22, 1987) interviewed a tearful housewife whose husband, smitten by Ramtha tapes, had abandoned her to live near J. Z.

Sandy Fallis, a good friend of J. Z. when she was Judy Hampton, a girl growing up in Artesia, New Mexico, told "20/20" about a prayer meeting in which Judy suddenly began speaking in a male voice that called himself a demon named Demias. (Mrs. Knight denied that this ever happened.) Steven Bakker, formerly J. Z.'s advance man, told how devastated he became when during a desert hike he observed Mrs. Knight smoking and practicing the Ram's gestures, slipping in and out of her Ramtha personality without bothering to have trances.

Now divorced, Knight continues the hobby she and her former husband had of raising Arabian horses. According to "20/20" she began selling them to followers who were told that the Ram had recommended the purchases. One woman paid a quarter of a million dollars for a horse. Washington State issued a cease and desist order, which J. Z. accepted. Naturally, she sees nothing wrong about such trance chiseling because she sees nothing wrong about anything.

In *Dancing in the Light*, MacLaine gives dramatic accounts of her many sessions with Mrs. Knight. When she first heard the name Ramtha, she writes, it aroused such a "strange soul-memory" that she broke down and sobbed. Using Knight's arms, the Ram once picked her up bodliy. On another occasion Shirley says she saw "him" pick up a two-hundred-pound man. Ramtha frequently laughs and weeps, and enjoys kissing the laughing-weeping women who sit transfixed in his audience. Sometimes he gets drunk on wine and poor Mrs. Knight has to suffer the hangovers.

Dancing in the Light comes to a climax in Galisteo, New Mexico, a village near Santa Fe where Shirley goes to see a woman called Chris Griscom. Chris uses acupuncture to help people remember past lives. Her long sharp needles jab into various "galactic points," especially into the third eye. The third eye is a term used by theosophy and some Eastern religions for the pineal gland (occasionally for the nearby pituitary gland)—a small knob about the size of a cherry pit that lies behind the forehead between the eyebrows. In Hinduism the region is called the *anja chakra*. The seven *chakras* are psychic centers associated with *kundalini*, a cosmic energy said to be responsible for sexual potency and higher awareness. It is often pictured in India as a serpent coiled asleep at the base of the spine, in the *muladhara chakra*. Some far-out parapsychologists believe the third eye is responsible for psi powers. The Hindu god Shiva uses his third eye to see the future.

While Chris waggles her needles in Shirley's *chakras*, and gushes over the shifting colors of Shirley's auric field, Miss MacLaine has kaleidoscopic visions of her past lives. Shirley is a pirate with a wooden leg. She dances in a harem. She is a Buddhist monk. She lives in a jungle where she communicates with elephants by telepathy. She has a hand in framing the U.S. Constitution. In talk-show interviews Miss MacLaine likes to recall her many incarnations as a prostitute. She thinks they gave her empathy for the hooker roles she has played. Louis XV had her beheaded because, as a court jester, she told improper jokes. Shirley's only child, her daughter Sachi, was her sister in one life, her mother in another.

Her most hair-raising incarnation was as a Mongolian nomad. After she is captured by a bandit, a jealous suitor slits her throat. Who was the murderer? Shirley recognized him as none other than her ex-husband, Steve Parker!

During her sessions with Chris, Shirley has a momentous meeting with her Higher Self—a tall, imposing androgynous figure with high cheekbones and deep blue eyes. He is more masculine than feminine, more Oriental than Western. The Higher Self, or H. S., as Shirley prefers to call him, reinforces what she has learned from the Ram. She is identical with her H. S. and he in turn is identical with God. To love God you must love yourself.

Well, there's no denying that in this sense Shirley has an overwhelming love for His Royal Isness. Egoism and altruism, intelligence and gullibility, curiosity and willful ignorance—it is a droll mixture. But Shirley MacLaine's obsession with herself is accompanied by a canny (and highly profitable) capacity to touch the same qualities in the American public. All four of her autobiographies are available as a boxed set, and she is now working on a fifth. Who can guess what new astral adventures she will have to report? What will she learn next from Ram and other friendly spooks, from the occult junk books she keeps reading? Miss MacLaine is now on tour through sixteen cities, giving weekend seminars ($300 per person) on how to get in touch with your Higher Self. She is also teaching how to heal yourself by visualizing colors—blue for throat problems, orange for the liver, green for the heart, yellow for the solar plexus.

II.

When I wrote the preceding chapter I had not read *Out on a Broken Limb* (Harvest House, 1986), by F. LaGard Smith, a professor of law at Pepperdine University, in Los Angeles. A neighbor of Shirley, in Malibu, Smith is a Protestant fundamentalist who believes in hell, Satan, the Second Coming, and creationism, and that paranormal phenomena associated with spiritualism is the work of demons. His flimsy book is not worth reading, but I mention it here because it has some amusing pages about Kevin Ryerson.

Smith attended some of Ryerson's trance sessions without revealing his skepticism. When he falsely told Tom McPherson that his mother was dead, Tom replied to questions as if she were. "Wouldn't the Akashik Records *know* whether or not my mother were still on the earth-plane?" Smith sensibly asks.

Smith also told Tom he had dreamed that he and Shirley were friends. Tom instantly revealed to Smith that yes, he and Shirley had been pals in eleventh-century China. Shirley was a puppeteer and Smith was a Taoist scholar. Smith found Kevin bright and likeable, performing an act that "is simply one of the best road shows in America."

On a late-night radio show (January 17-18, 1987) I heard Ryerson talk and answer phone calls for several hours. He had high praise for trance-channeler Edgar Cayce, parapsychologist Thelma Moss, Jeffrey Mishlove's

Roots of Consciousness (a monstrous addlepated book published by Random House), several books about OBEs and NDEs (near-death experiences), and the books *Mind-Reach*, by Russell Targ and Harold Puthoff, and *Mind Race*, by Russell Targ and Keith Harary, though he was a bit confused about the authors. He credited *Mind-Reach* to "Russell and Targ" and *Mind Race* to "Russell and Harary."

It is hard to keep up with the hundreds of new trance channelers who are popping out of the woodwork—the greatest concentration is in the Los Angeles area—but here are some more who have been in the news. The *Cleveland Plain Dealer* (January 23, 1987) featured a local medium who calls herself Coyote Powhatan. Her entities include Alaric, a philosopher, and a vegetarian called Produce. Channelng sessions are free, but it costs $25 to have Coyote interpret your aura and give a tarot-card reading.

Penny Torres, a Los Angeles housewife, was featured in the *Globe* (March 24, 1987). Penny channels a 2,000-year-old man named Mafu. According to Mafu, extraterrestrials live among us and humanoid colonies flourish under the earth. (Ramtha also speaks of a hollow earth and underground races.) Mafu says a giant pyramid will soon rise from the ocean off Florida and cause many wonders. Someone named Tom Massarri is channeling Seth, but whether this is the Seth of Jane Roberts is not clear. A dozen other Seths are coming through other mediums. Richard Lavi, on the Phil Donahue show (February 24, 1987), went into a trance and channeled an entity called Exton, who spouted the usual platitudes and answered questions from the audience.

Still other channelers are mentioned in Kathleen Hughes's article on channeling in the *Wall Street Journal* (April Fools' Day, 1987). Hughes toured the Los Angeles area. In addition to performances by channelers already mentioned, she caught the following acts: Taryn Krive channeling Bell Bell, a giggling six-year-old from Atlantis, a Hopi Indian named Barking Tree, and an entity from Western Europe called Aeffra; David Swetland channeling Matea, a 35,000-year-old black female spice trader; Shawn Randall channeling Torah; Diana Hoerig channeling Merlin of Camelot. The funniest act of all is by Neville Rowe, who channels a group of dolphins. In the trance state he picks up their vibrations and translates them into English.

"I'm amazed," said a woman after one session, "that such wisdom and truth is coming from a dolphin. I didn't know they were so evolved."

"Very much so," said Rowe.

Here are some more channelers. William Rainan and his student Thomas Jacobson both channel Dr. Peebles. Vernon Yater channels Indira Latara, a nineteenth-century Hindu woman. Rhea Powers channels Sanat. Jessica

Lansing channels Michael, a "recombined entity" who consists of more than a thousand souls. Pat Rodegast channels Emmanuel. Her *Emmanuel's Book* has a fulsome preface by Ram Dass. Scores of channelers—Virginia Essene, Elwood Babbitt, William Tenuto, and Annie Stebbins, to name a few—channel Jesus.

Fate magazine ran a series of three articles on channeling (May, June, and July 1987) by Craig Lee, reprinted from *L.A. Weekly.* J. Z. Knight, he tells us, first encountered Ramtha when she was experimenting with pyramid power. She put a model of the Great Pyramid on her head, and there in the doorway stood an apparition of the Ram. She has had the word *Ramtha* copyrighted, a fact that strikes Lee as like the Catholic church's copyrighting "Jesus." For a while Knight was telling her Ramsters that the money they spent on Ramtha was tax-deductible, but the IRS ruled it wasn't, since Ramtha was not a nonprofit organization.

Dozens of Ramsters have lately become disenchanted and are contemplating legal action against Knight. (According to Lee, Shirley MacLaine is among this group.) Pam McNeeley (mentioned earlier) spent more than $10,000 on Ramtha and is now one of his most vocal critics. Pam is single, 32, and works for a computer firm in Sausalito. She was horrified by what she heard the Ram say in 1985. He predicted that in three years there would be a great holocaust in which cities would be destroyed by disease before the coming of "Twelve Days of Light." A trio of gods—Yahweh, Ramtha, and Id (How did Freud's id get into J. Z.'s mind?)—will then arrive in great ships of light to battle the evil Old Testament god Jehovah. AIDS, said Ramtha, is nature's way of eliminating gays. In addition to disease, there will be major earthquakes. "Don't live on a major fault line," the Ram said, "It's a zipper." Ramsters were urged to buy pigs and chickens, move to the Northwest, and start farming. Ramtha warned his listeners that if they told anyone about all this he would destroy them.

Ram's predictions for the close of 1984 were wild. A great pyramid would be found in Turkey, with a shaft leading to the earth's center. Sabotage of the World Bank, by a high official, would plunge the United States into a major war. MacLaine, by the way, isn't much better as a prophet. In a *Playboy* interview (September 1984) she predicted that George Bush would get the '84 Republican nomination for president. Maybe she got the year wrong and really meant 1988.

Jack Pursel, a retired Florida insurance supervisor who channels Lazaris, seems to be the rising superstar of the mania. Like J. Z. Knight, he's getting rich from lectures, seminars, cassettes, and audiotapes. This rotund, bearded medium runs two New Age galleries in San Francisco, Illuminaria and Isis Unlimited, and heads a corporation called Concept: Synergy, Inc. He seems to have as many followers among movie and television celebrities as Knight has. Michael York and his wife brought him to the "Merv Griffin Show." When Sharon Gless (of the "Cagney and Lacey" show) accepted her Emmy award in September 1987, she included Lazaris among the people she thanked.

Like most channelers, when Pursel enters a trance state he first goes through a ritual of facial grimaces before Lazaris takes over. The entity, unlike most others who speak through mediums, has never lived on Earth—indeed, he is pure consciousness, an entity who has never had a physical body. This may explain why his accent is so hard to pin down. Fashionably dressed women in the audience, fondling quartz crystals, weep over the beauty of his messages. He tells them that many of them once lived in Atlantis. They were so frustrated over being unable to prevent the destruction of Atlantis that they have been reincarnated today to prevent the world from destroying itself in a nuclear holocaust. Like J. Z. Knight, he urges them to forget about the Judeo-Christian theology that says they can't create their own realities. They must stop thinking negatively and turn instead to "love, joy, and possibility," and so on.

Craig Lee was amused when Lazaris/Pursel, in the middle of a lecture, turned on a tape recorder that played "Theme from Lazaris." According to Lazaris, predictions found in the Great Pyramid and those made by Nostradamus and others stop around the year 2000. That will not be the end of the world, but the beginning of the New Age, when everyone will cooperate to create a new reality. In an interview with Lee, Pursel warned against bad entities. They come through careless channelers to mislead the unwary. He admitted that some channelers—not him, of course—are out-and-out fakes.

Potboilers about channeling are starting to flood the New Age sections of bookstores. Jon Klimo, a California psychologist, has surveyed the scene in a book titled *Channeling*, published by Jeremy Tarcher, a specialist in New Age literature. (I wonder if his wife, Shari Lewis, the ventriloquist, takes seriously the crap he publishes?) William Kautz's *The Intuitive Connection* (Harper & Row) has a foreword by Kevin Ryerson. Warner Books is publishing the first of what may be several volumes of autobiography by J. Z. Knight. Titled *A State of Mind: Ramtha, the Adventure Begins,* it covers her career up to her meeting with her present husband, and I have no doubt that tens of thousands will be eager to pay for the cloth edition before Warner issues a paperback.

Shirley MacLaine's fifth and most boring autobiography, *It's All in the Playing* (Bantam), also published in 1987, is all about the making of her television miniseries. No new lovers are on the stage, but spooks Tom McPherson and John are back, spouting platitudes through the mouth of Ryerson. John reveals that he is none other than the John who wrote the Bible's Book of Revelation. It never occurs to MacLaine that theologians and Bible scholars can now, at long last, find out exactly what the prophecies in that book mean—just ask the author!

Chris Griscom returns with her acupuncture needles, and there is a new medium, Adele Tinning, of San Diego, who tips tables: one tip for *no*, three for *yes*, a wobble for *maybe*. J. Z. Knight, with whom MacLaine has had a falling out, is nowhere to be seen. In her place is her chief rival, Jack Pursel. MacLaine is now a great admirer of his entity, Lazaris. She likes to call Pursel on the phone to get advice from Lazaris.

Gerry, Shirley's composite lover in *Out on a Limb*, dies in a car accident in France, though how a composite character can die except in fiction is not explained. Shirley keeps feeling his presence. He appears to her in a vision to say how wrong his skepticism was, that the two of them are one, and that he'll always be with her in spirit.

Shirley has other visions. Tom McPherson told her she was developing "mediumistic potential," and so she is. Once when she sought vainly for a spot in the Bible where Jesus seems to refer to reincarnation, she went into a quick meditation, got in touch with her Higher Self, and asked for the reference. The answer came in "clear English," telling her she would find it in the Book of Matthew. She turned to Matthew, and the Bible opened on the very chapter she was looking for.

In another vision she saw a huge pack of cigarettes of the brand she smoked. When she climbed into it and found it empty, a voice said: "See to it that it stays empty." She hasn't had a puff since.

The book closes with Shirley's vision of a huge gray UFO that hovers over her head. The craft vanishes, replaced by a "spectacular ocean of liquid crystal shimmering in front of me." MacLaine dances on its waves— "It was glorious." She tells us that she had touched the "Christ consciousness" in herself. Jesus only walked on water; Shirley danced on it.

To me the most interesting aspect of the book is the disclosure that Shirley is teetering on the edge of solipsism, the ultimate in self-absorption. If each of us creates his or her own reality, she writes, then "Objective reality simply does not exist." Could Gerry be nothing more than a creation in her dream? "Perhaps he didn't exist for anyone else at all!"

She seems serious. At a New Year's Eve party, a crystal was passed around, and everyone, when they held it, told what they wanted for the new year. Shirley began by saying she was the only person alive in her universe. Shock waves went around the table. Since everything is her dream, Shirley went on, the best way she can improve the world is to improve herself. When scandalized guests raised objections, Shirley felt she was "creating them to object . . . I hadn't resolved myself. In other words I *was* them. *They* were *me*."

If so, someone asked, wouldn't it follow that everything you do for others you are doing for yourself? Here is Shirley's incredible reply:

> And the answer is, essentially, yes. If I fed a starving child, and was honest about my motivation, I would have to say I did it for myself, because it made me feel better. Because the child was happier and more fulfilled, I would be. I was beginning to see that we each did whatever we did purely for self, and that was as it should be. Even if I had not created others in my reality and was therefore not responsible for them, I would feel responsible to my own feelings which desire to be positive and loving. Thus, in uplifting my own feelings I would uplift the feelings of my fellow human beings.
>
> How do we change the world? By changing ourselves.

Later on she puts it this way:

> If I created my own reality, then—on some level and dimension I didn't understand—I had created everything I saw, heard, touched, smelled, tasted; everything I loved, hated, revered, abhorred; everything I responded to or that responded to me. Then, I created everything I knew. I was therefore responsible for all there was in my reality. If that was true, then I *was* everything, as the ancient texts had taught. I was my own universe. Did that also mean I had created God and I had created life and death? Was that why I was all there was?

If Shirley believes this, and the trend continues, she may be dangerously close to the mental snapping of the young cleric in a G. K. Chesteron story about which I wrote in the first chapter of my *Whys of a Philosophical Scrivener*. Perhaps if someone like Chesterton's poet-detective would pin MacLaine's neck to a tree, between the two prongs of a pitchfork, and leave her there for a few days, it might persuade her that *she* didn't create the universe. As Chesterton's cleric says, after his radical therapy, he stopped imagining he was God. It was too big a strain.

Shirley has purchased 800 acres of ranchland in the San Luiz Valley of southern Colorado on which she plans to build Uriel Village, a world center for teaching spiritualism, numerology, reincarnation, color therapy, and other wonderful things. "The seminars will be state-of-the-art metaphysics," said one of her spokeswomen, "with top metaphysicians from around the world to serve as teachers."

On August 20, 1987, the *Minneapolis Star and Tribune* reported that Charles Hurtado Silva, 43, who claims to have been Shirley's guide when she went to Peru, pleaded guilty to two charges of fourth-degree criminal sexual conduct. A native of Peru, Silva was in the city to conduct workshops on miracles and prophecies. Two local women charged him with "therapeutic deception" that forced them to sleep with him. Silva says he has lived in the United States for 26 years. A spokesperson for MacLaine told the paper that Silva was one of several men Shirley had in mind when she shaped the composite character of David for her book *Out on a Limb*. Was Silva the flimflam artist who performed the no-hands drive through the mountains? Silva wrote a book called *Date With the Gods*, published in 1977 by Living Waters. In December 1987 the publisher and Silva filed a million-dollar lawsuit against MacLaine claiming she stole material from this book.

Psychoanalysis is no longer chic. Encounter therapies and group grope have gone with the New Age winds. *Est* can rest in peace. The dead are alive and talking to us. The occult revolution shows no sign of abating.

UFO-ABDUCTIONS: DANGEROUS GAMES
Philip J. Klass

"Missing-Time" Victims

Budd Hopkins is an "internationally acclaimed artist whose paintings hang in many major U.S. museums," according to the jacket of his first book on UFO-abductions, *Missing Time,* published in 1981. The jacket adds that "he has been fascinated by UFOs since 1964." By his account, he was "not particularly interested" in UFOs during his high school and college days in the late 1940s and early 1950s. But during the summer of 1964 on Cape Cod, late one afternoon, he and two companions sighted a UFO that he concluded could not possibly have been a balloon because it appeared to be moving in a different direction from that of nearby clouds.

This prompted Hopkins to read some UFO books in which he says he found "sightings like mine." (Hopkins does not inform his readers that experienced investigators, even those who are "UFO-believers," acknowledge that at least 90 percent of such sightings have prosaic explanations, no matter how inexplicable they seem to the observer at the time.)

Hopkins says that, while he could accept the possibility that his UFO might have been an extraterrestrial craft, when he first read about the famous Betty and Barney Hill case, he concluded it was "foolishness." However, after Hopkins bought and read John Fuller's book on the incident, *Interrupted Journey: Two Lost Hours Aboard a Flying Saucer,* his views changed and he "began to feel that the Hills were recalling precisely what had happened to them, and the fact that it emerged the way it did, *under hypnosis,* in two separate accounts, gave it *unusual validity.*" (Emphasis added.)

Philip J. Klass, for thirty-five years a senior editor with *Aviation Week and Space Technology* magazine, is recognized as the world's leading skeptical authority on Unidentified Flying Objects and has written three books on the subject. This essay is excerpted from his latest, *UFO-Abductions: A Dangerous Game* (Prometheus Books), with permission.

If Hopkins had read the book more carefully, particularly the chapter by Dr. Simon, he might not have made so gross an error about the "magic powers" of hypnosis. But fantasies of the mind are the source of most modern art and that is Hopkins's trade.

By the late 1960s, Hopkins had become so hooked on UFOs that he admits he would bring up the subject at dinner parties, which often would evoke reports by others of their UFO sightings. In 1975 Hopkins investigated a series of UFO sightings that had occurred near his summer home on Cape Cod, but again could find no prosaic explanation for them. His first big UFO case investigation came in late 1975, after he had returned to his New York City home, when the co-owner of a nearby liquor store told him of his UFO sighting, which had occurred many months earlier.

Seeking the aid of a more experienced UFO investigator, Hopkins soon was joined by Ted Bloecher, a UFOlogist who had been active in the field for 25 years and who then was the Mutual UFO Network's New York State director. Their investigation led Hopkins to conclude that a UFO had landed in North Hudson Park, directly across from Manhattan, at 3:00 A.M. on January 6, 1975, had returned briefly five nights later, then four hours later had returned again to land so UFOnauts could dig up soil samples, and then had departed. Hopkins also concluded that the mischievous UFOnauts had fired some sort of projectile that had broken a plate-glass window in a nearby high-rise apartment building, although the projectile was never found.

Hopkins next joined Bloecher in his longtime project of collecting "humanoid" reports from people who claimed to have seen strange-looking creatures. From almost the earliest days of the UFO era there had been such reports. People claimed to have seen humanoids near UFOs or walking along deserted areas with no flying saucer around; sometimes they claimed to have seen their strange faces peering in at windows. For two decades, many UFOlogists—like Donald Kehoe, of the National Investigative Committee of Aerial Phenomena (NICAP)—dismissed such stories as fanciful. But others, such as James and Carol Lorenzen of the Aerial Phenomena Research Organization (APRO), gave them more credence.

Ted Bloecher was one of the first UFOlogists to search obscure newspaper accounts looking for such reports. A significant number of these reports of humanoids came from young children, who might claim to have seen one or two small men wearing silvery or gray suits who mysteriously disappeared when they realized they had been seen by the children. Anyone familiar with the fanciful stories often told by young children who have been raised on a diet of fairy tales should be cautious in accepting a child's humanoid-sighting report as fact. But such caution is not characteristic of most UFOlogists, and certainly not of Hopkins.

For Hopkins, one of the most impressive aspects of the Hill case was the two hours of "missing time." Had he read Fuller's book more carefully or talked to Dr. Ben Simon, a psychiatrist who hypnotically regressed the Hills, he would have known that the Hills themselves originally were not particularly surprised that they had arrived home later than originally planned, considering their diversion to rural side roads to escape the UFO that seemed to be following them. It was not until Betty told NICAP investigators about her dreams of abduction and one of them suggested that this could explain why they arrived home late that "missing time" emerged as a possible fingerprint of abduction.

So "missing time," as the title of Hopkins's first book suggests, became for him the first indication that a person might have experienced a covert UFO abduction. (Is there anyone who has not at some time looked at a clock or watch and discovered that it was much later than he or she expected, or driven some distance and arrived at a destination later than originally expected, thus experiencing "missing time"?)

Hopkins soon decided that if any of those who reported humanoid sightings in their childhood, or many years later said they recalled them, could also recall an instance of missing time, then almost certainly they had been abducted. If the person had no memories of being abducted, that was not important because probably those memories had been intentionally suppressed by the UFOnauts, in Hopkins's view. Fortuitously, the UFOnauts had not yet learned that Earthlings had discovered hypnosis—the magic key that could unlock the door to memories of UFO encounters!

But Hopkins admitted to being troubled by the fact that, in a number of cases he investigated, the subjects *were* able to recount details of their alleged UFO abduction *without* hypnosis. This implied that UFOnauts sometimes *forgot* to suppress memories of abduction in their victims. (Perhaps UFOnauts who come on abduction missions should carry a "check-list" reminder, such as those used by human pilots before take-off and landing.)

The importance of missing time, even as little as several minutes, is shown by the case featured in Hopkins's first book of a 35-year-old businesswoman whom he refers to by the pseudonym of Virginia Horton. He met her after he appeared on a television program on UFO abductions broadcast in New York City in early 1979.

She told Hopkins that twenty-nine years earlier, in 1950, when she was only six years old and living on her grandfather's farm in Canada, she had had a "weird" experience. Virginia recalled that she had been outside playing, then decided to go into the barn to gather some chicken eggs. "All of a sudden, I was in the yard and I didn't remember going from the barn into the yard toward the house." Here it was, a few minutes of "missing time," the all-important clue for Hopkins of a possible UFO abduction.

Virginia recalled that her leg itched and she reached down to scratch it. But for some inexplicable reason she pulled up her blue jeans to scratch the itch and discovered there was blood on the back of her calf. She recalled that the wound was about an inch long and half an inch deep, and today she has a scar that substantiates this part of her recollections.

The woman told Hopkins she recalled no feeling of pain twenty-nine years earlier, but, "doubly strange," she had no recollection of how she had cut her leg. But she had gone into the house and shown the wound to her mother and grandfather, who bandaged it. She admitted that there were things in the barn that could have caused the wound, but her jeans had not been cut! Even though she was only six at the time, the woman told Hopkins, she realized that there was "something very weird about the cut."

If Virginia's 29-year-old recollections were correct and even a six-year-old child recognized there was something "weird" about how she had acquired the wound, surely her mother and grandfather would have been even more puzzled at the time. But when Hopkins talked to Virginia's mother, she did not even recall the incident! (She did recall another incident, in Europe during a picnic when her daughter, then age 16, had emerged from a wooded area with blood on her blouse. After hypnosis, Hopkins concluded that this too was the result of a UFO abduction.)

One possible explanation for the discrepancy between Virginia Horton's account and her mother's is that Virginia's 29-year-old recollections of what happened as a child of six are confused and the source of her wound did not seem unusual at the time to her mother and grandfather. But Hopkins abhors a prosaic explanation as Nature abhors a vacuum.

Hopkins asked Virginia if she had ever had any dreams that might bear on UFOs, which he explains to his reader is a question he *always* asks "in cases which may have a time lapse or other clue which suggests a possible abduction." Earlier, Virginia had told Hopkins of her longtime interest in space travel and that even as a teenager she had wanted to be an astronaut.

In response to Hopkins's question about dreams that might be UFO-related, she told him that when she was about 13—seven years after her leg wound—she had dreamed "about traveling in outer space and going far, far away and meeting people that I knew like they were old friends, and I talked to them about things and they explained things to me. . . ." Hopkins, naturally, asked if she remembered how she had traveled or the type of vehicle, undoubtedly hoping she would recall a circular or saucer-shaped craft. But she had no recollections of any vehicle.

Nevertheless, Hopkins now suspected that Virginia might have been abducted at age six, and so she underwent hypnosis, administered by a psychologist, Dr. Aphrodite Clamar. Under hypnosis, Virginia relived the experience of discovering the cut on her leg, much as she had told Hopkins, except now she said, "I think my leg was cut with a scalpel." Knowing of Hopkins's strong convictions on UFO abductions, and his lengthy pre-hypnosis discussions with the woman, I suspect that he may unwittingly have planted this "pseudo-memory." For instance, while examining her scar, he may have said "this almost looks as though it was made with a surgeon's scalpel."

At one point in hypnosis when Virginia presumably was regressed to age six, she suddenly recalled something that had happened much later in her life, raising the question of whether she was really in a deep-trance state.

Under hypnosis, Virginia said that, shortly after discovering her wound, she found herself in a conversation with an elderly UFOnaut, who reminded her very much of her grandfather. Her recollections have a dreamlike quality and their contents sound very much like the space-travel dream she had had as a 13-year-old girl that she had earlier mentioned to Hopkins.

For example, at least some of her recall under hypnosis indicates she did not actually see an elderly UFOnaut. When she tried to describe the UFOnaut's hands, Virginia said that he "says he has hands," and later "I don't remember if he says how many [fingers] he has." She said that "the eyes are different than ours, I don't remember exactly how . . . and they might not have two eyes; they might have *three* or they might have two. I'm not sure about that. . . ." (Emphasis added.)

Most other claimed abductees report two eyes, which are described as being large, dark, and slanted, and they are the best-remembered detail of the UFOnaut's appearance. Virginia was not sure if they had two or three eyes and could not recall their appearance. Yet Hopkins writes: "So many things [in Virginia's story told under hypnosis] coincided with other abduction cases; in fact, all during the hypnotic session, little bells of recall kept sounding in my mind, as detail after familiar detail surfaced."

At no time during this hypnosis session did Virginia report having seen a UFO at or near her grandfather's farm on the day she cut her leg. Nor did she recall any details of being taken aboard a flying saucer. (She would vaguely recall such details in a later session intended to explore the blood on her blouse when she was sixteen. But by the time of this second hypnosis session, knowing that Hopkins was convinced she was an abductee, she probably would have read one of the many books on the subject simply out of curiosity, or this could have been pseudo-memory acquired from conversations with Hopkins and his descriptions of other abductee tales.)

Hopkins concludes that the most plausible explanation for Virginia's childhood wound, and for her seven-years-later dream of pleasant conversations with an elderly UFOnaut, is that UFOnauts cut the deep one-inch-long gash in the leg of a six-year-old child and removed a large sample of flesh for some extraterrestrial experiment.

It never occurs to Hopkins to ask himself where such surgery was performed. In the barn? If inside a flying saucer, why didn't Virginia recall seeing a UFO parked in the backyard? And why didn't the kindly old UFOnaut have the decency to at least put a bandage on the child's leg? Hopkins doesn't even consider such questions. He has discovered one more UFO-abductee to add to his growing list.

Another case selected for inclusion in *Missing Time* that Hopkins investigated in early 1979 was a UFO sighting that had occurred about ten years earlier involving persons whom Hopkins identifies as Denis McMahon and Paul Federico. The incident had occurred when both were age seventeen. Hopkins soon discovered what he believed to be two hours of "missing time" *that the principals themselves had never noticed.* As a result, Hopkins reports in his book, "I suspected [the incident] might have been an abduction."

As McMahon recalled the incident for Hopkins, it was a Friday night and after having dinner at his home, he had driven to West Nyack, New York, to pick up his friend Federico. The two young men then had driven to a road overlooking DeForest Lake, where they had parked to discuss events of the past week and decide how to spend the rest of the evening— "where there was a dance that night and where they might find some girls."

McMahon recalled that Federico had seen a reflection on the dashboard of a bright light that increased in size and brightness. He said both got out of the car and saw "the underside of an oval UFO hovering about thirty-five feet above a nearby telephone pole. The object had a large beam of light radiating downwards . . . ," McMahon recalled. When they returned to the car, Hopkins was told, its engine refused to start. When it finally did, McMahon said the two of them drove to the Clarkstown police station to report the incident. Later, when Hopkins was able to make contact with Federico, he told "essentially the same story."

Because McMahon's memory was "hazy about everything" except what had happened initially, Hopkins suspected there might have been an abduction, with UFOnaut-imposed amnesia. When he later visited the Clarkstown police station, he was able to find the original report made by the young men on April 5, 1969. Not surprisingly, the story the young men told the police immediately after the incident was less dramatic than the one McMahon had told Hopkins. The UFO originally was reported to be hovering "about 150 feet over their heads." There was no mention of any difficulty in starting the car's engine. And the original report indicated that after a few minutes—seemingly not enough time for an abduction and physical examination—the UFO had taken off to the west.

But for Hopkins, the most important detail in the police log was the fact that the youths had not made the report until 10:23 P.M., suggesting there were more than two hours of missing time! Both men recalled that they had had dinner before departing for DeForest Lake, so Hopkins estimated that the UFO incident must have occurred shortly after 7:30 P.M. Further, he estimated it should not have taken more than 30 minutes for them to drive to the Clarkstown police station, so they should have arrived by 8:00 P.M.—*if the youths had parked by DeForest Lake at 7:30 P.M. as Hopkins estimated.* But the log showed 10:23 P.M. Clearly, there was the all-important "missing time."

The police report yielded one more new fact, which I consider important but which Hopkins barely notes. McMahon had forgotten that he had *two* companions with him on the night of the UFO sighting, not just one. The "forgotten" companion was Douglas Sharkey, also age seventeen at the time. Neither McMahon nor Federico can be faulted for this lapse of memory, considering the incident had happened ten years earlier. But this meant that after McMahon had finished his supper (and Hopkins does not say where he then lived), he had to drive to West Nyack to pick up Federico, and then they had to drive to pick up young Sharkey (and Hopkins does not say where he lived) before they could have driven to the parking spot.

Considering that the young men were hoping to find female companions, surely it is possible that they might have stopped at a tavern or two before they finally drove to DeForest Lake. If McMahon and Federico had forgotten after ten years that they had had another companion that night, surely they could have forgotten what seemed to them to be unimportant events that occurred prior to the UFO sighting itself. How could they know that Hopkins would attach such great importance to the *timing* of events *prior* to the UFO sighting?

Both McMahon and Federico were quite willing to appear on a television show dealing with UFO abductions being produced in early 1979 by New York's NBC affiliate station. While Hopkins was driving the two men to DeForest Lake to film their on-site account of the UFO sighting, he told them that dreams sometimes reveal details of forgotten UFO-abduction experiences. By a remarkable coincidence, Federico promptly recalled a dream in which he saw a UFO land nearby and shine a beam of light on him. Hopkins suspicions were confirmed—the young men had indeed been abducted by a UFO.

Further confirmation came a few weeks after the UFO-abduction program was telecast, when McMahon called Hopkins to report that his recollections of what had occurred ten years earlier were now "flooding back." McMahon now remembered the UFO landing and the beam of light shining on him exactly as Federico had "dreamed" it. Still better, he also said he recalled being "inside the ship and being examined by small, frightening beings."

Soon afterward, without the need for hypnosis, McMahon described his abduction experience in considerable detail for Hopkins. McMahon said his UFOnauts looked much different from sketches of UFOnauts shown on the New York television program, which were based on the hypnotic recall of another of Hopkins's subjects. Whereas the other subject had described UFOnauts with very narrow shoulders and skinny arms, McMahon said his UFOnaut abductors were "built powerfully . . . there were no skinny arms."

Hopkins now was eager for both McMahon and Federico to undergo regressive hypnosis by psychologist Clamar in the hope of obtaining many more details. Federico told Hopkins he would like to oblige but he lived too far from New York City and his time was severely limited. Eventually, McMahon agreed to meet with Clamar so she could explain hypnosis and give him a brief "dry run" experience, in which it was agreed that there would not be any probing of his UFO recollections. But after McMahon arrived in Clamar's office he changed his mind and declined even to try the "dry run."

This has not shaken Hopkins's confidence one iota that the two men were abducted by a UFO on the night of April 5, 1969. Thanks to Hopkins, the two have become celebrities, at least to their friends and neighbors. In return, they have provided him with two more UFO-abductees to add to his long list. This strikes me as a fair exchange.

* * *

Communion?

In February 1986, Budd Hopkins received a telephone call from Whitley Strieber, who was eager to tell of an unusual experience that he said had occurred on the night of December 26, 1985. At their first meeting Strieber was so "very, very distraught" that Hopkins "immediately suggested that he seek some kind of therapeutic help," as Hopkins recalled during an interview on a Houston television talk-show on April 16, 1987.

Although Hopkins had by then worked with 135 subjects, all of whom he claims showed some signs of trauma because of their (alleged) experiences, he said that Strieber "was the first" he had ever suggested see a professional psychotherapist. In *Communion,* Strieber says that "Hopkins explained that he was not a therapist but could put me in touch with one if I wanted that." Hopkins suggested Dr. Donald F. Klein, director of research at the New York State Psychiatric Institute, in New York City, who would administer the four regressive-hypnosis sessions that soon followed. Klein is also professor of psychiatry at Columbia University's College of Physicians and Surgeons.

Hopkins participated in several of these sessions and thus is mentioned often in *Communion.* But, curiously, Strieber is not mentioned even once in Hopkins's *Intruders,* which he was then in the process of writing. During the April 16 Houston talk-show, when I asked Hopkins about this curious omission, he explained that Strieber's account was "rather irrelevant" for his book. Yet Hopkins said he was "thoroughly convinced that Whitley is a UFO abductee."

Strieber, by his own account in *Communion,* is a person whose life seemingly has been filled with many extraordinary, even bizarre, events. He now admits that some of these oft-told tales are not true. For example, Strieber writes: "A dozen times I have told a story of being menaced by an old college acquaintance, whose terrifying appearances and phone calls had driven us from our 76th Street walk-up [apartment in New York] to Cos Cob [Connecticut], then from there to the East 75th Street high-rise, and finally to [Greenwich] Village." Shortly thereafter he writes: "But it didn't happen; none of it happened."

Another example: When Strieber was interviewed in the early 1980s by Douglas E. Winter for his book on famous authors of horror-fiction, *Faces of Fear,* Strieber vividly described how he was almost killed by a sniper in a tower at the University of Texas in July 1966. As recounted by Strieber in Winter's book, the mad sniper "shot two girls in the stomach right behind me. And they were lying there in the grass, screaming, begging, pleading for help. . . . One was vomiting pieces of herself out of her mouth. And I could smell the blood and the odor of stomachs."

In *Communion,* Strieber admits that "for years I have told of being present when Charles Whitman went on his shooting spree from the tower in 1966. *But I wasn't there.*" (Emphasis added.) However, shortly after his book was published, Strieber again changed his story in an article written for the January/February 1987 edition of *International UFO Reporter (IUR),* published by the J. Allen Hynek Center for UFO Studies, and once again claimed that he *was* on the scene at the time of the sniper incident.

In Winter's book, Strieber described his troubled childhood: "My uncle was murdered brutally and his body left on his mother's own doorstep. My grandfather . . . died in front of my eyes in abject agony. Shortly after that, the wife of the uncle who had been murdered was burned in a fire from head to toe. . . . Shortly after that, my father . . . lost his vocal chords to cancer. . . . Right in the middle of all these catastrophes, *our house burned down*." (Emphasis added.) But in *Communion,* Strieber admits that the house did not burn down—"Only the roof over the wing containing my bedroom" caught fire.

Strieber claims that his life has been filled with bizarre experiences, some of which he barely noted when they occurred. For example, he claims that in April 1977 he and his wife had just finished playing a phonograph record on their stereo system in their New York apartment when they heard a human voice coming over the system, as can occasionally occur due to harmonic frequencies unwittingly radiated by a "ham" radio operator or a taxi radio.

But, according to Strieber, *"the voice held a brief conversation with us,"* despite the fact that Strieber's stereo "had neither a microphone nor a cassette deck." (Emphasis added.) He says he does not remember any details of the conversation except that the mystery voice's last words were: "I know something else about you." This implies that the mystery voice had revealed knowledge about Strieber's life not generally known, which would be especially astounding. Strieber admits that, in retrospect, "I cannot understand why we didn't make more of" the incident, other than to check with someone at the Federal Communications Commission who told him that such an incident was "impossible."

In Winter's book, Strieber revealed the genesis of his book's title when he characterized himself as a "contentious, rebellious Catholic, sometimes an Episcopalian." He said: "I have been a witch. I have experimented with worshipping the earth as a goddess/ mother." He also said he was a "student of Meister Eckhart, the great thirteenth-century German mystic," but that his present religious views in some respects were close to those of Zen Buddhism. Strieber notes that he spent "fifteen years involved with the Gurdjieff Foundation," which promotes the views of a Russian "mystic."

In Strieber's article in *IUR,* he summed it up more succinctly, saying: "[I] have experimented with everything from mystical Christianity to Zen to witchcraft (of the white variety)." But he denies that he ever experimented with hallucinatory drugs as did many other college students during the mid-1960s.

According to Winter's book, between 1970 and 1977 Strieber wrote nine novels but was unable to get any of them published and earned a living working in a New York advertising agency. One night while walking in Central Park, he discovered a pack of wild dogs, which prompted him to write *The Wolfen,* a novel focusing on a pack of "werewolves" running in Manhattan. This "horrorfiction" book, published by Morrow in 1977, was an instant success and was made into a movie in 1981. His next book, *The Hunger,* dealt with vampires. His next two books, published in 1982 and 1983, dealt with the invasion of Earth by alien races and powers.

Even more significant in terms of its implications for Strieber's more recent UFO-abduction tales is his commentary on dreams in Winter's book: "There is no fear in the outside world as great as the fear that can be generated by a nightmare." While a nightmare can indeed be frightening, Strieber's extreme assessment indicates that he himself was prone to terrifying nightmares even before his alleged UFO-abduction. This could help explain his success as an author of horror stories.

Strieber, his wife, and his young son spend about half their time in a New York City apartment and the rest in a second home, which he refers to as an "isolated cabin" in upstate New York. He describes the isolated area as a "peaceful, crime-free corner of the world." Nevertheless, he had installed an elaborate burglar-alarm system, similar to one in his New York City apartment, which he is careful to activate every night before he retires.

Despite this, Strieber admits that he feels impelled in the middle of the night to search his isolated cabin, "opening closets and looking under beds . . . especially the corners and crannies." He adds: "I always looked down low in the closets, seeking something small." He admits that this obsession with possible small intruders "has been going on for a long time, although in 1985 [the year of his UFO encounter] it became much more intense." Surely this is unusual behavior for a man of forty, especially when he is living in so isolated and seemingly secure an area and has outfitted his cabin with an elaborate burglar-alarm system.

Prior to Strieber's December 26, 1985, experience, he admits that he had "read a book or two" about UFOs and that "maybe I could remember seeing something years ago in *Look* magazine about somebody named Hill being taken aboard a flying disk." Strieber's claim that he had scant interest in UFOs in recent years is challenged by the fact that his brother sent him a book dealing with UFOs as a Christmas present in 1985, shortly before his reported UFO encounter. Strieber claims that he had read no more than five or six pages of the new book prior to his December 26 experience because the book "frightened" him.

Considering that Strieber is accustomed to writing books intended to frighten their readers and that the book he was reading (by British UFOlogist Jenny Randles and astronomer Peter Warrington) is mild for this genre, his reaction is surprising. Strieber admits that the book contained a description of what he called an "archetypal abduction experience" and that he had learned of Hopkins's work with "abductees" from the book.

On the night of December 26, after an afternoon of cross-country skiing, Strieber turned on the cabin's burglar alarm, "which covers every accessible window and all the doors. . . . I made a tour of the house, peering in closets and even looking under the guest-room bed for hidden intruders." By 11:00 P.M., he and his wife were asleep in their bedroom.

Some hours later, according to Strieber, he was awakened by a "peculiar whooshing, swirling noise coming from the living room downstairs . . . as if a large number of people were moving rapidly around in the room." He reports that he checked the burglar alarm, which appeared fully operational but which had not sounded any alarm. "Then I saw . . . a compact figure. It was so distinct and yet so completely, impossibly astonishing that at first I could not understand it at all. . . . The next thing I knew, the figure came rushing into the room. I recall only blackness after that, for an unknown period of time. . . . My next conscious recollection is of being in motion. . . . Next thing I knew, I was sitting in a small sort of depression in the woods," according to Strieber's account in his book. (There is no recollection of snow, although Strieber earlier informed his readers that there were eight inches of snow on the ground near his cabin.)

In Strieber's conscious (pre-hypnosis) recollections, he described a "person . . . wearing a gray-tan body suit . . . [with] two dark eyeholes and a round smooth mouth hole," and another "working busily at something that seemed to have to do with the right side of my head. . . . It wore dark-blue coveralls," he said. Later, he recalled sitting in a small circular chamber, a shape often reported by "abductees," which is not surprising considering that UFOs are reported to be circular. But, whereas others describe the interior as being spartan clean, Strieber characterized it as "messy . . . [with] some clothing thrown on the floor." This prompted him to admonish the UFOnauts: "This place is filthy."

Strieber said he recalled *four* different types of UFOnauts. The first was small and robotlike. A second type he described as "short and stocky," with deep-set eyes, pug noses, and somewhat human mouths, and wearing blue coveralls. Inside the circular room, Strieber reported seeing two more types that "did not look at all human." One of these, he said, was about five feet tall, very slender and delicate, with "mesmerizing black slanting eyes." The fourth type was somewhat smaller with black eyes that resembled buttons.

Strieber's first session with Dr. Klein must have been disappointing to Hopkins because Strieber's recollections were so rambling. He told of a UFOnaut who touched his head with a silver-tipped wandlike device, enabling him to see pictures of the world blowing up in a nuclear holocaust. He recalled that the previous November he had dreamed of seeing Cleveland destroyed by a nuclear explosion, and had recently coauthored a book with that theme called *Warday*.

Strieber comments in *Communion* that although his account of a UFOnaut "practicing psychotherapy with a fairy wand . . . is almost unique [among 'abductee' accounts], the being I saw wielding it is of a type commonly reported." During Strieber's first session, he also described disturbing recollections of his father's death, which he admits "did not reflect what really happened."

Four days later, Strieber returned to Dr. Klein for his second session and was regressed back to December 26—the day of his presumed UFO-abduction. When Strieber was asked about his state of mind in late December, he reports that he was scared and unhappy: "I felt like the world was caving in on me. Kept thinking there were these people hiding in the closet. Went through the house every night. Checking." He revealed that two months earlier he had purchased a "riot gun" for "protection." When Dr. Klein asked what he wanted protection from, Strieber replied: "Not sure. I just have the feeling sometimes . . . there are people in the house."

During this session, Strieber provided new details of the appearance of the UFOnaut that allegedly came rushing into his bedroom that night. "He looks like he's wearing cards. On his chest, this big, square blue card on his chest. An oblong one down on his middle. And he has on a— a round hat. And he's wearing a face mask with two eyeholes." But earlier in the book, Strieber mentions that the only illumination in his bedroom was that coming from a tiny pilot-light on his burglar alarm monitor, which surely would not be sufficient to see the details he described.

In addition to this UFOnaut, Strieber described many others in "blue coveralls" who marched into the room—"two rows of them." Meanwhile, Strieber's wife, Anne, remained asleep at his side, completely oblivious to what (allegedly) was occurring. According to Strieber, "They're little bitty people. I feel like I could almost pick one of them up with one hand." Despite their tiny size, they somehow transported Strieber downstairs to the front porch, where he reported seeing "a sort of black iron cot," which was used to fly him to the UFO.

When a female UFOnaut, who looked "like a person made out of leather," told Strieber that an operation would be performed on him and he realized they planned to insert a shiny thin needle into his brain, he warned them, "You'll ruin a beautiful mind." This prompted her to ask (in what Strieber said was a "startlingly Midwestern" accent): "What can we do to help you stop screaming?" Strieber responded: "You could let me smell you." When she agreed, Strieber reported "a slight scent of cardboard" which, he said, "gave me exactly what I needed, an anchor in reality."

Under hypnosis Strieber said that after the female UFOnaut agreed to let him smell her, "she drew something up from below. 'Jesus, is that your penis?' I thought it was a woman . . .—that goes right in me . . . punching in me." Despite this dreamlike sex-role contradiction, Strieber continues to refer to that particular UFOnaut as a female. At one point, he recalls that the female UFOnaut asked him "if I was as hard as I could get," and he realized he was sexually aroused. This is especially curious because he described her as "old . . . bald . . . she's got a big head and her eyes have bulges" so that her appearance reminded him of "a bug."

Later, Strieber said he was shown "an enormous and extremely ugly object . . . with a network of wires on the end . . . at least a foot long . . . and triangular in structure," which he said was inserted "into my rectum." Still under hypnosis, Strieber said he saw his now-deceased father and relived a childhood train trip with his family.

Following the fourth, and last, session with Dr. Klein on March 14, Strieber reported that his nocturnal visitors returned, jabbing him on the shoulder to awaken him. According to Strieber, he could see three small people standing beside the bed, their outlines made visible by the glow of the panel on his bedside burglar alarm. He described them as stocky, dwarflike, with gray humanoid faces and glittering deep-set eyes.

Additionally, barely two feet away, was one of the thin variety, a female, with big round eyes instead of the traditional slanted eyes. According to Strieber, she appeared to be wearing "an inept cardboard imitation of a blue double-breasted suit, complete with a white triangle of handkerchief sticking out of the pocket." But when Strieber smiled at the visitors, "they dashed away with a whoosh and I was plunged almost at once back into sleep." He said he is "quite certain that the beings I saw were not a dream, and probably not a hallucination."

After his second session with Dr. Klein, on March 5, Strieber said: "[I] was doubly worried now for my sanity. First, I still felt that I might be the victim of some rare disorder. Second, I questioned my ability to live with the notion that my whole life might have proceeded according to a hidden agenda," i.e., that the many bizarre events that he believed he had experienced from his childhood might be part of a UFOnaut master plan.

Strieber added: "Neither of these alternatives was acceptable—hardly endurable—and yet one of them had to be true. . . . If I did not accept that something real was hiding deep in my life, then I had to accept myself as a disturbed man. But I did not feel or act disturbed." Strieber said that following this second session, Dr. Klein told him that "he thought I was sane." Yet later in the book, Strieber admits that after his fourth hypnosis session with Dr. Klein, on March 14, "our interest shifted . . . *to discovering some physical cause for it.*" (Emphasis added.)

Several months later, on July 26, Dr. Klein wrote a letter to Strieber "in which he mentioned that many of my symptoms were consistent with an abnormality in the temporal lobe" of the brain. Strieber explains that "people with temporal-lobe epilepsy report déjà vu, unexplained panic states, strong smells, and even a preoccupation with philosophical and cosmic concerns. They also sometimes report vivid hallucinatory journeys."

According to Dr. Barry L. Beyerstein, a psychologist in the Brain Behavior Laboratory of Canada's Simon Fraser University, persons suffering from temporal lobe epilepsy—referred to as TLEs—are characterized by "their humorlessness, excessive moral zeal, and tendency to find profound meaning in mundane events." Based on a controlled study of behavioral traits of TLEs conducted by Dr. David Bear, cited by Beyerstein, I learned that TLEs have a "penchant for somber moralization, idiosyncratic cosmological speculation, and suspiciousness toward those who question their ideas."

Further, TLEs have a "preoccupation with religious and mystical matters" and many have a history of multiple conversions from one religion to another, according to Beyerstein. He cited other studies that show that TLEs are "particularly likely to have experienced a variety of spontaneous events widely regarded as paranormal. . . . Reports of 'mystical-religious presence' were especially prevalent," he said. Also, TLEs often experience olfactory hallucinations and report a wide variety of odors.

If Dr. Klein's suspicions were correct, this would explain the many bizarre experiences Strieber recounts in his book that seemingly have plagued him since his childhood. And it would explain why Strieber could repeatedly tell extraordinary tales that he honestly believed at the time to be true, yet later would recognize were simply fantasy.

But Strieber seemingly rejected Dr. Klein's diagnosis, characterizing it as "nothing more than another speculation, essentially no different and no more supportable than the [alien] visitor hypothesis."

The week after Strieber received Dr. Klein's letter, he met a woman who claimed to be an abductee and described how "a needle with a small, knifelike handle" had been inserted in her nose. When Strieber mentioned this to Hopkins, he was told that of Hopkins's more than one hundred subjects, four (including Strieber) had reported UFOnaut "intrusions in or behind the ear, three under the eye, eleven, again including me, up the nose . . . right into the olfactory nerve with its connection to . . . the temporal lobe."

The pieces of the puzzle fit together nicely in Strieber's mind. If UFOnauts were penetrating the brain with their nasal probes, Strieber writes, "then it may not be possible to decide between the temporal-lobe-epilepsy and visitor hypothesis. It could easily be that the visitors are affecting the temporal lobe in such a way as to induce abnormalities that would later be diagnosed as epileptic conditions." Yet if this were true, why did not the other ten subjects who claimed nasal probe experiences also exhibit the temporal-lobe-epilepsy symptoms noted by Dr. Klein?

Strieber did follow Dr. Klein's recommendation to undergo the painful laboratory tests designed to detect temporal lobe epilepsy, involving the insertion of electrodes deep into the nasal cavity. Strieber claims that the analysis of the resulting temporal-lobe electro-encephalograms is "such a subjective business" that he had his own analyzed by two different neurologists, one of them a specialist recommended by Dr. Klein. (It would be more accurate to say that detection of temporal lobe epilepsy is complicated by the fact that it is a transient condition so that a single test is not necessarily conclusive.)

Strieber reports that both neurologists concluded that his brain exhibited "absolutely normal temporal-lobe function. . . . So whatever the visitors did, they did not damage me in a way detectable to our science. I am not a temporal-lobe epileptic," he said. However, this claim was contradicted by Strieber in his letter to me of May 3, 1987, in which he admitted that one of the two neurologists had not yet finished his investigation.

The appendix of *Communion* contains a statement by Dr. Klein that at first seems to give Strieber a "clean bill of health," but which on closer reading leaves a different impression. Dr. Klein's statement says he sees "no evidence of an anxiety state, mood disorder, or personality disorder." But he adds: "[Strieber] has approached the dilemma of *what is happening* to him in a careful and forthright way. . . . After an initial period of stress, he became much more calm about *his situation* and soon learned *to deal with it in a psychologically healthy way.* He appears to me to have adapted very well *to life at a high level of uncertainty.*" (Emphasis added.)

In correspondence with Dr. Klein, I learned that when Strieber called him to request a statement on his "clinical condition" for use in the book, the psychiatrist sought guidance from Strieber as to how much he should reveal and what Strieber might consider to be confidential. It was agreed that Strieber first would draft a statement indicating the range of information he was willing to reveal. Then Dr. Klein would revise the statement so it "accurately portrayed my view of his situation within the limits of his authorization." Clearly, Strieber did not invite Dr. Klein to offer a candidly complete statement.

On May 9, 1987, in my reply to Strieber's letter of May 3, I wrote: "It is my long-standing procedure, both as a journalist and an investigator of UFO cases, to seek firsthand technical expertise. In that connection, will you authorize Dr. Klein, Dr. [John] Gleidman and Dr. [Robert] Naiman to talk to me and to make full disclosures of their professional assessments of your reported experiences and the state of your physical and mental health as the latter might impact on the former?" Strieber never responded to this request.

The strongest endorsement on the jacket of *Communion* for Strieber's belief that he has been subjected to terrible indignities at the hands of strange creatures comes from Dr. Bruce S. Maccabee, a Navy physicist and longtime "UFO-believer" who heads the Fund for UFO Research, which financed Dr. Elizabeth Slater's psychological study of nine of Hopkins's subjects. Maccabee has had the opportunity to get to know Strieber personally as a result of being a guest on several occasions at Strieber's second home, in upstate New York.

Maccabee characterized Strieber's book as: "The gripping story of one man's repeated contact with apparent aliens or visitors. Taken in the context of the numerous similar reports which have been investigated by qualified researchers and scientists, the events so well described in *Communion* become extremely significant. Assuming that these events are factual—and I think they are—then we human beings must begin a reevaluation of ourselves and our place in the universe."

This is the appraisal of one of the UFO movement's most technically competent and rigorous investigators. It differs sharply from that of Strieber's own psychiatrist, Dr. Klein, whose assessment is based on scientific fact rather than fantasy.

*　　*　　*

Rivals

In the spring of 1986, as Hopkins was completing the manuscript of *Intruders*, he tried to persuade Strieber to "postpone" writing his own book about his perceived experiences. The reason, as Budd Hopkins explained during his appearance on a Houston TV talk-show on April 16, 1987, was to enable Strieber to "sort out the nightmares and fears of his discovery and what to put in the book."

Strieber chose to ignore Hopkins's advice and his publisher, Beech Tree Books (a division of William Morrow), was able to get *Communion* into the bookstores by late January, roughly two months ahead of Hopkins's new book. Sales of Strieber's book quickly zoomed and by late March it was in the number two position on the nonfiction best-seller list of both the *New York Times* and the *Washington Post*, and shortly moved up to number one. As of this writing, it has been on the national best-seller list of *Publishers Weekly* for nearly six months. This indicates that many hundreds of thousands of copies of *Communion* have been sold to date in hardcover form and millions more probably will be sold when it emerges in paperback, justifying the $1 million cash advance Strieber received.

Hopkins's book, published by Random House, was eclipsed by Strieber's success and has so far failed to make any of the best-seller lists. In an effort to overcome Strieber's head-start, Random House published a most unusual statement, signed by its publisher, Howard Kaminsky, in the form of a full-page advertisement in the *New York Times Book Review*.

Kaminsky's statement began:

> The last thing the world needs is yet another kook-book about UFOs and extraterrestrial visitations. And the last thing a quality minded publisher needs is to put its name on such a book. Those were my thoughts as I began reading *Intruders* for the first time.
>
> Four hundred and fifty manuscript pages later, I knew we had to publish this book. And, as the manuscript made its way through Random House, I began to hear my judgment echoed by some of the most brilliant, least gullible, and most savvily skeptical people I've had the pleasure to work with. Put simply, we had to publish *Intruders* because it made all of us think about extraterrestrial phenomena in a completely different way.
>
> None of us who read the manuscript *wanted* to believe in UFOs; many of us still don't . . . *totally*. Yet the events described in Budd Hopkins' manuscript—and frankly, many of them will strain your credulity almost to the breaking point—are so objectively and convincingly set down, and so compelling in themselves, that in the end, I found myself actually considering the impossible . . . that extraterrestrial visitations might, in fact, be occurring *now*.
>
> At this point you may think that both the author *and* his publisher are kooks. But it is Hopkins' calmness, objectivity and cogency—as well as the mass of medical, physical, and psychiatric evidence he presents—that make *Intruders* so *un*kooky. He is as intelligent and thoughtful as anyone I know, and questions his own evidence as severely as any skeptic would. He sympathizes with the doubter—but answers that the true skeptic is one who cannot deny the possibility of anything. . . .

As I read Kaminsky's statement, my thoughts went back twenty years to mid-November 1966, when I was weighing expressions of interest from both Random House and Doubleday to publish my first book on UFOs.

I received a telephone call from Random House's founder and chief executive officer Bennett Cerf, who sought to convince me that I should select his company.

Cerf invited me to join him and "a few friends"—including Frank Sinatra and "Mike" Cowles, whose publishing empire included *Look* magazine—for Thanksgiving dinner at his New York townhouse, and I accepted. Following dinner, Cerf assembled about twenty of the male guests and asked me to speak to them on UFOs. One of these was Cowles, who, I later learned, was favorably inclined toward UFOs and had often tried to convince Cerf. After my talk, Cerf invited Cowles to challenge my skeptical views, but he declined. Not surprisingly, Random House published my first UFO book in 1968, and a second on the same subject in 1974 prior to Cerf's death. Cerf would have been terribly embarrassed over the Random House endorsement of the Hopkins book and delighted to know that within six months Kaminsky would be replaced as second-in-command.

The first indication that relations between Strieber and Hopkins were not all "sweetness and light" came when Strieber wrote Kendrick Frazier, editor of the *Skeptical Inquirer,* a quarterly published by the Committee for the Scientific Investigation of Claims of the Paranormal (CSICOP)— an international organization of skeptical scientists, educators, and journalists. In Strieber's letter of February 1 to Frazier, he enclosed material on his just-published book, hinting that he hoped it would be reviewed in the *Skeptical Inquirer.*

Strieber's letter also mentioned that Hopkins's new book, and another on UFOs, would be published in March. He said it was terribly important that these books be reviewed in the *Skeptical Inquirer* and suggested that *he* was the logical person to write the reviews. Strieber explained that, while he considered Hopkins a friend, he disagreed with his approach because Hopkins failed to consider that some of the abduction tales might not be "entirely real."

In his letter, Strieber said that, although his book had only recently appeared in bookstores, he already had received ten letters and eight telephone calls "from people who have had experiences similar to mine." (Although Strieber did not specifically ask persons with similar experiences to contact him, as Hopkins did in both of his books, the last page of Strieber's book prominently displayed his mailing address for those wishing to write.)

Strieber concluded by stating, "I have the respect of the UFO community, and deserve it, because I have been honest and forthright with them about my experiences." He would soon be surprised, and hurt, by the UFO movement's somewhat cool reaction to his story and his book.

Budd Hopkins had long been active in MUFON, the nation's largest and most active UFO group, and had presented papers on UFO-abductions at its annual conferences in 1981, 1984, and 1985. At the 1986 conference, Hopkins received the "1985-86 MUFON Award for outstanding work in the UFO field." Strieber, on the other hand, was a newcomer and his article in the January/February 1987 issue of the *International UFO Reporter* (mailed in late April) suggested that he aspired to become the chief guru of UFO-abductions, perhaps even a spokesman for the UFO movement.

In the article, Strieber cited his appearances on more than 40 television and radio programs, including ABC-TV's popular "Good Morning America" and "The Phil Donahue Show." He said he had "taken 218 telephone calls on the air." More important, he said he had received more than five hundred letters from readers of his book and was then receiving letters at the rate of twenty a day. (By May 6, when Strieber appeared on NBC-TV's popular "Tonight Show," with Johnny Carson, he reported he had received forty letters on that day alone.)

In Strieber's article he said that 85 percent of the letters described "some sort of visitor experience." "About 40 percent report an actual abduction," he said, and added that five of the letters "appeared to be from seriously disorganized minds."

"These letters probably represent one of the largest repositories of the visitor experience ever assembled," Strieber said. He disclosed that he recently had created a nonprofit organization that would employ "professional psychologists" to catalog the reports and conduct an "extensive array of mental and physical tests" on selected volunteers. The new organization, he said, would be called the Triad Group.

(In his book, Strieber noted that he had "always been fascinated" by the triangle and that Russian mystic G. I. Gurdjieff and his disciple P. D. Oupensky put great emphasis on the triad, or triangle, as a "primary expression of the essential structure of life." During the night of February 7, 1986, while Strieber was staying in his New York apartment, he said he "felt their [UFOnaut] presence." The next morning, according to Strieber, he found "two little triangles inscribed on my left forearm.")

Strieber's article in *IUR* expressed views that would please pro-UFOlogists. For example: "For the past ten years the 'scientific debunkers' have had almost sole access to national media," Strieber claimed. Despite this, he observed, "Apparently the public simply hasn't bought a word of it. The success of *Communion* strongly suggests that the public cannot be made to believe a lie, no matter how highly placed those who promote it might be." He urged "the UFO community" to refuse to debate the skeptics, explaining that "there is no reason why people holding mainstream opinions [i.e., pro-UFO] should expect to be paired off with obvious fanatics [i.e., skeptics]."

Strieber concluded his article: "If we are to move toward the truth, it will be because the open-minded majority has found an open-minded leadership from within the UFO community. The community must have the courage to tell the truth: we don't know what is going on, but it is very real and very strange."

The May 1987 issue of the *MUFON UFO Journal* carried a rather critical analysis of *Communion* by Dr. Michael Swords, a professor of natural sciences at Western Michigan University, suggesting that Strieber's perceived experiences might be due to "internal" causes. This prompted a harsh response by Strieber, published in the same issue, in which he said: "I am increasingly becoming certain that there are large elements of the UFO community who cannot successfully address the issue of abductions in general, and my own case in particular." Strieber said:

> [I had been] warned by the other abductees before writing *Communion* that it would be dismissed by the scientists and engineers in the UFO community because it dealt primarily with the spiritual and metaphysical aspects of the experience. . . . The abduction experience is *primarily* a mystical experience, in the sense that stresses generated are similar to those created by initiation into the mystery cults of the old animist religions. And the postlude experienced by abductees . . . is usually replete with spiritual and paranormal life events. . . .
>
> I suspect that all or most of the abduction experiences as reported by UFO investigators may suffer from an unintentional fictionalization. They have been subtly altered to suggest that a quite comprehensible force is behind them. The strangeness of my account makes some UFO investigators hasten to conclude that it must represent an *internal* experience. . . .

One of Strieber's most curious statements claimed that he has "little interest in identifying the force behind the abductions." He wrote, "The issue of whether or not UFOs are real doesn't much concern me. . . . If visitors are real, *they* appear to me to be in almost total control of the situation. Therefore the search is useless because it will not bear fruit until and if *they* want it. And when *they* are ready to reveal the answer, the mystery will at once be solved." (Emphasis added.)

Such views would not endear Strieber to many in the UFO movement who get their "kicks" from investigating UFO sighting reports, speculating on such things as where the UFOnauts come from and what kind of propulsion system is used in their craft, and from being interviewed by the news media. If Strieber was correct, MUFON might as well disband

and UFOlogists should find a new hobby.

Thus it is not surprising that when MUFON held its annual conference in Washington, D.C., on June 27-28, 1987, attended by more than four hundred enthusiastic UFOlogists, Strieber was accorded a respectful, but cool, reception.

Two evening sessions on UFO-abductions were held on June 27. The first featured Hopkins, Dr. David Jacobs, a professor of history who recently started working with "abductees," and Indiana University professor Thomas E. Bullard, who obtained his Ph.D. in folklore and has made an analysis of about three hundred abduction reports. Despite Strieber's announced plans to create an organization for UFO-abduction research, he was not invited to participate on this panel to describe his planned effort. Instead, he was one of eight "abductees" who appeared on the subsequent panel.

When his session began, Strieber was introduced by Jacobs as the author of the book that had achieved number-one best-seller status, the first time that a book on UFOs had achieved such distinction. None of the panelists had prepared remarks but responded to questions from the audience if they wished. In response to the first question about the difficulty of "going public" with the abduction stories, Strieber said he had made 225 public appearances on radio and television since January. He acknowledged that he had been paid $1 million for his book, adding that "I have cried all the way to the bank . . . but I've earned every penny of it." He revealed his hurt at being ridiculed during his appearance on the "Phil Donahue Show."

The following morning Strieber gave one of several dozen "contributed" papers that had been volunteered by authors, each of whom was given fifteen minutes time, as distinguished from "invited" papers, which were allotted thirty minutes. Strieber reported that his experiences with his "visitors" during the past year had been "very unlike what happened to me before." Some of them were "so subtle" that he would have discounted them but for the presence of other witnesses. "If this isn't an experience with real visitors, then it becomes certainly the most witnessed paranormal experience I have ever heard of," Strieber said.

He also revealed plans to write a new book, detailing his more recent experiences, and explained that he has gained important insights that the public needs to know. He reported "removal of fear by confrontation with it, and eventually leading to understanding of what was happening to me to where I really don't fear any more." More important, he said, was "a response from the other side [i.e., the 'visitors'] that was intelligent and effective. . . . This was followed by what I can only describe as a period of psychological probing, which is the part that I would have personally discounted if this thread [*sic*] of witness had not been present," he added.

In *Communion,* Strieber wrote that he had "received a great deal of material about the perilous condition of the earth's atmosphere" from his "visitors," which he included in the book *Nature's End,* coauthored with James Kunetka. In March 1986, he said, he had held a press conference in Washington "to warn about the serious implications of the hole that had been detected in the ozone layer over the Antarctic. My apparent visitor information suggested this hole would lead to further holes over the Arctic and thereafter a thinning of the ozone layer over the Northern Hemisphere, with measurable crop damage from excessive ultraviolet light beginning to occur in the 1990–1993 period. At the time I gave this warning, the only stories about the hole were saying that its significance was not understood. I had also been told that the atmospheric problems will cause a reduction in immune system vitality in all animals, and the consequent resurgence of disease." Strieber admitted in *Communion* that he did not reveal to reporters at his Washington press conference that his "visitors" were the source of his predictions for fear "my credibility would be destroyed."

In Strieber's more recent MUFON conference paper, he said he had just heard from an Australian scientist that a new hole in the ozone layer over the *Arctic* had just been discovered, as he predicted, but he admitted that he had no hard confirmation. (Nor has there been any confirmation as of this writing.) He said there had been a 200-percent increase in rabies in the Northeastern part of the United States during the past two years and a comparable increase in Western Europe during the past five years, confirming his earlier prediction of damage to immune systems.

Strieber also reported that the "amount of atmospheric haze is rising, at least in my perception and . . . [according to] a friend who is a meteorologist." Strieber said the haze "is very dangerous" and that it "would spread over the Northern Hemisphere of the planet over the next three to five years rather dramatically." He admitted that he lacked the scientific background to evaluate the information provided by his "visitors," but offered to make available tape recordings he has made.

Strieber concluded by saying that "if this experience emerges in the direction that it appears it's going to, there are going to be made—not by me—some extremely controversial, startling and profoundly upsetting revelations in the next year or so. If that happens, we're going to end up with a very different view of ourselves than we have now. . . . It's going to be extremely hard. . . . We're living on a planet which is in the process of deteriorating in very unpleasant ways which we will be able to predict the outcome of but not able to affect to any great degree because of what has already gone on in the past.

"At the same time, many of the mythological underpinnings upon which we have relied for the sense and coherence of our cultures will be shaken, as well as our understanding of our own purpose and meaning in life. We could not have chosen—any of us—a more difficult time in which to be alive [or] a more challenging one. See you next year," Strieber said.

Strieber's remarks suggest that he now sees himself as a modern-day messiah who has been chosen to warn the people of this planet, bringing them not the Word of God, but of the omniscient UFOnauts.

"A VAST SPIRITUAL KINDERGARTEN": TALKING WITH BRAD STEIGER

Robert Basil

Brad Steiger has been a part of the mystical counterculture since 1957, when he wrote an article on reincarnation, "How Many People Are You?", for the now-defunct magazine Exploring the Unknown. *Since then he has written more than a hundred books propagandizing nearly every aspect of what is now called the New Age movement: trance-channeling, UFOs, UFO-abductions, psychic powers, superadvanced ancient civilizations, crystal magic, Native American and Eastern religions, and so forth. His most famous books are* Divine Fire, Gods of Aquarius, The Fellowship, *and* Indian Medicine Power. *But he is probably best known for his frequent appearances in magazines like* True Psychic Inquirer *and* Inner Light, *where he can be seen hawking crystals and telling stories of "invisible entities that possess and destroy!" So, while Steiger has been successful in establishing a large and loyal audience, he is not regarded highly by the skeptics movement, which questions the scientific validity of his work.*

But Steiger doesn't consider himself a scientist, nor is he especially concerned with scientific rigor. He describes himself as a "communicator" more interested in getting people to develop their spiritual potential than in establishing objective facts. The following interview, which took place in September 1987, explores the tension between these two different projects.

BASIL: And where were *you* during the Harmonic Convergence?

STEIGER: My wife Sherry and I spent a very quiet evening meditating— just reflecting, I guess, on what we hope will be symbolic of a better time for the species and for the world.

BASIL: You use the word *symbolic*, which is at the center of the debate on the New Age movement. The genesis of the Harmonic Convergence is the Mayan calendar, about which José Arguelles has made many exorbitant claims. Are we really about to move off of the track of a tremendous "light beam" and zoom into the millennium? Do you regard this forecast as having scientific precision, that we are on the verge of a brand new astronomical order?

STEIGER: We need always to maintain the attitude of hope. I look at so many of these things as traditions, and to me an effective tradition is one that supports you *in the now*, and that continually moves into the future. Traditions that keep us in the past, stuck in old attitudes, and that have not proven to be positive or beneficial to the community at large need to be tucked into another category.

BASIL: You're saying, then, that the benefit of Harmonic Convergence is symbolic, that it's a projection of our desires and needs, not an actual spiritual fact.

STEIGER: So much of what we are talking about is symbolic to me. What is our archetypal apprehension of the world? How are we able to make it meaningful for us? When people came to me and talked about the Harmonic Convergence being the end of the world, my reaction was, "Well, it is the end of the Mayan calendar." And I think it is marvelous how accurate the calendar is. But, surely, any people who lived in a temporal society are going to run out of time sometime, and their calendar is going to come to an end. However, if people build upon the image of the calendar's end as a way of trying to fashion a new world and really resolve to start a very new beginning, then, again, that to me is symbolical of our resolve as a species to try to do better. And I certainly always applaud that kind of attitude. As far as what happened on August 17, 18, and 19, I have talked to several people who had meaningful visions. They felt that space brothers communicated to them on those dates. And some felt that the essence of Quetzalcoatl entered their being.

BASIL: From all the people I talked with at Niagara Falls, the sacred site I was closest to, I got no dramatic reports like that. I got hopeful ones, no dramatic ones.

STEIGER: Yes, I heard *many* dramatic reports. We don't know whether these experiences were the product of expectancy; I am not in the position to judge that. If they feel that what they experienced is going to help them put their reality together now in a more positive way, I would tend to regard those things as symbolic inner visions. And I am comfortable with that—as long as no one tries to force the visions he or she received during the Harmonic Convergence on *my* reality.

BASIL: Do you think Arguelles and others looked at it in a symbolic way?

STEIGER: From what I can see—and a friend of mine just did an interview with him—it would seem to me that he looked upon it as an actual event. And, of course, on one level of reality it *was* an actual event. The calendar *did* end. In terms of the Harmonic Convergence, many of those things become, to me, a little amorphous, but they become significant in what they may mark for us.

In other words, let us say that everyone in the world did join their energies—and, of course, whether it is Hands Across America or whatever, we know regretfully that it is always a small percentage of people who do become concerned or even reflect upon these things. But if enough people joined in their energy to say, "Let's make tomorrow a better day," what could be bad about that? It's positive, and it becomes a real thing that happens. Many people may have made a new year's . . . er, a *new age* resolution, to become a better person. That's a positive experience.

BASIL: The New Age is clearly a kind of religious movement. What is your religious background?

STEIGER: I was brought up in an evangelical Norwegian-Lutheran church. It was a meaningful part of my life. I am, in fact, now married to an ordained minister who attended the Lutheran School of Theology in Chicago and is licensed and ordained by a mainstream Protestant church.

For me, the spiritual world, or the religious world, has always been an important part of my life. I see absolutely no dichotomy, nor have I ever, in embracing the several worlds of our reality. I guess I have always wanted to be a Renaissance Man in that sense. I come from that kind of background. Tor Heyerdahl (the author of *Kon Tiki*) is a cousin of mine, and, according to family tradition, Hans Christian Andersen is a great great uncle. My grandmother was a tall, six-foot matriarch who said that a true man must be able to write poetry, should be a good horseman, should be a good hunter, and also an explorer—her brothers were all outdoorsmen or explorers and that to her was the ideal, that was the tradition. So, in the Scandanavian tradition one was expected to balance the two, to be poetic and creative and also a person of action and accomplishment.

The fact that I very early on had a mystical bent did not alarm the family; I guess in terms of the Kierkegaardian or even Swedenborgian atmosphere it doesn't hurt if a Dane is a little bit mystical. I certainly was regarded as a very pious lad. And, in a sense, I was probably annoyingly pious. I was conditioned to be a Lutheran clergyman, and that was my orientation and desire for quite some time. As a child of thirteen or so I would sometimes take over the church service when the minister went on vacation—I did not give sacraments, but I could do the sermon and much of the service. This was in Iowa. In our particular public school—since it exists no longer, I am not tattling on them—but through all of grade school the Bible was taught as part of the curriculum. (Catholics were excused.)

My mother had visions, materializations, and dematerializations ever since she was a young girl—materializations that occurred with her sister as a witness and that actually left imprints of sandals in the soil as an angelic being manifested before her. My father, on the other hand, always insisted that everything had to be documented, that you don't accept anything unless you can see it, smell it, taste it, touch it—and, of course, if it fit the precepts of the Lutheran church. So in this very interesting blend of mystical mother and practical father, my visionary nature was tolerated.

BASIL: But your father surely must have been dismayed by the turn you took since your youth. UFOs, crystals, and reincarnation aren't found in the Lutheran litergy. What made you convert away from the dogmas of Lutheranism?

STEIGER: Nothing—it was a process of evolution, which began, in a sense, when I died at the age of eleven . . .

BASIL: You died?

STEIGER: . . . in an extremely distasteful and gory farm accident. It was a classic near-death experience. I saw what I somehow sensed was me, and I looked like an egg yolk, an orangish amoebic type thing, and I was moving toward this remarkably beautiful light. I would feel this tension—"I don't want to die"—and then I would be pulled back to the consciousness of my body, which was awful, because blood was in my eyes.

There was no pain, because I had received a mortal wound, and I guess nature provides in that way. I left my body, and I was then literally able to be wherever I thought—I didn't want to leave my mother, and suddenly I was with my mother in the kitchen as she was preparing lunch. I thought of the trauma of my friends hearing about my accident, and

I then saw all of them on their respective farms as they were helping their fathers. I had that kind of limitless consciousness.

I was then shown or I saw what I can only describe as a multicolored geometric design, and I can see it as clearly now as I saw it then, but I can't put it into words. But as I saw that, it suddenly put in me a marvelous euphoria, that the world would go on and, more importantly, through my interpretation, that there is a pattern and a meaning to this incredible drama that we call life. That totally reassured me. And then I suddenly came back into my body when I was on the operating table in Des Moines.

I was in a Roman Catholic hospital . . . so my first audience was a group of Roman Catholic nurses, who sensed that I had had some kind of experience, that I had "been somewhere." There was a child in my room who was dying, and her parents wanted me to reassure them by telling them what their daughter would soon be seeing. That was when I first recognized the universality of the spiritual experience. Here were these people—who, according to certain prejudiced adults, were, regretfully, supposed to be on their way to hell because they were Catholic; but now I saw that we had the same concerns. Indeed, it was because of them that I was living. This insight had a tremendous effect on my eleven-year-old psyche, this plus my near-death experience. I suppose it is not strictly medically accurate to say I died, because I am here. I didn't have the experience of a master telling me, "Brad, you have marvelous work to do," but, like many others who have returned from death, I did have that experience of going toward "the light."

BASIL: In many ways the New Age movement is a reprise of an older "Age," the age of spiritualism at the turn of the nineteenth century, which featured standing-room-only performances by the infamous Fox sisters as well as the bewilderingly complex theosophical systems of people like Madame Blavatsky and Rudolf Steiner, who led mystical occult movements that are now being revived.

STEIGER: Steiner I very much appreciate, and I suppose in many ways his ideas have influenced me. Blavatsky, in contrast, I find a fascinating *character* study. Her writings, however, which depict all these cosmological levels, hierarchies, and different masters are a basic turn-off to me. I don't see "the higher realms," because of my own personal experience, as being that complex. But by the same token I can go along with some of her concepts and say that there is hierachy, that we are a part of a larger brotherhood and "fellowship"—which is, by the way, the title of my new book. I see the value in those people, and I see their particular role in the sequence of the philosophical development, but a lot of Theosophy is just too weighty for me.

BASIL: There is convincing evidence that Blavatsky was caught in various frauds.

STEIGER: I am fascinated by the Madame Blavatskys, the people who start movements. I guess my basic feeling is, and I am quoting William James, all religions and all philosophies begin with the individual mystical experience. And then, generally speaking, their followers begin to add dogmas and ecclesiasticisms and create miracles and miraculous experiences that the leaders have supposedly undergone. There seems to be a ritual dance that spiritual leaders are supposed to follow, a very precise cosmic choreography.

BASIL: But it was Madame Blavatsky, not her followers, who was caught red-handed. Are you saying that a fraud was enacted on her retroactively?

STEIGER: I don't know enough about her. I was speaking of the founders of spiritual movements in general. I see her and people like her as flamboyant characters. I have seen so many fine physical mediums prime the pump a little bit with out-and-out stage magic. I think they feel in their own minds, however, that they are justified in what they have done, and no doubt they would be shocked and annoyed at the accusations of fraud.

BASIL: Well, people like Uri Geller do claim to be shocked and annoyed. In fact, there is nothing keeping frauds from being shocked and annoyed by skeptics—or one-time believers—when they've been caught lying and cheating. So let's move outside of their minds and follow the standards of your typical Los Angeles police officer, who "just wants the facts." Would it be fair for him or her to describe these mediums and spiritual leaders as frauds?

STEIGER: Yes. Phony spiritualist mediums who seek only to bilk money from the gullible would definitely attract the attention of the bunko squad, and probably for good reason. But the majority of mediums are practicing their beliefs; I don't really have any particular complaint against them. If they have assisted people in finding a way or in getting through the night, they have provided a certain kind shamanistic function.

BASIL: Doesn't the fact that these people encourage credulity before false evidence outweigh any benefits?

STEIGER: But let us always consider *motive*. If the medium is merely a charlatan who has come up with another method of deceiving the public for gain, your concern is justified. If we are speaking of a spiritualist minister devoutly channeling messages for his little group of followers, then we are speaking of belief structures. I would hate to see all Catholic priests arrested for the doctrine of transubstantiation—that the wine becomes the blood of Christ during the Eucharist. Are they also encouraging "credulity" based on "false evidence"? Should science attempt to legislate matters of belief?

BASIL: How about Uri Geller?

STEIGER: To me, Uri represents a lot of what we are talking about. I have seen Uri at times when I am personally convinced—and that's all I can ever say—that he was serving as the conduit for an energy that we are still trying to describe and understand.

BASIL: But James "The Amazing" Randi and others have shown that Geller is perfectly capable of claiming that simple magicians' tricks are psychic powers. As evidence there are photos, there's the testimony of his ex-manager . . .

STEIGER: I take a somewhat different approach to this issue. I'm an amateur magician, and my particular hobby is mentalist tricks, so I understand what Randi is doing. Of course a magician can replicate 99 percent of what the most accomplished psychic sensitive can do, or maybe 100 percent. So can a film studio's special effects department. But the fact that we have been able to replicate a flower in plastic does not mean that there are no real flowers. God is still making real flowers, even though we are beginning to be able to replicate them. I would say that sometimes I have seen our finest psychic sensitives "prime the pump." I have caught them at it. I am disappointed, but to me what they have done makes sense. They have put themselves in a position where their audience will not allow them to fail. I, for example, am a professional writer, and right now I am pressured with a deadline, and I have to produce because I am taking the publisher's money. When you are a professional psychic, you have to produce, you sold tickets. I think that is a very unfortunate position for a serious psychic sensitive to be in. Psychic powers are spontaneous; largely, they happen like the creative impulse. If I have a terrible headache and an upset stomach, I may not feel particularly creative that day. It would create a great deal of stress if I had to write for an audience, and I probably wouldn't be as effective as I would be normally. When you put yourself in the structure of being a professional psychic, you are promising to deliver on demand an ability that is most often the product of spontaneous creativity. A magician—Randi—can still perform if he is ill, because he is admitting he is a performer.

When a psychic sensitive, who has developed some kind of ability, puts himself in that kind of show-business situation, I think he's asking for it; it is a very hazardous thing to do.

* * *

BASIL: Define the New Age.

STEIGER: I wouldn't even try. I don't like labels, and I don't like categories. All my life I have tried to resist being labeled. I know that when I was in the evangelical-fundamentalist school as a child, we were told there was a New Age coming, that that was something that Jesus had promised. Now that I am a mature author, certain people say I am in the New Age movement, so I am on the side of Satan. I am very confused. Is the New Age a part of Jesus, or a part of Satan? I recently saw a little tract printed by an extremely fundamentalist church: It was called "A New Age Dawning" and had a big rainbow on the cover. But you also have Constance Cumbey, a fundamentalist, writing an attack on the New Age called *The Hidden Dangers of the Rainbow*.

I don't know for certain what we are talking about when we say "New Age." I don't think that there is really anything new under the sun. I see things in terms of cycles. And I think this kind of response to organized religion and what people feel as the betrayal of technology and science have been with us in many centuries.

BASIL: The New Age movement deviates from Christian dogma in a couple of key ways. It moves away from the historicity of Jesus and from Christian institutions; you don't need the church to have direct experience of the divine anymore. You say that over and over in your book *Revelation: The Divine Fire*. People have made God a *personal experience*—not a transcendent being. They are more protestant than the Protestants.

STEIGER: I agree, it's kind of a delayed reaction to the Reformation, like a spiritual landmine that didn't go off right away in that particular conflict.

BASIL: What do you keep of the New Testament?

STEIGER: Most of it, except for some of Paul, because of his misogyny and what I consider his neuroses, which I think were expressed in prejudicial ways toward certain people. As far as the teachings of Jesus, and especially as we are now finding them in the Qumran, the Dead Sea Scrolls, and the Nag Hamaddi gospels, I see a different picture of Jesus, which I feel very comfortable with.

Instead of speaking of Christ, the New Age people speak of "being Christed." Jesus wasn't saying "I am the Way." If we look closely we can see that he is saying "There is a way . . . I have a way and you too can follow it, you too can create miracles"—which he says repeatedly.

BASIL: Do you believe in the Resurrection?

STEIGER: It is not important to me whether Jesus appeared to Mary Magdalene and the disciples in a physical body or a spirit body. To me, the story of the Resurrection is a powerful metaphor, a promise that we have within us an essential self that does survive physical death.

BASIL: The institutions of Christianity don't buy your "powerful metaphor" idea. They say that Jesus was *bodily* resurrected. But you would say they are mistaking mythic truth for physical truth?

STEIGER: To me, these things are living truths, that, in the archetypal level of our consciousness, mean a great deal to us. They give us an expression, a promise that we can realize in our personal lives. Would I tell this to an orthodox Christian? No, I don't have the right to tell anybody else what to believe, just as I don't want anyone telling me what to believe.

I don't see these differences as the problems so many other people perceive. I emphasize repeatedly our universal aspects. So many of these things are semantical difficulties. I like to quote Edward Arlington Robinson, the American poet, who said that the world is a vast spiritual kindergarten and we are all trying to spell God with different alphabet blocks. I am dismayed when I hear people condemning other people to hell. The way these people perpetuate prejudice! Jesus said love was being one. Now if you say one, "one world," that's satanic in the view of certain Fundamentalists.

BASIL: You tend to look at things for their *symbolic* value. Skeptics scold you, however, for not attending to the *literal* aspect. It is very important to know the metaphorical and subjective qualities of existence, but isn't it just as important, if not more so, to know when something is literally true and when something's a personal projection? You seem to be saying that it is not important to know the difference. Christianity posits the *historical reality* of the Resurrection. Saint Paul even said, "If the resurrection didn't happen, our faith is all for naught." The truth has to be *literal.*

STEIGER: I would say *universal* instead of literal. Of course it makes great difference to the individual percipient, to the one who is having the experience. What I'm saying is this: The teachings of Jesus are a promise to everybody, not just to those who do the dance a certain way. Try to reason with a fundamentalist; it's impossible, because you have to say absolutely everything exactly their way. If you deviate by two words then you are still in error, you still haven't "accepted Jesus Christ as your personal savior." I want to look upon this *as a consciousness*—the resurrection as a universal promise—recognizing the temple, the God, *within.* The transcendental experience is there for each of us.

BASIL: For many, the phenomena of channeling has been the most dramatic development of New Age practice. Let's talk about one of the most famous ones—J. Z. Knight, who claims to channel the spirit of Ramtha, a 35,000-year-old semidivine warrior from the sunken continent of Atlantis. Tell me: Do you think there was an actual person named Ramtha, who existed 35,000 years ago, who is now a spiritual entity who comes to inhabit J. Z. Knight when she goes into a trance?

STEIGER: I have seen Hal Holbrook channel Mark Twain. I have seen George C. Scott channel George Patton, and various other actors channel and become a personality that is deceased. J. Z. Knight puts on a little pageant play that some people feel comfortable with.

BASIL: George C. Scott and Hal Holbrook don't make the same kind of claims for themselves that Knight claims for herself.

STEIGER: I would have to put Knight in the category of Scott and Holbrook.

BASIL: You are a very diplomatic person! Indeed, shouldn't you go further—and say that Scott and Holbrook haven't tried to become prophets or attract thousands of money-paying acolytes. You look at Knight on stage. . .

STEIGER: . . . as *entertainment.* That is not channeling, that's *platform trance mediumship,* which totally disappeared in the '60s. Why it has come back is a mystery that fascinates me. I'm not really keen on movements, denominations. We are all one, we shouldn't be putting up any barriers that prevent people of spirit from communicating freely with one another. What I am seeing is New Age denominations growing up around trance channelers. We have enough movements and sects, we have enough cults. We have all these people who have left the pews of the Baptists, the Lutherans, and the Catholics, and now they are forming other denominations built around new prophets, the channelers. Sadly, at too many New Age conferences, it has become, "My trance channeler can beat up your trance channeler."

I don't want to mention names, but some of these channelers, who ten years ago were lucky to get twenty people in their audiences, now suddenly have received exposure on television and they get 5,000 people. A channeler comes out with an Irish accent or a pseudo-Jewish-prophet-Old-Testament-type accent, whatever that is, and he or she says, "It is marvelous to behold that the sky is blue. We should all work together in an attitude of peace and love." That's fine, but do we need this from someone who allegedly is speaking from 40,000 years ago? What is wrong with someone simply declaring it for him- or herself?

BASIL: Are they putting on an act? Or is there a profound psychic dissociation going on?

STEIGER: I started sitting with trance mediums when I was eighteen years old. I saw numerous cases of psychic dissociation, individual psychic mechanism. I don't know what would convince me. A discarnate entity would have to come up with something that would be representative from the time or place from which he claims to emanate.

BASIL: In *Divine Fire,* you quote at length a young man who claims to channel Jesus. You don't seem to be appalled by him.

STEIGER: We are talking about different things. If someone tells me that he is channeling the spirit of Jesus, I would have to say that this is what he understands this energy to be. In fact, I believe that what he is experiencing is a revelatory mechanism that is helping this person to put his life together. We all have the ability; it's not so bizarre.

BASIL: Do you believe that people have objective contact with discarnate entities?

STEIGER: I think that this is possible. I think it does happen.

* * *

BASIL: UFOs. Something interesting came across my desk last week, a magazine you coedited, called *The Allende Letters: Has the UFO Invasion Started?* It came out in 1968. I wanted to ask you whether you believe that UFOs—with extraterrestrial physical beings inside of them—have come down to earth and abducted people, as Whitley Strieber in *Communion* and Budd Hopkins in *Intruders* claim. Or do you believe that UFOs can be better explained by scientific and/or psychological explanations?

STEIGER: Here is where I frustrate skeptics. Check all of the above. I don't see why I have to take just one point of view. It seems to me to be a viable hypothesis that we have had some kind of contact and interaction with alien—what I call *multidimensional*—intelligence ever since we straightened our spines. Again, for people who claim *regular* contact I would suggest that they are in contact with something, which, because they live in a technological age and are used to things flying around the skies, choose to think of as UFOs.

BASIL: You would be suspicious of "repeaters," then. The statistical improbability of seeing UFOs time and time again would make you go to the psychological hypothesis more quickly for those who claim to do so.

STEIGER: Yes, which is what I say in *The Fellowship*. I see a very fascinating phenomenon occurring here. I started researching the "contactee" phenomenon in about 1967. I found people who convinced me that they had had a physical, material, *objective* interaction with something. Many of these people would appear to have burn marks, scratches; I saw people who had grid patterns on their chests. Unless in a state of ecstasy or hysteria they somehow mutilated themselves, what we are dealing with is some kind of physical evidence.

BASIL: Isn't your latter hypothesis so much more easy to accept than the "alien" one, that entities have traveled over two light years to get to our solar system?

STEIGER: But perhaps they are here *all the time*, in our ocean, or in *another dimension*.

BASIL: But aren't these hypotheses likewise less credible than the self-mutilation one?

STEIGER: At this point, I have to stay open. I don't think any of us has enough evidence to be dogmatic. Several publications have reprinted my eighteen theories of what UFOs might be.

BASIL: Some people believe in the "dero" hypothesis, that the earth is hollow and houses a variety of alien creatures who swoop up through a hole in the Arctic.

STEIGER: I think that's metaphorical. But there are people who seem to give a demonstration that a physical something happened, and they are totally befuddled, shocked, and confused by it, and they really give a convincing demonstration that they have had a physical interaction with something of another world. And many of these same people have had their lives completely transformed, some even becoming channels. Now, what has happened there to cause such a conversion experience? What made Saul become Paul? What is this mechanism within humankind that is blinded by the light?

BASIL: You emphasize again and again your belief that abductees seem "sincere." This raises two points. James Randi's "Project Alpha"—in which he convinced skilled scientific researchers that two young magicians possessed a wide range of paranormal powers—has called into question *everyone's* intuitive sense of another's "sincerity." It's a sad fact, and also kind of scary; but truth-seekers in science as well as spirituality, it seems to me, have no choice but to accept it. So, how can you be sure that you can't be fooled? My second point is this: Even granting the sincerity of an "abductee" or of someone who claims to have impressive mystical or magical powers, cannot somebody be sincere, not to mention highly intelligent, and still be profoundly mistaken?

STEIGER: Of course. I would never be so presumptuous as to claim that I could never be fooled. But once again we are talking about two different things. Randi, as a professional magician, is a trained deceiver who deliberately set out to deceive others. I have accepted on faith that you are taking my time and my words to publish my thoughts in a book. If you are lying and you only wish to burn the manuscript or to expose my gullibility in trusting your intentions, then you have accomplished your deceit.
    Over the years, I have heard from literally thousands of people—ranging

from common laborers to heads of physics departments at major universities—who have chosen to tell me of their individual mystical experience or their UFO encounter. These are more in the nature of confessionals than projects intended to deceive. Their motives were: "At last maybe someone will listen and understand." When one is revealing an intense, subjective experience, how can anyone deny the internal validity of that experience? What I am dealing with is the transcendental experience, and I am reporting instances in which it would seem that the transcendental capacity within a person was somehow touched or manifested. And I am open-minded enough to say that maybe there is this extraterrestrial or multidimensional or "divine" intelligence that communicates to humankind through such a capacity.

BASIL: In an earlier conversation we had, you criticized Mr. Strieber and Mr. Hopkins and their two fairly successful books. You said that you've been writing about abductions seriously for years and it was unfair and ironic that these two men got all the attention. You raised, of course, a more profound objection: Their abductees described their experiences as horrifying—indeed, they felt "raped." But people you talked to, and you say you still get several letters a week, were much more positive. Now, that suggests one of two things: either Hopkins and Strieber happened into a completely different sampling or that the whole thing is metaphorical (or fradulent) and that their psychic drama is much darker than your own.

STEIGER: Let me clarify. First, it was just humorous sour grapes when I joked that those guys were standing in front of the cosmic slot machine when it paid off. Second, I also have received many reports that speak of UFO encounters in a frightening, traumatized way—Close Encounters of the Most Frightening Kind.

BASIL: Your sample is not qualitatively different from theirs, then.

STEIGER: No, I only objected to their single emphasis. There is another kind of contactee who recounts positive, spiritual experiences, who believes that it is wonderful to participate with their space brothers. Largely it depends upon your level of spiritual awareness, your attitude of openness toward strangers, your prejudice or lack thereof toward people who look different from you, your level of technological awareness, and educational background.

*   *   *

BASIL: Let me read some of your own work back to you. I find a startling amount of variation in your tone and sense of audience. Frankly, in many articles you seem to be appealing to the most paranoid and alarmist contingent of the UFO crowd. For example, in the magazine *The Allende Letters: Has the UFO Invasion Started?* you coauthored an article called "Three Men in Black—The UFO Terrorists," which begins this way:

> In September, 1953, three men dressed in black visited flying saucer researcher Albert K. Bender at his home in Bridgeport, Connecticut. The men told Bender something about flying saucers that so frightened him, he never again participated in organized UFO research.
>
> In February, 1955, in New Zealand, John H. Stuart came into possession of a grey white metal fragment from a UFO. The next night a man in black called on Stuart, collected the fragment and told Stuart to stop all his saucer research.
>
> In April, 1959, brilliant astrophysicist M. K. Jessup was found dead in his automobile in a Florida park. Jessup was reportedly conducting research that would zero in on the UFO mystery. Certain intimate friends say Jessup had been warned to cease prying into the flying saucer enigma.

And you go on:

> In all the theorizing about the identity of the mysterious group, one disturbing fact remains constant. Whoever comprises the ranks of the men in black knows, or gives the impression of knowing, a great deal more about the secrets of the cosmos than we at our present level of science and technology have been able to discover. . . .
>
> This thesis creates yet another enigma in an area where puzzles and paradoxes abound. Are the [Men in Black] persecutors or pals? Are they strong-arm agents of a hostile group or forceful friends using stringent measures to keep us from moving into areas where we can get hurt?

STEIGER: No doubt there have been occasions when people, for whatever reasons, have interfered with certain UFO percipients. These may truly have been intimidating agents of some government agency or, in other cases, members of civilian UFO-research groups who handled their investigations in an authoritarian or clumsy manner. Just to give you a bit of historical context, the prevailing mood of UFOolgy in 1968, when that magazine from which you quoted was published, UFOs were strictly "nuts and bolts," very physical things, and no other theories were tolerated. As you already stated, I was the coauthor of that article, and the thoughts expressed were really more hers than mine.

BASIL: Your name was on the article.

STEIGER: That magazine was spun off a book of mine that had begun as *Strange Flying Saucer Mysteries*. One of the chapters dealt with the Allende Letters, a series of bizarre communications allegedly written by one Carlos Miguel Allende to the author and well-known astrophysicist M. K. Jessup. The letters told of a secret United States Navy experiment that supposedly teleported a warship from Philadelphia to a dock near Norfolk by successfully applying Einstein's unified field theory. The publisher became so fascinated by this chapter that he changed the book's title to *Allende Letters: New UFO Breakthrough*, which was an embarrassment to me because the Allende letters had been a part of the UFO mythos for years. The flying saucer mystery of the three men in black was another facet of the phenomena that I dealt with in the book. When the magazine was spun off the book, the person in charge of the project rewrote a number of the articles using language that neither I nor the other authors would have used.

BASIL: Are you saying that "the three men in black," these "UFO terrorists," was taken out of context, or that it was rewritten?

STEIGER: The three men in black were very much a part of the UFO mythos at that time. Rumors flew about who had been "silenced" by the three men in black. A lot of UFO investigators really bought into this scenario, and I reported a number of alleged encounters with the UFO terrorists.

I guess one of the most difficult aspects about being an author is that things you wrote years ago when your thinking was at a certain level can always surface to embarrass you. There may be a whole lot of thoughts that you wish you could somehow erase. On the other hand, I try to indicate that I am presenting theories or alleged experiences of others, so that I leave myself open to evolution and growth. Since I came to UFOs from the area of psychical research, I began more and more to see that so much of the UFO mystery seemed to me to be paraphysical or multidimensional in nature. In my *Mysteries of Time and Space*, I compare the men in black to the trickster in American Indian culture. And, in occult traditions, when people feel that they are on to the truth, very often this type of pageant gets enacted: Challengers arise to test the seeker.

BASIL: So the mysterious men in black don't in fact exist. They are UFOlogists' projections of fear. Why didn't you say *that*?

STEIGER: I am not saying that there were not prototype experiences for the allegations that some people had physically been threatened by persons unknown and told to cease their UFO investigations. I am stating that I believe that in the great majority of cases individual ego came into play: "I'm onto the secret and there are people who are opposed to my finding out about it. I am therefore in danger."

BASIL: In the article you don't get *any* sense that you believe these men are merely projections of fear. You claim that they work for a large and powerful organization. You ask, "Are these strong armed agents of a hostile group or forceful friends using stringent measures from moving into areas where you can really get hurt?" But you don't add, "Or are they very fascinating trickster projections, common in American culture, of people who think they are on to something."

STEIGER: I couldn't add that in 1968 because I wouldn't write it until 1974 in *Mysteries of Time and Space*. I did not spring full blown from the brow of Zeus. I am learning, growing, evolving in my thoughts, words, and deeds. There was a quantum leap forward in my own work and in the publishers' attitude toward my work in those six years from the magazine article from which you quote to the book published by Prentice-Hall. In a great deal of my earlier work, my theories, mysterious reflections, were very often edited out. I might theorize on the true nature of ghostly phenomena, and all that would be left was, "My God, something is coming down the staircase!" I have had many projects not work out the way I had hoped that they would. I try always to do the best that I can, and if a project fails, I pick myself up, dust myself off, and start all over again. Until I developed a demonstrable following for my kind of book, I had to suffer through a lot of really bad covers and cover copy, which caused me a great deal of embarrassment, a great deal of pain. Most of the time I didn't even get to see the galleys. Remember, I was teaching college when a lot of these things were coming out.

BASIL: What about magazines like *True Psychic Inquirer* and *Inner Light*, in which you frequently appear? Neither could be designed with university tenure in mind.

For a recent issue of *Inner Light*, for example, you wrote a cover story called "Invisible Entities that Possess and Destroy." More distasteful still, however, is an advertisement for your book *Demon Lovers*, which takes up the entire centerfold. "Brad Steiger, America's Leading Parapsychologist Warns . . . THE DEVIL WANTS YOUR BODY AS WELL

AS YOUR SOUL! Startling—But All True—Modern Cases of Possession and Lust Between Humans and Vampires, Poltergeists, Werewolves, Ghouls, Astral Entities and Lucifer Himself." Those who order the book from the magazine receive a "FREE Devil's Trap" talisman, "to protect you from harm" and "ward off evil."

In an advertisement in another issue, "Brad Steiger Tells You How To Tap The Cosmic Source Using Crystals, Chants & Charms in the Proper, New Age Way." The ad continues: "Use the powerful force of New Age magic to achieve all you desire"; "Use crystals to banish evil & negativity"; "Tune into timeless realms"; "Explore the future with crystal vision"; "Astral project using the 'Aztec Ritual' method"; "Travel into space in your own crystal starship"; "Receive instant awareness"; "Use amulets, rings, as well as stones & gems for a wealth of positive benefits"; and "Breathe color to balance your energies." The advertisement also promises "Luxuries Unlimited" and "Huge Lottery Winnings."

STEIGER: These magazines are like psychic fairs, newsstand appeals to reach the broadest audience. But you are touching on perhaps the most sensitive area that exists for the serious artist in any area—the marriage between art and commerce. *Demon Lovers*, for example, is a reprint of my earlier work *Sex and the Supernatural*, which has always garnered serious reviews from thoughtful people, but which has never been advertised successfully.

BASIL: But how do you feel about your audience? You know that you are writing for people who might not always understand the difference between the poetic, metaphorical, psychological, and the literal.

STEIGER: I revere my audience, and I have a great sense of responsibility toward them. I have always received a large volume of reader mail, and I do a rather extensive program of lectures, seminars, and workshops. Let me tell you my grand plan. I do books like *Divine Fire, Gods of Aquarius, Mysteries of Time and Space*, and *The Fellowship* in which I theorize my heart out, really express what I think is happening. Then, because I truly have a sense of mission and purpose—that is, I want to tell the broadest audience possible that they have a nonphysical capacity, that they can be so much more than they probably have accepted, that they can eliminate their negative programming, and that they can truly in that sense have choices—I take my larger philosophical books and serve as my own translator and interpret those concepts that may be too heavy for the average person, though I try not to be condescending. My greatest delight is when I get fan letters from Ph.Ds and eleven-year-old kids reading the same book.

By and large I kind of like the fact that I can assume different styles. In lectures especially, I have to come from the audience's specific background, use words and phrases from their profession or from their cultural environment so they can understand the concepts I offer.

BASIL: You say that your interest is in the spiritual, and in assisting a wide variety of people to locate their own spirituality. But the ad I quoted earlier appeals less to spirituality and benevolence than it does to avarice.

STEIGER: You're getting back to commerce and literary expression once again. I don't even accept the concept of a devil walking about as a roaring lion seeking whom he may devour, but an ad writer may interpret my concept of negative energy as "the devil." I tell people that true magic is in one's mind. I have developed numerous mental exercises and techniques with colorful titles that will expand one's consciousness and hopefully make that person a more creative, more productive individual in the here and now.

BASIL: In the ad, though, published in a magazine for which you are listed as "contributing editor," you say, "align yourself with angels."

STEIGER: Don't hold me responsible for ads! You cannot believe that I write the ads, the cover blurbs, the press releases. I write for major publishers. I am not a one-man show. I keep alluding to the fact that a serious writer must first accept "what is." And what is is that the publisher wishes to sell books and how that is accomplished is out of the hands of the writer.

BASIL: People are making a lot of money off the New Age. There are about a dozen mail-order companies I'm aware of that specialize in "mysticism" but use the crassest of marketing tactics. They exploit people's spiritual yearnings, and often their helplessness, as a way of making heaps of money. This is far removed from Christ throwing the vendors out of the temple! How can you, someone who emphasizes spiritual growth, tolerate this kind of marketing?

STEIGER: That's so difficult to answer. I don't know a single author who is comfortable with the marketing aspect. If you are at all serious about your work, you bleed a little inside. God has not yet granted me complete control of the publishing industry. When this occurs, I shall, of course, run things differently.

BASIL: The medium ridicules, even extinguishes the message.

STEIGER: In some cases that may be true. I can only wince and go on with my work. You have to become somewhat detached to the marketing aspect of it, because some of the finest companies commit the most grievous misrepresentations. I have gone on talk shows not realizing that the publisher's publicist has inadvertently provided the host with a list of hostile questions for him to hit me with. I'm in the trenches and the generals are out throwing me curves, so to speak.

The mail-order audience is a totally different audience. This is something I have come to observe. The audience that reads my book may or may not come to my lectures and seminars. The audience that buys magazines really doesn't buy the book. In short, I have a book audience, a lecture and seminar audience, a magazine audience, and a mail-order audience. Of course there is some degree of overlapping, but it is much less than what you might expect.

BASIL: Which audience is the most lucrative?

STEIGER: The book audience, of course, then the lecture audience. But, as I said, as much as I try, it's hard to mix them. Let me tell you what happens in my seminars, which are very experiential. I lead the audience through creative visualization, which is very popular. I give people tools they can use in their personal life, and they say, "Brad, this is marvelous, you have changed my life." And then I might say very humbly, "Here is my new book." And they will pick it up, say, "Isn't it nice! I love the cover," and put it down. The audiences are different, which explains my different tones and approaches.

*   *   *

BASIL: Many skeptics think you purvey nonsense. Undoubtedly, they would be surprised that one could enjoy an intellectual conversation with you. On the other hand, in some aspects you bring a certain amount of skepticism that they would share. Do you think their debunking is harmful or helpful to the general climate of critical inquiry in this culture?

STEIGER: Mostly it's helpful. They say I am a purveyor of nonsense. But I see and hear some of these guys, and they are so narrow-minded, they are the Fundamentalists of the scientific movement. God, I would hate to live in their world.

BASIL: What's your primary criticism?

STEIGER: Their will to disbelieve. I think the will to disbelieve is as strong as the will to believe.

One thing you would get from me is a general moderate approach. Let's see what's going on, let's try to approach these matters without prejudice.

BASIL: Let me quote from your credo, "This I Believe": "I believe that man's one truly essential factor, his spirituality, may never be fully susceptible to scientific elucidation. I believe that the artificial worlds to which man has given the designation of sciences are no truer than dreams, visions, or inspirations. Since all thought is subjective, man-made criteria may never be objective. The quest for absolute proof or objective truth may always be meaningless and unattainable when it seeks to define and to limit one's soul." Your credo seems to reflect a defensiveness before the skeptics and the scientists. What is your position toward science?

STEIGER: I, too, am a child of this century. I esteem science and technology and all the marvelous fruits thereof. We are speaking about attitudes here. I simply have no trouble accepting both the mechanics and the physics of the material world together with the reality of the spiritual world.

I think that too many scientists judge the situation before examination. Science to me is openness, exploration, and the willingness to accept new concepts and new ideas. And I think certain scientific traditions, as well as certain religious traditions, can tie us to various kinds of superstitions. I think that scientific superstitions and falsehoods can be maintained. No scientist can ever really say that something cannot happen. Science should be like the street system in any large city—always under examination and always under repair.

BASIL: No scientist, of course, would disagree with that statement. Aren't scientists merely upholding the high standards of replication, corroboration, and evidence—which have moved technology and science so quickly to where it is—when they show skepticism before potentially revolutionary paranormal and New Age claims?

STEIGER: To me, someone who *embraces* a word like "skeptical" is not unlike a believer in a fundamentalist sect: He is already announcing his prejudice. Skeptics say, "I am a disbeliever and proud of it," in the same way a fundamentalist says, "I believe everything the Bible tells me because it is the literal word of God." Avowed skeptics already have their minds made up.

BASIL: Carl Sagan would say that there is so much to be in awe of in the physical world—that, for example, there are black holes the size of my office—that there's no reason to look to the paranormal or the psychic or any of these occult matters to retain awe, because true science really does maintain awe. Of course, he is skeptical when it comes to UFOs and various paranormal matters. But, in fact, he spends most of his career now searching for extraterrestrials, so he is harshly critical of people who say there is enough evidence to say we have already had contact with them now. Your definition of a skeptic does not apply to him.

STEIGER: I don't think one should ever attempt to derive definitions that fit all people. There are scientists who accept the spiritual world, just as there are transcendentalists who revere science. But I am uncomfortable when somebody says, "I am a skeptic." If you asked me what I am, I would say I am a searcher, an explorer, a communicator; I'm not saying I'm a believer or disbeliever. Moreover, I am also admitting that spiritual element of life—I do not see the conflict in being both scientific and spiritual, in being a complete person. But skeptics announce their positions ahead of time. I just don't see any openness. I have to keep going back to works like Burt's *Metaphysical Foundations of Modern Science* and my own understanding that in the beginning of humankind's intellectual-spiritual searchings science and religion were one. I am also convinced that many new discoveries in physics and mathematics will reunite science and the spirit and not keep them separate as so many people seem to want to do.

BASIL: You think skeptics are "spiritually closed."

STEIGER: Yes, and that is what disturbs me. In the so-called skeptically inquiring groups I have never been able to sense that they wish to be anything other than what they are now—skeptical inquirers.

*   *   *

BASIL: Let's talk about reincarnation and hypnotic "past life" regression, the technique you and others use to get people to purportedly remember earlier lives. Dick Sutphen, who has written many books on this hyponotic technique, claims that it doesn't matter whether people do in fact re-experience their past lives. The key is that the therapy makes them feel better.

STEIGER: Right, you can't prove it; but he doesn't seek to prove it. What is important in past-life regression therapy are the positive results—and so he very ably deflects criticisms of the literal veracities of these people's memories.

BASIL: This is spiritual machiavellianism—the ends justify the means, the means in this case being the unsubstantiated claims that hypnotic regression can bring you in contact with memories of a former life. Don't you have problems with that?

STEIGER: No, it is the same attitude I have. I have been doing past-life regression since the Sixties, and what I have been able to accomplish with people is truly remarkable. When people are able to separate their phobias and compulsions from themselves and see their lives as a kind of psychodrama, an incredible kind of therapy is accomplished. And this therapy has often been more successful for people than years of conventional pyschiatric therapy. I would say, instead of a machiavellian, I look upon myself as a pragmatic mystic. Am I a pure scientist? No, I don't claim to be. But I consider myself a pragmatic person.

BASIL: Does this therapy work for those who don't believe in reincarnation?

STEIGER: Yes, they don't have to believe.

BASIL: People are moved by the images they have in the trance state.

STEIGER: Exactly, profoundly. I have had total atheists, total skeptics, cynics, and so forth, moved by the psychodrama.

BASIL: You, however, believe in God.

STEIGER: I don't believe in the large man with the great beard, but I do believe in an eternally powerful energy source with which humankind can interact—a Holy Spirit, if you will. Surely this spirit can externalize itself in many guises to accomplish a goal of spiritual evolution.

BASIL: Do you believe in a "personal" energy, then?

STEIGER: As I say in the close of the *Divine Fire*, I guess I have a sense that there is an external force or intelligence that we, through the "God spark" within, are able to make connections with and receive that eternally powerful source of strength and inspiration.

BASIL: Looking into the future, what project, what idea, offers the best chance for a convergence of the skeptics and people like yourself, who more often entertain the paranormal hypothesis. Where will the common ground be?

STEIGER: A common ground? In this dialogue we came together from supposedly "enemy camps," yet we shared concepts and respected our differing points of view. So dialogue, dispassionately employed, would, in my opinion, be the most likely way to find common ground. But please understand that I am not an evangelist. I am not trying to sell anyone anything. I am a creator and a communicator. I want people to come to their own place, where they feel comfortable, fulfilled, and enriched.

I don't debate, because to me a debate is where previously biased people entrench their own beliefs.

BASIL: Isn't there a necessity to come to a common answer? In science if perhaps not in religion?

STEIGER: How can we ever have a common answer when we have a vast universe of creative minds seeking their own fulfillment, their own intellectual expression, their own spiritual expresssion, and having the cosmic birthright to do exactly that, to explore and express the type of reality that is comfortable for each person?

NEW AGE MUSIC?

Leslie Berman

Recently I boarded Rockbottom Airline's transatlantic commuter bus to fly home from a weeklong blitz of Dublin and London, overtired, restless, and dreading what I knew would be a cramped, noisy flight. I don't like to fly when I'm feeling my best, but when I'm cranky, I hate it. So I was instantly relieved when I found a New Age music channel listed in the in-flight entertainment guide. Solace, serenity, even sleep were just a few dreamy tunes away. Plugging in my headset, I twisted the dial to find the selections captioned "Smooth As Ice." Eleven album tracks from artists released by Global Pacific, Windham Hill, and even CBS Records were promised. But when I found Channel 9, instead of the soothing instrumental sounds of Paul Winter's "River Run" (*Living Music*), Acoustic Alchemy's "One for the Road" (*MCA*), Gabriel Lee's "Nature Cycle Variations" (*Narada*), or Mark O'Connor's "Opus 35: Send Rainbows" (*Warner Bros.*) listed in the log, I heard strident comedy, pulsing Latin beats, and hard-rocking country. Twisting the dial again, I tried alternate channels 7 and 11 (on some aircraft). No Ice.

"Last month's programs," I grumbled to the flight attendant, who fluttered his dismay and hurried off to locate the correct tape. Soon he was back, extremely apologetic, but unsuccessful. Now I was really irritated. I know I pulled a face, my trembling chin signalling distress, because he became overly solicitous, like I do when I'm trying to calm my petulant nephew before he throws an all-out tantrum. But his tactic didn't work with this baby, because I refused to be cajoled. After failing to tempt me even with complimentary helpings of everything on board, he finally slouched away, a sorrowful look conceding defeat. None of this had lightened my mood, but as I watched his retreat I found I was stifling a smile. "I don't

---

Leslie Berman is a prolific free-lance music critic whose work has appeared in the *Village Voice* and *High Fidelity*.

even like New Age music," I reminded myself. "Why am I acting so testy?" The subject was already in mind, but that momentary revelation gave me another disquieting, juicy bone to gnaw on: The New Age had arrived when I wasn't looking.

I worry about music for a living, so I like to think I'm on the cutting edge of the trends, but I have to admit that my real awareness of New Age music coincided with the spread of popular interest in the form. That was in the mid-Eighties. I'd heard vague somethings about it before, but the phrase "new age" had the curious effect of clogging my New York ears. Blissfully deaf, I was able to avoid the distasteful-sounding West Coast aberration for a long time. "It's a fad," I confided to an editor in my best self-satisfied manner. I believed that, and expected it would just drift away. Then one day the first wispy fingers of New Age music began to invade my folk and pop turf.

First, a number of folk-fusionists, whose works were similar to or compatible with the hazily defined form, tried to distance themselves from the quaintness associated with their rigid folk pasts and to generate greater public visibility and music industry credibility by banding into a "school." Fiddler Darol Anger coined the term "new acoustic music" to describe instrumental experiments that featured mandolin, fiddle, banjo, and guitar, experments that reached out primarily from the strict tempos and pat formulas of blue-grass music to the freedom of jazz. The press and the folk-music industry latched hungrily onto the term, linking every young musician who'd played even one composed or improvised bluegrass-plus-other-definable-musical-genre piece. In her July 1987 "New Acoustic" roundup for *Jazziz,* Jo Ann Guido even roped in electronic keyboardman John Jarvis. But the name stuck to only a few composers and groups. Very quickly, Anger and several others who'd been featured on Rounder Records' much-hyped "new acoustic music" sampler (featuring only their own previously-placed-under-contract contemporary string players), moved on to even softer compositions, Windham Hill Records, and inclusion in the New Age.

Of course, that forced me to privately reevaluate my anti-New Age prejudice, though I remained cutting and skeptical in public. And soon I became troubled, as well as fascinated, by the meteoric rise of this so-called "new" music form. I was afraid of a quiet revolution because I had come to believe—from the snatches I'd heard and my colleagues' reactions to those tid-bits—that New Age music was like other reduced-calorie consumer items: not quite as tasty as the originals it was meant to imitate. Through repeated letdowns when fickle audiences favored mediocre knockoffs of my favorite artists, I'd found that the general public's palate is far from sophisticated—and that loyal consumers don't remember how the real thing tastes once they've grown used to the "lite" version. I believed that New Age music would diminish the musics it borrowed from if audiences learned to like music served with sugary strains masking the dischords of passion.

At the same time I was fascinated by New Age music, because it spread like kudzu across every musical genre, was embraced by a few fine musicians and composers, multiplied rapidly from what seemed to be a tenuous toehold to choke off venues and outlets for better musical forms—even sneaked into the homes of my friends and family. When I thought about its widening acceptance, I had to wonder why so many people whose tastes I otherwise respected could find enjoyment in anything so feeble and bland.

By 1985 I'd listened to very few compositions I would have described as New Age, though I could name several jazz, pop, contemporary classical, and folk musicians who'd been ridiculed as New Age by rock critics of my acquaintance. And in 1985 I was nearly immune to the momentum-gathering sales pitches and growing presence of New Age music in America's record racks and on the airwaves. The first East Coast wave of marketing leveled at the consuming critical mass began as I left New York in 1984, on my personal odyssey to find Paris in the twenties by living in the squalor of London's East End in my thirties. I wrote my first review of a New Age record while living there, but relating this experience to my English friends didn't even raise eyebrows. The Londoners I knew were by and large indifferent to what I described offhandedly as another doomed-to-cult-status California sound.

When I reviewed that LP my definition of New Age (derived from glib debates with, and harangues from, various critic friends) was as impressionistic as the form itself. Before the emergence of the name my circle had discussed *Ambient Music,* a series of albums created to satisfy an aesthetic/philosophical premise proposed by former Roxy Music band-member Brian Eno. The first LP of the group, entitled *Ambient 1: Music for Airports,* was a pastel wash of tinkly, treacly repetition. I hated it instinctively, and I embellished this unhappy first impression without subjecting myself to repeated listenings. Of course, I was predisposed to scorn: I'd read the press release accompanying reviewers' copies of this LP that had included Eno's grandiose defense of his barely audible mood-musings. Eno defined "ambience" as "an atmosphere, or a surrounding influence: a tint," explaining that ambient music "must be able to accommodate many levels of listening attention without enforcing one in particular; it must be as ignorable as it is interesting."[1] This manifesto infuriated me: I'd been a fan of Roxy Music and had looked forward to a new Brian Eno project. But I found little to appreciate in *Music for Airports'* vague ramblings and missed the grittier styles I'd championed in print. So my friends and I harpooned *Ambient Music*. Not only did I say that it was self-dismissive in its mindlessness and passivity, but I rejected intentionally designed background music as the antithesis of proper composition. Moreover, I was dismayed by Eno's complicity in reducing the value of his own and others' hard work by purposely recording Muzak. When asked later whether I knew about or was interested in New Age music, I responded by equating it with Eno's wallpaper-of-sound.

Four years later I've changed my tactics if not my tune. I've written a bit about New Age, listened to a little more. Instead of simplistic dismissal, when I speak about New Age I try for debate. My brother, who loves his music as much as I do mine, moved on with his favorite artists as they slipped from soft jazz and jazz-rock fusion into New Age. And my California-based music-business friends became agents and managers of New Age artists. Musicians I adored flowed into the New Age stream. It seemed clear that New Age music had come to play and I could no longer avoid it. Then came the moment-of-truth plane ride, and I really began to stew.

Is There a Definable New Age Music?

To worry effectively about New Age music, I needed to define it. Was it a distinct musical category or just a marketing phrase?

Record-company staffers, who uniformly declined to be named in this article, admitted that, in their experience of the term, New Age had positive value in a retail sales pitch but negative impact on their performers. "If it's a legitimate label for a specific form of music, why do they dislike the term?" I asked.

"Let's just say the name has a ring of faddishness," one publicist said. "It would be more meaningful and more acceptable if it were called New Ageless."

Synthesizer innovator Wendy Carlos echoed that sentiment—she considers New Age a marketing term: "What will they call it ten years from now?" WFMU (New Jersey) radio host Steve Dondershine agrees that New Age is a convenient handle but believes there are some definable qualities that separate this from other forms of instrumental music. "It's mind-expanding, dream-inducing. You can broaden your thinking listening to this music," he says.

New Age publications rhapsodize over the music, calling it a natural byproduct of New Age thinking. These publications skirt the issue of musicality, reviewing instead the music's *intent* and its value as a therapeutic catalyst.

Journalist Jennifer King called it "a tonic for the physical and emotional toil of twentieth-century stress"[2] and likened New Age to music made by primitive societies, the ancient Chinese, and other "enlightened" groups who recognized music's ability to "harmonize body, mind, and spirit." In a "New Age Music and Video" column in *The Guide to New Age Living,* the music is defined as "contemplative, mellow, introspective," and it is praised for its purpose—"fitting accompaniment to healing practices and spiritual values often associated with New Age groups. . . . It is meant to be conducive to meditation, stress reduction, communion with nature, making love, or whatever else puts you in touch with a more peaceful state of being."

But one thoughtful assessment by a radio show host, who occasionally programs New Age music, specifically condemns the attention paid to the music's mission: "electronic [New Age music] is almost exclusively designed for meditation or stress reduction—and therein lies its weakness: The quality of the music itself often suffers. In all too many New Age works, any compositional merit is of secondary importance to extra-musical concerns."[3]

Whether New Age is a music genre or simply a publicist's catchphrase, few names have caused so much contention. Antilles/New Directions (a division of Island Records) Records chief Jean-Pierre Weiller-Letourner, whose label features instrumental artists ranging from innovative modern classical musicians and fusionists to jazz and ethnic-based composers, resents the implication that his label's acts could be called New Age. "New Age has no meaning as a musical term. Many of my records are instrumental, and some of the compositions are quiet. But that doesn't make their jazz less than jazz. Following that theory, you could take a slow, quiet passage from any of the great classical compositions and play it on a New Age radio station. Will that make it New Age music? Where do you draw the line?" Weiller-Letourner suggested that New Age music should not be marketed through record stores; it should instead be "sold in drugstores as a sleep and relaxation aid." International Music Network president Anne Marie Martins has suggested that the division in New Age music between artists whose compositions are created as emotionally stimulating interactive art and those whose music more properly belongs in the holistic therapist's lounge is not accounted for by the single term New Age.

WNYC (New York) radio host John Schaefer attempts to blur the divisions between many "new" musics, including those lumped together as New Age, while avoiding linking together "Difficult Music," minimalism, New Age, and others with a common label. In his pioneering abecedary-cum-history titled (after his show) *New Sounds: A Listener's Guide to New Music,* the heading "New Age" appears only twice in the index—the first is a listing for a German electro-acoustic duo by that name, and the second, the title of a compilation album of artists on the IC label (unfortunately, inadequately cited for uninitiated readers like myself). In the book's first chapter, "The Electronic Age," two pages refer to New Age (this mention doesn't make the index[4]). In this brief space, Schaefer explains that his difficulty with the term arises from the users' definition of New Age, which is often expressed philosophically rather than musically: "The name itself is based on the astrological premise that Earth is entering a new age—the 'Age of Aquarius,' as the musical *Hair* told us. The movement seems to believe that this new age will usher in an era of worldwide peace and harmony. The main objective of New Age music seems to be combining electronic and/or acoustic sounds in a way that is conducive to meditation, relaxation, etc.; the music sometimes reflects a concern with ecology, conservation, and occasional mysticism, especially in works with sung or spoken texts."[5]

A musician, Windham Hill recording artist and former *Keyboard Magazine* assistant editor Ted Greenwald has a musical description for the New Age sound, which he feels is identifiable by its "tendency toward stasis—harmonic, rhythmic, and especially dramatic—and an avoidance of such 'commercial' staples as vocals, distorted guitars, and pounding drums." In lauding Brian Eno as the first electronic New Age composer, he suggests that Eno's works "legitimized the absence of melody, harmony and rhythm—in traditional terms, the very content." Greenwald further contends that "treating these elements casually has continued to be the hallmark of much New Age music."[6]

A more general definition is made by *New York Times'* chief pop critic Jon Pareles, who says New Age music is uninterestingly repetitive: "'New Age' has come to mean instrumental music that soothes and tinkles. It might use solo piano or guitar, quasi-chamber ensembles, synthesizers, or a mixture of acoustic and electronic instruments. It's usually improvisational, with little structure beyond the performer's whims; now and then it borrows a folk tune or a Bach prelude. Almost invariably the tempos are slow, the harmonies simple, the timbres rich and the recording quality full-bodied and noiseless."[7]

All this debate still hasn't nailed down a solid definition of New Age music, though within these four attempts there are options for every spiritual and musical taste. Simply browsing through a mail-order catalog or New Age record bin will turn up music by many stylists who've been placed together by a gimmick-hungry sales manager unable to find more appropriate display space, just because their overall sound is delicate, though their work in widely differing musics would otherwise have prevented their being racked together.

The musical ground covered by the term New Age is therefore wide open—it may range from purely emotive or visceral Eastern folk and trance musics through cerebral syntheses of Western-influenced electronic and acoustic instrumental sounds. In many products described as New Age music there is evidence of Westerners embracing Eastern philosophies and semiclassical, pseudo-jazz, and soft-rock fusions. New Age music may be played on popular instruments such as guitar, synthesizer, piano, and electric bass, but many performers prefer to use harps or more exotic stringed instruments and "color" percussives—like gongs, bells, chimes, and finger cymbals. One of the prior-to-New Age compositions that's been accorded New Age status is multi-instrumentalist Michael Oldfield's "Tubular Bells," which was popularized when its opening bars were repeated throughout the soundtrack of *The Exorcist*. (The tubular bells of the famous title aren't even featured in the well-known section of that album-length work.)

I Defined it Gently My First Time

My first assignment to review New Age music came about accidentally. While living in London I traveled to several European festivals where the love affair between European audiences and exotic (read *non-European*) artists had begun to permeate folk music events. At many of the festivals I attended there were performances in a variety of distinctly non-Western music fusions. In the festival context—outdoors, in a sunny field under blue skies, a vacation atmosphere all around—even the least inspired instrumental achievements seemed fresh and friendly. At the Nyon Folk Festival held on Lake Geneva's shore in Switzerland, I heard a sampler of Windham Hill's artists. The label had had their own evening up the lake at the previous week's Montreux Jazz Festival, and several of their acts had been secured for Nyon. I was immediately taken with guitarist Michael Hedges, whose cool sonic imagery and pyrotechnical finger theatrics caused the weekend's biggest commotion. Rapt and hushed crowds filled the tents where he performed; camera crews zeroed in on his left hand technique. I went back to London, and to editors in New York, raving about Hedges and eager to hear a few of his formerly folk labelmates.

The first new LP to cross my desk was recorded at that "Windham Hill at Montreux" event. By the time I reviewed the Darol Anger/Barbara Higbie album titled *Live at Montreux*, the term "new acoustic music" had already fallen into disuse and was virtually replaced by "New Age." In my review of that project, I made a stab at pinning down the elusive "new" form:

> The first few times I listened to *Live at Montreux*, the duet-plus-ensemble recording by "new acoustic" musicians Barbara Higbie and Darol Anger, I

dismissed its soft sounds as it faded away, barely heard. As on many releases of this "new age" label, a delicate musical interplay predominates; there are few obtrusive junctures, no abrasions. This is Windham Hill's signature sound—a pastel wash, moody and flowing. . . . Hidden away in the narcotic repetition are the duo's warm improvisations drawn from jazz- and Eastern-inflected bluegrass repertoires (the basis for Anger's catchy coinage, "new acoustic music"). And like the sound of waves reverberating in a conch shell, the record's overall effect is hypnotic. . . . "New age" is a catchall term that connotes to its proponents an introspective spirituality and wholistic perspective, for which Windham Hill's meditations provide a soothing backdrop. . . ."[8]

When I reread that critique in preparation for writing this essay, I remembered why I had soft-pedaled my disapproval. During the edit, Georgia Christgau and I gnawed over the meaning and shape of New Age at great length, her deft editorial probing and willingness to treat the subject as sufficiently serious for debate encouraging me to find the value in New Age. My old notes for that essay include a defense of the form, as I perceived its effect on the Montreux Band: "New Age affords its performers the freedom to work in modern idioms with delicate music, to imply silences through passages and phrases that imitate natural sounds, to embrace several eccentric or little-known styles without sacrificing popular musical language (and a pop audience) as other more experimental contemporary hybrids have done."

But that positive sentiment failed to make it into the review, and I soon forgot it as copycats followed New Age imitators onto vinyl. If I thought at all about the pros and cons of New Age, it was the rise of the form, like that of any other minority musical interest, that made my cocktail chit-chat. At the time it hardly seemed like earth-shaking stuff, and yet my negative reaction was very strong. I tried to overcome my dislike, subjecting myself to self-criticism as I half-heard more New Age music, because I realized I would have listened to the music with greater objectivity if it were labelled anything else. After all, I'd enjoyed Oregon, Tangerine Dream, Kraftwerk, Wendy Carlos, Terry Riley, and dozens of other musical innovators who were cited as early New Agers. I began to be perturbed about my continuing inability to coherently articulate first my negative, and later my ambivalent, feelings about New Age.

Reductio Ad Absurdum

The phrases used to denigrate New Age music were delicious—I could hardly keep from snickering. The form's amorphous nature lent itself to snubbery. But if the considered definitions sound ambiguous, the spontaneous descriptions are even more so: "audio Valium . . ."; "Yuppie Muzak . . ."; "just plain noodling . . ."; "hot tub and BMW music . . ."; "soothing semimusical sounds that don't challenge listeners or require their complete attention . . ."; "non-music by nonmusicians . . ."; "New Age is what's left after you take the music away . . ."; "A mixture of musical naiveté and urbane sophistication. . . ."

Now, separate the pros from the cons. Hard to do? That's not surprising, because most of these were expressed by both devotees and detractors. Common knowledge says no publicity can be bad publicity. But when I conducted the interviews that form the background for this essay, I was surprised to discover that those working most closely with New Age music were unable to sell it in phrases differing from those tossed off in derision. Perhaps that's why it's so hard to take New Age seriously: In praising New Age music with faint damns, even the believers sound like infidels.

Arguably, It's Music, But Is It New?

Just as there are no clean breaks with the past or clear beginnings for other modern musics, there are no absolute "firsts" in New Age; no one can point to the date of its invention, no one can claim to have coined the phrase, no self-conscious intellectualization of a musical aesthetic can be attributed to any one composer or school of artists. The term surfaced in the alternative-healing community to link meditative and devotional or spiritual music to the practices associated with a New Age lifestyle, and it was picked up by a Boston pundit. But it came into the public domain with the release of guitarist/entrepreneur Will Ackerman's first album, *In Search of the Turtle's Navel*, which he issued on the Windham Hill label, named for his carpentry business. The success of his own LP encouraged Ackerman to expand the label to include his cousin, guitarist Alex De Grassi. Their records and those of the winsome guitarists to follow were so successful in their uniformity of quiet pleasure that for a while pop critics reviewed other nonfolk or nonclassical acoustic guitarists as "Windham Hill-like."

In some literature, the first New Age artist title is accorded to woodwind player Paul Horn, whose recordings in the jazz field through the Sixties were highly esteemed. Horn receives this tag for the release of the first of his "Inside" LP series, *Inside The Taj Mahal* (Kuckuck), an album of flute solos that uses the reverberation and audio enhancements of the space in which it was recorded (literally the Taj Mahal) as an instrument.

Soprano saxophonist/composer Paul Winter, whose musical experiments include the use of natural sounds and the vocalizations of whales, wolves, and loons in conjunction with standard Western instruments, is also considered an early New Age stylist. Like Horn's *Inside* series, Winter's work often makes use of the sound quality of the setting in which it is performed. For the album *Canyon* (Living Music) and a video documentary about the Paul Winter Consort's 277-mile rubber-raft journey down the Colorado River, *Canyon Consort* (A&M/Windham Hill, 1985), Winter employs the cavernous reaches of Manhattan's Cathedral of St. John the Divine to evoke the majesty and hush of the Grand Canyon.

Synthesizer innovator Wendy Carlos, known for her soundtrack to *A Clockwork Orange,* gave birth to the modern synthesizer movement with the 1968 recording *Switched On Bach* (Columbia). Carlos's first album of self-penned works, a four-suite exploration of the seasons (*Sonic Seasonings,* Columbia, 1971), is often cited as the first electronic New Age record.

Musician/writer Ted Greenwald believes Brian Eno's *Ambient Music* is the first electronic New Age composition, while reviewer Jeff Nesin believes that it is an earlier Eno work, "the remarkably atmospheric *Another Green World* (EG), on which he extends avant-Easy Listening to a new plateau with fourteen short tracks, half of them cool yet evocative solo instrumentals laced with sound effects" that heralds "as Lou Reed said in an entirely different context, 'the beginning of a new age.' "[9]

It's clear that artist and record-label publicists who find use of the term financially advantageous like to point to their own product or artists as New Age originators. But others prefer to move back in time, to link New Age with prominent musical antecedents in the early part of the twentieth century. Narada Records' publicity, for example, suggests that New Age music was preceded in spirit by the "impressionistic works of composers such as Debussy, Saint-Saens, and Eric Satie, and centuries ago by musicians such as Japanese shakuhachi flute players and Indian sitar masters."

But the stars credited with the form's birth are almost immaterial. As *New Sounds* author John Schaefer says: "The market is now so filled with this type of music that really important works have been lost in the crowd of cheap imitations. . . . It seems as if everyone with a working wall outlet is making electronic music in this vein. . . ."[10]

Among the acoustic instrumentalists, recent releases feature the nondescript works of harpists Georgia Kelly (Global Pacific), whose *Seapeace* is a New Age bestseller; Amy Shreve (Meadowlark Records/Capitol), solo performer on her own *Peace In the Puzzle* LP; and Andreas Vollenweider (CBS), who received the first New Age Grammy award for 1986's *Down to the Moon.* Of these, Vollenweider's works are the most masterly, but his tunes remain as repetitive and self-referential as those of his competitors. Guitarists abound, from the Windham Hill family's founder William

Ackerman and Robbie Basho through Narada's Eric Tingstad and David Lanz, to Global Pacific's Teja Bell and Joaquin Lievano. These virtually interchangeable musicians are put to shame by Windham Hill's Michael Hedges, an innovator on the instrument who would have been an asset to any non-New Age company. GRP's Lee Ritenour, a soft jazz player smooth enough for New Age listeners, is another formidable opponent, as, to a lesser extent, is Friedemann (Narada Equinox), whose tunes more than hint at creative potential.

All instruments used for New Age music offer the inexperienced composer substantial room for noodling, but the piano and synthesizer keyboards seem to demand it. Pianists such as Narada's Spencer Brewer, or Windham Hill's George Winston (a big fan of Vince Guaraldi, composer of the "Peanuts" theme music), and their synthesizer counterparts, Eddie Jobson (Private Music), Narada's David Arkenstone, and Bruce Mitchell, as well as Japanese synthesizer superstar Kitaro (Geffen)—whose works pre-date New Age but now help to define it—tinkle, swell, tiptoe, and wind endlessly through chord after rainfall-imitating single-note melody. Only a few of these keyboardists even try to work with rhythm sections or textural interplay. Cycling around like students practicing Czerny exercises, they go nowhere very, very, very slowly. Pianists with more talent, like the Hungarian artist Szakcsi (GRP), who wants to "combine European romantic classical music with traditional Asian, (East) Indian, and African musics and to that [his] own Gypsy background," and synth players like Keith Emerson, whose orchestral thrummings were the underpinning for the pop group ELP's signature sound, are unfairly diminished by comparison with unoriginal New Agers.

New Age, New Market

Whether revolutionary or evolutionary, the term gained general acceptance after it was used by music critics and reviewers as a catchphrase to identify both the style and its likely audience of buyers. And with public acceptance of the name came increased sales of the music to a wider audience. Dozens of independent labels sprouted, hoping to catch a free ride on the back of Windham Hill's success. Copying their successful format of clean graphic album covers, audiophile-quality sound recording, and alternative sales outlets, record companies that had been around before Will Ackerman and his partner Anne Robinson perfected the New Age look, sharpened their own corporate images. New Age music distributors created "house" labels and began marketing their own releases. Global Pacific, founded in Kamuela, Hawaii, in 1979, and Milwaukee, Wisconsin's Narada, which opened its doors in 1978, are the two majors. Narada landed a distribution deal with MCA records in fall 1986, and Global Pacific went with CBS in 1987. Together with Windham Hill (now distributed by A&M), independent companies emerged from their meditation/healing cubbyhole to record-store stacks alongside releases by Vollenweider, Kitaro, and Polygram's Vangelis.

But within a few years of startup, only a few companies called themselves New Age labels or defined all their artists as New Age. As with other half-breed forms, the title proved restrictive; the growth of acceptance of the music failed to dispel the New Age term's "woo-woo" image. (George Winston, interviewed in *The Guide to New Age Living*, explained "woo-woo": "There's real New Age stuff, that has substance, and then there's woo-woo. A friend of mine once said, 'George, you really love these woo-woos, don't you?' and I said, 'Yes, I do love them,' and I do. I mean, I'm half woo-woo myself."[11]) New Age music, the term, has begun to dismay a few of its earliest users: Windham Hill's publicists and owners have rejected the name as their star has risen. But the New Age sobriquet is not all bad—it spells dollars to those who know how to make use of it.

Major labels, whose fortunes rely on rock, find that New Age sells slowly but steadily, free from the constraints of radio promotion and the bread-fresh shelf life of their pop products. Those who eyed Windham Hill's successful marketing technique and growing audience with favor, acquired or created their own New Age subsidiaries. MCA, in addition to distributing the Narada family of labels, began their own "Master Series," which they hype as the meeting of jazz and New Age; RCA introduced "Novus"; even tiny Vanguard, the home of Sixties folk music and later a classical outlet, inaugurated the "Terra" label, before they sold the firm to the Welk Music Group, which has since dropped it. The majors have drawn away some of the independent labels' most prominent and creative artists with offers of life-size recording and promotion budgets. Alex de Grassi has left Windham Hill for RCA/Novus, as has another Windham Hill artist, pianist Liz Story; guitarist Pierre Bensusan has gone from Windham Hill to CBS/Masterworks; multi-instrumentalist Mark Isham has left Windham Hill for Virgin Records; Mark O'Connor has moved from Rounder (and the new acoustic music category there) to Warner Brothers.

But, despite pressure from major recording companies, small New Age labels and distributors continue to spring up and to thrive. Private Music, Living Music, Celestial Harmonies, Fresh Aire, and Expansion are only a few of the labels advertising regularly in New Age publications and racked in bookstores, health and natural food stores, yoga and exercise facilities, beauty salons, and art galleries—the forum that Global Pacific Distributing has trademarked as the Alternative Music Market. Other marketing ploys are also successful: Narada has determined that the New Age compact-disc buyer is even more narrowly focused than the old record buyer. They've subdivided their share of the market into three divisions, labeled "Equi-nox" (the fusion label), "Mystique" (the electronic arm), and "Lotus" (the acoustic instrumentalists' home). These three subgroups alert specialty audiences to the "new" artists guaranteed to be as satisfying as those they've previously purchased.

Brand-name loyalty has always been a factor in the selling of New Age; uniform packaging, which downplays artistic individuality, creates quality expectations that can be met regardless of specific content. New Age buyers have been trained to recognize that clean photos and hand-colored soft-focus pastorals outside mean quiet pleasure inside. The ploy has been so successful that Anne Robinson's much-imitated Windham Hill album jackets have been dissected and praised in publications as diverse as the *Wall Street Journal*, *USA Today*, and *Frets Magazine*. And the packaging doesn't end with the covers: New Age artists are promoted as endlessly interchangeable, one soothing, mellifluous tune rolling into another, one gentle artist seguing into another, one seamless whole. Finally, the packaging helped sell New Age music to the toughest trend-setters: radio programmers.

Radio For a New Contemporary Adult Easy Listening Age

Radio is not only the primary marketing tool for popular music but a very competitive and tightly formatted medium, leavning little room even for small innovations. Many commercial stations subscribe to a consulting service that provides them with short playlists and specific recommendations for frequency of airing the various songs. The programming services eliminate the need for guesswork, but they also restrict their audiences to music by well-known artists. For several years, New Age music was unable to break the airwave barrier. Then, tentatively, it began to appear: a cut here, aired on a few noncommercial and public radio stations; a few songs there, added to "Quiet Storm" formats. As New Age picked up a few radio fans, consultants like "Musical Starstreams" producer/host Frank Forest created local New Age music shows in markets where the music had its greatest word-of-mouth sales. The shows generated immediate advertising support, which encouraged the syndication of individual shows and part-time formats in a variety of marginal stations eager to build flagging ratings. Easy Listening formats and Adult Contemporary stations were ripe for conversion to New Age.

On September 11, 1987, *Radio & Records*, an industry weekly, touted the rise of New Age radio in its contents listing this way: "NEW AGE BANDWAGON ROLLING—What a week for New Age and Jazz on the radio!" "This is the first genuine new format since 1967, when progressive rock was created," said WBMW (Washington, D.C.) Program Director John Sebastian, quoted in a *Baltimore Sun* New Age music story. His station became "Radio for a New Age" in July 1987 with an ad campaign that featured ex-Watergate figure G. Gordon Liddy intoning the following: "In Washington, D.C. for the past twenty years, a conspiracy has existed— a conspiracy to keep you from hearing innovative, stimulating, fresh music— music too good for radio. The conspiracy has ended." But Sebastian chose to distance his format from New Age radio's most popular programming, a service that originated on Valentine's Day, 1987, in Los Angeles, when station KMET became KTWV, better known as "The WAVE."

The new KTWV format—consisting of little talk, no back-announce-ments of artists or album or song titles—formed a seamless fabric of mood-ring music, substantially raising the Arbitron rating of faltering KMET. (Arbitron ratings indicate listenership and are the measurement that allows a commercial radio station to set or raise advertising rates.) On September 24, 1987, The WAVE became a programming service, distributed live nationally by Satellite Music Network (SMN) from their Mokena, Illinois, headquarters. Within thirteen weeks of its national offering (as the company's industry-wide publicity campaign boasted), ten stations in major markets—including those in Chicago, Detroit, Dallas, Cleveland, Seattle, Miami, San Diego, and Kansas City—had become subscribers. The format proved so successful that Program Director Frank Cody, who had guided KMET into KTWV, became a hero. Cody was upped to Vice President of Programming for the station and then was given a vice presidency with SMN after its acquisition of The WAVE. In 1988, he moved on to form a consultancy with researcher Owen Leach. Cody/Leach was quickly snapped up by Pyramid Broadcasting, and it now develops ideas for radio programmers and provides research for nonradio companies as well as for Pyramid stations.

WBMW's Sebastian, who argued from the outset that his station's format was warmer, more personable, more one-to-one than that of The WAVE, claimed he had tried to start a service similar to that offered by The WAVE as early as 1982, when he hosted parties for "focus groups" of twenty-five-to-forty-year-old adults to introduce his Eclectic Oriented Radio (EOR) format. But that idea never got off the ground. When the New Adult Contemporary (NAC) format (yet another euphemism for New Age, debuted in a chart published by industry weekly *Radio & Records* in January 1988) became the watchword, Sebastian left his station to return to consulting full-time, forming his own firm, Eclectic Radio.

Other radio consultants and programmers boarded the New Age bandwagon, new format succeeding new format—the Burkhardt/Abrams group inaugurated "Jazzage" on the former "beautiful music" KLRS in Santa Cruz (which later became "Colors"). That station claimed to be the first twenty-four-hour all-New Age music station, though they inaugurated their brand of New Age/no-live-disc-jockey programming after The WAVE had rolled in. Burkhardt/Abrams also became marketing and sales consultants to The WAVE, though SMN continued to staff the creative, programming end. Then Progressive Music Network (PMN) offered "The Breeze." Other programming services and syndicated shows known variously as "The Oasis," "Lights Out," "Music From the Hearts of Space," "Musical Starstreams," and "New Sounds," to name just a few, began to criss-cross the country.

The WAVE service is broadcast for immediate consumption, and it is heard around the United States simultaneously. SMN produces The WAVE in its studio in Mokena, Illinois, sending its signal up to a satellite, which redirects the signal to blanket the country, where it is picked up by licensed stations and fed through a local transmitter to individual markets. The WAVE is operated almost entirely automatically. Many songs, all commercials, the between-songs commentary (including pre- and back-announcements of song titles and artists), and the signature logo tones are pre-recorded on cartridges (known colloquially as carts), then stacked in a computer-driven playback machine. The Mokena engineer who actually starts the machines sends strings of information to the computer, which plays the carts in order of preprogramming. Included in the cart lineup are tone signals that trigger the computer playback machines at the individual subscriber stations, turning on their prerecorded local commercials and announcements. This process not only eliminates the live disc jockey— it has other financial advantages as well: WAVE subscriber stations can be operated virtually staff-free.

If the radio stations eliminated the individuals on the staff, they also seemed to try to eliminate the individuality of the musicians whose records they played. In the beginning, New Age format shows didn't even identify the artists. Complaints by record companies and artists failed to initiate pre- and back-announcements, but listener complaints resulted in more identifications. The WAVE now prerecords artists announcing their own song titles and includes a number of these each hour, though they still identify a limited percentage of their music, circumventing some listener disgruntlement by offering a staffed telephone "song identification line."

This isn't solely a New Age format issue, as Don Ienner, Senior Vice

President of Marketing and Promotion for Arista Records, recently pointed out in a Billboard "open letter" to radio programmers: "You think audiences don't really care, so you feel free to treat music as just background, a filler between commercials and station identifications. But you're wrong. Research shows time and time again that this is a major frustration for listeners. It's as though you were broadcasting a baseball game without saying who hit the tie-breaking homer, who has come in from the bullpen, or who is coming up to pinch-hit. As the old saying goes: You can't tell the players without a scorecard. On radio, very often you can't tell the real players at all."

WNUA, the Chicago WAVE subscriber, offers several non-WAVE New Age shows during the listening day. "Lights Out Chicago" and "Musical Starstreams" are moodier programs broadcast at night, the first created locally. During the day, The WAVE broadcasts light jazz and soft vocal music that can also be classified as Easy Listening. Anne Marie Martins, president of International Music Network, an artist-management firm whose client roster includes the Montreux Band, believes the combined New Age and Adult Contemporary formats usually program 40 to 60 percent instrumental music, the rest being comprised of "easy listening" vocals.

Counting Up New Age

The influx of New Age music formats and shows around the country made industry insiders take notice. As they're big on quantifying success, *Radio & Records* and the *Gavin Report*, two radio reporting publications, added New Age charts—*Radio & Records* calling its "New Adult Contemporary" to differentiate between the soft-rock easy-listening formats of Adult Contemporary and to avoid the New Age term already shunned by *Billboard*, who'd earlier inaugurated a contemporary jazz chart. But the National Academy of Recording Arts and Sciences (NARAS) was less leery of the New Age title. Recognizing the surge in interest and participation in the New Age field by their members, NARAS instituted a New Age Grammy award category. As I noted before, the first award in 1987 went to harpist Andreas Vollenweider for his (Columbia) LP *Down to the Moon*, chosen from a field of nominees including Paul Winter (*Canyon*) and two Windham Hill samplers. In 1988 Yusef Lateef, the jazz flutist/saxophonist who used to play in John Coltrane's band, won it for *Yusef Lateef's Little Symphony* (Atlantic) over the Montreux Band's *Sign Language*. In 1988 you can find New Age music in almost every setting offering any other kind of music.

New Age Nightclub, the Concept for the Nineties

In New York City, Stephen Santa Romita and Charles Schnall have just opened Sanctuary, the first New Age nightclub, down the street from Crazy Eddie's discount records, tapes, and stereo-equipment outlet (which does fine thank you *without* a New Age section), and opposite an upstairs rock-and-roll-memorabilia shop, in the rapidly upscaling western half of Greenwich Village. Sanctuary is said to be on the site of the old club Bon Soir, purported to be the setting for triumphs by young Barbra Steisand.

Schnall was very involved with the Harmonic Convergence Council, and both he and Romita are into the "initiatic sciences"—a term Stephen uses as an umbrella for New Age inquiry. Their dance floor is for nonsmokers (a small room offers sanctuary for the nicotine-inclined) and their bar is for nondrinkers—"crystal essences" and upward of a dozen mineral waters are the drinks of choice (except in that aforementioned sidebar with the smoke crowd). On New Year's Eve they opened the club early for meditation and chanting on the dance floor; at ten to midnight New Year's Eve the excitement built until finally on the stroke of midnight the room resounded with omming.

What kind of music do they play in their New Age nightclub? "Third stream" music—the amalgam of East and West named by Guenthur Schuller; ethnic musics from Africa, Latin and South America, and modern Asia; and rock and roll on Tuesdays. Thursdays, if they succeed, will be their New Age music nights, featuring a radio-show disc-jockey specializing in the genre. Following its opening, Sanctuary was covered in the *New York Times*. At the party, eighty-two-year-old Harper and Row author Andrew Da Passano (*Inner Silence*) sat under a copper pyramid and said: "Nobody will listen to me here. For them, the New Age is a fad, like the new Coke." Santa Romita, once a successful real-estate entrepreneur, now hoping to turn a profit with Sanctuary, bets the prediction is wrong.

Save Which Baby?

Summing up New Age music in 1988 I find myself returning to the view I held when I covered *Live at Montreux* in 1985: Though the term has gained acceptance, it's grown even more slippery, offering a forum for increasing numbers of mediocre musicians and half-baked knock-offs of more successful and imaginative purveyors. Critics laugh at it, but audiences are drawn to it. Jon Pareles of the *New York Times* suggests that New Age is popular because it takes the work out of listening to music, offering its audience a different kind of reward:

The music itself, often described as dreamy, suggests a restricted kind of dream: smooth, assured, cushioned, imperturbable, safe. Hints of traditional music . . . are like a postcard collection that proves the listener is cosmopolitan. Album covers and recorded natural sounds insist on the music's connection to unspoiled landscapes, a long way from the urban grind. And quasimystical song and album titles, not to mention the connotations of "new age" itself, imply that the listener still has some connection to the idealism of the late 1960's. All this in music that rarely diverges from predictability. The music promises an exotic sanctuary, but it's a sanctuary furnished like a playpen.[12]

And, as I feared it would, the term "New Age" is now regularly used to describe "sonic wallpaper," lumping together unfairly the best of its proponents with the worst of Muzak. (The annoying cloudiness of the term has likewise made it extremely difficult to separate the good from the bogus throughout the entire New Age movement.)

A final question: What's wrong with Muzak? Art is an *interactive* experience, the artist joining in partnership with the audience to communicate a new message, reflect our world, or reinterpret old ideas. Art that's meant to be ignored is a palliative that keeps us from exploring and thinking, that numbs us to bad and good feelings. In the late 1970s, music critic and "new" music composer Tom Johnson wrote about the pleasure of "overheard" music for the *Village Voice*. He described a music festival featuring many artists who would now be claimed for New Age. But Johnson could only say it was pleasurable, not that it was *necessary*. Muzak is not only forgettable, it is unnecessary. Music, like the other arts, makes society. Some artists linked with New Age have experienced musical growth, have made music that is necessary. In so doing, they have helped to shape the age to come.

Notes

1. John Schaefer, *New Sounds: A Listener's Guide to New Music* (Harper & Row, New York, 1987), 12–13.

2. Jennifer King, "Soundtracks to a New Age," *New Age Journal*, November/December 1987.

3. John Schaefer, 11.

4. The book's most serious flaw is its capricious index. Some subjects are catalogued meticulously, others haphazardly. Nevertheless, Schaefer's essays provide some of the most informed writing available to the casual reader on the subject of contemporary music.

5. John Schaefer, 11.

6. Ted Greenwald, "New Age Now: An Introduction," *New Age Musicians*,

GPI Collectors' Edition, March/April 1988, 7.

7. Jon Pareles, "New-Age Music Booms, Softly," *New York Times*, November 29, 1987, Section 2, 28.

8. Reprinted by permission of *High Fidelity*. Leslie Berman, "Pleasantly Surprised," *High Fidelity*, August 1985, 65.

9. Jeff Nesin, "Special CD Report: Brian Eno," *High Fidelity*, April 1988, 89.

10. John Schaefer, 11.

11. Rex Wyler, "George Winston's Pure Piano," *The Guide to New Age Living*, adapted from an article originally appearing in *New Age Journal*, July 1983.

12. Jon Pareles, Section 2, 1.

THE POLITICS

I t is a debilitating error on the part of anyone concerned with American
culture to flush away the broader banalities of the New Age with
the rest of the foul muck we have to dispose of every day. To
do so, according to Jay Rosen in his dark but powerful essay, is to
miss what the New Age movement has to tell us. The appeal of the
New Age is the same appeal made by the ascendent gods of our culture:
television and advertising. "The typical New Age commodity," writes
Rosen, "is promoted in exactly the same way as a new car or a pair
of jeans: as an instant, total, and enchantingly easy solution to a deeply
felt problem." The New Age movement claims to be a great alternative
to contemporary consumer culture, "the spiritual emptiness of which
the New Age movement often claims to reject." But it is *one* with that
sick culture. "The habits of mind encouraged by television are not only
analogous to New Age ideas; they enable those ideas to take hold."

An ugly yet wholly appropriate manifestation of this bond between
the New Age and "the worst consumer capitalism has to offer" was
the Airplane Game—a pyramid scheme, disguised as a "prosperity
workshop," that swindled thousands in New York and other cities in
1987. "That the New Age would victimize itself with a pyramid scheme
is not surprising, given its hostility to skepticism of any sort and its
enthusiasm for 'everybody wins' economics," Rosen writes. Rosen applauds
Marc Medoff, the editor of *Whole Life*, a New York-based "holistic"
magazine, for his high-energy attacks on the game. "In declaring 'a phony
a phony,' Medoff was attempting to restore some connection between
the language of his community and objective reality. But his plea reverses
the entire logic of New Age linguistics, in which language is meant to
refer primarily to an inner reality, to wishes and fears rather than facts."

A revised version of Medoff's controversial piece appears here—
retaining all of its original indignation, adrenalin, and invective. "We
live in a community," writes Medoff, "where crimes become 'workshops,'

stealing becomes a 'growth experience,' and lying becomes 'empowerment.' Well, I don't buy any of that bullshit. A fool is a fool . . . and a parasite is a parasite."

In "New Age Economics," Carl Raschke shares Medoff's scorn as he assesses the movement's influence on corporate and economic policy. The movement's "strange Cuisinart mush of pop mysticism and utopian politics," writes Raschke, can't help but make our foreign competitors sigh in delight.

OPTIMISM AND DREAD: T.V. AND THE NEW AGE

Jay Rosen

Television is not in the business of disputing beliefs. It is more likely to *entertain* them, as a way of entertaining us. When New Agers appear on such programs as Phil Donahue or Oprah Winfrey, they are there to discuss holistic health or reincarnation as "controversies," equivalent in their entertainment value to incest, patricide, and men who love fat women. The hosts may stir up some opposition in the audience, or invite a skeptic on to dispute the New Agers. But as representatives of an emergent lifestyle, New Age thinkers are likely to be greeted with the different-strokes-for-different-folks attitude that serves as the unofficial ideology of the Donahue-Winfrey format.

At a somewhat deeper level, one can point out the compatibility between the New Age idea of personal transformation by spiritual enlightenment and the underlying message of most television commercials, which is, "Buy this product and change your life." The connection becomes stronger when the New Age is seen as a business, a way of moving merchandise. Whether the product is a book, a tape, a seminar, or a magic crystal, the typical New Age commodity is promoted in exactly the same way as a new car or a pair of jeans: as an instant, total, and enchantingly easy solution to a deeply-felt personal problem.

The aim of the present essay is to suggest a structural similarity in the way television and the New Age movement approach their audiences. The similarity can be stated as follows: Both seek to dissolve the boundary between the self and the world, because both treasure the sort of self that results—fluid, formless, open to any incoming messsage; in a word, a self that is weak but impressed by the strength of the forces bearing down

Jay Rosen is assistant professor of Journalism at New York University.

on it, believing that they somehow "come from within." In a sense they do. Both television and the New Age return to the audience its own inclinations, often by giving them another name. It is the circularity of this communication—common fears and desires recycled as statements about the world—that makes both TV and the New Age so successfully unreal.

The shameless flattering of an insecure audience, the overblown rhetoric of worldly crisis, the upholding of commonplace truths as remarkable discoveries, the mass-produced appeals to uniqueness, the reification of newness and change, the promise of magic cures and instant solutions, the mindless assertion that anyone can "have it all"—all are prominent in New Age thinking and the television discourse, especially the news, talk shows, and commercials. More than a series of coincidences, these common features arise from the similar projects television and the New Age movement undertake. "Nothing is more American than optimism accompanied by a pervasive sense of dread," writes Ruth Rosen in explaining the appeal of daytime soap operas.[1] As representative American institutions, TV and the New Age movement participate together in this truth: They reinforce a sense of dread in order to peddle an optimism that fails to provide the promised relief, leaving their audiences open to yet another round of appeals.

Blurring the Boundaries of the Self

Let us begin with the concept of marketing, an approach to communication that television and the New Age movement share. It is helpful to think of marketing as an effort, not to sell the products you have, but to have the products that sell.[2] A good marketer begins with the consumer rather than the goods to be consumed. What the consumer already desires, already believes—in effect, what he has already bought—these are the starting points for marketing as a communication activity.

The media consultant Tony Schwartz calls this the "resonance principle" of communication. The task of the communicator, Schwartz says, is not to get a message across but to "strike a responsive chord," by offering something that resonates with material already present in the audience.

> Resonance takes place when the stimuli put into our communication evoke *meaning* in a listener or viewer. That which we put into the communication has no meaning in itself. The meaning of our communication is what a listener or viewer *gets out* of his experience. . . . The communicator's problem, then, is not to get stimuli across, or even to package his stimuli so they can be understood and absorbed. Rather, he must deeply understand the kinds of information and experiences stored in his audience, the patterning of this

information, and the interactive resonance process where stimuli evoke this stored information.[3]

This is the task of any good astrologist, palm reader, or inspirational author: to offer as "advice" or "insight" something the audience is inclined to believe anyway because it conforms to some common wish or fear. Obviously, to succeed at such an enterprise one ought to be indifferent—or, at the very least, flexible—toward what is actually said. A popular astrologist has no message or ideology; she doesn't look to the heavens to determine "what the stars say." She looks at the stars in her customer's eyes, which become the content of her advice.

Because of its strong association with advertising, marketing is frequently misunderstood. In fact, there is no necessary connection between the two. The perfectly marketed product would not need to be advertised, because it would announce itself immediately as something the consumer desired; indeed, it would *be* desire, presented as an object. Honda dealers in the New York City area have recently made this the theme of their advertising. A car salesman complains that he has nothing to do because he sells Hondas—"The car that sells itself." Of course, the claim is ironic, being itself a form of advertising, but the logic is sound: The ideally marketed car would sell itself by giving form to certain ideas about a car that buyers already have.

An example of near-perfect marketing is the pop song that becomes an instant hit as soon as it reaches the radio. Here, what happens is that the music somehow conforms to what listeners have heard and liked and want to hear again. At the same time, the song sounds new, or at least fresh. Presented as a message from the outer world, as the latest thing, the newest sound, the perfect pop tune is derived from the listening tendencies of the mass audience, as expressed in and refined through earlier hits.

Lionel Ritchie has been an extremely successful pop balladeer during the 1980s. He cannot read or write music; he composes by humming to himself and then working the chords out on the piano. With Ritchie and many others like him, there is no clear difference between composing and recollecting. When working out a new song he merely struggles to hear the sound of earlier hits arriving at his ear in some slightly altered form. One is right to call his music formulaic, but the formula does not belong to Ritchie; it is the collective property of the audience, much as folk tales belong to everybody in the culture.

For song-marketers like Ritchie, the trick is to find a sound that is both new and familiar; a fresh sound must resound in an audience that has already heard and enjoyed something like it. When the trick works the results can be curious: One may hear a song for the first time and seem to be remembering it. Followers of pop music often report being obsessed by a new song: As soon as they hear it, they have to hear it again; if it doesn't come on the radio soon enough they start singing it.

Such is the goal of the jingle writer—to produce a little tune so "catchy" that listeners start humming it, thus repeating to themselves the name of the product through a process akin to religious chanting. The jingle is an interesting hybrid: It seeks to transfer the appeal of a perfectly marketed item, the irresistible tune, to an imperfectly marketed product, a car or soft drink that must be introduced to the buying public via the jingle. Like the pop song that becomes an "instant classic," the jingle is heard as both a message from the outside world and a desire from within. It seems to come *at* the listener, in one sense, but also to *be* the listener.[4] By singing the song to him- or herself the listener recreates it as something produced internally. This is what marketing is all about: producing objects that seem to already be the subject. Thus the advice we may give to a friend contemplating a purchase: *It's you.* Thus also the discovery a New Age convert may make in coming upon the philosophy that inspires him: *That's me.*

The goal of marketing, then, is to erase the boundary between the product and the consumer, so that the consumer sees the product, not as an object worth owning, but as a fragment of his subjectivity floating by. Buying things becomes a kind of reclaiming of the self—not "I want that" but "I *am* that." Or, to look at it another way, the self expands, amoeba-like, to include the desired item, which is not seen as an item but a way of being. The logical result of the marketing enterprise is thus a certain confusion about where the self leaves off and the world begins. Historian and culture critic Christopher Lasch has made this point in his writings on narcissism as a cultural condition. Mass-produced images that attempt to mirror the desires of the audience promote, he says, "the insubstantiality of the external world."

> Commodity production and consumerism alter perceptions not just of the self but of the world outside the self. They create a world of mirrors, insubstantial images, illusions increasingly indistinguishable from reality. The mirror effect makes the subject an object; at the same time, it makes the world of objects an extension or projection of the self. It is misleading to characterize the culture of consumption as a culture dominated by things. The consumer lives in a world that has no objective or independent existence and seems to exist only to gratify or thwart his desires.[5]

Lasch reminds us that, in the Greek legend, it is the "confusion of the self and the not-self" that does in Narcissis, not some rampaging "egoism." The kind of personality that results from this confusion Lasch calls the "minimal self," which is "uncertain of its own outlines, longing either to remake the world in its own image or to merge into its environment in blissful union." Culturally, the minimal self arises from the panic people feel in a threatening world and from "the replacement of a reliable world of durable objects by a world of flickering images that make it harder and harder to distinguish reality from fantasy."

Television is deeply involved in both these conditions: it helps produce the sense of panic by presenting worldly events as a series of disasters, and it is the primary means for distributing the "flickering images" that, as Lasch says, "seem to refer not so much to a palpable, solid, and durable reality" as to the "inner psychic life" of the viewer-as-consumer.[6]

New Age Thought and the Oceanic Feeling

Many of the most common messages of the New Age movement are unmistakeably wish-fulfillments.

You have unlimited potential.
You are infinitely creative.
You are unique.
You can have it all.
Your problems are all under your control.
You can tap the unlimited power of the universe.
You can change the world by changing yourself.

In each case the statements refer directly to the desires of people who are vaguely dissatisfied with their lives and achievements, who feel underappreciated at work and unloved at home, who have been made to doubt their own capacities for change and growth, who sense their isolation even in the most intimate settings, who see government and other institutions as huge forces resistant to change and oppressive to individuals—in short, contemporary people, struggling with the contradiction between the panic and emptiness of daily existence and their very human desire for a secure and meaningful life. The "market" the New Age addresses is for relief from this contradiction.

Perhaps the key word in New Age thought is "transformation," emphasizing the speed and exent of the change individuals can expect. Marilyn Ferguson's *The Aquarian Conspiracy* is subtitled "Personal and Social

Transformation in the 1980s."⁷ Shakti Gawain goes even further, offering "A Guide to Personal and Planetary Transformation."⁸ The stress on the word "transformation" shows how the dominant model for change in New Age thinking is *the wish*. In a wish the world is altered instantly according to the individual's desires; one is projected into a happier reality like a child in a fairy tale. Ferguson writes that the millions who have come upon the various New Age techniques for self-improvement "discover that they don't have to wait for the world 'out there' to change. Their lives and environments begin to transform as their minds are transformed." Shakti Gawain puts it more dramatically: "As I am healed and transformed, the whole world is healed and transformed."⁹

In Ferguson's book, often considered the authoritative guide to the New Age movement, the language for describing change is extreme, almost violent. It repeats over and over that a new era is upon us, a sudden and all-encompassing shift in consciousness that has been gathering throughout history. The power of this shift is promised to the self, located again and again in individuals. But described in such millennial terms, it cannot help but intimidate:

> Broader than reform, deeper than revolution, this benign conspiracy for a new human agenda has triggered the most rapid cultural realignment in history. The great shuddering, irrevocable shift overtaking us is not a new political, religious or philosophical system. It is a new mind—the ascendance of a startling worldview that gathers into its framework breakthroughs in science and insights from earliest recorded thought.¹⁰

Despite the disclaimer, language of this sort is transparently religious: It announces an ascendant age "overtaking us" with irresistible force. True, there is no messiah (or at least none as traditionally conceived—Ferguson depicts New Age people as all-powerful self-redeemers). But there is also no mistaking the apocalyptic tone of Ferguson's warning. Here is an important feature of New Age thought. At the same time that it builds up the power of individuals to "transform" themselves and their world, the New Age bears down on the individual with a fearsome message: *The world is rapidly altering, no one can stop it, get on board or be left behind.* Such a message can do little to secure the power the New Age attempts to give the self, for if the world is indeed in the midst of a "great, shuddering, irrevocable shift," then ordinary men and women have no choice but to go along. All they can do is open themselves up to the power of the universe and merge with the onrushing force. Gawain writes:

. . . as I surrender and trust more, I find my relationship with this higher power becoming more personal. I can literally feel a presence within me, guiding me, loving me, teaching me, encouraging me. In this personal aspect the universe can be teacher, guide, friend, mother, father, lover, creative genius, fairy godmother, even Santa Claus. In other words, whatever I feel I need or want can be fulfilled through this inner connection. I seldom feel truly alone anymore. In fact, it is in physical aloneness that I often find the most powerful communion with the universe. At such times, the previously empty places inside me are filled with the light.[11]

This is what Lasch means when he describes a self that, "uncertain of its own outlines," longs to "merge into its environment in blissful union." A New Age convert quoted in Ferguson's book describes his spiritual awakening in similar terms: "At that moment I knew I was being heard, that I was dissolving and becoming food for the great transformation process that was taking place in the universe."[12] Such imagery is very close to what Freud called "the oceanic feeling," in which the suckling child feels no boundary between its body and that of the mother, between getting food and being food. This is the original "blissful union" for which we long the rest of our lives, according to Freud. Psychoanalytically, New Age thinking is often a glorification of the boundlessness the infant feels in the pre-Oedipal stage; thus the New Age hostility to divisions of any sort.[13] "There is no dualism," Ferguson writes, "no separation of mind and body, self and others."[14]

Against the tragic divisions that Freud said would plague us forever, the New Age asserts the power of "wholeness" and its operating principle, "flow." A series of buzzwords helps to emphasize these two values: "connectedness," "unity," "relatedness," "oneness," "energy," "flux," "process." Promoted as a means of empowering the self, of restoring to individuals their grip on the world, the typical New Age philosophy is an invitation for the self to dissolve away until it, too, becomes a "process," part of the endless flow of the cosmos.

Buy All That You Can Be

What is striking about this invitation is its deep compatability—and complicity—with the consumer culture, the spiritual emptiness of which the New Age movement often claims to reject.[15] In the consumption universe "endless flow" is provided by the stream of product images, each an invitation to become a better, happier, richer, more glamorous person.[16] Obviously, if these images are to succeed, they must loosen the sense of self enough to suggest that a better self is always possible; they must create the desire, not for products worth owning, but for a self more worth having than the one the consumer has now. Critical to a consumer culture, then, is a sense of anxiety, from which the idealized images of products offer a blissful relief.[17] The ideal consumer is uncertain about himself and insecure about his place in the world, and the ideal advertisement reinforces this feeling even as it promises to banish it.[18]

If New Age thinking and the consumer culture share a reliance on mass-produced insecurity, they share as well a strategy for perpetuating it. Addressing themselves to real concerns—the need to be loved, for example, or to be in control of one's fate—they offer unreal solutions: magic crystals, instant transformations, unlimited choice, psychokinetic powers, daily contact with spirits and extraterrestrials.

Weakened further by these illusory promises, the fractured self is ready for a new round of appeals. Like the whirling carnival of product images, the outpouring of New Age advice cannot help but undermine the confidence of the consumer-believer and dissolve any lingering resistance.[19] Not all New Age groups are cults; many people participate without any drastic loss of self. But the cult is the logical conclusion of the New Age enterprise, for it draws all of its strength from the individuality its members give up.

The consumer culture and the New Age, equally dependent on mass-produced doubt, are both hostile to any tradition that anchors the self in a world of expected roles and inherited aspirations.[20] Personal identity must become permanently problematic; all structures that once supported identity come under attack. David Reisman in *The Lonely Crowd* was one of the first to analyze this process in the consumer culture. He noted, for example, that the commercial mass media support the rise of the adolescent peer group as a socializing force, with a corresponding decline in the authority of the family. While not totally dependent on the media for clues, the peer group is a weaker structure than the family and thus more open to the blandishments of commercial culture.[21] The power of the peer group to erase personality is taken to an extreme with the cult, which often forces members to sever all ties to the past, especially the family.

Ferguson does not go that far, but she makes no secret of her hostility to traditional structures like family or religion. The progress of her argument is instructive. Initially it is the power of the individual self that is upheld against institutions. But the individual self turns out to be an impediment as well, which must be dissolved into a universe of dissolved selves. "The separate self is an illusion," Ferguson declares. "The self is a field within larger fields." At the moment of enlightenment, when what she contemptuously calls the "little, local self" is abandoned,

> Brotherhood overtakes the individual like an army . . . not the obligatory ties of family, nation, church, but a living, throbbing, connection, the unifying I-Thou of Martin Buber, a spiritual fusion.[22]

Ferguson is aware that this fusion of freed selves can be impeded by any sort of social structure. In discussing couples she is mostly upbeat about how much growth and change come after enlightenment. But, she warns, if one of the partners remains struck in "old ways" of thinking there is no choice for the enlightened person. "Whatever the cost in personal relationships," she writes, "we discover that our highest responsibility, finally, unavoidably, is the stewardship of our own potential—being all we can be."[23] No one on Madison Avenue could have put it better. The pursuit of one's "potential" outside of existing social structures is the perfect formula for a consumer culture, which profits from the seasonal turnover in conceptions of self, the model for which is fashion.

The Rebellion Against Tragedy

Released from the "obligatory ties" of family, religion, and romantic love into a world of seemingly limitless "choices," the consumer/believer may find it difficult to choose anything at all and in response attempt to choose everything. On one level this is simple immaturity, a longing for a state in which desire is immediately and totally gratified. But in a deeper sense the New Age is in rebellion against both the idea and the reality of tragedy. It announces this rebellion by mocking the necessity of painful choices: "You don't have to choose involvement on a community or a global scale," writes Ferguson, "You can have both." On the classic problem of the individual's rights versus those of the community, she announces a "refusal to make that choice." Individual and community interests, she says, are "reciprocal."

The "you can have both" philosophy is only a slightly more modest version of the "you can have it all" credo by which the New Age movement and a culture of consumption entice and frustrate their members. On the plane of politics, a similar message is contained in the claim that "growth" will solve all problems without the necessity for difficult choices, and without discussion of how to make those choices wisely and equitably. Ferguson signs on to this attitude explicitly in rejecting a "win/lose orientation" toward politics in favor of a "win/win orientation."[24]

This "win/win" rhetoric is one of the many ways in which New Age thinking is hospitable to the ideology of a free market, where the untrammeled pursuit of profit is always in everyone's interests. The blind acceptance of this notion is taken to a hallucinatory extreme by Shakti Gawain in her discussion of money. Money, she says, is merely "a symbol of our creative energy." Since "the creative energy of the universe in all of us is limitless and rapidly available, so, potentially, is money." Those who lack money, she advises, simply have "energy blocks" within themselves.

> Your ability to learn and spend money abundantly and wisely is based on your ability to be a channel for the universe. The stronger and more open your channel is, the more you will flow through it. The more willing you are to trust yourself, and take risks to follow your inner guidance, the more money you will have. The universe will pay you to be yourself and do what you truly love![25]

The fraudulent reasoning of New Age economics gave way to simple fraud in the spring and summer of 1987, when the "Airplane Game" swept through New Age communities in California, Texas, and New York. The Airplane Game was an old-fashioned pyramid scheme in which those at the top of the pyramid were called "pilots" and new recruits "passengers." People typically invested $1,500 on the promise of getting $12,000 back when they reached the top of the 15-person pyramid and "piloted out." Wholly unoriginal as a con, the Airplane Game relied on the rhetoric of self-improvement and positive thinking to appeal to the New Age community, the leaders of which often organized games and "piloted out." Organizing sessions were called "prosperity workshops," the aim of which was to "create wealth." The con was presented as a "growth experience" in which the feelings individuals had in working toward a common goal could be openly discussed. But not too openly. Anyone who asked too many questions would be scorned for "lacking commitment" to the group.

That the New Age would victmize itself with a pyramid scheme is not surprising, given its hostility to skepticism of any sort and its enthusiasm for "everybody wins" eonomics. What the Airplane Game demonstrated, however, is the complete harmony between New Age attitudes and the worst that capitalism has to offer: moral bankruptcy practiced for profit. Marc Medoff, the courageous publisher of *Whole Life* magazine, came to this realization when he investigated the Airplane Game scam during the summer of 1987. In accepting a variety of "liars, thieves, and frauds" as leaders, the New Age has created a "sick community," Medoff wrote, "one that thrives in a fantasy world where the normal laws of logic and reason don't apply." Medoff went on:

> We live in a community where crimes become "workshops," stealing becomes a "growth experience," and lying becomes "empowerment." Well, I don't buy

any of that bullshit. A fool is a fool, a phony is a phony, and a parasite is a parasite. And if you want to know what the Airplane Game was, it was a phenomenon of fools, phonies, and parasites, and the story of how these people used and exploited each other in search of instant riches. It is a story of shameless greed, and little else.

In declaring that "a phony is a phony," Medoff was attempting to restore some connection between the language of his community and objective reality. But his plea reverses the entire logic of New Age linguistics, in which language is meant to refer primarily to an inner reality, to wishes and fears rather than facts. The Airplane Game eventually collapsed by the laws of mathematics, not because its language became disfunctional. Indeed, the language continued to work after the game broke down. Medoff was startled to find that victims who had lost all their money were still calling it a "growth experience."[26]

But why the surprise? After all, the notion of a "growth experience" was never intended to refer to the outside world (which is where the victim's $1,500 went). It is simply a name for an inner state, masquerading as a statement about an event from which one might learn or "grow." Were it to be put in more direct language, this inner state can only be described as the most innocent sort of longing possible, in which one hopes that everything will turn out all right but fears that it won't. A New Ager who speaks of having a "growth experience" is merely noting the existence of this longing, which remains regardless of whether growth (or loss) actually occurred. That is why everything can be a growth experience, even the shrinking of one's savings.

New Age language may seem like a collection of tired cliches. But it is more than that. It is a kind of short-circuited communication, in which utterances lead back to the inner life of the utterer without passing through the world first. Promoters of the Airplane Game merely saw the opportunity this provided for profit and took it. Their con was extreme enough to be called a crime. But the theory behind it is standard practice in New Age scams, most of which are perfectly legal. The same short-circuiting of communication is constantly at work in a consumer culture, which, at its deepest level, would like to convince us that changing your hair color in fact changes the world.

Neither the New Age nor the consumer culture makes good on its claims, of course. History does not obey the law of desire. In reality, people cannot always "have it all" (as the comedian Steven Wright says, where would you put it?). In the real world the opportunity to "be all you can be" is contrained by larger forces than one's personal "energy blocks."

Granting all of this, what is it that keeps either the New Age or the consumer culture from collapsing under its own contradictions? What makes these antirationalist attitudes *functional* for people who, sooner or later, must run up against reality? English critic John Berger considers this question in his discussion of advertising, for which he substitutes the term "publicity." Publicity, he says, is always about the future, about the enviable person buyers will be when they reach the ideal world portrayed in the ads. Like any sketch of paradise, the world on view in advertising is "endlessly deferred," Berger writes.

> How then does publicity remain credible—or credible enough to exert the influence it does? It remains credible because the truthfulness of publicity is judged, not by the real fulfillment of its promises, but by the relevance of its fantasies to those of the spectator-buyer. Its essential application is not to reality but to daydreams.[27]

Again, this is the sort of truth an astrologist or inspirational author deals in. The marketer of New Age ideas takes aim at a spot in the target audience where desire fills a void. The aim must be true, not so the idea. The process is essentially therapeutic, and the logic of therapy allows any problems that arise when the therapy fails to themselves become the subject of therapy. The problems do not go away, of course, but neither do they emerge in their full dimensions. A man may lack for money not because of his own "energy blocks" but because the skills he has to trade in the labor market are no longer of any value. There *is* a kind of value, however, in insulating the man from such a fact—therapeutic value for him and economic value for whoever sells him the insulation.

This is the sort of "good" the New Age produces using the resonance principle of communication. The principle is useless for adjusting people to the realities they face—in cybernetic terms, it can offer only redundant information—but whatever resonates is capable of eclipsing reality for a time, or pushing it so deeply into the unconscious that it can emerge only as a violent, overwhelming blow, the latent fear of which must itself be soothed. Thus the banality that pervades so much of New Age thinking and the mass media, the tired surfaces which carry more and more subconscious traffic.

Television's Law of Return

Nothing is more American than optimism covering up for dread. It is dread that underlies both the New Age movement and the consumer culture;

fear that things are falling apart, that the world is out of control, that meaning has gone out of existence, that the past is no help and the future not even certain to arrive, that not everyone can have it all, that we are not in a "win/win" situation but one in which we will win a little now and lose it all later.

As one of the engines of consumption, television both reinforces such fears and offers different forms of relief from them. And it does so by the same method the astrologist uses: Give back to the audience its own inclinations toward optimism and dread. Television presents people with what they desire to watch, the New Age movement with what they desire to believe. Both wear away at the notion of an objective world that exists independent of the self.

The habits of mind encouraged by television are not only analogous to New Age ideas; they enable those ideas to take hold. One can even see the New Age movement as a philosophy formed for the television age, in which objective reality has been abolished in favor of the endless flow of images. The New Age offers an answer to the problem of how to live in the world television portrays—a world that is out of control and impossible to understand, and yet filled with magic promises and instant transformations. The answer the New Age gives is "accept everything, contradictions included, and become part of the flow."

Let us look more closely at the features of television that make it so compatible with the New Age. As everyone knows, "success" in commercial television means big ratings. The more people who watch your program, the more money you make. Getting good ratings is an extremely abstract goal, the weirdness of which is rarely noticed by anyone. With no way to deem one message any more significant than another, the TV programmer is almost forced to be a nihilist. As Tony Schwartz put it, "that which we put into our communication has no meaning in itself." The bizarre juxtapositions that are routine on television—a laxative commercial following a terrorist bombing—do not disturb TV people because, in order to be disturbed, one would have to believe in a hierarchy of meanings, the disruption of which is unsettling to the believer. No such hierarchy exists in the television world.

In an effort to ground their own behavior in something rational, television programmers turn to the audience. The viewing habits of the audience, it is hoped, will provide an end or goal toward which TV can move.[28] If television has a teleology it is this: to perfectly reflect the desires of its viewers. Of course, things are not as simple as that. What people tend to watch is partly a function of what they have been watching. By presenting a very limited range of programs, television obviously influences the "choices" people make in selecting what to watch. An appetite for quick-moving imagery, for example, is partly a result of the blitz of such imagery during every hour of network television. But this problem in locating the origins of desire, while important to any serious student of TV, does not disturb the creators of programming, who can (and do) insist that they are merely giving people what they want.[29]

As David Marc has written, "The aim of television is to be normal," to become so much a part of people's lives that they don't see it any more as an alien object that invades their living rooms with a parade of mishaps and misfits.[30] As viewers relax and identify with television, especially with its regular characters, television attempts to identify with the audience, to ingratiate itself by giving back to viewers what it presumes they desire: more sit-coms, more cop shows, more good-looking people chatting happily with one another, more "lifestyles of the rich and famous."[31]

This in-bred familiarity, a structural feature of a commercial broadcasting system, has led NBC to promote its own shows with the slogan: "Come Home to NBC." On one level this means, "When you come home, turn on NBC." But on another level NBC wants to present itself *as* a home, your home, the place where you are known and loved and sure to be protected. There is even a third meaning: coming home as a return to origins, to a beloved past when things were safer and simpler. At this level, "Come Home to NBC" implies that you have been away, wandered far from home by leaving your television set.

The ease with which we fall asleep in front of the set is perhaps the best illustration of NBC's point: By presenting its audience with the already familiar, television loosens the boundary between the self and the screen. With this looseness comes the floating feeling on which one is carried off to sleep. We drift off because we are in a familiar world, made familiar by television's law of return—give back to the audience what it said it desires. What results from this process is often given the name "entertainment."[32] Entertainment can be understood not as a genre of programming or a division within a network, but a process by which programs are created in the image of the audience's presumed desires. In cybernetic language, entertainment is simply redundancy, predictability, refined through repetition and audience feedback.[33]

Self and Screen Lose Their Boundaries

Redundancy applies even to the news, which would seem to be the one area in which television attempts to offer information about the outer world and refer to reality rather than daydreams.[34] On the local news especially the principle for determining which items will be included is the same one for "entertainment" programming: Give back to viewers what seems to draw them to the screen most regularly. In the case of news this usually means fires, floods, violent crime, auto accidents, abandoned babies, telegenic anchors amiably kidding one another, and, of course, sports and weather. Anyone who travels widely in America and turns on television knows that the formula for local news is virtually identical in every market; in every city, every night, the "film at eleven" is about whatever calamities befell the world that day, packaged to fit the severe time constraints inherent in commercial TV.

We can be fairly sure that the events portrayed on a typical newscast actually happened—there was a three-car pile-up on Route 19, there was a warehouse that burned out of control. But this does not mean that the news is primarily *about* events in the outer world. It would be possible to produce the eleven o'clock news entirely from file footage; who could tell the difference between last week's three alarm blaze and this one? Indeed, such a production would not be fundamentally misleading, for the simple reason that TV news is not designed to lead the audience out into the world but back toward an inner realm of secret desires and half-articulate fears, back to TV.

What is it that viewers learn about a cocaine murder in the Bronx or the tornado that struck a tiny Texas town? They don't *learn* anything; they *experience*, from a safe distance, the horror and destruction, the craziness and brutality of a threatening world. It is the job of the television news team to find material that fits these themes; whether the material comes from the streets or the film vaults makes little difference. The reports that seem to come from the field are better understood as messages sent from the collective unconscious to the minds of individual viewers, reminding all concerned that the world is a dangerous and hostile place.

Terrorists comprehend this better than anyone. They know that the realm in which their bombs need to explode is the subconscious: The television audience is their true target. To reach this realm they simply detonate a "real" bomb in a "real" place so that news directors all over the world have something to show that evening; indeed, so that it *has* to be shown because it "really" happened. A true terrorist couldn't care less about reality. That is one reason his targets seem so random, his victims so unrelated to his supposed "cause." The terrorist's deed need only conform to a half-hidden fear already present in the audience—that history does not proceed in any sustained fashion but *explodes* out of nowhere like a bomb hidden in the trunk of a car.

To set off this reaction in the audience is the terrorist's only aim. His detour into the outer world, into history, as it were, is only a tactical decision, like leaving the studio to shoot a scene on location. True terrorism has no location, and no use for history; a man is propelled into terrorism because history has passed him by. Television and terrorism agree, then, on one very important principle: that history is just material for a nightly drama called the news, in which the real events are all psychological. As critic Martin Esslin observes, "*In the end the terrorists might be said to be actually working for television* by providing the thrills and violence that enable the news shows to compete with the fictional thrillers and an endless stream of often sadomasochistic drama."[35]

Tuning in to see "what's happening" in the outer world, viewers greeted by another terrorist bombing meet up with themselves again. Self and screen lose their boundaries. People feel personally assaulted by attacks occurring half a world away. Television does shrink the world, as it so often claimed, but not in the utopian sense implied by Marshall McLuhan's "global village."[36] The world is shrunk by the closing distance between pictures and reality, drama and life, feelings and facts, inner and outer realms. The world seems closer on television because in some sense it is happening inside us, which is the territory TV newsmen and terrorists both want to claim.

MTV and Self Transformation

This, of course, is the delusion from which the New Age suffers: that everything that happens happens inside the self. "As I am healed and transformed the whole world is healed and transformed," writes Shakti Gawain. If I am oppressed the whole world will be oppressed, says the terrorist. The blurring of boundaries between inner self and outer world, so necessary to New Age thought, is inherent as well in commercial television's structure. The nature of the medium itself (especially the reliance on visuals), the demand to hold the attention of huge audiences, and the feedback system that allows producers to adjust their programs to proven tendencies in viewers combine to wear away at the boundary between the viewer and the screen.

This tendency in television has given rise to a new form of programming, in which a succession of dreamy images is presented without any reference to a realm other than that of imagery. Music videos signal a new stage in the history of commercial mass media, in which the recruiters of audiences jettison all traditional formats—the news, the ballgame, the speech, the movie, the show—and turn the bid for attention into the content of television. Previously, television invited viewers to "watch this program"; music videos reduce the message to "watch this," or even to just "watch."

The stripping down of television's functions causes the collapse of certain common sense distinctions, especially the difference between ads and programs. TV critic Pat Aufderheide sees videos as part of an "aesthetic-information" that, when applied to art, goes under the name of postmodernism. Among the distinctive features of this aesthetic "are the merging of commercial and artistic image production, and an abolition of traditional boundaries between an image and its real-life referent, between past and present, between character and performance, between mannered art and stylized life."

In her recent study of music videos, E. Ann Kaplan argues that MTV, the cable channel devoted twenty-four hours to videos, is an extreme case of a programming strategy basic to commercial television. Because MTV's "programs" are so short (four minutes or less), they "maintain us in an excited state of expectation," Kaplan writes. "We are trapped by the constant hope that the next video will finally satisfy and, lured by the seductive promise of immediate plentitude, we keep endlessly consuming the short texts." Kaplan sees MTV as an outcome of a long series of developments in mass media that accomplish "the reduction of the old notion of 'self' to an 'image' merely."[37]

Images, of course, are easy to change, and therein lies the logic of music video in a consumer culture. The videos themselves are blatant advertisements for the performers who star in them. But in a deeper sense they support the kind of anxious search for identity on which consumption as a way of life is based. Music videos, says Aufderheide, "nicely match the promise and threat of consumer-constructed society, endlessly flexible, depending on your income and taste." By presenting the star in a series of dreamy poses that function as signs of an invented self, videos suggest that identity can change "with a switch of scene." The world portrayed in music videos is

> one of cosmic threat and magical power. The self-transforming figures [seen in videos] are menaced by conglomerate figures of authority, which often trigger all-powerful fantasy acts of destruction and salvation.

All of this, of course, is identical to the apocalyptic element in New Age thought and the promise of transformation that follows from it. According to Aufderheide, the major premise of the video form is "the constant permutation of identity in a world without social relationships." They may be fun to watch, she says, "but the process that music videos embody, echo, and encourage—the constant re-creation of an unstable self—is a full-time job."[38]

This points us toward a conclusion, for the relevant question about such a "job" is this: For whom are you really working? Who benefits from the "constant re-creation of an unstable self" that both television and the New Age movement encourage their audiences to undertake?

The answer is the forces that destabilized the self in the first place: the dislocations of modern capitalism, the scarcity of meaningful work, the strain the economy places on marriage and childbearing, the emptiness at the heart of a culture that values movement and change often for their own sakes. Powerful currents like these uproot all forms of identity but those that can be gained in the marketplace. "Uprootedness uproots everything but the need for roots," Christopher Lasch once remarked.[39] In reply to this very human need the New Age movement has nothing to say. The unwitting partner of the culture it claims to reject, it can only carry the uprooting a little further, building up the self with a cheery optimism that dread will later undo.

Notes

1. Ruth Rosen, "Soap Operas: Search for Yesterday," in Todd Gitlin, ed., *Watching Television* (New York: Pantheon, 1986), 66.
2. For this view of marketing see Michael Schudson, "Criticizing the Critics of Advertising: Towards a Sociological View of Marketing," *Media, Culture and Society* (1981:3), 5. See also the same author's *Advertising, the Uneasy Persuasion: Its Dubious Impact on American Society* (New York: Basic, 1984).
3. Tony Schwartz, *The Responsive Chord* (Garden City, N.Y.: Anchor/Doubleday, 1976), 25. See also Marshall McLuhan's little known first book, *The Mechanical Bride: Folklore of Industrial Man* (1951) (Boston: Beacon, 1967), esp. 47–50.
4. On the mingling of outer and inner worlds by mass media see also Jay Rosen, "TV Criticism: A Self-Less Pursuit" *Etc.* 43:3 (Fall 1986), 303–5.
5. Christopher Lasch, *The Minimal Self: Psychic Survival in Troubled Times* (New York: Norton, 1984), 30. Equally important to the themes of this essay is Lasch's *The Culture of Narcissism* (New York: Norton, 1978). On the troubled relationship between the public world and the private self see also Richard Sennett, *The Fall of Public Man: On the Social Psychology of Capitalism* (1976) (New York: Vintage, 1978); Hannah Arendt, *The Human Condition* (Chicago: University of Chicago Press, 1958), esp. Part II; and Arnold Gehlen, *Man in the Age of Technology*, trans. by Patricia Lipscomb (New York: Columbia University Press, 1980), esp. 74–81.
6. Lasch, *The Minimal Self*, 19, 34. On images wearing away at the solidity of the external world see also Susan Sontag, *On Photography* (New York: Farrar, Straus and Giroux, 1977), 141–3, 157–8.

7. Marilyn Ferguson, *The Aquarian Conspiracy: Personal and Social Transformation in the 1980s* (New York: St. Martins, 1980). On transformation see 20–21.

8. Shakti Gawain, *Living in the Light: A Guide to Personal and Planetary Transformation* (San Rafael, Calif.: Whatever Publishing, 1986). There is nothing particularly distinctive about this book. Indeed, I choose it for that reason. It is a fairly typical representation of the kind of advice one finds in any New Age publication or seminar, so it provides a useful supplement to Ferguson, whose view of the New Age is more official and therefore more concerned with how the movement looks to outsiders.

9. Ferguson, 32; Gawain, 187.

10. Ferguson, 10. For a similar passage see Gawain, 3.

11. Gawain, 8.

12. Ferguson, 12.

13. Philip Rieff's *The Triumph of the Therapeutic: Uses of Faith After Freud* (New York: Harper & Row, 1966) examines the link between psychoanalysis and what are now called New Age ideas. Chapter 6 on Wilhelm Reich is particularly relevant to the point being made here. Rieff's book is a brilliant anticipation of the therapeutic climate that has become so familiar on the American scene. Any sociological critique of the New Age would do well to begin with Rieff's insights.

14. Ferguson, 372.

15. On the New Age movement's alleged rejection of consumer capitalism see Ferguson, 323–30.

16. See the interesting discussion of "flow" as a dominant aesthetic in television in Raymond Williams, *Television: Technology and Cultural Form* (New York: Schocken, 1975), 86–96.

17. The relationship between consumption, anxiety, and advertising is discussed in Judith Williamson, *Decoding Advertisements: Ideology and Meaning in Advertising*, esp. chap. 2. See also John Berger, *Ways of Seeing*, (London: BBC and Penguin, 1976), 129–154; and Stuart Ewen, *Captains of Consciousness: Advertising and the Social Roots of Consumer Culture* (New York: McGraw-Hill, 1976).

18. On the consumer culture generally see Richard Wightman Fox and T. J. Jackson Lears, *The Culture of Consumption: Critical Essays in American History, 1880–1980* (New York: Pantheon, 1983); William Leiss, Stephen Kline, and Sut Jhally, *Social Communication in Advertising* (New York: Methuen, 1986), esp. chaps. 4, 10, and 11; Schudson, *Advertising, the Uneasy Persuasion*, chap. 5; and Frederick Jameson, "Postmodernism and Consumer Society," in Hal Foster, ed., *The Anti-Aesthetic: Essays in Postmodern Culture* (Port Townsend: Bay Press), 111–125. Of particular interest to the present essay is Lears, "From Salvation to Self-Realization: Advertising and the Theapeutic Roots of the Consumer Culture, 1880–1930," in *The Culture of Consumption*, 1–38. Lears traces the historical connections between the therapeutic ethos and the consumer culture, both of which administer to the same ills. See also Philip Gold, *Advertising, Politics and American Culture: From Salesmanship to Therapy* (New York: Paragon, 1987) esp. 21–30,

45–54, 85–96.

19. That advertising contributes to the ills it addresses is argued in Raymond Williams's excellent essay, "Advertising: The Magic System," in *Problems in Materialism and Culture: Selected Essays* (London: NLB, 1980), 170–195.

20. On the uprooting of personal identity by mass culture see Christopher Lasch, "Mass Culture Reconsidered," *democracy* 1:4 (October 1981) 7–22. On this theme more generally see Marshall Berman, *All That is Solid Melts Into Air: The Experience of Modernity* (New York: Simon and Schuster, 1982).

21. David Reisman with Nathan Glazer and Ruel Denney, *The Lonely Crowd: A Study of the Changing American Character* (1950) (New Haven: Yale University Press, 1961), chap. 3.

22. Ferguson, 100; ellipsis in original.

23. Ferguson, 391.

24. Ferguson, 214, 212, 211.

25. Gawain, 142.

26. Marc Medoff's investigation of the Airplane Game was published in *Whole Life* (Sept./Oct. 1987), 53–68. See esp. 54, 63–4. A revised version of this article is published in this volume.

27. Berger, *Ways of Seeing*, 146.

28. On the audience as a guide for TV programmers see Todd Gitlin, *Inside Prime Time* (New York: Pantheon, 1983), chaps. 1 and 2, esp. 29–30, 38–39.

29. On the problem of how well television reflects viewers' choices see Marc Crispin Miller, "Prime Time: Deride and Conquer," in Gitlin, ed., *Watching Television*; Martin Esslin, *The Age of Television* (San Francisco: W. H. Freeman, 1982), 44–45; and Todd Gitlin, "Prime Time Ideology: The Hegemonic Process in Television Entertainment," *Social Problems* 26:3 (Feb. 1979) reprinted in Horace Newcomb, ed. *Television: The Critical View*, third ed. (New York: Oxford, 1982), 426–454.

30. David Marc, *Demographic Vistas: Television in American Culture* (Philadelphia: University of Pennsylvania Press, 1984), 5.

31. That TV returns to viewers what it presumes they desire is a point made by Esslin, 433–45. On the ways in which television incorporates its audience see two suggestive essays in Robert C. Allen, ed., *Channels of Discourse: Television and Contemporary Criticism* (Chapel Hill: University of North Carolina Press, 1987); Robert C. Allen, "Reader-Oriented Criticism and Television," 74–112; and Sandy Flitterman-Lewis, "Psychoanalysis, Film and Television," 172–210. For a discussion of the uses of repetition and audience familiarity in popular culture see Umberto Eco, "Innovation and Repetition: Between Modern and Post-Modern Aesthetics," *Daedalus* 114:4 (Fall 1985), 161–184.

32. Neil Postman analyzes entertainment as a cultural practice in *Amusing Ourselves to Death: Public Discourse in the Age of Show Business* (New York: Viking, 1985). See also Jay Rosen, "That's Entertainment," *Propaganda Review* 1:1 (Winter 1986/87), 27–31. For theoretical and international perspectives see Heinz-Dietrich Fischer and Stefan Reinhard Melnik, *Entertainment: A Cross-Cultural Examination* (New York: Hastings House, 1979).

33. My understanding of the cybernetic concepts of information, redundancy, and feedback is taken from Norbert Wiener's classic, *The Human Use of Human Beings: Cybernetics and Society* (1950) (New York: Avon, 1967), and Jeremy Campbell, *Grammatical Man: Information, Entropy, Language, and Life* (New York: Simon and Schuster, 1982).

34. On TV news as akin more to fiction than reality see Esslin, *The Age of Television*, 61–62. See also Robert Stam, "Television News," in E. Ann Kaplan, ed., *Regarding Television: Critical Approaches—An Anthology* (Los Angeles: American Film Institute, 1983), 23–43.

35. Esslin, 64; emphasis is in original. On television, terrorism, and the viewing audience see Michael Ignatieff's moving and highly original essay, "Is Nothing Sacred? The Ethics of Television," *Daedalus* 114:4 (Fall 1985), 57–58.

36. Ferguson declares that the "global village is a reality" since electronic media and supersonic travel have knit the world together. See 408–9.

37. E. Ann Kaplan, *Rocking Around the Clock: Music Television, Postmodernism and Consumer Culture* (New York: Methuen, 1987), 4, 45. On MTV see also *Journal of Communication Inquiry* 10:1 (Winter 1986). The entire issue is devoted to the subject.

38. Pat Aufderheide, "Music Videos: The Look of the Sound," in Gitlin, ed., *Watching Television*, 112, 122, 127, 135. On the atomizing effects of images see also Sontag, *On Photography*, 20.

39. Lasch, "Mass Culture Reconsidered," 22.

NEW AGE-GATE: THE AIRPLANE SCAM HITS NEW YORK

Marc Medoff

One day in March 1987 I received an angry phone call at my office from a long-time *Whole Life* advertiser. Since it was one of those rare occasions when the person's anger had nothing to do with me, I took the call. The person was phoning to ask whether I had ever heard of something called "The Airplane Game." I hadn't, and he proceeded to briefly describe the essential elements of the game. The caller further informed me that the Airplane Game was being fraudulently hawked and promoted by individuals in the holistic community as a "prosperity workshop," and he expressed his alarm and disgust at these activities.

My first reaction was boredom. What he was describing was obviously a variation of an age-old pyramid scheme in which a handful of con-artists make a killing while everyone else gets ripped off. In this latest scam individuals were induced to put up $1500 in cash in hopes of getting back $12,000 in a short period of time. The entire swindle centered around dragging in more and more people to "invest"—until finally almost everybody lost their money, except those who started the pyramid. I told the caller that it seemed unlikely that such a transparent scam could get very far and therefore I wasn't particularly interested. I told him that he could keep me informed of any further developments if he'd like, but the whole thing was such an out-and-out swindle that I doubted that anyone with half a brain or a teaspoon of integrity would get involved. I hung up the phone, quickly forgot about the call, and went about my business. I figured that it was just another tip that meant nothing. Well, to say that I was wrong would be quite an

Marc Medoff is the editor and publisher of *Whole Life*. In 1985 he was honored by the Center for Science in the Public Interest for his investigative reporting on food-label fraud. An earlier version of this essay appeared in the September-October 1987 issue of *Whole Life*. Research assistance was provided by Rose Spector and Sean Mulligan.

understatement. That call was followed over the next few days by several dozen others, all expressing their outrage at the pyramid scheme and telling us that it was spreading like wildfire throughout the city. Over a period of weeks we were deluged with the names of people who were playing, locations of apartments and lofts where meetings were scheduled, and rumor after rumor about the amounts of money that people were winning, and losing. After sifting through that first flood of information I got very excited, and very scared. Something very big was taking place, and there was an incredible story to be pursued. But, as more and more facts about the Airplane Game were coming known, it was also apparent that something was seriously wrong.

As a team of *Whole Life* investigators began to file their reports from meetings they'd infiltrated, individuals they'd spoken to, and leads they'd followed up on, the depth and scope of the Airplane Game fiasco became staggeringly clear. A community had gone mad. Completely and totally stark raving mad. And some of the community's best-known, most respected, and well-connected "movers and shakers" were not only involved in the insanity, but they were promoting and exploiting the scam for personal monetary gain. Behind the bold-faced lie of being a "prosperity workshop" and a "growth experience," New Age leaders were brazenly raping their flock. And indeed, the flock seemed to be very willing victims. It was, as I think back to late March and early April 1987 when the Airplane Game fever reached its peak, unbelievable. In fact, as *Whole Life* undercover reporters began to piece together the sordid tale in our Fifth Avenue offices, there was a persistent atmosphere of incredulity, as we literally had trouble believing that such an outright swindle could be embraced by such a wide cross-section of people. On more than one occasion I had to listen and relisten to tape recordings we made of Airplane Game meetings to confirm the corrupt, morally indefensible, and outright criminal behavior of some of the holistic community's most visible members. From a journalist's perspective it was a scandal too good to be true; it was a New Age Watergate if there ever was one. But, from the perspective of a responsible member of the holistic community, it was a New Age catastrophe of a magnitude that stretched beyond the point of anything we had ever seen or experienced before.

A New Age Scandal

The Airplane Game was and is (it is still going on in pockets of New York City, as well as in other parts of the country, under a number of new names, like "Corporate Raider," "Chairman of the Board," and "Network") nothing but pyramid scheme. An absolutely illegal, inherently unfair, and, by any civilized standard, immoral "game" that is promoted and perpetuated by one thing: vicious greed and the lust for a quick and easy buck. It is *not* a "prosperity workshop," a "growth experience," or anything of its kind. It's a game of greed, period.

The Airplane Game is a variation of an age-old con-artist's formula that has been used and reused for decades. In fact, out of all the con-schemes that have surfaced in this culture, it is perhaps the crudest and clumsiest type of hoax you're likely to run across. And, of course, that's what makes the whole thing all the more disturbing—if such a large segment of the holistic community fell so easily for such a transparent scam, can you imagine what would happen if a scheme with the slightest bit of sophistication were introduced? Not since the similarly promoted Circle of Gold scam in the late 1970's (another illegal pyramid swindle that was cloaked in New Age jargon, it involved mailing sums of cash to complete strangers in anticipation of a big payoff) had so many people from so many different walks of life been suckered so easily. In that sense the fact that the Airplane Game is even the subject of so much discussion, and so many pages of this publication, is absolutely mind-boggling. The Airplane Game should never have happened in the first place; it should have been dismissed the same way we laugh off three-card monte dealers, street-corner "gold-watch" salesmen, and people who contend the earth is flat. These aren't matters that are worthy of any thought, let alone discussion or debate. And, accordingly, there is no "controversy" about card sharks, back-alley hustlers, or the Flat Earth Society. We just ignore them. But the New Age community is a bit different from the rest of the world. We're "open minded," so "open minded," in fact, that occasionally our brains fall out. And that's part of why the Airplane Game became so popular and achieved such a degree of respectability in so many holistic quarters. If the Airplane Game atrocity has shown us anything, it's that we live in a community that over the years has become a haven for moral and mental misfits of every type.

There are no standards, ethical or otherwise, for being part of New York's community, and the Airplane Game painfully proved that. For it was during the Airplane Game insanity that the holistic woodwork opened up, and out poured every crackpot, snake oil salesman, and New Age hustler that was finally getting his or her chance to shine in the limelight—or, more to the point, the *slime*light. But where else can liars, thieves, and frauds attain credibility if not in the New Age community? My goodness, they'd have no place to go, except perhaps to jail. The fact is that the holistic community in New York, as well as across the country, has never had the guts to police its own, to reject the leeches and New Age scum that have permeated our ranks from day one. As a result, we've taken in and supported some of the lowest dregs that mainstream society has thrown away, and we've gone beyond supporting them: We've made them our "leaders." And, in doing so, we've created a sick community, one that thrives in a fantasy world where the normal laws of logic and reason don't apply. We live in a community where crimes become "workshops," stealing becomes a "growth experience," and lying becomes "empowerment." Well, I don't buy any of that bullshit. A fool is a fool, a phony is a phony, and a parasite is a parasite. And, if you want to know what the Airplane Game was, it was phenomenon of fools, phonies, and parasites, and the story of the scam is the story of how these people used and exploited each other in search of instant riches.

Here Comes the Scum

The Airplane Game arrived in New York City in March of 1987 after periods of intense popularity in California, Texas, Colorado, and other states. In New York City it was very active from March to mid-April 1987 and then began to slowly die out. While the names and precise formulas in each city varied, they were all based on the same illegal pyramid structure, and all had the same inevitable results. In every area where the Airplane Game was played, hundreds or thousands of people lost all of their "investment" to a small group of people who got in at the very beginning, and they usually lost it fast. Law-enforcement officials estimate that more than 90 percent of those who played lost all of their "investment" to the less-than-10 percent that got in early. The leading New York law-enforcement agency cracking down on the scam, the New York State Attorney General's Office, puts the matter simply, "Pyramids such as the Airplane Game require an ever-expanding number of participants. If a thousand games are operating statewide, 56,000 new investors will have to be found to pay off the so-called pilots, co-pilots, and some members who have already paid in their $1500. Those 56,000 new investors would have to find 504,000 additional investors in a matter of days. The numbers accelerate so rapidly the pyramid eventually collapses, leaving the latest—and most numerous—group of investors without any chance to recover their investment, let alone make a killing." Typically those who played paid in $1500 in the hope of reaching the top of a fifteen-person pyramid and "piloting out" with $12,000. In reality almost everyone lost their $1500. All told, it is estimated that tens of millions of dollars changed hands nationwide as part of the Airplane Game—money that for the most part will never be seen again by those who lost it.

The game was usually played under the ridiculous guise of being a "prosperity workshop," but in some quarters it was done more "honestly," with the players and promoters presenting it simply as a way to make a killing. Either way, wherever and however the game was played, it left in its wake a legacy of social and community destruction the likes of which haven't been seen in some time. Relationships were torn up, families were divided, friends were pitted against friends, business agreements went up in smoke, people lost their jobs, and the foundations of holistic communities across the country crumbled. Everywhere the game was played, lives were changed, for the worse, forever. But the most serious impact has been the damage the fiasco has wrought on the credibility of New Age ideology, as holistic adherents in communities all across the country are being forced to question their fundamental beliefs, their leaders, and ultimately themselves.

In New York State, thirty-seven people were arrested by the New York State Attorney General's Office for crimes related to playing and promoting the Airplane Game. A number of those busted have already been convicted or forced to make restitution to those they ripped off. Locally, two New Age circuit riders, Alan "Archangel" Leventhal of Manhattan and Josephine "Angel" Cardinale of Brooklyn, were arrested and later pleaded guilty to crimes connected to the Airplane Game. In New York the Airplane Game was embraced by a number of different groups, with the New Age crowd and theatrical/artistic community being two of the most heavily involved. The reason people played was greed. It was seen as a way to make a lot of money in a very short amount of time without having to work for it. This hit home with New Agers on a number of different levels, with the most significant being that a lot of holistic types aren't particularly wealthy and are always in search of a dollar. The contention that people played because it was a wonderful "growth experience" is complete nonsense. None of the people who played would have done so if the prize were jelly beans or wooden beads; they were playing for the bucks. Of course, there are a lot of people who need money in this city, but not everyone will break the law, lie, and rip off their friends to get it.

Certainly the least culpable, but the most laughable, participants in the Airplane Game debacle were those simpletons who sincerely believed that such a scheme could work, that it was a "prosperity workshop" which "created" money. It's difficult to accept that anyone past the age of eighteen would be so incredibly naïve and stupid—but, as stated earlier, the Airplane Game clearly demonstrated that there is no minimum IQ requirement for acceptance into the holistic community. As a result, many foolish but sincerely motivated people made excellent dupes. Nevertheless, such individuals, and adults, have to take responsibility for their role, however innocent, in perpetuating the scandal of the Airplane Game, and in doing so making a laughing stock of this community. But, as fools rather than calculating criminals, the appropriate place for them is probably on a psychiatrist's couch rather than in a jail cell.

The New Age phonies who took part in the Airplane Game must bear much more of the responsibility for what took place over those several months. Who are the phonies? Well, they're people who are basically professional New Age fakes, individuals who ride the circuit spouting inane spiritual jargon while their real agenda is one of money and ego gratification. If you have spent any time interacting in the holistic community you've probably come across a lot of people who fit this bill—those who talk out of both sides of their mouth, who profess certain ideals but practice others, who will justify and rationalize anything they do as long as it serves their own self-centered goals. These individuals were the main cog in the well-oiled machinery of the Airplane Game, where lying, deception, and distortion are all essential parts of the game. These two-bit frauds were right at home with the Airplane Game, making speeches at meetings, rounding up an endless stream of suckers to fork over their cash, and coming up with whatever lies and New Age bullshit were necessary to keep the pyramid alive. When it comes to any sense of ethics or morality, these individuals draw a blank.

The parasites who promoted and profited from the Airplane Game are in a special class all their own. These are the individuals who used their positions of leadership and public visibility to seduce, and then rape, this community. These are people who have achieved certain degrees of success within the holistic community—whether it be in the areas of business, communications, or health care—and, as a result, have attained a level of public acceptance and trust. They are the "movers and shakers," people with their own television or radio shows, large prosperous holistic health practices, or schools or learning centers of some type—people who, because they wield a certain amount of influence over those around them, have a special responsibility (as does any public figure) not to abuse their positions of trust, and certainly not to abuse them for personal monetary gain at the expense of others. It is these people who acted with the most wanton disregard for the welfare of others during the Airplane Game fiasco. Instead of using their positions as a platform to stem the debacle, they ·turned into the most predatory of New Age cannibals, using their names, networks, and communication vehicles to spread the Airplane Game cancer and line their own pockets. As people who could have done so much to *prevent* the pyramid scam but chose instead to promote it, these individuals have to be seen as the most vile, the most culpable, and indeed the most dangerous of all those who played a role in the Airplane Game. For them, the Airplane Game was nothing more than a passing opportunity, and you can bet the same group of New Age degenerates will be ready to pounce again once the next scam comes through town—that is, if we let them.

Rationalizing Fraud: A New Age Way of Life

The so-called "arguments" of those who promoted the Airplane Game are embarrassingly self-serving, fundamentally illogical, and based on some of the most bizarre theories and principles this side of Bellevue. With few exceptions, those "defending" the game are either ones who made money from it or who played it so long and hard that they have a vested interest in not admitting what dopes they were. When *Whole Life* ran its ad last summer asking for Airplane Game losers to come forward, we received hundreds of calls from individuals who were ripped off. We got only three callers who "supported" the game. None of the three had the guts to give us their names or detail their involvement in the game; they just wanted to babble on about what a "wonderful experience" the Airplane Game was. All of them seemed to be suffering from a similar type of dementia as they spoke of "prosperity and growth" and "creating wealth." They said the only reason the game "failed" was because of "bad press." One woman told me she lost $5000 playing, but that it had been worth it because she had "grown so much." The woman said she was a working single mother who was "not rich." I asked her what she was going to tell her child when he was ready to go to college and found himself $5000 short for tuition. She replied that it was irrelevant because her son was so smart he was going to get a full scholarship. I told her that her son should be thankful he got his father's genes.

Although the Airplane Game promoters talked long and loud about the "beauty" of the con-scheme while it was going on, most have since crawled back under their rocks and don't have very much to say on the subject these days. When we were able to get someone who was "pro" Airplane Game to talk with us, we usually found he or she wasn't much good under fire. Most we spoke with moved from one argument to another as each transparent rationale fell into the flames. In fact, in the course of many of our interviews a number of individuals actually changed their positions and proceeded to condemn the activity they were praising only moments before. All told, the efforts to philosophically justify the scam were downright pathetic, with even the most eloquent Airplane Game defenders presenting the most inconsistent, contradictory, and illogical of positions. The most ardent of the scam supporters still claimed there was nothing wrong with the game. People's "lack of commitment" and "bad press," they said, caused the collapse. These poor creatures still couldn't bring themselves to concede the mathematical reality of a pyramid that seals its fate from the beginning. In a few cases, where we were able to convince these New Age tweety-birds that 2 + 2 does equal 4, and that the press didn't cause the Airplane Game disaster any more than it caused Watergate, Contra-Gate, or any other scandal, we would start getting back-up excuses. For those finally able to concede the mathematical impossibility of the game, and therefore acknowledge that it falls apart on its own, back-up excuse number one was usually, "Well, okay, so you lose your money, but the experience is so beneficial and worthwhile that it's worth the money." (Of course, the person making this statement is invariably *someone who didn't lose any money*, so how convenient that they are telling the poor suckers they swindled that they shouldn't feel bad—it was "worth it.")

Of course, it is very difficult to argue with people whose mental faculties operate on such a twisted plane (pardon the pun), but let's make a statement for the record. There was and is no "spiritual component" to the Airplane Game, any more than there is a "spiritual component" to molesting a small child, robbing a bank, or pistol-whipping a senior citizen. The wackos who claim such a "component" existed contended that the activity of going to Airplane Game meetings, listening to lunatics praise the game, spending hours on the phone trying to convince your friends to hand over their cash, and arranging secret money drop-offs constituted a "growth experience" that was the real point of the game. The game's proponents (read "the few that cashed in") state that the "feelings" that you had "working with other people toward a common goal" substantiated their claim it was a "prosperity workshop." This type of rationalization could be applied to anything one does, no matter how dishonest, destructive, or illegal. The moral criterion for taking part in any activity is not, by any stretch of contemporary civilized Western or Eastern standards, what you think you may have gotten out of it. If you beat someone up, and for some reason feel you benefited from it because you are a sadist, that does not in any way morally justify your actions. Let's say, for the sake of this discussion, people did "benefit" from it. So, if that's the case, we shouldn't have any problem with something called the Bank Robbery Game, where a bunch of people get together and attend meetings to plan the heist (and of course discuss their "feelings") and then try to get their friends to come in and help them work toward the "common goal" of knocking off this bank. Finally you all join together to rob your neighborhood bank, and the money you get will be just icing on the cake, because, of course, the Bank Robbery Game "isn't about money" either. This "game" will have the effect of helping those involved "get in touch with their feelings about money," and for them, why, it might even be, my goodness, a "prosperity workshop."

If a bunch of dopes want to get together to discuss their "feelings" and "work together," that's fine, but if the activity that they are involved in is unethical and destructive, then such "benefits" are irrelevant. This is simple moral logic that anyone with an ounce of human decency applies, without even thinking, in the general course of life's affairs and activities. The fact that such fundamental common sense was abandoned by those pushing and defending the Airplane scheme only speaks to the moral degeneracy of the characters involved. Now, as for these alleged "benefits" that those who played (and lost) purportedly derived from being defrauded, give us a break. No doubt there are a few airheads out there (or masochists) who will state that they enjoyed being ripped off and have no regrets about their experience. All we can say about that is to encourage everyone to give generously during Mental Health Week this year. Actually, you've got to hand it to the folks who "piloted out" for developing what has to be considered a revolutionary new technique for criminal behavior— getting crime victims to enjoy being screwed over.

For those players who operate somewhat within the borders of sanity and don't try to stake a claim to the "spiritual experience" rationale, there still are a couple of back-up excuses that come straight from loonytoon land. One "pro" Airplane Game argument is that the game is a "redistribution of wealth in society," that playing the game is a way to help our fellow man. Sure, it's a redistribution of wealth: The Airplane Game took the majority's money and handed it over to a small minority. Then, for those really running out of excuses, there is the oh-it's-just-a-form-of-gambling rationale. These pathetic folks try to palm off the multimillion dollar swindle as being akin to "betting on the Super Bowl."

Many Airplane Game defenders shamelessly contended that, since all types of crimes went on all the time, playing the Airplane Game was just the New Age's way to "get theirs." At Airplane Game meetings speakers and those in attendance would often refer to scandals on Wall Street and in the Reagan Administration as justification for playing the game. Their attitude was, "Well, they're corrupt, so why shouldn't we be also?" This type of convoluted hypocrisy requires no comment other than a personal note: As a result of working on this story and hearing the type of garbage logic described above, I now take special care to make sure my apartment door is always double-locked before I go to sleep at night. God knows when some group of New Age retards is going to decide that "everyone else's" apartment in New York is being burglarized, so "why don't we try Marc's out."

When an Airplane Game apologist is finally at the end of his morally tenuous rope trying to justify his crimes, he usually comes up with what has to be considered the most self-serving (and simultaneously revealing) "argument," which once and for all shows his, and the game's, true stripes. Those who played "weren't forced to play," so the "winners" are not responsible for those who lost. These individuals place the onus of responsibility on those who lost by saying, in essence, that they weren't clever, fast, or manipulative enough to win, "so we took their cash." Sure, the people who played were idiots, even if they were "informed, consenting" idiots, but that has nothing to do with the legitimacy of ripping them off. That's why there are consumer-protection laws and antifraud statutes on the books, to protect both the imbecile and the non-imbecile from society's leeches. Those promoting the game seem to think they have some karmic right to rob those who are too blind to see them coming. I say *bullshit*. If you decide to take a walk through a crime-ridden part of town at night and as a result you are mugged, there's no question you did a foolish thing. But that's a separate issue from the mugger's guilt in stealing your money. The mugger can't stand up either in a court of law or in the court of public opinion and say, "Well, the guy knew it was a bad neighborhood, and that he was taking a chance walking through, so he got what he deserved, and I should not be punished or asked to return what I stole." In other words, Airplane Game losers, you were mugged because you were *real* fools, but don't let your foolishness so blur your vision that you don't see that you were mugged by *real parasites*.

Of Thieves, Frauds, and Charlatans

Law-enforcement officials estimate that thousands, if not tens of thousands, of people participated in the Airplane Game throughout New York State. The individuals who played came from all walks of life and represented a broad cross-section of society. Men and women played, as did young and old. There were as many doctors, chiropractors, lawyers, politicians, government officials, and radio broadcasters taking part as there were yoga instructors, astrologers, numerologists, crystal salespersons, reflexologists, channelers, and health-food-store employees. Although those who became involved came from a wide variety of backgrounds, they all shared the motivation of greed. In terms of the holistic community, many of those who took part and played key roles in pushing the scam were the same New Age retreads and workshop junkies who have been circulating throughout the community for more than a decade. While the swindle brought out a lot of fresh New Age blood, most meetings that were presented as part of the "prosperity workshop" rap were heavily populated by faces familiar to anyone who travels in New York's holistic circles.

Although there were no organizations that officially sanctioned the game, we came across unusual numbers of DMA instructors and graduates, Direct Centering instructors and graduates, and Rajneesh followers who were going at it full throttle. As we followed the Airplane Game trail we found ourselves not being too surprised at many of the people we found to be heavily involved. We have dealt with a number of these individuals in a variety of capacities, and they had already built up wide reputations as some of the slimiest phonies the New Age has to offer. In other cases, though, we were genuinely surprised to find individuals who we thought were of sound mind and morals taking part. In conducting our investigation we were mainly interested in individuals who were heavily involved in promoting the scam and in some of the more well-known New Age movers and shakers who used their names and positions to climb quickly up the pyramid of greed. In New York City those actively involved included natural-foods chef David "King" Townsend of Manhattan, Sunrider sales representative David "Captain Kirk" Cameron of Locust Valley, hellerworker Josephine "Angel" Cardinale of Brooklyn, spoon-bender Diana "Aunt Mary" Gazes of Manhattan, former WBAI Radio broadcaster Mary "Abundance" Houston of Manhattan, carpenter John "Sunshine" Knox of Manhattan, film-lab operator Elliott "Moses" Landy of Manhattan, perennially un-employed Alan "Archangel" Leventhal of Manhattan, "psychotherapist" Cese "Vision" MacDonald of Manhattan, crystal salesman Andrew "Bear Man" Nevai of Arizona, reflexologist Laura "Maja" Norman of Manhattan, Rayviserve Inc. owners Kurt "Sunshine" Rayvis and wife Liz "Samurai" Rayvis of Brooklyn, yoga instructor Ravi "Yogi" Singh (a.k.a. Neil Hackman) of Manhattan, and convicted-cocaine-trafficker Jonnie "Harmony" Winchester of Manhattan..

One of the Airplane Game's most notorious promoters was Mary "Abundance" Houston, who was indefinitely suspended from her broadcast position at WBAI Radio for using her program to defend and promote the scam on the air. Houston, who has been involved in New Age issues and alternative media for many years, jumped into the Airplane Game as soon as it was introduced to New York, and organized and ran a number of Airplane Game meetings at various locations throughout Manhattan. Houston, usually accompanied by boyfriend/attorney Alfred Labremont Webre III, gave fiery evangelistlike speeches before small and large groups to extol the "beauty" of the swindle, while Webre would usually follow with a more composed sermon claiming the game was "legal" and urging people to play. Those who "played" with Houston were struck by her aggressiveness as she bullied, taunted, and manipulated those around her to "pay up" quickly and to bring new suckers into the game. On occasions when people involved with Houston would express their doubts about the legality or ethics of the scheme, they would be treated to wild outbursts in which they were blamed for "slowing everyone else down." During the game Houston told others she had piloted out at least once (meaning she had made $12,000), and perhaps many more times, as she hopped from plane to plane. When a Manhattan office worker balked at giving Houston the $500 balance she "owed" for "purchasing" a $1500 "seat," Houston flew into a rage, telling the reluctant sucker that she (Houston) wasn't really "concerned with the money," because she had "made so much money from this" that $500 was peanuts. Houston apparently only wanted the five bills because she believed it was "rightfully owed" her. Houston's spirited but twisted defense of the Airplane Game's legality, ethics, and "spirituality" came to a head on April 10, 1987, when she devoted her two-hour WBAI radio program, "Radio Live," to a "discussion of the Airplane Game." The program, which was "cohosted" by boyfriend Webre, was little more than an unabashed promotion of the pyramid scheme and a repetition of the many lies that were commonly circulated at the time to justify the game. During the course of the broadcast the pair read extensively from the "Airplane Game Newsletter," *Wings*, and made scores of preposterous statements, including the contention that the Airplane Game was "creating monies that didn't exist before." The duo battered down a number of callers to the show who challenged the legitimacy of the scam. But the most outrageous aspect of the show had to do with what *wasn't* said over the air: Both Webre and Houston were *personally involved* in the swindle and stood to profit by its proliferation. At no time during the entire show did either host reveal this blatant conflict of interest or discuss their personal participation in the Airplane Game. Houston's concealment of her involvement violated just about every accepted journalistic ethic in the book and amounted to an outright deception of her audience.

Ironically, during the show Houston lambasted the media's coverage of the scam as "yellow journalism" and charged them with "hanky panky," while at the same moment it was *she* who was perpetuating one of the most monstrous journalistic frauds ever witnessed in the annals of modern radio broadcast history. During the broadcast WBAI Program Director John Scagliotti became so concerned over the content of the show that he had the station's attorney call Webre aside to find out what they were up to. Scagliotti says that Webre and Houston were instructed to "publicly identify" their connection to the game, but neither did. Scagliotti says he was unaware that both Webre and Houston were organizing Airplane Game meetings at the time (although Houston had previously told him the Airplane Game was "wonderful"), but had he known, it "would have compounded the situation." Still, Scagliotti was so disturbed at what he termed Houston's "outrageous statements" that he immediately suspended her and canceled further broadcasts of her program. Scagliotti called Houston's broadcast "sick" and said WBAI was still investigating the entire incident.

WBAI wasn't the only place that banned Houston and her cronies as a result of her illicit Airplane Game activities. On April 1 Houston ran an Airplane Game meeting in rented space at the World Yoga Center at 265 West 72nd Street under the guise of holding a "meditation class." (The Center is utilized for a number of ongoing holistic classes and spiritual activities, and it has a solid reputation for integrity.) Houston organized and conducted the get-together without the knowledge or permission of the Center's owners (at a rate of $15 an hour). Once the deception was discovered, she was barred from further use of the facility. Ann Farbman, the founder and executive director of the Center, told *Whole Life* that she was "furious" at Houston's deception and said her facility was no place for "lies." "We want the World Yoga Center to be a refuge and place of healing from this type of greed," she said. "We feel betrayed and violated that this took place here."

Houston has not only become persona non grata with the folks she was renting space from, but has since come under fire from people she took money from during the game, including three local residents who have filed lawsuits against her. John Percik, a Manhattan-based massage therapist, attended a number of meetings run by Houston and Webre and was impressed enough to give Houston $1500 in cash on April 2 in her fourth floor apartment at 741 West End Avenue. When the game went down the tubes a short time later, Percik, recalling all the love and kisses and New Age claptrap that Houston had been preaching, nicely and quietly asked for his cash back. In response Houston went berserk, threatening to sue Percik, saying *he* was mentally ill, and then claiming that she was "broke" herself, living off a loan from her mother. She also threatened to take criminal action against *him*, bragging, "My brother's a cop and he's very high up in the police force," adding that "I have a lot of good friends who are lawyers." She accused Percik of being a "phony spiritual person" and ended her last conversation with him by screaming "Prove it! Prove it! Prove it!" "My friends," she said, "are going to drag your ass into court." Percik subsequently filed a suit in Small Claims Court.

Houston was not very cooperative when we called to talk with her, and in fact she wouldn't even let us ask her a single question as she screamed at us nonstop for about five minutes before hanging up the phone. She said she was going to "sue" and that I was a person "without much integrity." She said I was a "libelous person" and that she would "see" me "in court."

Previously Houston had told others that she was going to "sue *Whole Life* and Marc Medoff so bad their eyes are going to be twisted around in their head." *Whole Life* had previously received both a phone call and a letter from a Manhattan attorney claiming to represent Houston and fellow Airplane Game pusher Diana "Aunt Mary" Gazes. The attorney "ordered" us not to publish the article you are now reading and threatened various types of action if we did so. My only personal recollection of Mary Houston (other than one occasion when I think I met her in person for about thirty seconds) is an incident about one-and-a-half years ago, when she called the *Whole Life* office and got into an argument with one of my staffers. She then spoke to me and spent about five minutes screaming at the top of her lungs that she was going to "get" my assistant for being "rude" to her and would "personally" use her "power and influence" to have my assistant "blackballed" from working anywhere else again. She concluded by saying, "No one talks to Mary Houston that way." Well, *exccuuuuse me*!

We had absolutely no luck tracking down Houston's constant sidekick and sometimes money pick-up companion, attorney Alfred Labremont Webre III, but it was some small consolation to us that we're not the only ones who can't find him. It seems that Webre, who was licensed to practice law in the New York State Court System on June 27, 1969, had never registered with the state (as required by law since 1979) and owes $200 in back registration fees to the New York State Court Administration/ Attorney's Registration office. As a result he is considered "not in good standing." Until Webre pays up he is subject to disciplinary action for violating the state statute requiring his registration (and payment of fees). Webre maintains no published or unpublished phone number and is not a member of either the American Bar Association or the New York State Bar Association. We were going to ask Mary Houston where we could find Webre, but she hung up on us too fast. We wanted to ask Webre about his involvement in the Airplane Game and whether he thought his conduct might bring him under investigation by any state agencies. Although to date Webre has not been charged with any crime in connection with the scheme, he can be held responsible for unethical behavior by agencies governing his profession whether or not he is convicted of any wrongdoing.

One of the most unsavory characters involved in promoting the Airplane Game both in New York and Boston was well-known New Age leech Alan "Archangel" Leventhal. Levanthal has been involved in New Age-related activities in the northeast for about a decade, mostly in the area of coordinating health fairs and writing. While many people are familiar with the divorced father of one from his days as a radio broadcaster at WBAI (he was fired several years ago), there is another side to the smooth-talking con-artist that should leave no one surprised that he surfaced as a "big" in this latest scam. Leventhal is a criminal, in both the literal and spiritual meaning of the word, who has over the years built up a reputation with those who have worked closely with him as one of the most dishonest, irresponsible, and hypocritical people the New Age community has ever seen.

Anyone who has dealt with Leventhal over the years—ranging from his exwife, who denounces him as a "crook" for non-payment of child support, to the large numbers of people who have loaned him money never to see it again—knows he has a problem with money. The problem is that he doesn't have it, but that has never stopped him from just taking it—whether it belonged to him or not. Leventhal's ability to take other people's money and make it disappear began in the early 1970s, when he spent a year behind bars in Her Majesty's Prison in England after being convicted of bank fraud. Upon completion of his jail sentence in March 1973, he was deported from Great Britain and came to the United States to set up his sordid criminal shop on this side of the Atlantic. It was during this time that Leventhal began to rack up debt after debt, borrowing money from friends, relatives, and even strangers who were foolish enough to take seriously any of his hair-brained schemes for success. In the early 1980s Leventhal's attention turned mainly toward working with the then-fledgling *Whole Life Times* in a variety of editorial and promotional capacities. While Leventhal was known as a tireless worker, he was also known as a tireless moocher, and his reputation for borrowing money from coworkers and then "forgetting" to pay them back became legendary.

Leventhal's "problem" with money didn't stop even while he was employed full time with *Whole Life Times*, and he was constantly being embarrassed at the office by calls from sheriffs, marshalls, attorneys, his exwife, and other aggrieved parties who were looking for a piece of him. Leventhal hadn't learned his lesson from his jail term in England, and he was still looking for his pot of gold. In 1984 the deadbeat began an intense personal relationship with a convicted felon (named "Marcello") serving a jail term in Trenton State Prison in New Jersey. Leventhal fell for a common scam run by prison inmates to rip off gullible outsiders. The scam takes a number of different forms, but generally it involves some long-term violent offender convincing some idiot on the outside that before he got thrown in the can he pulled a big robbery and buried a ton of cash somewhere. The convict finds some sap (by writing or calling—inmates in many maximum security prisons pass around lists of such potential dupes) and tells him that if he helps him out, he will split the "money" with him. Of course, the money does not exist, but over the period of months that the two write to each other, call, and even visit, the inmate is able to extract all kinds of "gifts," "loans," and various types of "presents" hard to come by in the slammer. The rube, motivated by greed, is milked for all he is worth and is even often told he has to put up some money to "bribe a guard" as part of the "arrangement" to "dig up the cash." Well, you can see what type of hot attraction this would be for someone like Leventhal. Over a period of more than two years Leventhal defrauded *Whole Life Times* out of hundreds, and perhaps thousands, of dollars by accepting countless person-to-person collect phone calls from this bum to the *Whole Life Times* office. Although he was warned to discontinue this "relationship," and that he was being ripped off, he would not stop. He not only continued to accept the collect calls but he also began sending and delivering various "presents" to the inmate, including items that didn't belong to him. (I was a co-worker of Leventhal's at the time, and as a result my college typewriter is now occupying space in someone's prison cell.) Leventhal even arranged to meet the "bribable guard" at 2 A.M. one night in the *Whole Life Times* office, but the "guard" never showed up. Throughout this time Leventhal ignored pleas by myself and others to get out of the scheme and continued to insist that a "map" existed that would lead to a stash of cash amounting to something like $70,000. Finally, when it became known that this same inmate was calling a number of people who were featured on the editorial pages of *Whole Life Times* (no doubt reading about them in copies supplied to the inmate by Leventhal during his visits) and giving them the same rap, Leventhal appeared to concede that he had been duped by his own greed and stopped bragging to others that he was about to be "wealthy."

In any case, Leventhal's background of crime, deception, and delusional behavior provided him with the perfect credentials for vigorous participation in the Airplane Game; and, accordingly, he was one of the first to join the scheme. The impoverished (and, of course, still unemployed) Leventhal jumped onto the Airplane Game bandwagon with both feet, calling everyone he could think of to get aboard his "planes," telling them what a "wonderful experience" they would have. At meetings throughout the city Leventhal acted as leader and emcee, explaining the scam to crowds large and small, urging them to take part. A typical Leventhal presentation took place April 5, 1987, at 118 West 27th Street, where he convened a meeting of about seventy-five Airplane Game players and potential suckers. Leventhal told the packed loft that the Airplane Game was the cat's meow. "It's not a pyramid scheme, but it's something that generates money, and it does it in a most interesting way," he said with a straight face. "This game is about self-empowerment, it's certainly about prosperity. Many of us have begun to see it as a workshop." Leventhal's rap was the same warped pitch being given by other Airplane Game hustlers all over New York. "This game isn't about money, because you're involved in a process and you're getting to know a lot of things about yourself, your own life, your stuff, and why you're not moving or getting what you want. And you start learning about relationships at a very high level," he told the crowd.

Leventhal signed on to a number of different planes and bragged to people he had piloted out once or twice. Friend and fellow Airplane Game player John "Sunshine" Knox, a Manhattan construction worker, told a *Whole Life* reporter that Leventhal had piloted out twice (meaning he walked away with $24,000 in cash). Indeed, it was beginning to look like Leventhal had finally found his pot of gold when on the evening of April 9, 1987, he was arrested in an Airplane Game sweep carried out by a joint anti-fraud task force headed by the New York State Attorney General's Office. The 49-year-old con-artist and nine others, including hellerworker Josephine "Angel" Cardinale of Brooklyn, were arrested as a meeting broke up at the 118 West 27th Street location and charged with a variety of misdemeanor and felony counts in connection with their participation in and promotion of the Airplane Game. Leventhal was fingerprinted, mugged, and released under order to appear shortly in New York City Criminal Court, while Cardinale was kept in the can overnight after being charged. Now, you would figure that anyone with a thimble full of brains would call it quits at that point. The guy had made some money and was facing criminal chrages, so it would make sense to lay low, right? Well, not the greed-driven Leventhal. While awaiting trial and unknown to investigators at the Attorney General's Office, Leventhal continued to play the Airplane Game through surrogates in New York, and he along with fellow Airplane Game criminal Victor Zurbel (a Manhattan graphic artist who often "works" with Leventhal and is currently his roommate) made several trips to Boston in the weeks after his arrest to promote the scam there.

After Leventhal's arrest he told others that he was going to fight the charges and challenge the "constitutionality" of the law prohibiting such swindles. Leventhal bragged to acquaintances that his was going to be a "test case," that his Airplane Game activities were part of a "political statement" he was making (which, in Leventhal's perverted world, must make him some type of "political prisoner"). On October 9, Leventhal appeared before Criminal Court Judge Mary Bednar in New York City Criminal Court and, tail tucked firmly between his legs, pled guilty (as a result of a plea-bargain arrangement) to promoting a chain-distribution scheme and was fined $500 plus a $1000 civil penalty. In addition, the now twice-convicted criminal consented to a permanent injunction stating he would never again participate in any chain-distribution scheme.

Whole Life interviewed Leventhal on a number of occasions subsequent to his arrest and his conviction, and we were generally treated to a rather pathetic assortment of lies, excuses, and rationalizations regarding his actions. Often Leventhal would change his position or contradict himself in the course of trying to justify an obviously unjustifiable pyramid scheme. On June 5 we asked Leventhal why he was involved, and he responded, "I found the game philosophically interesting, and I also needed the money. I got into the game and got out of it very quickly. I wasn't involved after I was arrested. I didn't make very much money anyway."

When we first interviewed Leventhal, we were unaware of his travels to Boston and his use of surrogate players while awaiting trial. On August 25 we spoke with him for over an hour in the *Whole Life* office. Leventhal once again asserted he stopped playing the game after his arrest, but as soon as we told him we had evidence he was crossing state lines to promote the scam, he immediately changed his story, saying, "Oh yes, now I remember, I did go up to Boston a couple of times to play after the arrest." As the interview wore on, and it became clear to Leventhal that we knew the intimate details of many of his Airplane Game misdeeds, he told us he was not "proud" of his participation; it was "a circumstantial situation," he said. He refused to say how much money he had pocketed (though he did admit "piloting out" once), but claimed he had "given half back." We asked him to give us documentation or the names of people to whom he had returned money, but he refused. He said the reason the game fell apart was because people "became too greedy." Leventhal admitted it was he that "set up" the giant March 30 Airplane Game meeting in Manhattan's All-Craft Center, the meeting that helped propel the scam to all corners of the New York metropolitan area. Leventhal still mouthed the oft-repeated lie that the laws banning the Airplane Game "were being challenged in courts all around the country," but he could not produce any evidence to back up this ridiculous claim. "The Airplane Game was not bad for the New Age community. It allowed a lot of people to make money so they could leave jobs they weren't happy with," he said. Leventhal continued to call the swindle a "prosperity consciousness workshop" and declared that "no one is going to get their money back." He said that so many people he knew had gained "insight" from the "experience," and because he personally had met so many "high-minded people" during the game, that it was okay that virtually everyone lost their money.

Despite the countless inconsistencies, distorted logic, and outright falsehoods we pointed out to Leventhal during our conversation, he continued to mouth mindless New Age slogans, refused to concede to mathematical reality, and maintained that he was a very "moral" person. Our final conversation with Leventhal took place after his conviction, on October 14, where his out-of-wack reasonings and rationalizations had reached an all-time low. In response to our questions about the Airplane Game being a "con scheme," he replied, "Life is a con scheme."

Another hot promoter of the Airplane Game scam was Manhattan resident Diana "Aunt Mary" Gazes, producer of the now-defunct cable television show *Gazes Into the Future*. Gazes, best known for her "spoon bending" workshops, played the game rabidly, according to those who were involved with her, organizing meetings, presiding over Airplane Game get-togethers, and constantly haranguing those on her planes to move quickly to bring in more cash. One individual who was on one of her planes described Gazes as "being on a real power trip," and recalls her running around at meetings with "a stack of sheets of all the planes she was on." Over a period of weeks Gazes conducted a wide variety of illegal Airplane Game activities (meetings, money transfers, etc.) out of a number of Manhattan locations. At one point Gazes apparently tired of the formality of meetings and, according to one source, just wanted to work from her apartment and "pilot out over the phone." As a result of Gazes' highly visible conduct during the Airplane Game debacle (standing up in front of large groups of people and saying stupid things), her heavy involvement was a matter of public knowledge in New York's New Age community. But, when we called her to get her side of the story, Gazes suddenly adopted the rather novel position that "it was nobody's business if I played the Airplane Game or not." In an interview with *Whole Life* Gazes appeared shaken and constantly repeated the same inane line: "It's nobody's business but my own." In response to dozens of questions about her role in the Airplane Game, Gazes, who is usually anything but shy in moving whatever idiotic bandwagon she happens to be on at the moment, refused to confirm or deny that she took part in the scam in any way, shape, or form. "Money is a real personal issue," she told *Whole Life*. "It's my business whether I was involved or not, and I can't answer any direct questions about it." When we pressed Gazes for a bit more information, she began to digress and talk about unrelated subjects like rainforests, killing dolphins in Japan, and cutting down trees.

Gazes seemed to be trying to make a case for what she called the "ten to eleven years I've spent working to help humanity" to balance the recent scam she was promoting. Finally, we were able to get Gazes to shut up about all the wonderful deeds she had done for the world over the past hundred years or so and get her to comment, at least indirectly, on her part in the scheme. "My overview is that I think the Airplane Game served a lot of people, an enormous amount. A lot learned and grew from it," she told us. Gazes then went on to make what has to be considered one of the most preposterously deranged statements regarding the game (and there have been a few doozies) we've heard to date. "I think the key to planetary peace, the key to ecological peace on the planet," she said, "is consciousness, the lifting and raising of consciousness, and I think the Airplane Game served a lot of that." You heard it here first: The Airplane Game is the "key to peace." And all these years we thought it had something to do with nuclear weapons. What sillies we were.

One of the few Airplane Game promoters who expressed any regret about his role in the scheme is well-known Manhattan yoga instructor Ravi "Yogi" Singh. Singh (whose original name is Neil Hackman) has built up a solid reputation over the years in New York's holistic community as a top yoga and meditation teacher. He garnered a lot of publicity having a number of local celebrities as clients, including actress Liv Ullman and television talk-show host Bill Boggs. During the height of Airplane Game activity in March and April, Singh was holding several meetings a week at his 61 Fourth Avenue yoga studio. Singh presided over the meetings (turban and all), some small, some large, giving speeches about how great the scam was and how it was important to get involved quickly. Singh bragged to *Whole Life* reporters that he was riding on three planes at once and proudly pointed out all the "respectable" people who were pilots at his meeting, including well-known reflexologist Laura "Maja" Norman, whose role he described as being "very hot." Indeed, Singh spent a good deal of time trying to seduce a *Whole Life* reporter into signing on, calling the swindle a "networking phenomenon."

"For the time being it's a certain thing," Singh told our reporter at a meeting on April 2. "You get back $12,000 in about a week. I can guarantee you, if you get in now you'd pilot out." Singh lauded the "integrity" of the game, citing as evidence the short meditations that he conducted at meetings. When our reporter expressed doubt about the legality of the game, Singh uttered this incredible slander: "The Attorney General's girl-friend is doing it." Amusingly enough, during a long conversation with our reporter about various subjects, Singh, in between attempts to get our reporter to join the scam, expressed his own revulsion at New Age cons, saying, "A lot of people are just trying to cash in on New Age stuff. There are so many gimmicky things." Oh brother.

After the game fell apart we interviewed Singh. He claimed he had "come out about even" financially as a result of losing what he had won on other crashed planes. He "lost" $3000 in a game called "Top Gun," he said. In between threats to "take legal action" against *Whole Life* if we printed his "name," Singh said he became involved in the scam because he had a "gambling nature," but in retrospect he admitted he had made a "mistake." He called the Airplane Game "exploitive" and conceded the outcome of the episode was a "negative one." "If I had to do it all over again, I would not do it," he told *Whole Life*.

Singh's regrets look like an outright confession compared to the self-serving drivel others of his ilk are mouthing, but he still maintains many of the pointy-headed ideas of his cohorts, and an examination of the local record shows a wide disparity between his words and his actions. Singh told us repeatedly that he would "never" have participated in the game or have recruited others if he had "realized that the situation would fall apart the way it did." Well, that might be nice to say now, but the tapes of meetings recorded by *Whole Life* clearly show that Singh was keenly aware that the Airplane Game was on shaky ground even as he continued to try to bring others in, including our reporter. At the April 2 meeting he told some prospective new suckers, "This can keep going for about three weeks, but after that you have to be careful. The sooner you get in the better."

Singh said that he "didn't know if the game was illegal. I'm not convinced it is illegal," he told *Whole Life*, admitting that he continued to hold meetings after the widely publicized April 9 arrests took place. "Just because the Attorney General says it's illegal doesn't mean it is," said the legal whiz, adding, "I don't want to say something stupid and incriminate myself." (Too late, pal.) Singh blamed the "media" for many of the game's problems, and also blamed "greedy people" (like those on "Wall Street") for ruining such a good thing.

Laura ("Maja") Norman, kingpin of New York's reflexology scene (reflexology is a foot massage that purportedly cures a wide variety of ills), was identified by Singh at a meeting at Singh's yoga studio as a "hot pilot" whose large network of contacts would be ideal for the Airplane Game. Norman's voice shows up on our tapes of meetings, but she has steadfastly refused to discuss the matter with *Whole Life*. We called Norman right after the arrests in April and she pretended to be someone else "taking a message for Laura." She was obviously shaken up and suspicious. Our only other contact with the usually publicity-hungry Norman was a letter we received after we had left messages to speak with her about a dozen times. The letter was, in a word, bizarre. "Thank you for calling regarding your upcoming article. It is great *Whole Life* magazine consistently takes the lead in educating all of us about issues that affect the holistic community. . . . While I truly appreciate your interest in soliciting my views, I am currently not doing any media interviews/publicity until early 1988. I'm concentrating all my efforts on servicing my present clients and restructuring the training program." What? Laura Norman "not doing media interviews"? Quick, somebody check to see if hell has frozen over. At least people like Singh and Leventhal had the guts to state their views, however sick. As for Laura Norman, well, it's up to you to decide whether you want to put your feet in this woman's hands. (In any case, if Norman hasn't got the guts to speak with us, she will shortly be forced to speak to a judge. Norman has been sued by at least four of the suckers she ripped off, and she'll soon be standing trial in Small Claims Court, accused of stealing thousands of dollars from gullible followers.)

If the Airplane Game can be seen as having both a "moderate" and "extreme" component, then Manhattan-based crystal salesman Andrew "Bear Man" Nevai has to be considered the guru of its most outlandish lunatic fringe. Out of all the Airplane Game promoters we tracked and tried to interview, we came across no one with more bizarre and mentally unbalanced views than Nevai. Nevai, a portly man with long greying hair, made a full-time job of playing the Airplane Game, attending one or more meetings nightly during the period of peak activity in the early spring. Nevai, who like Alan Leventhal has been homeless for some time and generally bunks with friends or lives out of his black van, would often joke at meetings that he had "no time" to look for a place to live because he was "too busy playing Airplane." Throughout the tenure of the game Nevai was one of the community's most outspoken proponents of its growth, and he presided over, spoke at, and helped organize countless gatherings all around the city. Nevai's belief in the Airplane Game as a salvation for humanity was so strong that he preached its virtues like the gospel, launching into defenses of the game at every opportunity and battering down its critics with a vengeance. Nevai's numerous speeches to throngs of potential suckers were consistently replete with distortions, half-truths, outright lies, and some of the most nonsensical New Age ravings this side of Shirley MacLaine. Despite the obviously fraudulent nature of Nevai's presentations and promotions, he became a figure of "respect" during the game, and his name was often mentioned as a reference for a variety of inane rumors and lies. It's hard to say how much Nevai made in the scam, although in April friend and co-Airplane Game criminal John "Sunshine" Knox stated that Nevai had "been through it (piloted out) twice, and three times in a day or so." Nevai continually stated that the Airplane Game was serious business and spoke long and passionately about how important the Airplane was for the "survival of the planet." The game was about "relationships and learning," "learning about abundance on a very deep level."

At one meeting Nevai was given a chance to go through his entire demented monologue. He defended the "legality" of the Airplane Game by comparing it to jaywalking. "Almost everything is illegal. Overtime parking is illegal," he said. "My personal opinion is that the reason why these laws are on the books is because fifty to sixty years ago there were many scams. Some real slick guy would come into a small town and start a game like this, and that one person would collect more and more money and everyone else would be left at the bottom of the thing, and he would leave town with the money. These were innocent people, farm folk who just didn't know what was going on." But, said Nevai, this wasn't the situation with the Airplane Game. "The Airplane Game is being played on a level that puts it into a whole different arena. So the laws that were made a long time ago don't really apply today." What were the differences? Today, he said, "everybody gets to be pilot, not just one person"—a lie. "The game is played with a tremendous amount of integrity here in New York. People are tithing their money to churches, temples, organizations, and so on."

According to Nevai, "The Airplane Game is a model for the kind of economy we will be having twenty, thirty, fifty years from now, a 'win-win' economy. Those of us playing the Airplane Game are at the leading edge of humanity in getting into the game. The same people who are at the forefront of all kinds of change are involved in this." On April 27, Nevai was one of the star attractions at an Airplane meeting held in a basement at 32 West 89th Street, where perhaps the most outlandish incident of the entire Airplane Game fiasco took place. At the meeting Nevai presided over an Airplane Game "ceremony," where Elliott "Moses" Landy, another rabid Airplane Game promoter, was "decorated" with a silver-wings pin in recognition of his "contributions" to the swindle. Nevai called Landy to the front of the room and, as he placed the pin on him, made a short speech: "In every community there are people who do work that is above and beyond the call of duty. We have 'Moses' here, who, I feel, definitely fits that description in general and certainly as far as the particular community is concerned. I would therefore like to, on behalf of everyone here in this room, appoint you 'commander of the great feathers' and give you these silver wings." Then to loud applause Landy made an "acceptance" speech. Sick, sick, sick.

We first interviewed Nevai on May 10th after the Airplane Game fever had pretty much died out. At the time he was more than happy to share with us some of his more deranged ideas and opinions. "Most of the people I know wouldn't play just for money. There had to be a creative spark. The Airplane Game has a creativity and creativity is just a down-to-earth way of getting close to God." Prohibiting the game was a "violation of the Bill of Rights and the Constitution," he said. "As a result of the Airplane Game people now have the money to pay their bills and work on their projects. Many people who have a problem with money are now able to allow the universe to prosper them and become prosperous." But, for this crystal-hawker, the Airplane Game provides more than just personal eternal enlightenment; it is a spiritual path for the whole world. "The Airplane Game is a basis and model for a new economic, political, and spiritual order. It's a way of spirituality, economy, and politics. It's a model of the way things should be. It's like a family, rather than competition, where it's every man for himself. The Airplane Game is the Global Village coming into reality on the planet." When we talked to the New Age visionary a second time, however, he had changed his tune, claiming that "I don't know what you mean by 'participate.' I may have said something at a meeting. I may have asked some questions. It has been such a long time ago. I don't recall addressing any meetings, no."

Most of the other prominent Airplane Game promoters we contacted behaved in just about the same manner, lying about their participation, making absurd claims about the nature of the Airplane Game, threatening to sue *Whole Life*, and hanging up on us. Elliot "Moses" Landy, the owner of a Manhattan film lab called LandyVision, is currently the subject of one lawsuit filed by someone he swindled, and he has been named in sworn court testimony in another case as having been a key promoter of the fraud. Our reporters followed Landy from meeting to meeting, and he can be heard all over our tapes pushing the game and bragging about how much money he made and how many planes he was on (he piloted out at *least* once, according to his own statements). Many of Landy's outrageous comments rival those of friend and co-hustler Nevai. When Landy accepted the silver-wings pin from Nevai at the infamous Airplane Game Emmy Award ceremony, for example, he proudly promised to "try to uphold the tradition." "I did some channeling about this game," he said, "and got that this is in the tradition of a lot of metaphysical secret societies that have gone on through the ages where people were a little more adept at communing with the highest spirits. . . ." That's it, I can't even quote him anymore. Suffice to say that the only difference between Landy and Nevai is that Landy apparently still has a place to live. When I called Landy to ask him some questions, he said, and I quote, "I wasn't involved with the Airplane Game. In fact, I've never even heard of it, and I don't know anyone who was involved in it in any way."

I have never come across such a situation, such a "controversy," where the entire question at hand could be so easily decided by applying the "proof is in the pudding" test. And, in regarding the Airplane Game outrage, the proof is *very much* in the pudding. No matter what went on back in those few months in the spring of 1987, and who did what and said what, how these same individuals *now* take responsibility for their actions has to be the key consideration in evaluating their prior activities and motivations. How are they taking that responsibility? Not well at all. Back then these individuals were standing in front of large groups describing the game as a "fantastic experience"; they were calling every friend, associate, and even strangers to get them involved; they got on the radio to promote their scheme and even published a "newsletter" to push their "cause." During that time these individuals spoke shamelessly in support of the activity as a wonderful phenomenon, right? There was no reticence about it then, was there? Fine, so what's the problem now? Why all the hang-ups? Why all the threats to sue *Whole Life*? Why all the lies? If the game was such a great idea, and if you believed in it so sincerely, then why aren't you crooks sticking to your guns? Why aren't you happy to discuss the details of what you did, and just as happy to have your activities reported in the media? In fact, why aren't you doing something to *revive* the Airplane Game? If it was such a salvation for humanity, as was claimed back then, shouldn't it be a high priority to bring it back so we can all be delivered to Nirvana via the Wings of Greed? Well, I'll tell you why these folks are hanging up on us, lying through their teeth, and threatening to sue us. Because the proof is in the pudding, and the pudding is as sour as hell. These people know, and they knew it back then, that they were involved in an illegal, unethical activity that would hurt countless numbers of people. These people knew at the time that they were promoting an outright scam, and they did it anyway because they wanted to make a quick buck. And they were able to do it, and still sleep at night, because they are people without scruples, without values, and without an ounce of integrity. The New Age bullshit that they mouth means nothing. For these New Age scum, it's merely a means to an end. Why doesn't Mary "Abundance" Houston speak to us and tell us about what she did instead of hang up when we call and threaten to sue me? Why doesn't Diana "Aunt Mary" Gazes discuss her involvement in the scheme rather than conveniently claim it's a "personal matter" and threaten to sue us? Why does Elliott "Moses" Landy now lie about his role in the scam, claim he "never heard of it," and hang up on me? Why does Andrew "Bear Man" Nevai now claim "it was so long ago" that he doesn't "remember" what he did back then? Why does he lie about the money he made and refuse to discuss it? Because all of these guys and gals are nothing but a bunch of amoral opportunists, who managed to seize the moment to shake a lot of people down.

"Creating Your Own Reality"

In the early spring a crudely printed four-page "pro" Airplane Game news-letter called *Wings* was printed anonymously and distributed at hundreds of Airplane Game meetings throughout New York City. The newsletter recited most of the same New Age crap being repeated elsewhere. "The Game is, in its deepest essence, a spiritual growth prosperity workshop," it begins, calling the Airplane Game "as American as Barn-Raising and Apple Pie." It also carried a number of statements and excerpts from pre-viously published sources that were either untrue or distortions. There were also rather perverted pieces of journalism quoted from the Bible (the Book of John) and Benjamin Franklin to "support" their position on the game, which made the task of getting comments from these folks kind of tough. But there were a few things we were able to check out. The newsletter carried the bit about the Airplane Game being invented by monks in Texas, who "channeled" it. Well, those monks don't exist. We called virtually every New Age and holistic source available in Texas, and nobody there ever heard of the "monks," or even the "rumor about the monks," indicating to us that this particular piece of New Age bullshit was created much more locally. The newsletter also quoted the *TV Guide* in support of the game. We spoke to Julianne Hastings, the publicity manager for *TV Guide*, and read her what was printed. Hastings said she was unaware of *Wings'* use of its material and said her company was "not at all happy" about being used to promote the scam. The newsletter also carried a long excerpt from an interview with noted New Age leader Marilyn Ferguson (*The Aquarian Conspiracy*) that had originally appeared in a West Coast New Age publication called *Magical Blend*. While the interview had nothing to do with the Airplane Game, those putting together *Wings* were using the excerpt to try to prop up some aspect of the scheme. *Whole Life* spoke to Terry Martinez, the General Manager of Marilyn Ferguson, Inc. He said that Ferguson was, and we quote, "100 percent against the Airplane Game" and other similar scams. The folks at *Magical Blend* were also incensed. After the magazine's copublisher Jerry Snider reviewed what was excerpted, he told *Whole Life*, "We don't endorse this game or approve of it. If I received this newsletter I would have taken one look at it and thrown it in the garbage. If there were some sort of lawsuit against these people I'd be happy to join in. There are copyright laws, and they should have gotten permission from us, which we would never have given." *Wings* also carried a couple of paragraphs purporting to be "news" about the Airplane Game arrests: ". . . two women were subjected to personal violence and harassment while in overnight detention." This apparent lie was also repeated by Mary Houston on her radio program and others playing the game (obviously to garner symapthy and draw in new suckers) at the time. There were no charges filed against the police or against any law-enforcement agency that was involved in the handling of those two female prisoners that night. Yet the newsletter also goes on to claim that "We have presently retained a criminal attorney . . . to seek dismissal of the charges. In addition, we are interviewing prominent constitutional lawyers in the process of clarifying the legality of the Airplane Game seminar." Airplane Game promoters were constantly fueling rumors that "lawyers were working on making it legal," that it was "legal in other states," and that there were "constitutional challenges going on everywhere" that would soon vindicate this mob of morons and let the world play the game. In fact, it was even claimed to be presently "legal" in New York. At the Airplane Game meeting held April 5 at 118 West 27th Street, Andrew "Bear Man" Nevai told the packed loft, "They have since legalized (the Airplane Game) in Colorado and turned it into a workshop; and they're also doing that in California." All lies. In New York it is illegal; and, according to Chris Braithwaite, a spokesperson for the New York State Attorney General's Office, there was never, and is not now, any legal or legislative challenge to the laws prohibiting the game. It was an outright lie that any "constitutional lawyers" were being interviewed or engaged in any manner to "challenge" the laws in New York. Of course you can *try* to legalize anything. In Massachusetts, for example, there's an organization called the North American Man Boy Love Association (NAMBLA), which describes itself as an organization that is trying to "legalize" sexual contact between middle-aged men and little boys. It is nothing but a cover for a pack of degenerates trying to legitimize their perversion. So, if the Airplane Game folks want to put themselves in such ranks, I have no problem—but such a "challenge" would be on that same level.

As for other states, it's the same story. Gary Clyman, an investigator for the Colorado State Attorney General's Office-Consumer Protection Division, told *Whole Life* there were a total of twenty-two arrests made in Denver in connection with the Airplane Game and about ten more in surrounding cities. All of the twenty-two busted in the capital city had pleaded guilty and were put on probation and ordered to make restitution to those they ripped off. As part of their investigation Clyman said they had seized $30,000 from a bank account that was being used as a depository for Airplane Game revenues. Clyman said that there had been *no attempt* to "legalize" the game. "There was a lot of talk at the time about New Age philosophy and abundance, and it being a legitimate workshop, but that didn't make it legal to us," he told *Whole Life*.

In Texas we spoke to Ron Dusek, the Public Information Officer for the Texas Attorney General's Office. Dusek said the Airplane Game was "definitely illegal in the state of Texas," and he said there were no moves underway to challenge the constitutionality of the laws either through the courts or the legislature. Arrests and convictions were made in various cities throughout the state, according to Dusek. Howard Wayne of the Office of the California Attorney General's Department of Justice told us that there had been arrests and convictions throughout California and stated that there were no moves underway to challenge the constitutionality of the laws in any way. In fact, the only even remotely "judicial challenge" to the constitutionality of the laws barring pyramid schemes took place in Buffalo, New York, in January, several months before the game reached Manhattan. In that case, Buffalo City Judge Anthony P. LoRusso upheld the constitutionality of the state's ban on pyramid schemes, rejecting claims by a defense attorney (defending one of the Airplane Game scum) that the law prohibiting the scams was too vague. At that time the New York Attorney General's Office hailed the ruling as a great help in its efforts to stem the flow of the activity.

Another lie that was circulated around the game was that there existed, or was soon to exist, a "fund" that would provide money to people whose planes had crashed. This "fund" was said to contain anywhere from $50 thousand to $200 thousand (depending on which liar you were talking to) and was meant to provide a safety net for anyone who lost their money. In fact, although rumors and lies about such a fund were spread by Mary "Abundance" Houston, Alan "Archangel" Leventhal, Andrew "Bear Man" Nevai, and others, there is no evidence that any such fund ever existed. Indeed, in such a game of greed it would have been remarkable to see any of those players willing to part with even a dime of their ill-gotten gains for the good of others. But the rumor served its purpose, helping to calm the fears of nervous potential investors who were given false hope that in the event of a "crash" they would be bailed out. Well, the crash of course occurred, and nobody ever heard of this "fund" again.

Because those pushing the scheme feared they would lose out on bringing in fresh cash, they began spreading lies about the press coverage in order to deflect attention away from the game's imminent doom. (In fact, the media's response to the scandal was exemplary, rigorously attacking the scheme from its inception. Local television news crews infiltrated and filmed meetings, radio programs warned people away, and newspapers had a field day ridiculing the New Age sham.) Most of the lies were so unbelievably stupid that we felt embarrassed about even checking them out, but we did. Throughout the game Airplane Game promoters spread the absurd lie that the *Village Voice* had assigned a writer to do a "100 percent positive" feature story on the game after having "just piloted out." Of course this was wishful poppycock. *Village Voice* Executive Editor Kit Rachlis told *Whole Life* that the *Voice* never assigned any writer to do any such story. The *New York Times* became the subject of a particularly inane lie regarding an article they published on the Airplane Game on April 7. The article, entitled, "Airplane: High Stakes Chain Letter," was written by reporter Elizabeth Neuffer, and it was a basically innocuous account of the game that was buried in the back of the newspaper's second section. Still, the article, which reported that the Airplane Game was illegal, sent Airplane Game promoters up the wall. The lie that was manufactured, and repeated by a number of the scam's promoters, was that the reporter was "in trouble" with others at the paper for writing the small piece. At one meeting, Andrew "Bear Man" Nevai told the assembled group, after the subject of that morning's article was raised, "I'll tell you who's really in trouble, the writer who wrote that article is in deep trouble because she's a newcomer to the paper. She's trying to make a name for herself, and all her fellow reporters are playing the game." Nevai, who seems to know so little about so much, apparently doesn't know anything about journalism. One doesn't make a "name" for oneself by writing such unimportant filler. In addition, nothing is written without the assignment, go-ahead, and final proofing by an editor. *Whole Life* spoke to Elizabeth Neuffer, who found the charges quite humorous. Neuffer is hardly a "newcomer," having worked for the *New York Times* in a variety of capacities for four years. "No one I came across at the *Times* was playing the Airplane Game, and I didn't 'get into trouble' at all whatsoever for writing the article." One of the biggest jokes that was constantly being told at Airplane Game meetings was that money being "made" by pilots was going to worthy causes, ranging from Greenpeace to local synagogues. Of course, virtually no one has been able to substantiate any evidence of "tithing" being done by Airplane Game criminals. It doesn't really matter, anyway. If you rob a bank, you are not excused from your crime because you donate 10 percent of the stolen loot to an orphanage. The fact is, though, that no legal, credible, self-respecting organization would want, or would knowingly accept, donations from sources of such dubious legal and moral foundations.

Sifting Through the Wreckage

During the course of our investigation of the Airplane Game, those who promoted and defended the scam often told us that those who lost money in the swindle were not "victims," because under generally accepted principles of New Age ideology there is no such thing as a "victim." The New Agers who follow this particularly twisted concept found it came in handy during the pyramid scam, where this tenet was used to justify the most outrageous conduct by those promoting the scam. Indeed, following this course of "logic," there are also no "perpetrators," and therefore anyone can do anything they want, and whoever gets burned, well, that's just tough. That person's not a victim, he just "attracted that into his life." Of course, this perverted position, like all of the others put forth by the Airplane Game scum, can be used to rationalize doing *anything*, no matter how unethical or corrupt. The fact is that there *are* victims here, and I'm not talking about the morons who lost money playing the game. The *real* victims of the Airplane Game fiasco are people who have, over the years, contributed time, money, energy, and commitment to making a truly "holistic" community in New York a reality—people now routinely associated with the so-called New Age movement. Journalist Gary Null, known for his exposés of spiritual cults, says bluntly, "The New Age movement doesn't exist. Self-serving opportunistic predators have created a movement that serves its own interest. The New Age movement is really just an advertising scam, from crystal healers to weekend become-a-shaman workshops, to things like this, the Airplane Game."

Outside of New York and across the country virtually every responsible leader and public figure in the holistic "movement" repudiated the Airplane Game. Spiritual leader Ram Dass compared the Airplane Game with his own experience with such nonsense many years ago. "I was in the Circle of Gold, which cost fifty dollars," he told *Whole Life*. "It was ultimately a great embarrassment to me. I hadn't thought it through completely before I did it, and now I realize that these pyramid schemes hurt more than they help. The Airplane Game has nothing to do with spirituality, awakening, awareness, or any of those things." In Sausalito, California, a state where the swindle had periods of intense popularity, J. Baldwin, Technology Editor of the *Whole Earth Review*, called the Airplane Game, "an airhead scheme." He went on, "But it's airhead mixed with greed. There's a cumulative effect, so that eventually down the line someone does get hurt and the damage is big. Anyone who uses the phrase 'New Age' to promote something isn't part of it."

Yes, the damage is "big," and continues to be, for everyone, but mainly for those who have worked long and hard to try to create the type of community that serves the highest needs of its constituency, to create the type of community that operates on the most basic principles of integrity and honesty, and to create the type of community that can be a model for the way things should be, rather than the way they shouldn't. The real victims of the Airplane Game scheme are all the people who have worked and shared this ideal, only to see our community turned into a laughing stock, the target of scorn and contempt. And it is to those people, as much as to those who simply lost their cash, that the Airplane Game promoters should, if they truly "take responsibility" for their actions, apologize. Is there really a viable, alternative holistic community? Or are we all just a large pool of New Age barracudas, where the most cunning and predatory among us devour everyone else? I really don't know anymore.

Is it so difficult to conceptualize a community of people whose rank-and-file and leaders can be counted on to *reject* such frauds, rather than *embrace* them? Let me share with you a daydream I had the other day: *It is March of 1987, and a handful of people from California arrive in New York hell-bent on making a fast buck. They have a scam called the Airplane Game, and they are going to try to hook into New York's holistic community to make some money and run. But you know what? It doesn't work. As soon as they approach a number of local New Age movers and shakers, the word goes out: "Beware, there are con-artists within our midst claiming to be pushing a prosperity workshop, but it's all a scam. Don't fall for it." This group of New Age charlatans continues to approach people in the community to try to sell the scheme, but wherever they go they are rebuffed. Those pushing the scam are shocked. They expected to be greeted warmly by their New Age allies in greed, and not for a moment did they expect to run into a community whose leaders felt a deep moral and spiritual responsibility to expose such frauds. As soon as Alan Leventhal heard about this scheme he was shocked, and he warned the con-artists that he was not only going to turn them into the Attorney General's office, but that he was going to use his formidable networking abilities and contacts to put the word out about the scam. Leventhal told the would-be thieves that his name garnered a lot of respect in the community* (remember, this is a daydream), *and he would use whatever influence he could to thwart this swindle. When Mary Houston heard about the scam her reaction was immediate. She decided to take to the airwaves to use the considerable influence of her WBAI Radio show to alert her listeners and members of the community about this scheme. Houston immediately began to assemble a diverse group of guests to appear on her program to discuss the Airplane Game and expose it for what it really was. Houston told others that she felt it was her personal and professional responsibility to take a strong public stand exposing this fraud and to use her powerful communication vehicle to serve the community's right to know. At the same time Houston got on the phone, telling all her friends and associates to steer clear of the scam, warning them, "It's nothing but a bunch of fast-buck artists trying to capitalize on New Age rhetoric and bullshit. Let's stop them." Houston even went so far as enlisting her boyfriend, attorney Alfred Webre, to go with her to speak in front of large groups, explaining how the whole thing was illegal. Diana Gazes was equally disgusted by these California fakes. As a long-time member of the New Age community and veteran journalist, she knew a fraud when she saw one. No, there's no way she could be fooled. She immediately got on her phone, calling everyone she knew to spread the word. Gazes told those she spoke with that it "would be serving the highest good" if they too would contact their friends and associates to warn them about this unspeakable scam.*

When Ravi Singh got wind of this New Age bullshit, he too was outraged. Although he had a "gambling spirit," Singh knew this was an out-and-out swindle that would very quickly hurt a lot of people. Singh told everyone attending his yoga classes to be on the alert for the Airplane Game and to make sure they told their friends to steer clear of it. In fact, Singh was so upset that people would be hurt in this game of greed that he started to hold meetings in his yoga studio of people who were similarly concerned. At these meetings Singh would lead the group in discussions of ways that the community could be warned of this scam, ways that those promoting it could be stopped. Laura Norman was one of the many concerned New Agers who attended these meetings, and she offered to use her large network of clients and contacts to sound the alarm as far and as loudly as possible. Indeed, virtually every New Age mover and shaker made it their "personal responsibility" to use their positions of trust and influence to, as Diana Gazes puts it, "serve the highest good." As a result of this unified stand against this grotesque and obvious fraud, the California con-artists were totally thwarted. Although some people here and there did get involved, there was such an uproar of outrage from the community leaders that the game was effectively killed before it even got started.

Finally, with the scam stopped dead in its tracks, Mary Houston, Alan Leventhal, Diana Gazes, Ravi Singh, and Laura Norman stepped back, wiped their hands, and thanked each other for a job well done. They had fulfilled their responsibilities to themselves and, even more importantly, to the community that sought their guidance and leadership. Indeed, their actions represented the highest ideals of holism, and they had truly risen to the occasion. They all turned to one another, smiled, and in unison expressed the same thought and feeling: "Now, back to building."

An Epilogue

More than a year after the peak of Airplane Game-mania in New York City, the specter of its impact and the depths of its damage to our holistic community continue to be felt. And a complete accounting of its most grisly aspects are continuing to come to light. But the ongoing exposé of the Airplane Game disaster and its criminal promoters are not coming about as the result of any journalistic investigation or any law-enforcement activity. For New York's media it's "old news," and for the cops, well, they've got daily homicides to worry about. But for one group of New York New Agers the Airplane Game is not over, and its tenacity in seeking justice is forcing, once again, a critical examination both of the New Age leadership and of the concepts that precipitated the pyramid-scheme scandal.

By the time the fall of 1987 rolled around, these New Age phonies who had promoted and profited from the illegal pyramid scheme probably thought they could breathe easy. The game had died out just before the summer, and, with no more arrests or media coverage in sight, it certainly looked as though they had gotten away with it. But they hadn't counted on Iris Solow, and they hadn't counted on *Whole Life*. Solow, a Brooklyn resident, had been ripped off in the scheme to the tune of $1250; but, unlike the many thousands of similarly duped New Yorkers who lost their money, she decided to fight back. Solow filed suit in New York City Small Claims Court against the "pilot" who had taken her cash; and, after a trial on November 13, 1987, Small Claims Court Judge Marshall C. Berger found in Solow's favor, and ordered Mary Meuer, a Manhattan architect, to return Solow's money. As a result, Solow became the first person in New York, and perhaps in the country, to have a court rule that an individual ripped off in a pyramid scam has a legal and moral right to have it returned. News of what was immediately dubbed the "Solow decision" spread quickly throughout New York's New Age community and received coverage in the press. The verdict threw the fear of God into those Airplane Game criminals who had profited from the fraud, and it gave unexpected hope to the multitudes who had been ripped off. In all parts of the city the worms began to turn. Suddenly a "dead issue" became a very live one, as one by one Airplane Game losers began to file lawsuits against the creeps who had taken their cash. By the time *Whole Life* hit the stands in mid-December with a full account of the Solow decision, the steady trickle of Airplane Game lawsuits had turned into a flood. By January 1988 there was hardly a week that went by in which there wasn't at least one or two Airplane Game cases heard in New York City Small Claims Court. The cases that have already been tried or settled have produced a steady string of victories for Airplane Game losers looking to get their money back. To date, almost all cases filed have been won by those seeking their cash, and at the same time they have provided a close-up look at some of the most grotesque acts of New Age greed and trickery ever seen in this or any other holistic community.

The trials were remarkable not only for the behind-the-scenes look they provided of the inner-workings of the scam but also for the forum they created, forcing New Age degenerates to face those they had scammed and compelling them to admit to their misdeeds under oath. The result was a nonstop procession of some of New York's most notable New Age leaders, like rodents forced out from under their rocks, made to face the light of the day. And the brighter the light, the worse they looked.

If there was any doubt left as to the moral bankruptcy and criminally warped spirituality of those who had perpetrated the Airplane Game swindle, the trials put those questions to rest once and for all. Those pyramid-scheme hustlers who had the guts to take the stand in their own defense committed multiple perjury, most now pretending to be injured parties themselves. A number of the hustlers who had made a killing even referred to themselves in trial testimony as "victims," an ironic self-description from the same folks who, in best New Age tradition, hotly eschew the term and its implications. Others who had been major organizers of the scam now tried to portray themselves as innocent little lambs who had been duped by some mysterious power beyond their control. Virtually all claimed to have made no money in the swindle, and many said they had been ripped off, too. A lot of the New Age bandits employed high-priced legal counsel (no doubt paid for by their winnings from the scam) to try to get them off the hook—but to no avail. Some, unwilling to face public scrutiny, simply did not show up for trial—therefore losing by default—while others agreed to pay back the ripped-off cash before trial. Those who did show up for trial took their anger out on journalists covering the proceedings, sometimes even resorting to physical attacks. And still others skipped town altogether, content to lie low in other states with their ill-gotten gains.

The Airplane Game's most notorious promoter, Mary "Abundance" Houston, was sued by no less than three people she ripped off. At first Houston made a big squawk about how she was going to contest the charges against her. She appeared at numerous hearings seeking delays and screaming and crying about being "harassed" by *Whole Life*. At a number of hearings Houston engaged in long, unintelligible monologues on subjects ranging from the Soviet Union, her daughter's telephone number, the state of her mental health (at one point she said she was mentally/emotionally ill and under a doctor's care), to various obsessions she had with *Whole Life*'s article about her. The hearings, though, had nothing to do with anything she was talking about, and on more than one occasion a judge had to cut off her incoherent ravings and ask her to stick to the subject at hand. It was, for all those present, a pathetic spectacle. Finally, after Houston repeatedly lied to various judges and other court officials to gain delays in her trials, her time had run out, and she cracked. On March 18, 1988, she agreed to pay back nearly $1000 that she had stolen from Manhattan's John Percik. Houston made the payment rather than face a trial a week later. On March 21 Houston showed up in court to face a lawsuit by Michael Oles of Manhattan. But, before the trial started, Houston broke down in tears and, clutching a Bible (no joke, she carried it to court), agreed to settle the complaint.

Incredibly enough, despite all of this hoopla, the Airplane Game, in a number of different forms, is still going on in various parts of New York City (as of this writing in mid-1988), and more suckers are presumably being parted from their wallets. Its most current incarnation is called "Network," but it's based on the same get-rich-quick format that formed the foundation for the Airplane Game. And, just as incredibly, those who are pushing the scam are claiming that the "basis for the game" is still "sound," that it was just "the press," "the police," and "bad vibes" that caused everyone to get ripped off the first time around. As unbelievable as it may seem, the mentally disabled New Agers who promoted the scandal are still clinging to their "belief" that the game "worked" and, in the warped words of New Age looney Diana "Aunt Mary" Gazes, "served the highest good." Although they have been arrested, convicted, sued, and publicly exposed and ridiculed, these mantra-chanting screwballs have "kept the faith."

In other words, in New York's holistic community business is going on as usual. And what is "business as usual" for New Agers? Well, in New York it's the same rotten socioeconomic infrastructure that allows things like the Airplane Game to flourish in the first place. And that infrastructure is based on one evil, self-serving, and criminal precept: "If you don't blow the whistle on my scam, I won't blow the whistle on yours—and we'll both make lots of money."

In reality, the New Age community in New York is comprised of many daily mini-Airplane Games—acts of fraud and theft that go on disguised as "healing treatments," "enlightenment workshops," and "spiritual guidance sessions." And it's not that the community doesn't know who the snake-oil salesmen are. Everyone knows who's a crook. The community simply has never displayed the moral courage to throw the scum out. But why? How, on Manhattan's upper west side, does a man named Mark Becker, a convicted narcotics trafficker who organized a nationwide PCP-peddling ring, successfully operate a yoga studio, a mail-order herb shop, and other "New Age" enterprises? How, on Manhattan's lower east side, does a woman named Jonnie Winchester, another convicted narcotics dealer (coast-to-coast cocaine dealing) and a big promoter of the Airplane Game fiasco, now become a major figure in peace-activist circles in New York, playing a key role in the planning of antiwar actions throughout the city? How do these New Age dregs, and countless others like them, achieve such positions of respect and responsibility when they are so known for their slimy, unethical, and criminal dealings in their day-to-day activities? Why has the New Age become such a haven for these mental misfits and social misanthropes? They have been rejected from mainstream social and business circles for their morally reprehensible activities, so why do *we* embrace them? Is there something wrong with *us*?

Perhaps. New Agers are supposedly "open minded," "nonjudgmental." And that's fine. The problem with the New Age community is that these concepts have been taken to such an extreme that it is not unusual to come across New Agers who would refuse to condemn the mass murders of Charles Manson because it would be "judgmental" to do so, who would believe that a flying saucer had just landed on the White House lawn because it would be close-minded to doubt it. And that's the way it was with the Airplane Game, and with the general state of mental decay and lack of self-policing in the New Age community. In its zeal to embrace alternatives and better ways to live, both physically and spiritually, the community has abandoned all shreds of common sense. So what we have is a social circus: Anything goes, and nothing is wrong.

A truly progressive and enlightened people will never trade in their brains and common sense for mindless slogans and pie-in-the-sky propaganda. And, until the New Age movement becomes both discriminating and honest, we want no part of it. *Whole Life* no longer uses the term "New Age" on its editorial pages—that is, unless we are lampooning it. There are many wonderful things happening today in the fields of alternative health-care, spiritual exploration, and political/social consciousness-raising that are suffering unnecessarily because they are being swept into the same garbage pail occupied by bogus New Age scams and crooks. At *Whole Life* we are going to do our best to separate the good from the bad, the positive from the negative, the real from the bullshit. The "Airplane Game" is over, for the time being. And now begins the work to make sure it never comes back.

NEW AGE ECONOMICS

Carl Raschke

Theodore Roosevelt once said that what would destroy American civilization would be the growth of a style of thinking stressing "prosperity-at-any price, peace-at-any-price, safety-first instead of duty first, the love of soft living and the get-rich-quick theory of life." Old T. R., whose headstrong politics and bullnecked idealism kept him from appreciating what Reinhold Niebuhr once termed "the irony of American history," must have expected that such a default of collective values would result from inattention, lethargy, and the slow demise of a people's character. He surely could not have imagined it to arise from a glitzy and carefully marketed social and political agenda known as the "New Age movement." One of the most curious ironies amid today's headlines is the revel of handwringing over our national lack of will to compete in the global marketplace at precisely the same moment when many among our trend-drenched business and educational luminaries are partaking of a popular philosophy with a recklessly opposite clutch of objectives. The power of the so-called "New Age movement," which tells us that we all are gods immune to pain or struggle, to bewitch the minds of politicans, pedagogues, and management-training specialists is a present-day behavioral oddity comparable to the vacation habits of lemmings.

What Is the New Age Movement?

What exactly is the New Age movement? The expression itself seems to have gained currency several years ago as a packaging label for the 1980s designed to recycle within the kingdom of quiche the numerous "human potential" therapies, alternative mating styles, and sundry forms of self-preoccupation that historian Christopher Lasch a decade ago christened the

Carl Raschke, a widely quoted critic of the New Age movement, is professor of Religious Studies at the University of Denver.

"culture of narcissism." During the 1970s, supposedly a time of privatism and introspection, no one would have dared call such a social underworld a "movement." What writer Tom Wolfe sardonically named the "Me Decade" lurched along from Watergate through the Carter years as a melodrama of moral dissociation and political paralysis, highlighted by double-digit inflation and the simmering of one-time student activists in executive saunas and suburban hot-tubs. New Age seminars in the last few years have been all the rage not just among teacher groups, career-training specialists, and even some police departments, but many of the nation's giant corporations, like IBM, AT&T, and General Motors. Werner Erhart, the perverse genius who founded est, has recently been raking in the greenbacks with a new pitch aimed specifically at the corporate boardroom with a group known as the Forum. New Age thinking has also made inroads into the "economic development" efforts of the state government of Colorado. In the summer of 1987 the state's Department of Local Affairs unveiled what was known as the Economic Renewal Project (ERP). ERP has almost as much to do with serious economic development as Rocky Mountain oysters have to do with seafood. The ERP encourages rural residents to do such things as grow broccoli in their backyards and mushrooms in mineshafts with the aim of "enhancing community consciousness." The Colorado economy, it should be duly noted, has been slumping for most of the period the New Age mania has been spreading, while the rest of the country has been experiencing sustained growth. All along the expansion of the new culture had followed the maturation curve of left-leaning 1960s youth, who in slightly more than a decade were transformed from "hippies" into "yuppies." Though their demographics may have changed substantially, their "psychographics" have not been altered in any significant measure.

Sixties radical Jerry Rubin was recently quoted as proclaiming that "yuppies are challenging the ossified corporate structures, just as they once challenged the sacred tradition of academia." Rubin added, "We haven't sold out, we're taking over." The tendentiously named "counterculture" that spread amid the social wreckage of the Vietnam era was, and to this day remains, the ideological fodder of the New Age movement. In the 1960s there allegedly existed a functional split in motivations between drug-muddled "flower children" and SDS revolutionists. Twenty years later the split has been defined away by the New Age caption-makers. They are all part of "the movement," a 1960s term itself.

This strange, Cuisinart mush of pop mysticism and utopian politics was first codified, using the alleged imprimaturs of experimental psychology as well as theoretical physics, in 1980 with the publication of a book by Marilyn Ferguson entitled *The Aquarian Conspiracy: Personal and Social*

Transformation in the 1980s. Ferguson's book is for New Agers what *The Communist Manifesto* was for the First International. And there is even a kind of kitsch apocalypticism in the rhetorical opening of the book that sounds a lot like Marx himself. "A leaderless but powerful network is working to bring about radical change in the United States," Ferguson declares. "Its members have broken with certain key elements of Western thought, and they may even have broken continuity with history." Just as Shirley MacLaine's recent television miniseries played on the average housewife's soap opera sympathies to advertise the hackneyed seductions of the occult, so *The Aquarian Conspiracy* exploits the metaphysical yearnings of many a suburban American to push the dated agenda of what used to be called the "New Left." "The political system needs to be *transformed*, not *reformed*," according to Ferguson. Ferguson applauds the "revolutionary" striving of "a powerful, committed minority" that employs strategies of advocacy and infiltration of businesses and federal agencies to bring about what resembles quite strikingly the kind of anarcho-syndicalism espoused by student radicals of yesteryear. Anarcho-syndicalism is founded on a myth of active rebellion against state authority without the rational strategies of revolution common to Marxian socialism. That style of politics has been absorbed into the rarefied eschatology of the New Age. "The new collective is the new politics," Ferguson exults. Meditation, chanting, guided fantasy, hypnosis, and a Turkish bazaar of mind-altering technologies all become aids to the "revolutionary process," including the use of psychoactive drugs, which have "given a visionary experience of self-transcendence," says Ferguson, in order to "determine the future of human development."

Business pundit John Naisbitt, who plumps for Ferguson in his runaway best-seller *Megatrends*, genuflects in his own writings to her notion of the "conspiracy to enable transformation." Notwithstanding his repeated references to *The Aquarian Conspiracy*, Naisbitt does a quite effective job of soft-selling segments of Ferguson's acid-dreams social policy to America's manageriate by offering a respectable vision of the high-tech future, which fuzzes her more hard-edged fantasies of Santa Monica service-station attendants changing into superbeings. While avoiding Ferguson's cosmo-psychic patter about "the experience" as the substance of all things hoped-for, from nuclear disarament to sex without superego, Naisbitt dwells extensively on her prophecies about the imminent uprising of "leaderless" legions of New Agers. "The strength of traditional networks such as family, church, and neighborhoods is dissipating in American society," Naisbitt tells us in *Megatrends*, invoking certain commemorative codewords guaranteed to rekindle the subcortical consciousness of the Woodstock-nation generation, which has habitually substituted personal fantasy and altered states of consciousness for critical intelligence. "The gap is being filled with new networks functioning, as Marilyn Ferguson puts it, as the spontaneous modern-day equivalent of the ancient tribe." In *Re-Inventing the Corporation* Naisbitt characterizes "networking" as "the baby boom's management style of choice." It is supposedly a nonauthoritarian, antibureaucratic form of industrial organization where "everyone learns from everyone else." Naisbitt commends the networked, leaderless, "reinvented" corporation, which on close reading begins to sound like a *profitless* corporation, as an updated instance of what student activists twenty years ago called "participatory democracy"—democracy without democratic institutions, or what old-era, stodgy sorts of political thinkers have referred to as "mob rule."

Naisbitt also gushes about the "new worker" for the New Age—that is, the "knowledge worker" or reinvented employee whose intellectual skills and computer prowess are so valuable that he can demand to be compensated for his conviction "that work should be fun." The new worker, says Naisbitt, is "self-managed," which means he can be whatever he wants and live wherever he wants, and somebody will pay for it. Or, as a Naisbitt aphorism runs: "The world stands aside for the person who knows where he or she is going." Moreover, New Age management theory—which may be labelled "Theory N," for "narcissism"—holds forth tremendous opportunity to assist in the recovery of the American economy, hobbled by foreign competition, by creating an entirely new industry to compensate for the current surfeit of Wendy's franchises and Pizza Huts. Carolyn Corbin, futurist and author of *Strategies 2000: How to Prosper in the New Age*, predicts that by the turn of the century there will be countless unfilled niches for "those people [e.g., consultants] who know how to manage the New Age employee," who allegedly does not need to be managed anyway. The perspicacity of New Age economic nostrums may perchance be measured by the performance not only of those public figures pitching for Naisbitt on his book jacket but of the corporations that he contends have been reinvented for the sake of the greater social weal.

Aside from Ferguson's pro forma endorsement, *Megatrends* is touted by the CEO of a large company, who has recently cut back operations and had its bonds downgraded, as well as by one-time Democratic presidential candidate Gary Hart, one-time Colorado senator and "co-conspirator" in the new politics with former governor Richard Lamm. Both Hart and Lamm had sufficient New Age savvy to vacate elected office just as their home-state economy, once a national exemplar of prosperity and stability, was unravelling. It is significant that Naisbitt lends a lot of ink to profiling the airline People Express as the truly reinvented "American corporation of the 1990s." Since People Express recently teetered on the edge of bankruptcy, before its name vanished from history after having been absorbed into Texas Air, one must wonder whether the next chapter in the story of New Age "innovation" will be Chapter 11.

The Impact on Productivity

The New Age movement, should it continue to "catch on" with sundry professionals and pace-setters among the baby-boomers, will surely "transform" the American economy and social order in much the same way as AIDS transforms the body's immune system. The impact on economic productivity and America's capacity to compete in the global arena will doubtlessly be affected. Ferguson's gleeful boast that "it is impossible to overestimate the historic role of psychedelics as an entry point drawing people into [the] transformative technologies" of the New Age is a point well-taken. If psychedelics had not been hawked in the 1960s as, in her words, "a pass to Xanadu," we would probably not have the epidemic of middle-class cocaine addiction in the 1980s, not to mention the present billion-dollar "war" with drug-pushers, whom the U.S. Secretary of Defense recently delineated for the first time as a threat to national security. It would also not have been the case, again in Ferguson's *ipissima verba*, that "the changes in brain chemistry triggered by psychedelics cause the familiar world to metamorphose" for the armies of Aquarians. Such an Alice-through-the-looking-glass metamorphosis of common sense and critical intelligence may account for the fact that New Age themes are now slithering through the public-school curriculum, while the educational magisterium either smiles or looks the other way. The regular use of "guided imagery" in the classroom, where school children are hypnotized and taught to float out of their bodies, is the most egregious example of these tendencies.

Rocky Mountain Hype

California may historically be the intellectual fountainhead for New Age nincompoopery, but Colorado in the last several years has assumed the role of political showcase for the movement's strange sort of praxis. Shirley MacLaine's revelation that she would establish her multimillion-dollar "healing center" on private land by the "entrance to the hollow earth" near the Great Sand Dunes National Monument enhanced the state's reputation as the "roof of America" by promising to increase the indigenous population of airheads. The city of Boulder, already well-known for its eccentricities, was also the command post for the nationally publicized "Harmonic Convergence" (aptly dubbed by cartoonist Gary Trudeau as the "Moronic

Convergence"), where the presumed 144,000 invisible followers of Quet- zalcoatl, the Mayan "lord of unified opposites," held hands at "sacred sites" around the planet, hummed, chanted, and sought to make contact with UFOs high up in the ozone. As *California UFO* magazine laconically ex- plained the matter, "August 16 and 17, 1987, known collectively as 'Harmonic Convergence,' marked the beginning of a twenty-five year phase in which humankind will prepare itself to join the 'federation or league of galactic intelligence,' according to current readings of Mayan and other Native American prophecy."

In Colorado groups of parents vociferously objected to a foundation- financed, nationally published curriculum used for teacher certification which, mouthing much of the New Age agenda, encouraged such intel- lectually rigorous exercises as Chinese fortune-telling and learning how to commune with spirits of the dead. Their complaint was roundly ignored. Earlier, a Denver newspaper reported on the epidemic popularity of a "new- age version of the pyramid scheme," known as the Pilot Investment Program, which relies on "cosmic mumbo jumbo" (rather than plain avarice) "to attract its participant-victims." While district attorneys and local police around the state have been scrambling to squash the scam with the help of consumer fraud laws, Colorado's New Age dream-makers have managed to amass millions in funny money by sugaring empty investment promises with such Aquarian argot as "personal empowerment" and "getting centered."

From Economics to Enlightenment

The tacit purpose of such shenanigans may be to persuade the credulous and unsuspecting, by use of particular "initiation" ruses to disorient and confuse the adept, that the free-enterprise system itself is a "blockage" to universal enlightenment. New Age thought historically has tattooed itself with the fantasies of internationalist socialism. Alice A. Bailey, a highly influential occultist and political strategist who began popularizing the expression "The New Age" more than sixty years ago, wrote in her book *Serving Humanity* that the ultimate objective of what she equivocally named "The Plan" would be the elimination of "the greed of the capitalistic forces in the world" and making sure that "the principle of sharing" controls economic affairs. Indeed, the key concepts, shibboleths, prophecies, promises, and overarching motifs of the New Age movement can all be found in the publications of Bailey's Arcane School, otherwise known as the School for Esoteric Studies, a metaphysical organization responsible for giving broad currency to the term "New Age" itself, which recurs throughout her books and pamphlets. The Arcane School, in turn, derived from the revisionist wing of the Theosophical Society, which was founded in America in the 1870s by a Russian countess and seer named Helena P. Blavatsky. The teachings of theosophy include a pantheistic view of God; belief in reincarnation, and ancient "ascended masters" guiding the destiny of humanity, an idea that the soul evolves over many eons from an animal to a divine state; and an obsession with the so-called "ancient wisdom" formulated by priests of the lost continent of Atlantis. Theosophical doctrines have entered into the genealogy of various cults and political insurgencies of "true believers" throughout the twentieth century, including the Golden Dawn, the Ordo Templi Orientalis (OTO), I AM, the Church Universal and Triumphant, and German National Socialism. During the 1960s the phrase "Age of Aquarius," synonymous in the lexicon of the Arcane School with "New Age," prevailed. The term itself can occasionally be found in the mysteries and quasi-gnostic flights of speculation throughout the nineteenth century as part of what James Webb has dubbed the "occult underground."

The New Ager's obsession with redistributing world income and enforcing what he refers to as "the limits to growth" is a natural extension of his fundamental belief that, as Peter Russell puts it in *The Global Brain*, "humanity . . . is behaving rather like a malignant growth on the planet." If the "capitalistic forces" of the world are liquidated, then perhaps another, less obvious goal will be achieved—*a world without people*. The Khmer Rouge once attempted to excise the "cancer" in a local context. Perhaps that sentiment explains the motivation behind the staging of a New Age extravaganza last December known as "The World Instant of Co-operation," where millions supposedly jammed into sports arenas from Houston to Moscow in order to meditate and, by collective "mental imaging," to create a "planetary resonance" that would manifest world peace. If the event did not succeed, according to Texas-based New Age guru John Randolph Price in his book *Practical Spirituality*, two billion people would have to be "removed" from the planet. Such "purifications" are mentioned in many other New Age texts, including those of J. Z. Knight, José Arguelles, and Jack Underhill. The prediction is ubiquitous, and it tends to mask the underlying Manichean will-to-power of the movement, not to mention its submerged intolerance and incipient violence.

If T. R. were alive, he would be moved to drink. The Soviets may be clucking that we finally have manufactured enough rope with which to hang ourselves. And the Japanese are probably having a good giggle.

A MEMOIR

W hat happened to those West Coast visionaries and occultists—
pictured so well in James Webb's essay—after the hippie
counterculture went back under ground?

Ted Schultz went to San Francisco to sample its alternative spiritual offerings—from Buddhism to Sufi dancing. There, he founded the "Corps of Reality Engineers," an organization devoted to "creating new consensus realities," primarily by developing people's psychic powers and coordinating their belief systems. But Schultz came to doubt the efficacy of psychic power. "I noted with interest," he writes here, "that the world's greatest 'reality engineers' were scientists and engineers who had manipulated physical reality not by 'violating' its laws but by understanding and using them. . . . Diseases had been conquered not by positive thinking but by the discovery of microbes, antibiotics, and vaccines." Schultz is now a "reality engineer" at Cornell University, where he is completing a doctorate in evolutionary biology.

His critique of the New Age movement is sympathetic. "I suspect," he writes, "that most adherents are attracted to New Age belief systems less for the vague philosophies than for the tangible effects on their lives generated by practices like trance induction, meditation, physical therapies (e.g., yoga, massage), psychological counseling (e.g., within frameworks like astrology and psychic reading), and the pleasure of love and friendship within a shared social context. . . . I do not doubt that some of these practices work, having benefited from them myself." Schultz notes happily that it is not necessary to accept metaphysical explanations in order to enjoy the "beneficial" effects of some of the movement's "exotic" practices.

A PERSONAL ODYSSEY
THROUGH THE NEW AGE
Ted Schultz

Recently I received a letter from my old friend Tom. Back in 1973, when we were both twenty years old, Tom and I traveled west together to explore California's "New Age" movement. Sharing an apartment with a group of friends in San Francisco's Haight-Ashbury district, we immersed ourselves in the gamut of twentieth-century mysticism, spirituality, and alternative culture: yoga, Tai Chi, Buddhism, Taoism, meditation, vegetarianism, massage, Sufi dancing, spiritual gatherings, Hare Krishna parades, and various occult and psychic practices. Eventually we parted ways, and while Tom's path led to Theosophy and thence to Anthroposophy, mine led to the study of science. I am now a student of evolutionary biology; he's a eurythmy[1] instructor.

We'd been out of touch for a number of years, but Tom's letter wasn't your typical long-time-no-see gusher:

> Through the years I have observed you selling out to the big Satan of materialistic science—too scary out there on the edge so you thought you would creep back to the safety and security of Mother Earth while trying to maintain some credibility with your inner nature by surrounding yourself with alternative types. William Irwin Thompson [a New Age philosopher] has described how new knowledge streams down from the spiritual worlds, from beyond the threshold to earth: In four stages of development, an idea is first revealed to "crazies," then made more subtantial by artists, further clothed in substantiality by "savants," and finally drilled into the dirt by pedants. A sorry ending for your many talents if it is to this last that you pledge your life. And this never-ending obsession with objective testing—something to concern oneself with

Ted Schultz is a graduate student of biology at Cornell University and editor of the forthcoming *Fringes: The Whole Earth Catalog of Strange Beliefs and Eccentric Science.*

but not to be strangled by. Haven't you read some of these "new physics" people like [Fritjof] Capra, [Thomas] Kuhn, *et al.* on what a bugaboo some of this objectivity is? No more than a way of influencing the results to correspond to one's own theories.

Hmmm. I guess subtlety isn't one of the Anthroposophical virtues. Still, criticism from an old friend deserves consideration. Is Tom right? Have I "sold out"?

As a matter of fact, I have given the various New Age and spiritual philosophies a great deal of thought over the years, culminating in 1986 when I edited a special issue of *Whole Earth Review*[2] that critically examined some of the beliefs current in the New Age and in the paranormal world in general. Rather than turning my back on these exotic beliefs, as Tom implies I have done, I feel as if I have arrived at my current mindset as a direct result of such interests; indeed, I've come to realize that scientific methodology is the most direct way of evaluating the sizable subset of New Age claims that falls to the province of natural science.

The "New Age"—part media invention, part hype, and part genuine inquiry by sincere seekers—is a poorly defined amalgam of exotic beliefs that ranges through religions, cosmologies, ethical philosophies, spiritual disciplines (e.g., meditation), health practices, personal-growth systems, and theories supported by psychic and paranormal claims. Many groups eschew categorization under the New Age umbrella, but, insofar as there's a lot of trafficking of people and ideas within this burgeoning subculture, it's all New Age to me. Because the New Age is so poorly defined, it's impossible to characterize its disparate movements by a common philosophy. Still, certain broad generalizations can be made.

Tom's letter conveniently covers three recurrent New Age themes: (1) "Materialistic [a.k.a. Western] science" and rationalism in general are responsible for most of the evil in the world. (2) Objective truth is an overrated commodity, perhaps an illusion that doesn't really exist. (3) All knowledge originates from a spiritual plane (a.k.a. the "etheric" or "astral" world) that is "higher" or more important than the material world. Some extend this concept to condemn the material world as a "bad" place, the preoccupation with which is the source of all of humanity's problems.

I would include an additional point not covered in Tom's letter, but which has gained currency in recent years, especially with the rise of Shirley MacLaineism: (4) We are each "personally responsible" for the conditions of our lives. Some New Age systems (e.g., those of the channeled entities Ramtha/J. Z. Knight and Seth/Jane Roberts) carry this notion to an extreme, asserting that we have "chosen" our parents, physical ailments, and other life situations usually considered beyond our control.

For the rationalist, the above philosophical points may seem sufficient cause to dismiss the New Age out of hand. But most adherents are attracted to New Age belief systems less for the vague philosophies than for the tangible effects on their lives generated by practices like trance induction, meditation, physical therapies (like yoga and massage), psychological counseling within frameworks like astrology and psychic reading, and the pleasure of love and friendship within a shared social context. For most New Age adherents, it seems a small step from experiencing the noticeable psychological and physical benefits of a prescribed practice to accepting wholesale the accompanying philosophy and cosmology.

I do not doubt that some of these practices work, having benefited from them myself, and for this reason alone I consider them worthy of further study. Unlike many of my friends, however, I don't find it necessary to accept the proffered explanations behind these positive experiences, especially because they usually conflict with what is known about the natural world and because they are often half-baked and contradictory. I have, for instance, experienced profound physical benefits from the practice of yogic exercises, even though I've generally ignored pseudophysiological teachings about chakras, kundalini channels, and the like. A yoga purist might contend that in so doing I am missing out on the essence of the practice, but my experience is that yoga works fine without these beliefs. Since so much in the New Age is similarly dubious, I prefer to sample this colorful world of exotic beliefs with a mind that is simultaneously open and skeptical, so that I may enjoy beneficial experiences and entertain exotic possibilities but accept nothing as "true" that has not been objectively proven.

Materialistic Science

New Age philosophy in the 1980s owes a great deal more than most of its adherents realize to Helena P. Blavatsky and the other founders of Theosophy. Tom, for instance, echoes in his letter Blavatsky's 1888 occult classic, *The Secret Doctrine*,[3] which rails on at length against "materialistic science." This deep anti-science tradition in New Age thinking is problematic, in my opinion, not only for society as a whole, but for the balanced perspective of individual New Age adherents. A strong bias toward emotion, creativity, and intuition without any attention to rationality deprives one of the ability to fully enjoy or, indeed, to effectively interact with the world.

A poet may observe the beauty of nature with a different perspective than a biologist, and we are all richer for these two points of view. But consider the following poem:

Behold the butterfly.
Winged brother of the bird,
No cousin to worms.

Aside from being a bad poet, our bard would be quite wrong in literally deducing, based on the shared character of wings, a closer evolutionary relationship between insect and bird than insect and worm—something the biologist could tell him. This fact would not detract, of course, from the metaphorical nature of the poem (such as it is), and in fact it may be intentional. But now suppose a group of insistent pop philosophers were to arise, the "Aquarians for the Supremacy of Poetry Over Science," who, unable to make the distinction between metaphor and objective fact, asserted that, on the basis of poetic intuition, the butterfly and bird were *in fact* closely related organisms. This would resemble the character of current New Age attacks on "materialistic science." (In fact, Anthroposophy's version of biology makes this very claim that, because physical forms are generated by "ideal" patterns in the etheric plane, animals that look alike are the most closely related!) On the other hand, if the biologist were to decide that metaphors were improper unless they coincided with systematic biology, he would resemble the more extreme critics of the New Age, who fail to see anything positive about fictional cosmologies and who ascribe all of the reported benefits of New Age teachings to "self-delusion."

How sad that the situation has come to this, because a cooperative effort might instead produce a shared body of knowledge that nourished all of the realms of human experience (including emotion, creativity, intuition, and rationality) while recognizing the limitations of each. Science unguided by vision produces runaway pollution, nuclear stockpiles, and all the other abuses that have made my generation so misguidedly anti-science. On the other hand, creative vision without regard for objective truth produces unquestioning belief in Atlantis, alien entities, reincarnation, and the other highly improbable superstitions that run rampant in twentieth-century Western culture. What both sides really need to do at this point is to descend from their fortresses of opinion and meet on the common ground of allegiance to the truth—and to recognize the difference between metaphorical, intuitive "truth" and objective truth. The truth may fail to match our cherished preconceptions; that is the price few are willing to pay for the reward of a deeper understanding and experience of life.

The "Bugaboo" of Objectivity

My experience in the New Age has been with sincere people who, however misguided, genuinely believe in the systems they espouse, usually as a result of deep, meaningful experiences. In the early seventies the New Age community was small and the sincerity was more noticeable. Today it is a big, pop-culture business, and charlatans and scams abound. For example, some shameless New Age entrepreneurs are profiting from the current AIDS epidemic. Here in the San Francisco Bay Area, psychic healers and others claim that AIDS can be cured with the proper mental attitude. Local health food stores sell a 15-page typed, xeroxed pamphlet "channeled" by Kevin Ryerson, one of the mediums made famous by Shirley MacLaine, that describes a "holistic" remedy for AIDS.[4] Can Ryerson and others be so sure of their touted cures that they feel justified in parting the desperate and beleaguered AIDS victims from their last few dollars?

Another con game that recently emptied the wallets of Bay Area New Agers was the "Airplane Game," a pyramid scheme that required attendance in revivalist-style "abundance seminars." Participants paid $1500 (!) to buy in as one of eight "passengers," then worked to persuade friends and acquaintances to buy in as well so that they could advance to the next level as one of four "flight attendants." After advancing through one of two "copilot" positions to "pilot," the player of the Airplane Game was assured he'd "pilot out" with a $10,500 profit. The simple mathematics of how many more people must buy in as passengers (sixty-four, bringing in a total of $96,000) in order for a player to win, as well as the increasing difficulty of finding new players as the game progressed, was simply lost on the New Age participants, who preferred subjective enthusiasm to critical analysis. Worse still, the game violated all of the ethics that are cherished by sincere, thinking New Agers.[5]

It is not the purpose of this essay to address New Age scams and charlatans, except to point out that, in essence, the only method for separating deliberate falsities from the truth is the same as the one for separating sincere but mistaken beliefs from the truth: through a system of objective testing. When all the false and misguided beliefs are stripped away, it's my opinion that a body of genuinely useful New Age ideas will remain: a baby in a sea of bathwater. These ideas are currently obscured to a degree directly proportional to the amount of blurring that exists in the distinction between subjective, psychological experience and objective truth.

But is objective truth, as Tom wrote, an overrated "bugaboo"?[6] The assertion that objectivity is an impossible goal arises time and again in New Age writing. (Some "new physics" philosophers assert that this has been proven by Werner Heisenberg's "uncertainty principle," which describes the impossibility of simultaneously measuring the speed and position of an electron with unlimited accuracy. The specificity of this principle is a far cry from the New Age extrapolation.) If absolute objectivity is not possible, they conclude, then "truth" is either relative at best and not worth fretting over, or it is merely a matter of opinion, so that one thing may be "true for me" and a different, even contradictory thing may be "true for you." This line of reasoning is used by many well-intentioned people to explain the inconsistencies among belief systems practiced simultaneously in the New Age (e.g., differing schools of aura reading, or sidereal vs. tropical astrology), and to explain the obvious mismatch between some belief systems and physical reality (e.g., the poor success rate of health systems like iridology when subjected to objective testing, or the failure of anything monumental to happen upon the foretold date of the Harmonic Convergence[7]).

Paradoxically, many New Agers, having demonstrated to their satisfaction that objective truth is the unattainable bugaboo of thick-headed rationalists, often become extremely dogmatic about the minutiae of their own favorite belief systems. After all, if what is "true for you" isn't necessarily "true for me," should I really worry about the exact dates and locations of the upcoming geological upheavals predicted by Ramtha or the coming of the "space brothers" in 2012 predicted by José Arguelles? It's hard to imagine either of these things actually happening and not being "true for everybody"! Likewise, and perhaps for some less obviously, other New Age claims like the possession of psychic powers by some people, esoteric history (e.g., Atlantis), crystal "energy," and extraterrestrial entities (e.g., Whitley Strieber's *Communion,* or Ruth Montgomery's "walk-ins"[8]) must all, if true, be "true for everybody." The valid part of the "true for you" argument, as I see it, applies only to the individuality of subjective experience. It may indeed happen that dealing with one's psychological growth in the context of an astrological symbol system produces beneficial results for one person, whereas the symbology of past-life therapy may work better for another. It's a long leap from psychological experiences to extrapolating that either astrology or reincarnation is an objectively real phenomenon.

Recently I picked up a copy of *Plain Truth,* the fundamentalist magazine founded by evangelist Herbert Armstrong. One article promised to demonstrate, starting only from basic principles and using only logic, that Christianity is the one true religion. I read eagerly, having spent many hours as a devoutly Lutheran youth worrying over this very problem, but the promised proof was as disappointing as the best that my parochial educators could muster. The argument boiled down to: "If you try it and believe in it, you'll find Christianity works; the fact that it works proves it's true." Of course, as the author failed to point out, this argument can be applied to any religion.

Most New Age beliefs use a similar rationale. Because past-life counseling has produced positive results for a friend of mine, she is sure that reincarnation is a fact. But this argument from functionalism is a flawed one. Methodologies may produce results for reasons quite different from those suggested. Likewise, one part of a system may work while the rest of it may be completely wrong. The phenomenological similarity of past-life regression, channeling, mediumship, and guided visualization, for example, suggest to me that these states have a common, as yet poorly understood psychological origin, rather than that the different paranormal explanations for each practice are true.

Psychodrama, as I understand it, is a form of counseling that involves acting out, with the therapist and other, fellow patients, incidents from one's life, perhaps a confrontation with one's father or mother. While immensely life-changing revelations may result from these sessions, and while the interaction may feel completely real to the patient while it is taking place, I doubt that anyone would afterward contend that his mother or father was actually present, and that the drama was not a "drama" at all, but a real encounter in every respect. In the same way, the emotions, revelations, and understanding imparted in a New Age-style counseling session may be genuinely real and life-changing, but the context of reincarnation, tarot, astrology, meditation on "crystal energy," etc., may be imaginary. The temporary suspension of disbelief within the appropriate imaginary framework may, in fact, be essential for certain very real emotional and revelatory experiences. Some of the deepest experiences of my life have occurred while reading novels, also in a state of suspended disbelief. The fact that they are works of fiction does not diminish these lasting effects. Perhaps channeling and past-life regression at their best provide a context that frees the imagination of the subject, allowing him to spin his own personally symbolic and meaningful work of fiction. And perhaps the symbol systems of astrology, tarot, the I Ching, and other divination methods speak directly to creative and unconscious levels of the personality.

Unfortunately, most of the New Age folks I know don't see any problem with failing to make the distinction between entertaining a possibly-imaginary notion for the purpose of personal growth and assuming that this notion actually describes physical principles. Because they are relatively unconcerned with assembling an accurate mental model of how the natural world really functions, the radical paradigm shifts required to accommodate reincarnation, Atlantis, or visitors from other galaxies don't seem worth the additional trouble of mustering the evidence to validate such exotic claims.

But it matters a great deal whether or not these things are real. Our lives literally depend on understanding natural principles either directly or indirectly, by benefiting from the research of others. For all the New Age denunciations of "allopathic medicine," for example, it has been objective experimentation that has conquered many of the world's worst diseases. No amount of native spirituality made the people of India immune to the scourges of typhoid and cholera. Positive thinking and creative visualization may provide the inspiration and principles that serve as guides for our actions, but they are not a replacement for building an accurate picture of the natural world through scientific observation and experimentation.

Create Your Own Reality

In 1973 I read a book called *The Crack in the Cosmic Egg*[9] by Joseph Chilton Pearce. This book had a major influence on my thinking; it also influenced much of the New Age philosophy that was to come. Borrowing heavily from the writings of Teilhard de Chardin[10] (Jesuit paleontologist), Paul Tillich (theologian), Jean Piaget (child psychologist), Carlos Castaneda (author of *The Teachings of Don Juan*[11]), and others, Pearce's thesis is that we humans participate in the creation of physical reality. The impression that we are subject to unchangeable physical laws is an enslaving illusion; actually, according to Pearce, these laws exist only because we believe in them. The greater the number of people who believe in a particular "consensus reality," the more real it becomes. Usually the rules of this reality are imparted unconsciously, picked up during childhood as part of our unquestioned cultural heritage, and so we operate under the mistaken impression of an objective, external reality that we cannot change. Pearce's message is that by becoming conscious of our participation in the ongoing creation of the physical universe, groups of people can work together to actively change "consensus reality" into whatever they please.

Pearce has proof for his ideas. He reports that, in Ceylon, firewalkers regularly violate modern physics by stepping through coals at flesh-searing temperatures without getting a blister. Apparently, a different belief system has produced a different physics. For Australia's aborigines, according to Pearce, clairvoyance and telepathy are common, everyday experiences, again because their cultural beliefs include these phenomena. Pearce also cites the ability of hypnotized subjects to endure hot cigarette tips held against their skin without burning or needles poked through their flesh without bleeding. And, of course, the many experiences of Carlos Castaneda, described in the Don Juan books, can only be explained as evidence of "alternative," created realities.

Pearce was not the first person to suggest that, essentially, if you believe in something hard enough, it will come true, but he was the first New Age writer to intelligently articulate this idea in depth. In a subsequent book, *Exploring the Crack in the Cosmic Egg*,[12] he backed down from his premise a little: Reality wasn't the *totally* arbitrary invention of culturally defined consensus belief systems; instead, certain immutable biological laws always held true. But he still asserted that the laws of physics were subject to belief. Meanwhile, in 1973, I took Pearce's notions to heart. It felt good to know that I was an active participant in the physical world, not a victim in an unsympathetic cosmos. Changing reality for the better seemed like a worthwhile pursuit. I founded the "Corps of Reality Engineers" and began to work, with my friends, on "the deliberate engineering of selected realities."

In Berkeley, California, I helped to organize weekly assemblages of like-minded visionaries. Our meetings were optimism-charged sessions in which anyone could suggest an exercise or experiment, and during which any guest was welcome to expound. Once we listened to a long-haired saucer contactee describe how he could telepathically summon UFOs to hover overhead. His demonstration was fun, but the "saucers" only looked like stars to most of us. Often we practiced group meditation, during which we sat in a circle and "ommmmed" in unison. We found that, if nothing else, this practice helped us to achieve a mutual calm normally absent from large groups of people. At other times we played with "guided visualization," in which one person, the guide, described fantastic scenarios while the rest of us lay relaxed on the floor with our eyes closed, imagining ourselves to be participants in the fantasy. These "group hypnosis" sessions were an attempt to contact our unconscious minds and to achieve a shared consciousness. Much of what we did was fun and beneficial, but I had to admit that I could see no evidence that our combined efforts had altered physical reality one iota.

At the same time, I began to wonder about the logical extensions of "consensus reality," "personal reality," and the power of belief. Supposing a schizophrenic was totally convinced that he could fly. Could he? If so, why weren't there frequent reports from mental institutions of miracles performed by the inmates? What about large groups of people like the Jehovah's Witnesses, who devoutly believed that Jesus would return on a particular day? Hadn't he failed to appear twice in that religion's history (in 1914 and 1975), forcing the faithful to reset the dates? What if the inhabitants of some other solar system believed astronomical physics to work differently than we believe they do on earth? Could both be true at the same time? If not, which system would the universe align itself with? Does the large number of Catholics on earth make the Catholic God and saints a reality? Should I worry about the consequences of denying the Catholic faith? Before Columbus, was the earth really flat because everyone believed it to be? Did it only "become" round after the consensus opinion changed?

The more I thought about Pearce's premise, the more convoluted it became. I decided instead to take a practical approach, and looked around to see how humans had most effectively changed reality. My observations revealed that the most obvious changes wrought on "physical reality" had not been achieved directly through the psychic power of belief alone but by an indirect strategy of belief in a concept coupled with the step-by-step manipulation of physical reality within the confines of known and understood physical laws. I saw no evidence that faith alone had moved mountains, but I saw that plenty of mountains had been moved by a combination of faith and dynamite.

I noted with interest that the world's greatest "reality engineers" were scientists and engineers. The wonder of flying hadn't been achieved by negating the laws of gravity with levitation, yet it had become an everyday occurrence with the invention of airplanes. Diseases had been conquered not by positive thinking but by the discovery of microbes, antibiotics, and vaccines. The marvel of communicating over distances of thousands of miles had been made possible by the radio and the telephone, and was certainly more reliable than telepathy—if telepathy truly existed. (After all, even the psychics I knew owned phones) When it came to altering physical reality, it became increasingly obvious to me that the "magicians" who had produced the most consistently reliable results were scientists and engineers, not psychics and "believers." Perhaps Pearce was wrong, and there *were* physical laws that couldn't be changed by any amount of belief.

Nonetheless, a form of "reality engineering" was possible, and it seemed that the most direct route to it was the study of the laws of nature, so that one could work *with* them, rather than "will" them to change. This was not as easy to do as the "belief" route. The study of science was hard work but, it seemed to me, necessary if one was truly interested in altering physical reality. In a move that confused some of my New Age friends, I enrolled at UC Berkeley to study physics, computer science, and mathematics. This maneuver marked a kind of turning point in my life because, though I had always maintained a deep interest in science, during the next three years I acquired a profound appreciation for the monumental body of information about nature that had been painstakingly assembled by generations of researchers. Clearly, no world-view could ever hope to be complete without taking into account this accumulated knowledge.

I later found that some of Pearce's examples have alternative explanations. Firewalking has become a New Age fad, and New Agers pay hundreds of dollars to attend firewalking seminars that consist of a few hours of the "personal growth/revivalist" school of group affirmation, followed by the firewalk itself. In the Fall 1985 *Skeptical Inquirer,* physicist Bernard

J. Leikind and psychologist William J. McCarthy, both of UCLA, describe their own firewalks over 1500- to 1800- degree Farenheit coals while attending such a seminar, successful despite their agnostic attitudes. Leikind explains how this remarkable feat is made possible by the poor heat conductivity of charcoal and the insulating Leidenfrost effect,[13] not by a rewriting of the laws of physics. Another of Pearce's frequent references, Carlos Castaneda's Don Juan books, have been proven to be works of fiction.[14]

While a Berkeley student, I had the opportunity to attend a lecture given by Pearce in San Francisco. Quite by chance, I wound up standing next to him in an elevator after his talk. I complimented him on the lecture and commented on how his book had inspired me. When I told him I'd returned to school as a direct result of his influence, because "the methods of science and technology are the most direct strategies for reality change," he reacted with bemusement, as if I had missed his point entirely.

Empowerment and "Personal Responsibility"

Even though some of Pearce's assumptions are wrong and Castaneda's books aren't literally true, a core of useful metaphors can be gleaned from them: We are not "victims," we are creators. We can conceive of things that do not exist—and cause them to be. We can impose justice and morality into a neutral, impersonal cosmos. In a society that gives only lip service to independence and self-mastery while emphasizing one's subservience to authority, this is an attractive message. It's no wonder that many popular New Age systems stress "empowerment."

Curiously, this healthy message is frequently perverted. Newly liberated New Agers wind up exchanging one authority for another. People tell their bosses to shove it, then turn around and turn their life's savings over to Rajneesh or Ramtha. My friend Tom waged and won an inner battle to throw off the psychological shackles of a deeply ingrained Catholicism, only to eventually become a devoted Anthroposophist. Another friend joined the 3HO Yoga organization (the white-clothed, turbaned followers of Yogi Bhajan), initially to engage in meditation and yogic practices designed to improve mental and physical health. A few years later, he let me in on some of his guru's "revelations," including: that the hair on one's head serves as an "antenna" for certain "cosmic" forces, and that cutting it is unhealthy; and that bringing back rock samples from the moon by the Apollo astronauts constitutes a serious crime against nature sure to result in major geological upheavals and weather changes.

Another, even stranger perversion of the "empowerment" doctrine has produced the ideal Yuppie religion: a morally bankrupt rationalization for ignoring human suffering and giving free rein to one's own greed. In 1972, right around the same time as Joseph Chilton Pearce's book, a volume called *Seth Speaks*[15] appeared. The entity Seth, channeled by the late Jane Roberts (and now by many other mediumistic heirs apparent), teaches that we have not only "chosen" to be reincarnated into our particular lives but that we "choose" all of the details of our lives as well. A horrible accident is a lesson that we have unconsciously willed to happen. An illness is not simply due to exposure to a virus but a learning experience we have brought upon ourselves. By extrapolation, all suffering and misery in the world can be dismissed as valuable lessons the victims have "invited" into their lives. Every child killed by famine or war is simply completing some past-life "karmic debt."

In fact, such extrapolations have become doctrine in the latest wave of New Age beliefs, as one of Shirley MacLaine's favorite gurus, Ramtha, demonstrates:

> [Questioner]: So you're saying that even murder is not wrong or evil.
> Ramtha: That is correct. . . .
> The slain will come back again and again. For life is perpetual; it is continuous. . . .
> I do not abhor the act. I have reasoned it. I have understood it. I am *beyond* it.[16]

The ultimate guru for the eighties?

It's important to point out that this disturbing trend has been recognized and rejected by many thoughtful New Agers, including the *New Age* magazine reviewer who said of similar sentiments in Shirley MacLaine's new book[17]: "If I were a dictator, I could think of nothing better than to have a nation dedicated to following MacLaine's agenda."

Martin Luther, Flying Saucers, and Faith

I benefited from reading Pearce's book because I did not accept all of its ideas as a package deal but instead, after a long analysis, extracted what I could use. My guide was a form of objectivity: Does the evidence really support the contention that belief alone affects physical reality? Are there simpler alternative explanations that explain the facts just as well? Is there a compelling reason to reject the simpler explanation and to adopt Pearce's theory, other than just that it "sounds good" or that I want very badly for it to be so? This kind of reasoning isn't easy, and usually involves the checking of facts in other sources as well as the honest self-evaluation of one's own motives.

For many New Agers, whether or not an idea "sounds good" has unfortunately become the sole criterion for testing its validity. In her tremendously popular book *Out on a Limb*,[18] Shirley MacLaine describes how her acceptance of one New Age idea after another resulted from this "ultrasubjective" method of evaluation. Take for example Shirley's conversation with trance channel Kevin Ryerson following her first encounter with the "entities" that Ryerson channels:

> "My God," I said, "It was incredible. I just don't know what to think."
> Kevin straightened up in his chair and then stood up. "Just do what feels right," he said. "Did what came through *feel* right? They've told me to just trust my feelings. There's nothing else you can do once you begin to ask these questions."
> "But they were saying incredible stuff."
> "Like what?"
> "Oh, about previous lifetimes. A whole lot of stuff about people I know now that I'm supposed to have known in other lives. . . .
> "So?"
> "Well, do you believe all that?"
> "I believe what feels right."

Later Shirley asks Kevin about UFOs:

> "Have you ever seen a UFO?" I asked.
> "No," said Kevin, "I have not yet had that pleasure."
> "But you believe it anyway?"
> "Of course. It feels comfortable to me."

Or how about the reasoning that leads Shirley to believe in reincarnation? Here's where her friend David presents the best argument he can muster:

> "You mean you believe [reincarnation] is that firmly established as a fact?"
> [David] shrugged his shoulders and said, "Why, yeah, I do. It's the only thing that makes sense. If we don't each have a soul—then why are we alive? Who knows if it's true? It's true if you believe it and that goes for anything, right? Besides, there must be something to the fact that the belief in the soul is the one thing *all* religions have in common."

At another point David says:

> "Well, there's no question about it to me. I believe it. I know it. That's all. Of course there's no proof. So what?"

Unfortunately for the "if it feels good it must be true" school of New Age philosophy, we've all had experiences in life with ideas that sounded and felt good only to turn out to be either wrong or only partly true. The flat earth theory felt just fine to millions of ancient Babylonians, all of whom turned out to be in error. The modern national newspaper *Grit* publishes only the good news, and it is quite popular with its 575,000 subscribers. If your knowledge of current events was restricted to what you learned from *Grit,* I'm sure you'd feel very good indeed. But if you were to assume naively that this "feel good" news was the whole truth about world affairs, you'd be in for a particularly rude awakening the next time you booked a vacation flight to Lebanon or Palestine. In my experience, we must be *especially* suspicious of ideas that we would like to be true, for we have a vast capacity for self-delusion and rationalization. In fact, I would propose an exactly opposite strategy for determining the truth: to open-mindedly consider the point of view that *contradicts* what "feels good" to you.

I learned this kind of ruthless analysis not, I'm sorry to say, from grade-school teachers. In fact, my Lutheran parochial school instructors were busy telling me things like "dinosaurs never existed—God planted their fossilized bones in the ground to test your faith." My extracurricular reading told a different story about prehistory, and it was this and other contradictions that set my mind to whirring: These assertions were mutually exclusive; they couldn't *both* be right. During this same period in grade school (roughly around sixth grade), it began to dawn on me that other folks believed as sincerely in their religions as we Lutherans believed in ours (despite what we were told about Catholics worshiping graven images). The stakes for choosing the wrong religion seemed pretty high: eternal damnation; so what was it that distinguished Lutheranism from all the others? Try as I might (and I anguished over this for years), I could never locate that elusive "objective verification." It always seemed to boil down to "faith," and I respected my non-Lutheran friends enough to know that the faith they placed in the religions into which they were born was just as pure as mine. As a result of this kind of reasoning, by the ninth grade my faith in Lutheranism had crumbled and I had learned a valuable, lifelong lesson: Faith without evidence is self-delusion; when evidence is available, faith is not required.

My interests in high school included paranormal and occult subjects, as well as more normal fare (I wasn't a complete weirdo!). In 1966 I discovered UFOs via Frank Edward's classic book, *Flying Saucers: Serious Business.*[19] I consumed flying saucer books after that. The writers offered many different theories for the origin of UFOs: they come from space, they come from the interior of the hollow earth, they are vehicles driven by a "fourth reich" of Nazis living at the South Pole, they come from another dimension, they are projections of the collective unconscious, they are luminous creatures that live in the sky. Those who favored an outer space origin were further divided among those who believed they originated on the moon, from the Pleiades, from Sirius, from Zeta Reticuli. But I had learned about contradictory assertions from the problem of religion, and in this and other paranormal matters I maintained an agnostic attitude.

Later, I was to approach the New Age with these experiences already behind me. As with UFO and other paranormal theories, I open-mindedly entertained the possibility of the various claims I encountered. I enjoyed temporarily suspending disbelief as I read volumes of far-out New Age theories or participated in various rituals and practices. Like going to a movie or reading a work of fiction, I enjoyed fully experiencing, and therefore fully appreciating, what these systems had to offer. I suppose all along I was protected from "true believerhood" by my experience with Lutheranism. At the same time, I learned quite a lot and derived many lasting benefits. Best of all, by sampling and informing myself about a wide diversity of belief systems, I feel I gained some insights about the nature of belief, the will to believe, and the limitless capacity we all have for self-delusion.

What's *Right* With the New Age

I have referred to the positive aspects of New Age thinking that remain when the dogma is stripped away. What are these? In a nutshell, I think the New Age focus on higher principles—morality, meaning, development of creativity and intuition—provides a healthy and necessary balance in a society that emphasizes and rewards greed, materialism, and callousness toward one's fellow humans. Science can tell us whether a proposition about the natural world is or is not true; it cannot supply the morality or vision required to use this knowledge. This sphere of human affairs has traditionally been allocated to religion, but the cosmologies of most of the world's traditional religions have become rather unappealing in the light of both science and modern social mores. New Agers, to their credit, have rejected the religions into which they were born and have tried to access visionary experiences directly, using these to construct a newer, better morality and sense of purpose. It is perhaps inevitable that new dogmas have arisen, which in short order have equalled or surpassed the amount of superstition contained in traditional religions.

New Age teachings validate the realm of inner, subjective experience, thus satisfying a vital human need that is largely unfulfilled in modern, twentieth-century culture. It's not difficult to understand how New Agers, thrilled at the pleasures of acknowledging this newfound realm, tend to confuse the boundaries between inner experience and objective truth. When I began the practice of meditation back in the early '70s, self-taught mostly from books, I learned that the goal was to achieve an "empty" state of mind, devoid of thoughts. Such revelations and ideas as might occur as one passed in and out of the desired state were to be regarded not as objective truth, but as mental phenomena similar to imagination and dreams—useful, perhaps, as symbols and metaphors, but a distraction from the meditative goal. In contrast, today the emphasis is on "information": information from channeling, from past-life regressions, from psychic readings. I still believe as I did then that this information, often arising in genuine trance states, is indistinguishable from imagination or dreams. Perhaps these trance revelations originate in the same creative fount of the mind that produces the world's novels and works of art. It is a valuable endeavor indeed to invent new methods for contacting these sources of imagination (as anyone who has ever suffered from writer's block knows); it misses the point entirely to ascribe to them the same level of reality as scientific fact, and it robs us all of the legacy of the generations of researchers who have struggled to assemble this body of objective knowledge.

In their purest form, then, some of the New Age systems may provide methods for tapping into creative and visionary psychological states, whereby one may find calm and clarity, new ideas, and personal answers to the perennial human need for meaning and purpose. But what about the exotic claims made about the natural world by New Age doctrine, e.g., crystal healing, reincarnation, channeling, Atlantis, psychic healing, clairvoyance, new exotic medical systems? Should they all be dismissed as products of the imagination? Of course they shouldn't be dismissed, nor should they be accepted as true, without objective verification.

In an ideal world with unlimited funds for research, every such claim would be objectively verified or disproved. Unfortunately, we live in a world of limited funding and a finite number of researchers, and some form of screening must prevail. With rare exception, most exotic claims are immediately dismissed by scientists because they so obviously violate our current picture of nature. This dismissal is viewed by New Agers and other paranormalists as evidence of a crippling conservatism in science or, by the more paranoid, of a conspiracy of persecution. Occasional claims of genuine value undoubtedly slip through the cracks.[20] If, as I've argued, rationalism and scientific objectivity are to be encouraged as important facets of a balanced perspective, then it's important to correct this situation and for science to evaluate these claims that so many people regard as important.

In the meantime, the proper attitude to take toward such claims is one of skepticism, if a skeptic can be defined as one who neither believes nor disbelieves claims for which there is insufficient evidence. This agnostic attitude requires living with a large degree of uncertainty about many things —certainly a proper scientific viewpoint, but one that most people find very uncomfortable. Human beings crave certainty. We would rather know that something is "true" or "false," even if we have to delude ourselves, than file it into the category of "possible—not proven."

In this regard it is tragic that science education is so substandard. It's impossible to judge just how exotic a claim is, and thus the level of evidence one must demand in order to accept it, if one has no objective model of nature. Consider the evidence for the "lost continent" of Atlantis: It's mentioned once in a short allegorical morality play by Plato. That's it. Over two millenia later, in 1882, an author named Ignatius Donnelly revived the idea in a book, *Atlantis: The Antediluvian World*[21]; this book was plagiarized by the already-mentioned Madame Blavatsky, who incorporated Atlantis into her occult cosmology. Today, hundreds of channeled entities hail from Atlantis and thousands of New Agers remember past lives lived there. The New Age occultist is oblivious to the tremendous rearrangement of all that we know of world history, geography, and geology that would be required to accommodate Atlantis—certainly unwarranted on the basis of the evidence. Thus, the New Ager's world-view incorporates Atlantis with no trouble at all.

Or consider this passage from *The Complete Crystal Guidebook*:[22]

Energy, in the form of vibration, is projected from each crystal to form a field around it. This is often referred to as the power of the crystal. Each projected field varies in dimension with each crystal. Generally, a small crystal of approximately one-half inch in size will project a field of around three feet. . . .

Each quartz crystal contains a line of direction along which energy flows when it is transmitted through the crystal. The energy flow in the crystal runs up from the bottom where it enters, up through the crystal and then out through the point. If the quartz crystal has a point on each end, the energy comes and goes in both directions, as in a battery. As it transforms energy, it expands and contracts slightly at differing rates depending on the rate of vibration of the influence to which it is exposed. (This oscillation is what makes the crystal so essential in radio and television broadcasting.)

The author goes on to describe how crystals may be "charged" by running water, wind, sunlight, the moon, and psychic energies. She assures us that crystals can help us develop clairvoyance, clairaudience, and the ability to travel in our astral bodies, and that "crystal energy" is supported by the latest findings of physics. The scientifically minded reader may wonder what exactly "crystal energy" is. Like the once-popular "pyramid power" or the "subtle energies" that psychic healers claim to perceive and interpret, these "energies" resemble in name only the genuinely measurable forms of energy (e.g., heat, light, kinetic) described by physics.

What most New Agers fail to grasp is that postulating a new form of energy is a radical notion, and radical notions require radical evidence. Each of the forms of energy described by science can be directly detected and measured—it has a demonstrated existence outside the imagination of the perceiver. Crystal or psychic "energies," on the other hand, are indistinguishable from other forms of "creative visualization" common in New Age practices; their independent existence has yet to be demonstrated. This is not to say that such visualization techniques may not have a useful purpose; my own hunch is that these visualized "energies" may represent projections of the creative imagination that tell the imaginer something about him- or herself. Perhaps in the case of aura reading they symbolize what the reader has learned about his or her subject through unconsciously perceived sensory cues. This "unconscious projection" model is one of a number of alternatives that have the advantage of explaining the facts without requiring the acceptance of new forms of energy for which there is no evidence.

A Plea for Balance

The New Age is fraught with contradictions. Channeled entities like Ramtha and Seth emphasize a "personal responsibility" that runs so deep that we have "chosen" to be reborn to our current set of parents, to look the way we do, etc.; yet legions of the "personally responsible" dote slavishly on the words of their gurus. "Materialistic science" is blamed repeatedly as the source of the world's worst troubles; paradoxically, the trappings of science are greeted with enthusiasm when they support New Age expositions like *The Tao of Physics*.[23] Traditional religions are rejected, only to be replaced by new dogmas. "Alternate realities" are thought to be the rule; nonetheless, highly specific cosmologies are vigorously defended. "Body awareness" and "earth wisdom" are stressed, but we are also told that the "material world" is the source of pain and suffering and that it is only the disembodied "spiritual world" that counts.

I cannot understand how anyone could sample this array of mutually contradictory ideas without concluding that an objective standard is necessary for separating the wheat from the chaff, and that one must pick and choose carefully, extracting the good ideas from otherwise untenable doctrines. We cannot rely on our minds alone to supply the required objectivity; indeed, the human capacity for self-delusion is so great that, in science at least, elaborate methods have been devised to guard against it. Delightfully, when such methods are used, what seems intuitively obvious often turns out to be dead wrong.

On the other hand, it's important to remember that there are entire realms of human experience for which rationalism and the scientific method are useless. Humans are essentially irrational creatures. The subjective realms of art, creativity, feeling, and intuition, which include the major emphases of the New Age, are as important as those of rationality and intellect, and equally deserving of our attention. It's all too easy to mock the frequently brave, sometimes foolhardy explorers of these mysterious and difficult territories, but I think it a far more profitable enterprise to attempt to understand those unmet human needs that are compelling hundreds of thousands of people to turn to the New Age for satisfaction.

In my own life, I continue to seek to nourish these nonrational realms of human experience in ways that are not antithetical to rationalism and science. In this light, I find it convenient to regard most New Age ideas as "metaphors" and "myths," rather than as objective facts, with the result that the ideas of my New Age friends make better sense. "Changing reality" is understandable when reality is defined as "prevailing cultural myth" or "personal world-view" rather than "the laws of physics." "Worship of the Goddess" does not require me to accept the presence of an actual female supreme being if I regard this notion of my neopagan, feminist friends as a guiding cultural myth that resonates with unconscious archetypes of personality. "Learning to see" various "energies" within the body becomes acceptable when translated into "learning to visualize."

I have pointed out this careful distinction between inner experience and objective truth to my New Age friends, with mixed results. Some have no trouble with it, because they are primarily concerned with internal models that facilitate psychological growth. Others, who feel they are describing actual models of nature, dispute my interpretations of their beliefs. But even if they fail to value objectivity themselves, I try to remind myself that the best revelations of society's poetic visionaries are essential to balanced cultural and personal perspectives. At their finest they serve to reconnect us all with the deep and elusive wellsprings of inspiration that give meaning to life.

Notes

1. A discipline of dancelike body movement invented by the founder of Anthroposophy, Rudolph Steiner.

2. *The Fringes of Reason: Strange Myths and Eccentric Science* (*Whole Earth Review*, Fall 1986).

3. Unfortunately for the occult edifice that is built upon the cornerstone of Blavatsky's *Secret Doctrine*, most of her *magnum opus* is plagiarized from other sources. For an entertaining discussion of Blavatsky's literary indiscretions, see Bruce F. Campbell's *Ancient Wisdom Revived* (Berkeley: University of California Press, 1980).

4. *AIDS and Syphilis: Further Explorations Into Holistic Healing (A Trance Channeling With Kevin Ryerson, Conducted Dec. 8, 1987)*; The Holistic Group, P.O. Box 3073, Oakland, Calif. 94609; 1987. This pamphlet suggests, among other things, that AIDS (a virus) and syphilis (a bacterium) "have similar DNA codings which bring about similar symptoms and patterns which wear upon the immune system" and that "in the correct hands, syphilis could be used as a homeopathic compound to stimulate greater resistance to the AIDS phenomenon." Ryerson's channeled entities warn against any form of radiation therapy, except for "mild exposures" to naturally occurring "ore compounds." Instead of pharmaceutical penicillin, the entities recommend experimenting with moldy bread! Their prescribed bottom-line cure for AIDS—"stress reduction, embracement by a fellowship environment—that is, with individuals who give reinforcement to each other—and following effective dietary means that includes a much broader range and spectrum of the diet than currently suspected."

5. The Airplane Game has, in fact, been condemned in New Age publications, most notably in the November/December 1987 issue of *New Age* magazine. This issue comments on the New Age trend of "prosperity consciousness" and money-making scams in general, quoting Ram Dass (Richard Alpert, a former Harvard psychologist who is a strong moral force in the New Age and spiritual subcultures): "[The New Age movement is] a combination of some genuine spiritual awakening and a tremendous amount of power rip-off by worldly-preoccupied people in order to justify or rationalize their lust or greed."

6. Tom incorrectly attributes this notion in part to Thomas Kuhn, author of *The Structure of Scientific Revolutions* (Chicago: University of Chicago, 1962, 1970), who would no doubt be appalled to be called "one of the 'new physics' people."

7. In his book *The Mayan Factor: Path Beyond Technology* (Santa Fe, N. Mex.: Bear and Co., 1987), the art historian and mystic José Arguelles predicted that the "Harmonic Convergence" would occur on August 16 and 17, 1987. New Agers around the world gathered at "sacred sites" to usher in a "new awakening, a kind of planetary renaissance . . . or else, extinction." That neither happened seems pretty clear, except to many dedicated believers who insist that the profound effects are obvious to those who understand.

8. *Communion* by Whitley Strieber (New York: William Morrow, 1987) and *Strangers Among Us* by Ruth Montgomery (New York: Putnam, 1979) both describe alien beings already living here on earth. Strieber's aliens are nasty and weird-looking; Montgomery's are humanlike and benign, and intermingle in human society. Some of the psychics I know meet the latter variety on a daily basis.

9. Joseph Chilton Pearce, *The Crack in the Cosmic Egg: Challenging Constructs of Mind and Reality* (New York: Julian, 1971).

10. "Teilhard was the individual most often named as a profound influence by the Aquarian Conspirators who responded to a survey," according to Marilyn Ferguson's *The Aquarian Conspiracy* (Los Angeles: J. P. Tarcher, 1980).

11. Carlos Castaneda, *The Teachings of Don Juan* (New York: Ballantine, 1969). See also subsequent volumes in the series.

12. Joseph Chilton Pearce, *Exploring the Crack in the Cosmic Egg: Split Minds and Meta-Realities* (New York: Julian, 1974).

13. The differences in heat conductivity of materials at the same temperature are familiar to anyone who has baked a cake: The air in a 350-degree oven will not immediately burn your hand, nor will contact with the surface of the cake; but touching the metal pan or oven grating is sure to produce instant blisters. Charcoal's heat conductivity is closer to that of cake or air than to that of metal. The Leidenfrost effect explains why the heat-insulating properties of water make it possible to safely test the temperature of a hot iron with a moistened fingertip, but not with an unmoistened one.

14. See *Castaneda's Journey* (Santa Barbara, Calif.: Capra Press, 1976) and *The Don Juan Papers* (Santa Barbara, Calif.: Ross-Erikson Publishers, 1980, 1981), both by Richard de Mille, for a sympathetic exposé of the Castaneda books.

15. Jane Roberts, *Seth Speaks: The Eternal Validity of the Soul* (New York: Prentice-Hall, 1972).

16. From Ramtha, edited by Steven Lee Weinberg (Eastsound, Wash.: Sovereignty, Inc., 1986). Ramtha abandons the concept of karma, so that justice is not even an issue: "I do not recognize karma or perfection, for I see them as limitations, not gratifications. . . . You may see the slaughter of ten thousand innocents, and you may say, 'Woe unto such a misery. Why don't angels weep for this atrocity? Why do they sing to the glory of God?' Because they have not limited themselves by believing that life ever ends. They know that those who are slaughtered are immediately caught up into 'heaven' as you term it, for a greater learning and more experiences and what I call adventures." Shudder.

17. Shirley MacLaine, *It's All in the Playing* (New York: Bantam, 1987).

18. Shirley MacLaine, *Out on a Limb* (New York: Bantam, 1983).

19. Frank Edwards, *Flying Saucers: Serious Business* (New York: Bantam, 1966).

20. For instance, the claim that emotional well-being plays a significant part in the effective functioning of the immune system—made for years by the "positive thinking" contingents of schools of alternative healing—is now being taken seriously in scientific publications like the *Journal of Psychosomatic Research*.

21. Ignatius Donnelly, *Atlantis: The Antediluvian World* (Harper, 1882).

22. Uma Sibley, *The Complete Crystal Guidebook: A Practical Path to Personal Power, Self-Development and Healing Using Quartz Crystals* (New York: Bantam, 1987).

23. Fritjof Capra, *The Tao of Physics* (Berkeley, Calif.: Shambala, 1975).

THINKING OUR WAY THROUGH

P seudoscience and superstition are never sold as such. They are sold as hope, as vision, or as faith. But these are expensive euphemisms.

Why do we buy? According to Carl Sagan, our temptation is emotional—skepticism may guard us from inaccurate information, but it gives us no peace of mind. Skepticism is a *burden*: We must forgo certainty, and we give up a sense of humanity's centrality in the scheme of things. "When we recognize some emotional vulnerability regarding a claim, that is exactly where we have to make the firmest efforts at skeptical scrutiny." The *why* is simple: "That is where we can be had."

Proof for which Alan MacRobert amply provides—in his humorous yet cutting assessment of "New Age Hokum." MacRobert comes from a long line of spiritualists, so he has deep respect for what he calls "The Search"—just as he has little patience for persistent self-delusion. With a combination of bemusement and exasperation, MacRobert notes that cockamamie theories die only to be reincarnated. "The pattern is common: A new paranormal claim turns out to be a very old one, debunked long enough ago for the debunking to have been forgotten. The rate at which such old, disproven, and forgotten theories are being revived shows a certain unimaginativeness in the field, as if new paranormal theories cannot be invented fast enough to meet the New Age demand. And every time they are revived, these theories gain a little more venerability."

MacRobert's rule-of-thumb for assessing New Age claims is easy and nondogmatic: Claims are best judged *by their fruit*—do they produce new knowledge, or are they infertile?

Al Seckel—columnist for the *Los Angeles Times* and executive director of the Sourthern California Skeptics—sees the New Age as an educational problem. "The widespread and *growing* belief in various pseudosciences is just one small indication that people are not evaluating information properly." It is disconcerting, to say the least, that Seckel's recommendation is so sane that it seems radical: Combat irrationality, he writes, with the common sense your Momma gave you.

THE BURDEN OF SKEPTICISM

Carl Sagan

What is skepticism? It's nothing very esoteric. We encounter it every day. When we buy a used a.car, if we are the least bit wise we will exert some residual skeptical powers—whatever our education has left to us. You could say, "Here's an honest-looking fellow. I'll just take whatever he offers me." Or you might say, "Well, I've heard that occasionally there are small deceptions involved in the sale of a used car, perhaps inadvertent on the part of the salesperson," and then you do something. You kick the tires, you open the doors, you look under the hood. (You might go through the motions even if you don't know what is supposed to be under the hood, or you might bring a mechanically inclined friend.) You know that some skepticism is required, and you understand why. It's upsetting that you might have to disagree with the used-car salesman or ask him questions that he is reluctant to answer. There is at least a small degree of interpersonal confrontation involved in the purchase of a used car and nobody claims it is especially pleasant. But there is a good reason for it—because if you don't exercise some minimal skepticism, if you have an absolutely untrammeled credulity, there is probably some price you will have to pay later. Then you'll wish you had made a small investment of skepticism early.

Now this is not something that you have to go through four years of graduate school to understand. Everybody understands this. The trouble

---

Carl Sagan is the David Duncan Professor of Astronomy and Space Sciences and Director of the Laboratory for Planetary Studies at Cornell University. Dr. Sagan is the author, coauthor, or editor of more than twenty books, including *Broca's Brain*, *Comet*, *Contact*, *The Dragons of Eden*, and *Cosmos*. This essay is adapted from Dr. Sagan's keynote address to the 1987 annual meeting of the Committee for the Scientific Investigation of Claims of the Paranormal (CSICOP) upon receiving that organization's "In Praise of Reason" award, "in recognition of his longstanding contributions to the use of the methods of critical inquiry, scientific evidence, and reason in evaluating claims to knowledge."

is, a used car is one thing but television commercials or pronouncements by presidents and party leaders are another. We are skeptical in some areas but unfortunately not in others.

For example, there is a class of aspirin commercials that reveals the competing product to have only so much of the painkilling ingredient that doctors recommend most—they don't tell you what the mysterious ingredient is—whereas *their* product has a dramatically larger amount (1.2 to 2 times more per tablet). Therefore, you should buy their product. But why not just take two of the competing tablets? You're not supposed to ask. Don't apply skepticism to this issue. Don't think. Buy.

Or, there is now a commercial where someone reads the breakfast cereal boxes. Look what's in this one—huh, no calcium. Look at this one— no calcium in this one, either. But buy *our* product, it's *full* of calcium. True as far as it goes. But what the commercial doesn't tell you is that most people eat cold cereal with milk. Milk is well known to be a rich source of calcium. There's a reason why all those competing products don't have calcium in them. It's because that's what's in the milk. I maintain that such ads betray a real contempt for the intelligence of the listening and viewing audience, and the fact that they get away with it shows that that contempt is at least to some extent justified. If every time such a commercial appeared people would make a real attempt not to buy that product, you would see a sudden great rise in the caliber of commercials.

Recently, I saw a big sign near Kennedy Airport. It said "Stars fade, but (this particular brand of whiskey) never varies." Well, let's think about that a little bit. It is true, stars do fade. Of course, it takes rather a while. And not just that, but before they fade they get very bright; even those that just become red giants become very bright. This is something especially appropriate for the present moment, when there is this superb supernova in the Greater Magellanic Cloud. Sometimes, before the stars fade they get brighter than the entire galaxy in which they are embedded. So stars fade, but this particular brand of Scotch doesn't? A certain amount of relevant information has been swept under the rug.

Now the second half. This brand of Scotch that I'm making a valiant attempt not to give any plug for "never varies." Well, especially since they have made a comparison with the astronomical time scale, "never" is quite a claim. How long has this particular brand of Scotch been in existence? You can look it up. It's two to three hundred years at most. So, even if they did a controlled experiment—a glass of the Scotch here, a star here, let's compare (you can imagine this done "double blind")—I maintain there has been insufficient time to do a proper comparison. What is more, "never" embraces a still longer time scale than the mere stellar evolutionary time scale. "Never" is, you know, "not ever." Well, on some very long time scale all of the atoms in that glass of Scotch will radioactively decay. Even the ones that are usually called "stable" isotopes in a sufficiently long time will fall to pieces. So even if they beat out the stars they could not beat out quantum mechanics.

Such claims in commercial advertisements constitute small deceptions. They part us from a little money, or induce us to buy a slightly inferior product. It's not so terrible. But consider this:

I have here the program of 1987's Whole Life Expo in San Francisco. Twenty thousand people attended the program the year before. Here are some of the presentations: "Alternative Treatments for AIDS Patients: It will rebuild one's natural defenses and prevent immune system breakdowns—learn about the latest developments that the media has thus far ignored." It seems to me that presentation could do real harm. "How Trapped Blood Proteins Produce Pain and Suffering." "Crystals, Are They Talismans or Stones?" (I have an opinion myself.) It says, "As a crystal focuses sound and light waves for radio and television"—crystal sets are rather a long time ago—"so may it amplify spiritual vibrations for the attuned human." I'll bet very few of you are attuned. Or here's one: "Return of the Goddess, a Presentational Ritual." Another: "Synchronicity, the Recognition Experience." That one is given by "Brother Charles." Or, on the next page, "You, Saint Germain, and Healing Through the Violet Flame." It goes on and on, with lots of ads about "opportunities"—ranging from the dubious to the spurious—that are available at the Whole Life Expo.

*   *   *

If you were to drop down on Earth at any time during the tenure of humans you would find a set of popular, more or less similar, belief systems. They change, often very quickly, often on time scales of a few years: But sometimes belief systems of this sort last for many thousands of years. At least a few are always available. I think it's fair to ask why. We are *Homo sapiens*. That's the distinguishing characteristic about us, that *sapiens* part. We're supposed to be smart. So why is this stuff always with us? Well, for one thing, a great many of these belief systems address real human needs that are not being met by our society. There are unsatisfied medical needs, spiritual needs, and needs for communion with the rest of the human community. There may be more such failings in our soicety than in many others in human hsitory. And so it is reasonable for people to poke around and try on for size various belief systems, to see if they help.

For example, take a fashionable fad, channeling. It has for its fundamental premise, as does spiritualism, that when we die we don't exactly disappear, that some part of us continues. That part, we are told, can reenter the bodies of human and other beings in the future, and so death loses much of its sting for us personally. What is more, we have an opportunity, if the channeling contentions are true, to make contact with loved ones who have died.

Speaking personally, I would be delighted if reincarnation were real. I lost my parents, both of them, in the past few years, and I would love to have a little conversation with them, to tell them what the kids are doing, make sure everything is all right wherever it is they are. That touches something very deep. But at the same time, precisely for that reason, I know that there are people who will try to take advantage of the vulnerabilities of the bereaved. The spiritualist and the channelers better have a compelling case.

Or take the idea that by thinking hard at geological formations you can tell where mineral or petroleum deposits are. Uri Geller makes this claim. Now if you are an executive of a mineral exploration or petroleum company, your bread and butter depend on finding the minerals or the oil; so spending trivial amounts of money, compared with what you usually spend on geological exploration, this time to find deposits psychically, sounds not so bad. You might be tempted.

Or take UFOs, the contention that beings in spaceships from other worlds are visiting us all the time. I find that a thrilling idea. It's at least a break from the ordinary. I've spent a fair amount of time in my scientific life working on the issue of the search for extraterrestrial intelligence. Think how much effort I could save if those guys are coming here. But when we recognize some emotional vulnerability regarding a claim, that is exactly where we have to make the firmest efforts at skeptical scrutiny. That is where we can be had.

Now, let's reconsider channeling. There is a woman in the State of Washington who claims to make contact with a 35,000-year-old somebody, "Ramtha"—he, by the way, speaks English very well with what sounds to me to be an Indian accent. Suppose we had Ramtha here and just suppose Ramtha is cooperative. We could ask some questions: How do we know that Ramtha lived 35,000 years ago? Who is keeping track of the intervening millennia? How does it come to be exactly 35,000 years? That's a very round number. Thirty-five thousand plus or minus what? What were things like 35,000 years ago? What was the climate? Where on Earth did Ramtha live? (I know he speaks English with an Indian accent, but where was that?) What does Ramtha eat? (Archaeologists know something about what people ate back then.) We would have a real opportunity to find out if his claims are true. If this were really somebody from 35,000 years ago, you could learn a lot about 35,000 years ago. So, one way or another, either Ramtha really is 35,000 years old, in which case we discover something about the period—that's before the Wisconsin Ice Age, an interesting time—or he's a phony and he'll slip up. What are the indigenous languages, what is the social structure, who else does Ramtha live with—children, grandchildren—what's the life cycle, the infant mortality, what clothes does he wear, what's his life expectancy, what are the weapons, plants, and animals? Tell us. Instead, what we hear are the most banal homilies, indistinguishable from those that alleged UFO occupants tell the poor humans who claim to have been abducted by them.

Occasionally, by the way, I get a letter from someone who is in "contact" with an extraterrestrial who invites me to "ask anything." And so I have a list of questions. The extraterrestrials are very advanced, remember. So I ask things like, "Please give a short proof of Fermat's Last Theorem." Or the Goldbach Conjecture. And then I have to explain what these are, because extraterrestrials will not call it Fermat's Last Theorem, so I write out the little equation with the exponents. I never get an answer. On the other hand, if I ask something like "Should we humans be good?" I always get an answer. I think something can be deduced from this differential ability to answer questions. Anything vague they are extremely happy to respond to, but anything specific, where there is a chance to find out if they actually know anything, there is only silence.

The French scientist Henri Poincaré remarked on why credulity is rampant: "We also know how cruel the truth often is, and we wonder whether delusion is not more consoling." That's what I have tried to say with my examples. But I don't think that's the only reason credulity is rampant. Skepticism challenges established institutions. If we teach everybody, let's say high school students, the habit of being skeptical, perhaps they will not restrict their skepticism to aspirin commercials and 35,000-year-old channelers (or channelees). Maybe they'll start asking awkward questions about economic, or social, or political, or religious institutions. Then where will we be?

Skepticism is dangerous. That's exactly its function, in my view. It is the business of skepticism to be dangerous. And that's why there is a great reluctance to teach it in the schools. That's why you don't find a general fluency in skepticism in the media. On the other hand, how will we negotiate a very perilous future if we don't have the elementary intellectual tools to ask searching questions of those nominally in charge, especially in a democracy?

I think this is a useful moment to reflect on the sort of national trouble that could have been avoided were skepticism more generally available in

American society. The Iran/Nicaragua fiasco is so obvious an example I will not take advantage of our poor, beleaguered president by spelling it out. The Administration's resistance to a Comprehensive Test Ban Treaty and its continuing passion for blowing up nuclear weapons—one of the major drivers of the nuclear arms race—under the pretense of making us "safe" is another such issue. So is Star Wars. The habits of skeptical thought CSICOP encourages have relevance for matters of the greatest importance to the nation. There is enough nonsense promulgated by both political parties that the habit of evenhanded skepticism should be declared a national goal, essential for our survival.

*   *   *

I want to say a little more about the burden of skepticism. You can get into a habit of thought in which you enjoy making fun of all those other people who don't see things as clearly as you do. We have to guard carefully against it.

It seems to me what is called for is an exquisite balance between two conflicting needs: the most skeptical scrutiny of all hypotheses that are served up to us and at the same time a great openness to new ideas. Obviously those two modes of thought are in some tension. But if you are able to exercise only one of these modes, whichever one it is, you're in deep trouble. If you are only skeptical, then no new ideas make it through to you. You never learn anything new. You become a crochety old person convinced that nonsense is ruling the world. (There is, of course, much data to support you.) But every now and then, maybe once in a hundred cases, a new idea turns out to be on the mark, valid and wonderful. If you are too much in the habit of being skeptical about everything, you are going to miss or resent it, and either way you will be standing in the way of understanding and progress.

On the other hand, if you are open to the point of gullibility and have not an ounce of skeptical sense in you, then you cannot distinguish the useful ideas from the worthless ones. If all ideas have equal validity then you are lost, because then, it seems to me, no ideas have any validity at all.

Some ideas are better than others. The machinery for distinguishing them is an essential tool in dealing with the world and especially in dealing with the future. And it is precisely the mix of these two modes of thought that is central to the success of science.

Really good scientists do both. On their own, talking to themselves, they churn up huge numbers of new ideas, and criticize them ruthlessly.

Most of the ideas never make it to the outside world. Only the ideas that pass through a rigorous self-filtration make it out and are criticized by the rest of the scientific community. It sometimes happens that ideas that are accepted by everybody turn out to be wrong, or at least partially wrong, or at least superseded by ideas of greater generality. And, while there are of course some personal losses—emotional bonds to the idea that you yourself played a role in inventing—nevertheless the collective ethic is that every time such an idea is overthrown and replaced by something better the enterprise of science has benefited. In science it often happens that scientists say, "You know that's a really good argument; my position is mistaken," and then they actually change their minds and you never hear that old view from them again. They really do it. It doesn't happen as often as it should, because scientists are human and change is sometimes painful. But it happens every day. I cannot recall the last time something like that has happened in politics or religion. It's very rare that a senator, say, replies, "That's a good argument. I will now change my political affiliation."

*　*　*

In the history of science there is an instructive procession of major intellectual battles that turn out, all of them, to be about how central human beings are. We could call them battles about the anti-Copernican conceit.

Here are some of the issues:

• *We are the center of the Universe. All the planets and the stars and the Sun and the Moon go around us.* (Boy, must we be something *really* special.) That was the prevailing belief—Aristarchus aside—until the time of Copernicus. A lot of people liked it because it gave them a personally unwarranted central position in the Universe. The mere fact that you were on Earth made you privileged. That felt good. Then along came the evidence that Earth was just a planet and that those other bright moving points of light were planets too. Disappointing. Even depressing. Better when we were central and unique.

• *But at least our Sun is at the center of the Universe.* No, those other stars, they're suns too, and what's more we're out in the galactic boondocks. We are nowhere near the center of the Galaxy. Very depressing.

• *Well, at least the Milky Way galaxy is at the center of the Universe.* Then a little more progress in science. We find there isn't any such thing as the center of the Universe. What's more, there are a hundred billion other galaxies. Nothing special about this one. Deep gloom.

• *Well, at least we humans, we are the pinnacle of creation. We're separate. All those other creatures, plants and animals, they're lower. We're higher. We have no connection with them. Every living thing has been created separately.* Then along comes Darwin. We find an evolutionary continuum. We're closely connected to the other beasts and vegetables. What's more, the closest biological relatives to us are chimpanzees. *Those* are our close relatives—*those* guys? It's an embarrassment. Did you ever go to the zoo and watch them? Do you know what they do? Imagine in Victorian England, when Darwin produced this insight, what an awkward truth it was.

There are other important examples—privileged reference frames in physics and the unconscious mind in psychology—that I'll pass over.

I maintain that in the tradition of this long set of debates—every one of which was won by the Copernicans, by the guys who say there is not much special about us—there was a deep emotional undercurrent. The search for extraterrestrial intelligence and the analysis of possible animal "language" strike at one of the last remaining pre-Copernican belief systems:

• *At least we are the most intelligent creatures in the whole Universe.* If there are no other smart guys elsewhere, even if we *are* connected to chimpanzees, even if we *are* in the boondocks of a vast and awesome universe, at least there is still something special about us. But the moment we find extraterrestrial intelligence that last bit of conceit is gone. I think some of the resistance to the idea of extraterrestrial intelligence is due to the anti-Copernican conceit. Likewise, without taking sides in the debate on whether other animals—higher primates, especially great apes—are intelligent or have language, that's clearly, on an emotional level, the same issue. If we define humans as creatures who have language and no one else has language, at least we are unique in that regard. But if it turns out that all those dirty, repugnant, laughable chimpanzees can also, with Ameslan or otherwise, communicate ideas, then what is left that is special about us? Propelling emotional predispositions on these issues are present, often unconsciously, in scientific debates. It is important to realize that scientific debates, just like pseudoscientific debates, can be awash with emotion, for these among many different reasons.

Now, let's take a closer look at the radio search for extraterrestrial intelligence. How is this different from pseudoscience? Let me give a couple of real cases. In the early sixties, the Soviets held a press conference in Moscow in which they announced that a distant radio source, called CTA-102, was varying sinusoidally, like a sine wave, with a period of about 100 days. Why did they call a press conference to announce that a distant radio source was varying? Because they thought it was an extraterrestrial civilization of immense powers. That is worth calling a press conference for. This was before even the word "quasar" existed. Today we know that CTA-102 is a quasar. We don't know very well what quasars are; and there is more than one mutually exclusive explanation for them in the scientific literature. Nevertheless, few seriously consider that a quasar, like CTA-102, is some galaxy-girdling extraterrestrial civilization, because there are a number of alternative explanations of their properties that are more or less consistent with the physical laws we know without invoking alien life. The extraterrestrial hypothesis is a hypothesis of last resort. Only if everything else fails do you reach for it.

Second example: British scientists in 1967 found a nearby bright radio source that is fluctuating on a much shorter time scale, with a period constant to ten significant figures. What was it? Their first thought was that it was something like a message being sent to us, or an interstellar navigational beacon for spacecraft that ply the spaces between the stars. They even gave it, among themselves at Cambridge University, the wry designation LGM-I—Little Green Men, LGM. However (they were wiser than the Soviets), they did not call a press conference, and it soon became clear that what we had here was what is now called a "pulsar." In fact, it was the first pulsar, the Crab Nebula pulsar. Well, what's a pulsar? A pulsar is a star shrunk to the size of a city, held up as no other stars are, not by gas pressure, not by electron degeneracy, but by nuclear forces. It is in a certain sense an atomic nucleus the size of Pasadena. Now that, I maintain, is an idea at least as bizarre as an interstellar navigational beacon. The answer to what a pulsar is has to be something mighty strange. It isn't an extraterrestrial civilization, it's something else; but a something else that opens our eyes and our minds and indicates possibilities in nature that we had never guessed at.

Then there is the question of false positives. Frank Drake in his original Ozma experiment, Paul Horowitz in the META (Megachannel Extraterrestrial Assay) program sponsored by The Planetary Society, the Ohio University group and many other groups have all had anomalous signals that make the heart palpitate. They think for a moment that they have picked up a genuine signal. In some cases we have not the foggiest idea what it was; the signals did not repeat. The next night you turn the same telescope to the same spot in the sky with the same modulation and the same frequency and bandpass, everything else the same, and you don't hear a thing. You don't publish that data. It may be a malfunction in the detection system. It may be a military AWACS plane flying by and broadcasting on frequency channels that are supposed to be reserved for radio astronomy. It may be a diathermy machine down the street. There are many possibilities. You don't immediately declare that you have found extraterrestrial intelligence because you find an anomalous signal.

And if it were repeated, would you then announce? You would not.

Maybe it's a hoax. Maybe it is something you haven't been smart enough to figure out that is happening to your system. Instead, you would then call scientists at a bunch of other radio telescopes and say that at this particular spot in the sky, at this frequency and bandpass and modulation and all the rest, you seem to be getting something funny. Could they please look at it and see if they get something similar? And only if several independent observers get the same kind of information from the same spot in the sky do you think you have something. Even then you don't know that the something is extraterrestrial intelligence, but at least you could determine that it's not something on Earth. (And that it's also not something in Earth orbit; it's further away than that.) That's the first sequence of events that would be required to be sure that you actually had a signal from an extraterrestrial civilization.

Now notice that there is a certain discipline involved. Skepticism imposes a burden. You can't just go off shouting "little green men," because you are going to look mighty silly, as the Soviets did with CTA-102, when it turns out to be something quite different. A special caution is necessary when the stakes are as high as here. We are not obliged to make up our minds before the evidence is in. It's okay not to be sure.

I'm often asked the question, "Do you think there is extraterrestrial intelligence?" I give the standard argument—there are a lot of places out there, and use the word *billions*, and so on. And then I say it would be astonishing to me if there weren't extraterrestrial intelligence, but of course there is as yet no compelling evidence for it. And then I'm asked, "Yeah, but what do you really think?" I say, "I just told you what I really think." "Yeah, but what's your gut feeling?" But I try not to think with my gut. Really, it's okay to reserve judgment until the evidence is in.

*   *   *

There are many cases where scientists have concluded despite their most powerful predispositions and interests that the opposite is true of what they had imagined. Johannes Kepler and the discovery that the planets move in ellipses, not the perfect Aristotelian circles, is a famous example in the history of science. But let me give you a more recent one. There is a psychiatrist at Harvard Medical School named Lester Grinspoon, who is a specialist, among other things, in schizophrenia. In the seventies a new category of drug that treats schizophrenics came out, tranquilizers, thorazines, and so for the first time it was possible to do a set of controlled experiments. Grinspoon and his collaborators were then psychoanalytically oriented psychotherapists. They believed that there are important things you can do to help people by talking with them. They did a set of experiments in which different groups, properly normalized, of schizophrenics were given different treatments. Some were given psychotherapy only, some were given thorazine only, some were given both the thorazine and psychotherapy, and some were given (you would not do that today) placebos in place of the thorazine. What did they find? They found that thorazine alone was more beneficial than thorazine plus psychotherapy. The psychotherapists discovered that psychotherapy was worse than nothing, at least for schizophrenics. I find this absolutely stunning, that people committed to a kind of intellectual orthodoxy, which has great difficulty in justifying its underpinnings, would in doing such a controlled experiment conclude that their doctrine doesn't work. That's an example of scientists being able to change their minds.

*   *   *

After my article "The Fine Art of Baloney Detection" came out in *Parade* (Feb. 1, 1987), I got, as you might imagine, a lot of letters. Sixty-five million people read *Parade*. In the article I gave a long list of things that I said were "demonstrated or presumptive baloney"—thirty or forty items. Advocates of all those positions were uniformly offended, so I got lots of letters. I also gave a set of very elementary prescriptions about how to think about baloney—arguments from authority don't work, every step in the chain of evidence has to be valid, and so on. Lots of people wrote back, saying, "You're absolutely right on the generalities; unfortunately that doesn't apply to my particular doctrine." For example, one letter writer said the idea that intelligent life exists outside the earth is an excellent example of baloney. He concluded, "I am as sure of this as of anything in my experience. There is no conscious life anywhere else in the Universe. Mankind thus returns to its rightful position as center of the Universe."

Another writer again agreed with all my generalities, but said that as an inveterate skeptic I have closed my mind to the truth. Most notably I have ignored the evidence for an Earth that is six thousand years old. Well, I haven't ignored it; I considered the purported evidence and *then* rejected it. There is a difference, and this is a difference, we might say, between prejudice and postjudice. Prejudice is making a judgment before you have looked at the facts. Postjudice is making a judgment afterwards. Prejudice is terrible, in the sense that you commit injustices and you make serious mistakes. Postjudice is not terrible. You can't be perfect of course; you may make mistakes also. But it is permissible to make a judgment after you have examined the evidence. In some circles it is even encouraged.

*   *   *

I believe that part of what propels science is the thirst for wonder. It's a very powerful emotion. All children feel it. In a first grade classroom everybody feels it; in a twelfth grade classroom almost nobody feels it, or at least acknowledges it. Something happens between first and twelfth grade, and it's not just puberty. Not only do the schools and the media not teach much skepticism, there is also little encouragement of this stirring sense of wonder. Science and pseudoscience both arouse that feeling. Poor popularizations of science establish an ecological niche for pseudoscience.

If science were explained to the average person in a way that is accessible and exciting, there would be no room for pseudoscience. But there is a kind of Gresham's Law by which in popular culture the bad science drives out the good. And for this I think we have to blame, first, the scientific community ourselves for not doing a better job of popularizing science, and second, the media, which are in this respect almost uniformly dreadful. Almost every newspaper in America has a daily astrology column. How many have even a weekly astronomy column? And I believe it is also the fault of the educational system. We do not teach how to think. This is a very serious failure that may even, in a world rigged with 60,000 nuclear weapons, compromise the human future.

I maintain there is much more wonder in science than in pseudoscience. And in addition, to whatever measure this term has any meaning, science has the additional virtue, and it is not an inconsiderable one, of being true.

NEW AGE HOKUM

Alan M. MacRobert

Recently on display in bookstores throughout America was a flashy paperback entitled *Somebody Else Is On the Moon*. The cover depicts an astronaut coming upon huge tracks in the lunar soil and pipes sticking out of a crater. "For two hundred years astronomers have suspected—now we know!" proclaims the blurb. "Incredible proof of an alien race on the moon! The evidence: Immense mechanical rigs, some over a mile long. Lights, flares, vehicle tracks, towers, pipes, conduits."

To the connoisseur of crank literature, this book is a delight. It is the rambling narrative of how George H. Leonard, a retired public-health official, has identified amazing things in photographs of the moon that he gets by mail from NASA. (NASA, of course, is part of a governmental conspiracy to cover up Leonard's findings. The only reason the Apollo astronauts visited the moon was to study its inhabitants, and everything else is a government hoax that "dwarfs Watergate.") The chapters of Leonard's book bear such titles as "A Motor As Big As the Bronx" and "Service Station in a Crater?" Thirty-five pages of moon photos illustrate with circles and arrows the marvels discussed in the text. But the circles and arrows point to nothing unusual at all. The photos are just ordinary moonscapes of hills, plains, and craters.

The most interesting thing about *Somebody Else Is On the Moon*, however, is not its contents. It's the publisher's marketing strategy. The book was placed in bookstores among the offerings for "New Age" readers, including those like myself who like to think that we are in the vanguard, exploring important new ideas and philosophies. There, in fact, is where

Alan MacRobert is editor of *Sky and Telescope* magazine. An early version of this article appeared in the *Vermont Vanguard Press*. Here we reprint the piece as it appeared in the *Whole Earth Review*'s famous "Fringes of Reason" issue, which was edited by Ted Schultz.

all sorts of crank literature has migrated. That's where it sells.

In times past, purveyors of fringe and paranormal ideas bitterly charged that they were being censored out of print by conspiracies of publishers and orthodox scientists. No more; all holds are off. Firewalking, sunken continents, astrology, psychokinetic spoon-bending, psychic readings, channeling, aura reading, remote viewing, psychic archaeology, scores of dubious holistic health systems, and a thousand other paranormal ideas have been getting a hearing like never before. And my generation, the supposedly "skeptical" generation, is eating it up.

The very abundance of such claims has made the "Search," as I like to call it, more difficult than ever. This Search is a tradition in my family. My grandfather was a devout spiritualist. He held séances with the great mediums of the day—Arthur Ford, Eileen Garrett—and he took my mother and father to all the main spiritualist camps. My parents were somewhat more skeptical. My father joined the American Society for Psychical Research and became one of its directors, investigating haunted houses, poltergeists, clairvoyants, and telepaths long before such investigators were guaranteed a spot on the "Merv Griffin Show." Up in the attic we still have a set of fake spirit photographs a medium tried to pass off on him; spirit photography was the popular equivalent in those days of psychics' key-bending stunts now.

Some of my earliest reading materials were the "psychic books" that filled my family's bookcases. In one of them, I ran across an engraving of my great-grandfather, Emerson J. MacRobert, a spiritualist in London, Ontario. At a time when such activities were scandalous and possibly illegal, he had held séances in a top-floor room of an old house with velvet tacked over the windows. Word got out and he was nearly forced from his post on the London School Board by righteous churchgoers. In my childhood reading, I also ran across an old reference to something called a "Treborcam Ethereal Healing Machine." The name is my own spelled backwards.

Descended from two generations of spiritualists, my father was always noncommittal. He had run across plenty of frauds and exaggerations, but, even at its best, the Society for Psychical Research seemed only able to draw blanks. Under close scrutiny, psychics failed because they were "having a bad day" or because their powers were impeded by the presence of skeptics. Modern parapsychologists excuse the "nonrepeatability" of their experiments with much the same rationale.

This lifetime exposure to the paranormal has left me somewhat disillusioned and impatient with the intellectual credulity of my generation—no improvement on that of my grandfather's. Still, I'm ready for the day when UFO creatures land on the White House lawn and are interviewed by Dan Rather, or when one single psychic somewhere can predict the future or reliably levitate paper clips so that anyone can see it's so. In the meantime, here, culled from all the time I've spent in the Search, are some guidelines by which to evaluate the flood of paranormal claims. These guidelines, carefully applied, should help eliminate the claims that are worthless—at least 98 percent of them—and will provide grounds for evaluating anything that's left.

1. Looking the Other Way

Almost everyone with a paranormal theory to tout, I have discovered, is *unwilling to scrutinize the phenomenon*. Whatever the claim, chances are he won't examine it closely even when he gets an excellent chance to do so. I get the impression that, deep down, paranormal claimants are afraid they'll see there's nothing there. Because science, *the art of looking carefully to determine the truth*, is precisely what they're afraid of, they'll reject its ability to assess their claim, perhaps with a snide reference to the inadequacy of "linear, left-brain, Western science."

Somebody Else Is On the Moon contains a fine example of this fear of scrutiny. All of Leonard's moon constructions are at the very limit of photo resolution. When he had a chance to get better photos and to see the same terrain more clearly, he didn't.

On the other hand, you might expect John Taylor, a physicist the *New Scientist* called one of the top twenty scientists in the world, to be suspicious of psychics who attempted to avoid his close scrutiny. Yet his 1975 book *Superminds* enthusiastically described his experiments with "Geller children," kids who could bend forks and spoons "psychokinetically," just like Uri Geller. The trouble was, they could only do it when no one was looking. Taylor even gave this aversion to scientific scrutiny a name: the "shyness effect." He accommodatingly designed "sealed" tubes with the objects to be bent placed inside, and sent them home with the children. When they returned bent the next day, still sealed in the tubes, he considered this proof of psychic abilities.

Taylor refused to see the magician, the Amazing Randi, who felt he could explain the shyness effect in more prosaic terms: cheating. Perhaps Taylor himself had become afraid of close scrutiny. Randi called on him anyway, disguised as a reporter, and found Taylor particularly easy to fool. In his book *The Truth About Uri Geller*, Randi describes having no trouble at all opening and closing the crudely sealed tubes in Taylor's presence, even managing to bend an aluminum bar while Taylor was momentarily distracted, scratch on it "Bent by Randi," and replace it among Taylor's collection undetected!

The final blow to Taylor's shyness effect occurred when an alternative team of scientists decided to replicate Taylor's findings. Six of his metal-bending prodigies were tested in a room with one observer, who noticed no cheating even though "psychokinetic" metal-bending occurred repeatedly. But a hidden camera recorded the truth about the shyness effect, as reported by the investigators in the September 4, 1975, issue of the scientific journal *Nature*: "*A* put the rod under her foot and tried to bend it; *B*, *E*, and *F* used two hands to bend the spoon . . . while *D* tried to hide his hands under a table to bend the spoon." Today, Taylor has retracted many of his 1975 claims.

When my father was investigating mediums, they often claimed that the spirits would stay away if there was a skeptic in the room. So, if an investigator frisked the medium for gadgets, the spirits would fail to materialize. This is a very convenient explanation for why paranormal phenomena disappear when someone looks closely, and it is invoked in many ways by New Age theorists. The Amazing Randi is strongly disliked by the modern parapsychological community, and quite unwelcome at psychic demonstrations, because of this "skeptics effect." A simpler explanation for why something isn't there when you look carefully is that it isn't there at all. Beware of anyone who says you mustn't look closely.

2. Cloaks of Fuzz

This next guideline grows out of the first. Watch out for paranormal phenomena that are cloaked in *noise*.

"Noise" in this sense means any kind of confusion, static, or fuzz that obscures what you're looking for. Leonard's moon marvels are an example, lost as they are in the graininess of his photographs at the limits of resolution, where everything gets fuzzy and random.

Another example comes from the *Journal of the American Society for Psychical Research* on my father's bookshelves. One psychic investigator theorized that psychokinesis, the mind's alleged ability to move objects by will power, might depend on what elements the objects were made of. Zinc might respond differently than zirconium. The straightforward way to test this would be to suspend a piece of each element in such a way that the slightest force would move it, then sit back and concentrate on each one to see which moves in response. Of course, the objects would probably sit there and do nothing. The experimenter seemed to realize this unconsciously, so he instead fashioned dice out of different elements and rolled them thousands of times down a sloping board, concentrating on what numbers he wanted to turn up.

Obviously, the amount of force needed to influence bouncing dice is far greater than the force needed, say, to deflect a needle suspended on a string in a vacuum. But the rolling dice added statistical noise to the experiment, giving the researcher something to work with. His results were not clear-cut, but with a statistics-based experimental design a researcher can fiddle around endlessly, matching good and bad runs to mood, the weather, phases of the moon, sunspots, and so on, making a nice thick report for a psychical research journal.

Dr. J. B. Rhine of Duke University pioneered the statistical approach to the study of psychic phenomena in the 1930s, and it still dominates the experimental design of modern parapsychologists, who seem to delight in devising new ways to make their experiments more complex and the results more confusing. As Albert Einstein wrote of Rhine's experiments in 1946: "I regard it as very strange that the spatial distance between the [telepathic] subjects has no relevance to the statistical [ESP] experiments. This suggests to me a very strong indication that a nonrecognized source of systematic errors may have been involved."

This data-to-noise ratio can be applied to many popular paranormal claims, such as the Shroud of Turin. The Shroud is an ancient cloth bearing the image of a mournful looking man. It is widely claimed to be the burial cloth of Jesus, imprinted by a miracle, though it turned up in a church in the fourteenth century and is not known to have had a prior history. A team of modern Christian scientists has produced volumes of analyses of the Shroud in an attempt to demonstrate its extraordinary characteristics. But recently, secular researchers found that the image contained a red pigment commonly used by fourteenth-century artists (a conclusion that few newspapers bothered to report—the public always prefers a mystery). Even before this discovery, the Shroud could have been evaluated by the data-to-noise ratio guideline.

An immediate cause for suspicion is the presence of whole museum-loads of clearly false relics from the Middle Ages, when practically every church had to have a wood chip from the True Cross, a plate from the Last Supper, one of Jesus' sandals—any single item of which would be as hard to evaluate as the Shroud itself. The Shroud appeared in the middle of all this noise. Ray N. Rogers, a leading Shroud advocate, once said that he could hardly think of a better way for the deity to prove His existence to a skeptical modern world than to leave us the Shroud. I can think of plenty of better ways, perhaps something clean and clear like materializing as a figure fifty miles tall and speaking loud enough to rattle the earth. The Shroud was a pretty forlorn miracle by comparison, lost in the trivia of the Middle Ages like a needle in a haystack—a speck of dubious data extracted from a sea of noise.

Cloaks of noise by themselves are not proof of the Shroud's inauthenticity—nor that mind power doesn't occasionally tilt a zirconium die, nor that the moon is not covered with artificial objects just a little smaller than the best photographs can show. "Noise" in information theory means, literally, that you just don't know. Data swamped in noise are unworthy of belief, and it is suspicious that evidence for the paranormal is consistently cloaked in this way.

3. Believers

Watch out for "believers." Watch out for stories told and retold. Francis Bacon said, "Man prefers to believe what he prefers to be true." A believer doesn't have to be a zealot. Anyone qualifies who possesses imagination enough to get excited at the idea that the mysterious crashing sound in the woods just beyond the campfire might be Bigfoot. Or that Venus sparkling in the clear dawn sky might be a flying saucer. Our beliefs may predispose us to misinterpret the facts, when ideally the facts should serve as the evidence upon which we base our beliefs.

Garden-variety flying saucer sightings based on such misperceptions clutter up the UFO literature. Some UFO investigators, like the late astronomer J. Allen Hynek, have concluded that after the garbage is sorted out, a few unexplainable cases still remain. Others, like *Aviation Week and Space Technology* magazine editor Philip J. Klass, don't agree. "In twelve years of investigating some of the most famous and highly acclaimed UFO reports," says Klass, "I have yet to find one that could not be explained in prosaic terms. . . . I'm not skeptical on principle, just on evidence."

Often a paranormal claim gets thoroughly debunked but continues to travel far and wide. Belief, not evidence, supplies the fuel. Lawrence Kusche, a pilot and investigator for the Committee for the Scientific Investigation of Claims of the Paranormal (CSICOP), scrupulously examined every allegedly mysterious disappearance in the so-called "Bermuda Triangle," for example, and found nothing really mysterious about any of them. He reported his findings in two books, *The Bermuda Triangle Mystery—Solved* and *The Disappearance of Flight 19*. These books have sold very poorly compared to sensationalistic works like Charles Berlitz's *The Bermuda Triangle*. "I assumed that people who read the weird books would naturally want to read the other side of the story and find out the truth," he commented. "I was wrong." Bermuda Triangle lore continues to percolate through American popular culture. A movie on the Triangle was released a couple of years ago, claiming to be factual. Its television ads were filled with flying saucers, underwater horrors, time warps, and planeloads of screaming people.

Some skeptics have concluded that every last paranormal mystery can be accounted for by these twin forces of true believers and tales amplified in the retelling.

4. The Past Is Prologue

Check out the history of the claim. The past can put a currently popular paranormal belief in a perspective that can be gained in no other way.

Many of the paranormal claims and movements of the 1980s actually have long and colorful histories. One example that has made the rounds in New Age circles in recent years is the Bates vision-correction system, billed as a new, holistic way to treat poor eyesight with a series of easy exercises.

Dr. William Horatio Bates was born in 1860 and graduated from medical school in 1885. His medical career was disrupted by spells of total amnesia, but this did not prevent him from publishing, in 1920, his great work, *The Cure of Imperfect Eyesight by Treatment Without Glasses*: Bates claimed, contrary to reality, that the eye does not focus by changing the shape of the eye lens. He said that the lens never changes shape at all, and that the problems orthodox doctors attribute to imperfect lenses are actually caused by an "abnormal condition of mind" or "a wrong thought." He invented a series of exercises to correct these problems, such as "palming" the eyes with the palms of the hands, "shifting" and "swinging" vision from side to side, and reading under difficult conditions such as in dim light or on a lurching streetcar. He also advocated staring directly at the sun for brief moments (which can cause genuine eye damage).

Bates died in 1931, but disciples kept his theories alive. Dozens of popular books were published on the Bates method, and "Throw away your glasses!" became the rallying cry of an international movement in the Thirties and Forties. Thousands of people sincerely believed the Bates exercises had cured them of nearsightedness, astigmatism, cataracts, and glaucoma. Unfortunately, medical tests did not bear this out.

One of the most prominent converts to the Bates system was Aldous Huxley. His corneas had been scarred since childhood, but he believed the Bates exercises had repaired them. He wrote a book about it, *The Art of Seeing*, hailed as a vindication by Bates sympathizers responding to criticisms from opthalmologists. But Huxley could be an embarrassment, too. Bennett Cerf wrote this account of the time Huxley addressed a Hollywood banquet in the April 12, 1952, *Saturday Review*:

When he arose to make his address he wore no glasses, and evidently experienced no difficulty in reading the paper he had planted on the lectern. Had the exercises really given him normal vision? I, along with 1,200 other guests, watched with astonishment while he rattled glibly on. . . . Then suddenly he faltered—and the disturbing truth became obvious. He wasn't reading the address at all. He had learned it by heart. To refresh his memory he brought the paper closer to his eyes. When it was only an inch or so away he still couldn't read it, and he had to fish for a magnifying glass in his pocket. It was an agonizing moment.

Eventually the Bates movement ran its course. In 1956, a Manhattan optometrist, Philip Pollack, wrote the definitive book exposing its failures, *The Truth About Eye Exercises.* "It is a rare occasion indeed when anyone so well informed troubles to take apart a pseudoscientific cult in such a thorough and painstaking manner," wrote Martin Gardner in his 1957 book, *Fads and Fallacies in the Name of Science.* But today the Bates method has been resurrected, minus some of Bates's more obvious blunders and clothed in New Age "holistic" rhetoric. Meanwhile, the Pollack book sits forgotten on library shelves.

The pattern is common: A new paranormal claim turns out to be a very old one, debunked long enough ago for the debunking to have been forgotten. The rate at which such old, disproven, and forgotten theories are being revived shows a certain unimaginativeness in the field, as if new paranormal theories cannot be invented fast enough to meet the New Age demand. And every time they are revived, these theories gain a little more venerability. It is important to remember that tradition and venerability aren't necessarily related to *credibility.*

A few years ago I attended a "natural living" festival in Connecticut and noticed an iridiagnostician on the program. An iridiagnostician! I felt like a biologist discovering a living fossil.

Iridology was invented around 1880 by Ignatz Peczely of Budapest. He declared that every human disease can be diagnosed by studying the iris of the eye. He claimed—no one knows why—that the iris is divided into forty zones that correspond to the different body parts. The zones run clockwise in one eye, counterclockwise in the other. Peczely gained disciples, and in 1904 his works were translated into English. Orthodox doctors ridiculed iridiagnosticians, who failed to treat diseases accurately when tested. (Pranksters had their day, too. The *Textbook of Iridiagnosis,* fifth edition, 1921, carefully explains how to recognize glass eyes in order to avoid being caught making lengthy diagnoses of them.) The method never produced any results, and so it slowly faded away around the time of my grandfather.

I expected the iridiagnostician at the "natural living" festival to be a doddering old man in his eighties, full of reminiscences about Henry Lindlahr, J. Haskell Kritzer, and other bygone greats of the movement. But no. He was a young, hip-looking fellow as enthusiastic about iridology as if it were brand new.

Since then, iridology has become entrenched in the holistic health scene, believed in (and financed) by thousands who never bothered to check out its full history. It has, in fact, been around long enough in its current incarnation to have undergone another round of debunkings. In 1979, University of California at San Diego researchers A. Simon, D. Worthen, and J. Mitas tested three iridologists, including Bernard Jensen, the author of the modern textbooks on the subject. The iridologists scored no better than would be expected by chance at making correct diagnoses of the illnesses of 143 patients. And in 1981, D. Cockburn at the University of Melbourne in Australia had iridologists evaluate before-and-after photos of the irises of patients who had developed acute diseases. Not only did the iridologists fail to diagnose any of the illnesses, they could find no changes in the eyes whatsoever!

A similar resurgent alternative health practice is zone therapy, based on the belief that every organ of the body is connected to a different spot on the bottom of the foot, the roof of the mouth, and the hands. Zone therapy is often linked by its practitioners with acupuncture and shiatsu massage, an association from which it derives venerability, but the truth is that, like iridology, zone therapy was another turn-of-the-century invention, by a Dr. William H. Fitzgerald of St. Francis Hospital of Hartford, Connecticut. Zone therapy flourished for a while, aided by testimonials of spectacular cures. But the cures somehow didn't endure the test of time, and the practice slowly faded out. By 1950 it was nearly extinct. Now it has been resurrected as reflexology, and poster charts of the bottom of the foot can be found in health food stores everywhere. It is currently practiced without some of Dr. Fitzgerald's more unusual treatments, like the application of tight rubber bands and spring clothes pins to various fingers and toes.

Many other past systems of bygone medical quackery have been revived in recent years, including chromotherapy (healing with colored lights), colonics (enemas), and homeopathy (where medical tinctures are made so dilute that hardly a molecule of the active ingredient remains).

5. By Their Fruits Shall You Know Them

The preceding examples lead to the next guideline: Watch whether the field of study remains barren over time.

In the end, the most telling argument against the Bates system, iridology, and zone therapy was not that they were founded by cranks or were based on spurious theories, but that they bore no fruit. The Bates exercises had every chance to succeed. Thousands of people "threw away their glasses" and practiced the system religiously. Millions more gave it briefer tries. If palming, shifting, and swinging really could cure poor eyesight, glasses would be as obsolete now as horse-drawn carriages.

As physicist Rolf M. Sinclair pointed out at an American Association for the Advancement of Science meeting in 1980 in San Francisco, one of the key distinctions between science and pseudoscience is that science changes rapidly. New ideas are quickly accepted once they are proven, and disproven ideas are likewise quickly rejected. Most of the focus of current research involves ideas less than ten to fifteen years old. In contrast, pseudoscience clutches doggedly at ideas for their own sake. "Astrology froze about two thousand years ago and simply hasn't changed much," Sinclair said. "That unchanging character is what allows me to say astrology is a pseudoscience."

My father finally became inactive in the American Society for Psychical Research, partly because nothing ever seemed to lead anywhere. At home we have a shelf lined with issues of the Society's *Journal*, marching back through the decades. Unlike other scientific journals, it contains nothing that one can build upon. In essence, the Society is just where it began in 1885, and where its precursor, the London Society for Psychical Research, began before that. It has yet to demonstrate that psychic powers exist at all, much less learn anything about them.

6. Crank-Watching

If someone making paranormal claims compares himself to Einstein, Galileo, or Pasteur, dismiss him right away. Real geniuses usually let their work speak for itself. If he believes he is being conspired against by the A.M.A., "orthodox oxen," and "would-be scientists" with "frozen beliefs" and "hi-de-hi mathematics" (to quote George F. Gillette, discoverer of an incomprehensible something called the "spiral maximote"), then you may safely ignore him. Paranoia is a frequent refuge of the incompetent.

The crank usually works in isolation from everyone else in his field of study, making grand discoveries in his basement. Many paranormal movements can be traced back to such people—Kirlian photography, for instance. If you pump high-voltage electricity into anything it will emit glowing sparks, common knowledge to electrical workers and hobbyists for a century. It took a lone basement crank to declare that the sparks represent some sort of spiritual aura. In fact, Kirlian photography was subjected to rigorous testing by physicists John O. Pehek, Larry J. Kyler, and David L. Faust, who reported their findings in the October 15, 1976, issue of *Science*. Their conclusion: The variations observed in Kirlian photographs are due solely to moisture on the surface of the body and not to mysterious "auras" or even necessarily to changes in mood or mental state. Nevertheless, television shows, magazines, and books (many by famous parapsychologists) continue to promote Kirlian photography as a proof of the unknown.

And finally, of course, there are plenty of outright fakes.

A fake often gives rise to a movement that endures long after the fakery is exposed. Spiritualism, the religion of my family for two generations, began in 1848 when twelve-year-old Margaret Fox of Wayne County, New York, became the world's first medium. People sitting with her in a darkened room asked questions of the spirits, and unexplained rapping noises would reply. More and more people came to witness this marvel, and soon Margaret and her sisters went on tour. Much later, in 1888, she confessed that it was all a hoax; she did it by snapping her big toe joint against the floor. But by now spiritualism had grown far beyond the "spirit rapping" stage, and séances were full of flying spirit trumpets, spirit voices, gauzy figures appearing in the dark, and mediums foaming ectoplasm from all their body orifices. Spiritualists continued to revere Margaret Fox as the founder of their religion, even after her confession. Once, my grandfather took my parents to visit the Fox sisters' cabin, preserved as a sort of spiritualist shrine. My mother remembers sitting in Margaret Fox's chair. She also learned to do the toe-snapping trick, and she can still do it. She demonstrated it for my grandfather once, but "he was very out of patience with us for being so skeptical."

7. The Self-Defeat of the New Age

In the whole panoply of the paranormal, is there anything at all that an intelligent person can believe in? Perhaps *belief* is not the issue. The *possibility* is always there. Maybe a few of the spiritualists did get messages—no one can prove otherwise. Maybe the saucers will finally land next month and show up the skeptics once and for all. "If we are only open to those discoveries which will accord with what we already know," said Alan Watts, "we might as well stay shut." And that is as far as an honest person can go.

The real significance of the paranormal boom is that so many of us take it so uncritically. It is as if the question "Is this so?" has become irrelevant—and has been replaced by the attitude, "If it feels good, it must be right for me." This is a very fundamental shift. That an objective reality exists outside our internal viewpoints, and that this objective reality is worth studying, is a relatively new idea in the history of the world. It did not gain a firm foothold until as late as the Renaissance, and though it rapidly led to the sciences that have transformed the world, perhaps this idea is more alien to human nature than we might think.

Today, nowhere in the rationalist paradigm "Is this so?" more roundly attacked, and its replacement, "If it feels good, it must be right," more self-consciously advocated, than in the movements that go collectively under the name "New Age." I believe this paradigm has served us poorly. It has led countless good people to squander years of their brilliance and energy on shabby falsehoods. It has been responsible for trapping others in vicious cults. It may have even short-circuited just the sort of quantum leap in human thought that our theorists keep saying is just around the corner.

Historically, paranormal movements have drawn more adherents from the right wing than from the left. No nation has a more extensive crackpot literature than Germany, and never did paranormal beliefs of every kind get more of a hearing than as in that country between the two World Wars. The Nazis' racial theories were only a small part of the pseudoscience that overran Germany.

One of the most widespread beliefs was the World Ice Doctrine (Welt-Eis-Lehre, or WEL), which held that the Milky Way was not made up of stars but of blocks of ice spiralling toward the earth. This pseudoscience was somehow connected with Aryan racial superiority, and the WEL acted almost as a political party. So successful was it that the Propaganda Ministry was obliged to announce, "One can be a good National Socialist without believing in the WEL." Another Nazi doctrine was that the earth is the interior of a hollow sphere, so that a line directed straight up into the sky would hit the other side of the world. The sun and stars were thought to be optical illusions in the middle. This idea was so widely accepted that a military party of ten was dispatched to the Isle of Rugen to photograph the British fleet by pointing an infrared telescope 45 degrees up into the sky!

The sight of intelligent, educated people walking around with pyramids on their heads, a sight you are liable to witness at any New Age festival, is comical. Perhaps the next irrationalist movement will not be so funny.

Certainly the New Age will make no lasting progress, nor will it gain any more credibility, until we accept the fact that nature gave us heads as well as hearts. Maybe we were given heads for a good reason. Maybe it is because, in the end, only the truth can set us free.

A NEW AGE OF OBFUSCATION AND MANIPULATION
Al Seckel

In the spring of 1985, the new "Twilight Zone" series premiered with an episode called "Word Play." It was about a man who woke up to find that a few key words had changed in meaning. At work, his boss asked him whether he was ready to go to "dinosaur," rather than to "lunch." Obviously, the man became very perplexed as common words with definite meanings were substituted for other words with quite different meanings.

It appears as if I have entered the "Twilight Zone" every time I talk with or read the literature of people associated with the New Age movement. Terms that have quite specific meanings are often carelessly bandied about with the result that the message is either gibberish to someone who knows the proper usage of the terms or profound, esoteric, and sublime to those who do not.

An example: One of the local morning television talk-shows recently featured a woman who works with crystals. She wore a purple quartz crystal that she claimed liberated a "large magnetic field" from within her body, enabling her to give "psychic" readings. How did she know that her field was "magnetic"? Did she attract iron objects? Did nails, tacks, and paperclips fly up from the floor? And, when you think about it, why would a "magnetic field" help with psychic readings?

Another interesting example occurred on a television talk-show on which I was asked to appear to discuss various New Age concepts with a well-known parapsychologist and author of several popular books on psychic

Al Seckel, a physicist and molecular biologist, is executive director of Southern California Skeptics and a scientific consultant to the Committee for the Scientific Investigation of Claims of the Paranormal (CSICOP). He has edited two collections of the writings of Bertrand Russell and writes regular columns on pseudoscience for the *Los Angeles Times* and the *Santa Monica News*.

phenomena, ghosts, and other strange and seemingly inexplicable happenings. To give scientific credence to what the parapsychologist had to say, special attention was given by the talk-show host to the fact that the man had a Ph.D. (I later learned that the doctorate was in special education.) During the show the parapsychologist claimed that he had demonstrated in his "laboratory research" that an unknown force, or forces, were at play in the universe and were behind many psychic events. I decided to ask him a simple question: "Can you name the four *known* forces in the universe?" His puzzled response was slow in coming: "Friction?" His incorrect response made me wonder how he could decide what *unknown* forces operate in the universe before he first *really* understood those already known.

Another example appeared in a "New Age" item in the *Santa Monica News*: "This planet has been slumbering for eons and with the inception of higher energy frequencies is about to awaken in terms of consciousness and spirituality." Note the term *higher energy frequencies*. At least we know that the message will not come via radio or television, which operate at low energy frequencies.

I believe that there are four reasons for there being so much verbal obfuscation among New Agers.

First, the use of technical jargon in a popular format, whether the words are contained in the dictionary or freshly coined, is meant to impress the reader.

Second, the meanings of words are subtly changed as a way to intimidate people. It has become fashionable, for example, for those who advocate an unorthodox point of view to declare themselves "open-minded." If someone disagrees with them, that person is righteously denounced as not having an open mind. This rhetorical technique shuts down critical discussion in a hurry—after all, who wants to be labeled "closed-minded"? This charge is frequently hurled at robust scientific or medical criticism, and as a consequence many scientists and doctors have refrained from openly criticizing pseudoscience. "Open-minded" originally meant having the ability to consider novel thinking. Today, however, for the advocate of pseudoscience, to be open-minded means to willfully suspend disbelief.

Third, for many people obscurity equals profundity. An example from the same column in the *Santa Monica News*: "Masters of Limitation and Masters of Divination use the same creative force to manifest their realities; however, one moves in a downward spiral and the latter moves in an upward spiral, each increasing the resonant vibration inherent in them." What could this possibly mean?

Finally, a vast amount of New Age literature misappropriates scientific jargon: *electromagnetic, frequencies, energy fields, multi-* or *extra-*

dimensional spacetime, and so on, to give the impression of scientific accuracy.

It is interesting to note that all of traditional science is dismissed with a shrug of the shoulders when it challenges the validity of a New Age product—yet inventors and vendors claim that their products work because they are "scientific." A typical example is the "Amazing Nuclear Receptor" (available for $90 at a recent New Age fair in Southern California) created by the "science of counter technology." It consists of a patterned medallion with a rhinestone suspended over the center, which, according to its inventor, protects the wearer by changing "toxic pollution" into "beneficial energy." Nothing in the jargon-loaded pamphlet that comes with the device resembles any of the known principles of traditional science. Would it really be a good idea to send people to clean up toxic-waste spills armed only with their "Amazing Nuclear Receptors," based on the authority of an inventor who offers only his fervent belief in "alternative technology" to back up his extraordinary claims?

This love/hate relationship with scientific authority arises because the promoters of pseudoscience confuse science with technology and openly reject rationality. They argue the following: Rational thought brought us science, and science brought us pollution and the threat of thermonuclear war. Therefore, we should reject the use of rationalism and science to solve problems. The New Age argument against rationality and science simply ignores the complex relationship between science, technology, big business, and politics. Pure science is a careful, well-tested, and highly successful method for discovering and describing how our universe works. That's it; and, in and of itself, it involves no applications. One can use knowledge for any ends one wants, but it is the demand created by society that directs the application of that knowledge into destructive or benevolent technology. We should ask ourselves this question: What chance do we have of solving global problems like nuclear proliferation, acid rain, the depletion of our rain forests and topsoil, and overpopulation if rationality is forfeited?

The misappropriation of scientific terms and concepts by the New Age movement reminds me of the tribal natives in New Guinea who watched American soldiers during World War II build runways and control towers that enabled strange and magical objects, which brought food and material wealth, to land from the sky. After the soldiers left, the natives tried to bring back the cargo planes. They built runways, placed bonfires along the strip for landing lights, and constructed control towers out of bamboo and grass. The cargo cult even fashioned airplanes out of grass in the hopes of luring the cargo back.

They built the structure, it looked right to them, but the planes never landed! And their society suffered as a result of their obsession with their fantasy in the sky. In the same way, the New Age movement has built a strictly verbal structure that has little or no relationship to reality; hence one can hold out little hope that their planes or "multi-dimensional spacecraft" will land.

There is a problem, however, that is much broader and more far-reaching than the fact that many people believe in unfounded ideas that in themselves don't matter in the grand scheme of things. (After all, who really cares that Shirley MacLaine wears a crystal that is supposed to emit strange powers or that other people believe that we have been visited by extraterrestrials?) The problem, as I see it, is that the widespread and *growing* belief in various pseudosciences is just one small indication that people are not evaluating information properly. And this has serious consequences.

I used to think that overpopulation, starvation, the depletion of our rain forests and topsoil, the carbon-dioxide buildup, and nuclear proliferation were basic global crises, but it finally dawned on me that they were all merely consequences of the human mind, individually and collectively: how we think, how we build up belief systems, why we follow certain leaders, and how we see challenges and create institutions to meet them.

Every day people are bombarded by the media, by sales representatives, and by their friends with information that is highly questionable. They are asked to accept ideas that, after the smallest amount of probing, can be shown to be invalid. This in turn has caused us to vote for people who may be unfit for public office, to buy products that are useless and even dangerous, and to join and support groups that are manipulative and destructive.

This is largely a consequence of the fact that people are for the most part always told what to think—by their churches, by their governments, by their schools, and by their parents. The emphasis has always been to teach someone *what* to think rather than *how* to think. This emphasis can be tempting in an age that has been made bewildering and scary by the almost unbelievably fast expansion of technology and information. Where has this brought us? Educational studies have documented time and again that critical thinking skills are seriously declining among schoolchildren. And, without criteria for distinguishing science from nonscience and fact from fiction, teachers too can be caught in the trap of believing in and disseminating unsupported contentions. It is unfortunate, therefore, that most people are not learning the skills needed to analyze the claims being made.

This problem sometimes crops up even inside the skeptical movement. In the course of my affiliation with this cause I have heard some pretty specious criticism of ideas when, in fact, there had not been enough information available to come to a conclusion, much less a robust conclusion. Even skeptics must be able to say "I don't know," must be able to live without knowing the solution to a "mystery" rather than entertaining or providing answers that are wrong.

Since New Age spirituality is of considerable interest to many people, I believe that the skeptical movement has a marvelous opportunity to encourage the development of better thinking skills by discussing various pseudosciences in a particular way. For the most part, the refutations of pseudoscience that one finds in the available skeptical literature aim at "debunking" the "mystery" or pseudoscience. But what do we accomplish by debunking the Bermuda Triangle, the false visions of a tabloid psychic, or the latest UFO sighting? Possibly not much in the long run. Although the skeptics may have presented the solution to one "mystery," rarely do they explicitly provide means for the reader or listener to figure out the next one—and there will always be a next one: a new triangle will appear off some country's coast, another psychic will make stunning predictions, and reports about UFOs will constantly reappear in the media and hence in people's imaginations. Although the places, dates, and names will change from mystery to mystery, the same faulty reasoning patterns will no doubt recur. To be clear, I am not disputing the value of debunking. One need look no further than the groundbreaking work of the Committee for the Scientific Investigation of Claims of the Paranormal and its excellent journal, the *Skeptical Inquirer*, to see how valuable such an approach can be. Now is the time, however, to see some other methods emphasized as well.

The "Aha! Insight" Method

How then does one go about teaching reasoning skills? The answer may have been provided by Martin Gardner, former columnist for *Scientific American* and author of numerous books on mathematical puzzles and tricks, as well as *Fads and Fallacies in the Name of Science,* one of the landmark books in skeptical literature. The answer, however, does not reside in that particular book. It can be found in one of his volumes of mathematical puzzles, entitled *Aha! Insight.* This book is a careful selection of problems that seem difficult, and indeed are difficult if you go about trying to solve them in traditional ways. But if you can free your mind from standard problem-solving techniques, you can be receptive to an "Aha!" reaction that leads immediately to a solution. Perhaps skeptics could approach future discussions concerning pseudoscience and New Age claims with the general audience in a puzzle-solving way—and thus achieve a better rate of success.

In other words, treat so-called mysteries as puzzles to be solved *by your audience* in such a way that they produce an "Aha!" reaction. This pleasant and nondogmatic approach encourages an inquiring individual to probe a little deeper the next time, and it has the benefit of not making him or her feel stupid.

One of the most effective ways to deal with extraordinary claims is to begin by *asking the right questions* in order to separate the essentials from the nonessentials. For example, what is the claim being made? Are there alternative explanations? How can you test the various hypotheses offered? Have you been told the full story? You might try this approach the next time you are asked for the solution to a "mystery." Reverse the question and ask members of your audience or your friends in a curious tone what they think the solution might be. Can they think of any natural explanation or present an alternative possibility? How would they check out or test the various possibilities? The idea is to get your audience to compare the different explanations, distinguish between them, and then think of ways to test the various hypotheses. After all, before you can say that something is *out* of this world, you must first make sure that it isn't *in* it! Be encouraging, but give them as little help as possible. Once they have hit upon the correct solution, you can support their correct ideas with the facts gleaned from the work of the debunkers who have already gone through this process.

This approach, if properly executed, frequently produces an "Aha!" reaction from your audience. It gets them to actively participate; and moreover, a participating audience is an *attentive* one.

Avoid Jargon

Always give examples that people can relate to their everyday experience. Avoid jargon. For example, in some explanations of the phenomenon of firewalking speakers from the skeptical movement would tell their audience that moisture protects the firewalker's feet by means of the "Leydenfrost effect." The speaker would then give an example of the Leydenfrost effect by stating that water droplets will skip around on a hot skillet. First of all, this explanation is not the best one for a lay audience. Second, in this example, the audience would find it very hard to relate how water dancing around in a hot skillet protects a firewalker's feet from being charred. Instead, the speaker should have avoided the "Leydenfrost" term altogether and have simply stated that evaporating water vapor provides protection from heat. After all, how do you test a hot iron? Most people would be able to relate this to their own experience and get an "Aha!" reaction.

Don't Deny Experiences

There is an even more important point that needs to be stressed. Many of the so-called paranormal claims (out-of-body experiences, walking across hot coals, the fortune-teller's ability to perform "readings") are *genuine experiences*. People *do* have out-of-body experiences and *can* walk across hot coals; fortune-tellers and astrologers *can* sometimes reveal what appear to be specific personality insights about their clients. And many people have had some sort of "paranormal" experience they cannot readily explain. It does not help the skeptic's case to deny an experience that a person genuinely believes he had. It just sets up the skeptic as close-minded. Most people, however, will allow you to help them figure out *alternative* explanations for their experiences, providing you are not confrontational or smug.

Recognizing Unfair Rhetorical or Manipulative Techniques

> When you meet the friendliest people you have ever known, who introduce you to the most loving group of people you've ever encountered, and you find the leader to be the most inspired, caring, compassionate and understanding person you've ever met, and then you learn that the cause of the group is something you never dared hope could be accomplished, and all of this sounds too good to be true, it probably *is* too good to be true! Don't give up your education, your hopes and ambitions, to follow a rainbow. [Jeanne Mills, a former member of the People's Temple and a victim of assassination a year after the November 18, 1978, Jonestown suicides/murders of 911 adults and children]

It is tempting to view the New Age movement as a decentralized, do-your-own thing affair. In fact, the New Age movement—like its precursors *est* and Scientology—can be highly organized. Groups supposedly formed around the dual principle of "awareness" and "freedom" often employ subtle manipulative techniques to enlist and keep a strangling grip on their members. For example, several New Age self-awareness groups have adopted firewalking as a spectacular gimmick to prove to people that they can do or achieve the impossible only through proper "spiritual" training and meditation. Because firewalking seems to be impossible to most people, it can serve as a powerful psychological tool in convincing those who accomplish it that the charismatic leader is correct in all his claims, some of which may be of questionable validity. This appeal to "personal experience" is a powerful persuasive tool, even more convincing than logic or reason. In our cold world it is easy to understand why people might consider their personal experience to be their last hope for maintaining their personal integrity and individuality. However, if a person assumes that his or her "gut feeling" is immune to the corrupting influence of the outside world, that person will be left exposed and vulnerable. People are especially vulnerable to manipulation when they are faced with experiences that they do not fully understand. The Jonestown incident is an example of a group that used powerful and persuasive techniques to bring about drastic personality changes that completely destroyed the ability of its members to think independently.

Destructive and manipulative groups fall into four sometimes-overlapping categories: religious, self-awareness and personal development (pseudotherapy), political, and commercial pyramid enterprises and "training" seminars. A group can be deviant or even heretical *without* being destructive; conversely, a group can be destructive without holding particularly unusual beliefs. Destructive groups are not interested in helping you, only in helping themselves. Their hidden agenda reveals that they only want your free, full-time, and lifetime commitment as a recruiter and fund-raiser. It is important, therefore, to know when a group is being manipulative, deceptive, exclusive, psychologically or financially exploitative, totalitarian, or disruptive to families and friends.

On the surface, many destructive groups seem to offer a strong feeling of community, a sense of purpose, spiritual fulfillment, esoteric knowledge, and wealth. But behind these offerings usually lie two subtle strategies of psychological coercion: (1) If you can make a person *behave* the way you want, you can make that person *believe* the way you want. (2) Sudden, drastic changes in environment or experience can lead to heightened suggestibility and to drastic changes in attitudes and beliefs.

The following are characteristics of destructive and manipulative groups, sometimes not always apparent in the first stages of indoctrination:

Immediacy: Members are pressured into making important decisions right away.

Charismatic Leadership: The leader claims divinity or special knowledge and demands your absolute obedience.

Deception: In recruiting and fundraising, the group hides its true objectives, often using "front groups" with innocent-sounding names. Members are secretive or vague about their activities and beliefs.

Alienation: The group tries to separate members from their families, friends, and society, The group becomes the new "family."

Fatigue: Extended classes and/or training sessions, long working hours, and repetition of hypnotic practices (meditating, "speaking in tongues," and chanting), leave participants exhausted and hence less able to deal critically with specious arguments.

Lack of Privacy: The group interferes with members' private contemplation and independent thought—inhibiting their ability to question.

Financial Exploitation: Members are required to relinquish their worldly goods and monetary assets to the group as well as to work long hours without pay or benefits.

Physical Exploitation: Leaders use fear and/or actual punishment to keep members in line. (Reports of sexual abuse and child abuse are common.)

Totalitarian: Members are expected to think, feel, and act in a manner prescribed by the group.

Mystical Manipulation: The leader stages "miraculous" or "psychic" events to impress disciples with his or her special divinity.

Need for Purity: The group tries to convince new members that before joining the group they were hopelessly impure. No such group ever empowers its potential members with the suggestion that they can climb up even one rung of the spiritual ladder by themselves.

Confession: Members are coerced into openly discussing their deepest fears, anxieties, and secrets.

Loading the Language: New words with special meanings, understood only by members of the group, are created. Familiar words, in turn, are bent to mean something unfamiliar. In this way, the group takes over your very vocabulary.

Stifling Opposition: The leaders condemn those who disagree with the philosophy of the group as liars (or agents of Satan).

Exclusiveness: The group claims or implies that it has the only right answer to a specific question or problem.

Rules: The group requires strict adherence to trivial rules.

If you are asked to join a group that has any of these characteristics, here are some suggestions:

Ask Questions: Never accept vague generalities and inadequate explanations in response to your questions. Learn to recognize when a message or answer is actually confused or ambiguous, perhaps intentionally so. Beware of those who try to silence you through group intimidation.

Say "No": You can always answer "none of the above" to any multiple choice. Recognize group pressure to decide quickly. Sleep and carefully think before making a decision. After all, the group will not disappear in the next few days or months. Be willing to disobey simple situational rules when you feel you should. Never do anything you don't believe just to conform or to get someone off your back.

Keep Your Self-Worth: Try to focus on what you are doing rather than on thoughts about yourself. Avoid giving personal confessions that may be later used against you. Many destructive groups and mind-control systems use in-group confessions, self-exposure "games," and the like to catalogue the weaknesses of their members for later exploitation.

Look for the Hidden Agenda: What is really being said? What is not being said? Beware of invitations to isolated weekend workshops that have nebulous goals.

Keep Outside Contacts: Maintain outside interests and sources of social support. Reject the appeal that devotion to the cause requires severing these ties.

Physical Abuse: Remove yourself from situations in which you are exposed to or threatened with physical, emotional, or sexual abuse.

People who have left destructive groups must deal with feelings of victimization, isolation, repression, and worthlessness. When beliefs are shaken, it is difficult to start over. Still, it is good to remember that every exit is an entrance to somewhere else.

It is not my aim to encourage people to become cynical or unduly suspicious of everything that is said and written, but rather to continue to think about the ways we come to know the world. The scientific method is not something confined to a research laboratory; it is the best method that has been devised by the human mind for detecting error and, just as important, for confirming shared experience. It has shown us time and time again that there is no shortcut to knowledge.

People enjoy pseudoscience; a belief in the fantastic can fulfill many emotional needs. However, educational development and our chances for survival are dependent upon our ability not to rationalize, but to reason.